Megalithic Research in the Netherlands, 1547-1911

Sidestone Press

Artefacts from hunebed D19-Drouwen. This study ends in 1912, when modern hunebed research began with J.H. Holwerda's complete excavation of the hunebeds D19 and D20 at Drouwen. Now it became clear what bewildering masses of fragmented pottery could be found in Dutch hunebeds (photograph by P.-J. Bomhof, National Museum of Antiquities, Leiden). See further Appendix 3.

Megalithic Research in the Netherlands, 1547-1911

From 'Giant's Beds' and 'Pillars of Hercules' to accurate investigations

Jan Albert Bakker

Dedicated to the memory of

KONRAD JAŻDŻEWSKI [1909-1985]
*exemplary researcher of the regional TRB Groups,
especially the TRB East and Southeast Groups*

HEINZ KNÖLL [1911-1989]
*fundamental researcher of the typochronology
of TRB West Group pottery*

ULRICH FISCHER [1915-2006]
*much admired investigator of the
Neolithic and fatherly guide*

ALBERT ETTO LANTING [1945-2004]
*precise analyst of European and Near Eastern prehistoric
typochronology and a most helpful colleague*

JÜRGEN HOIKA [1941-2006]
colleague in TRB matters and friend

Published by Sidestone Press, Leiden
   www.sidestone.com

ISBN 978-90-8890-034-1

Cover Illustration: View of hunebed D6-Tynaarlo. School picture from 1901 by
Bernard Bueninck [1864-1933]. The image was mirrored for esthetical purposes.
Cover design: K. Wentink, Sidestone Press
Lay-out: P.C. van Woerdekom, Sidestone Press

Contents

List of Illustrations

A. General Introduction

Modern scientific excavations of Dutch *hunebeds* (megalithic grave monuments or 'tombs' of the Funnel Beaker or TRB culture)[1] began in 1912 with the complete excavation of two hunebeds in Drouwen in Drenthe. This book covers the Antiquarian Period of Dutch hunebed research, which lasted till the early 1870s, and the next 40 years, till 1910, when accurate plans of hunebeds were made and decorated hunebed pottery was precisely drawn.[2] In the eighteenth century, Joannes van Lier anticipated these new approaches in a first monograph on a Dutch hunebed (1760).

Part A briefly presents the general knowledge about the hunebeds and TRB culture in The Netherlands available to modern researchers, most of which the antiquarian researchers were ignorant.

Part B deals with the preceding development of ideas concerning hunebeds, the identity and age of the hunebed builders, the way hunebeds were constructed, their protection, the drawing of ground-plans and side views, recording of their particulars, and discussions of the artefacts within them, more or less in chronological order

A brief description of the form and research history of the 77-81 known extant and known or suspected former Dutch hunebeds[3] is given in Appendix 1 at the end of this book.

After the 'References' follow a German summary (*Zusammenfassung*) and an excerpt, also in German, of a study about megalithic graves and other antiquities in Schleswig-Holstein, especially on Fehmarn, by Georg Wolfgang Ulrich Wedel, from 1812, which is kept in a Dutch archive (Appendix 2A). This is followed by notes, from 1809, by H. Wilder and J.D. Gundelach about other megalithic

---

1 The term 'megalithic', which combines Greek *mega*s, 'large' and *lithos*, 'stone', was first used by Reverend A. Herbert in 1839, in Brittany (Giot 1985, 16). 'Tombs' is used here in the sense of 'sepulchral monument'. *Hunebedden* is the local name for these tombs (see section A1); I use the shorter English term 'hunebeds' in this book, which was introduced by A.W. Franks (1872) and J. Fergusson (1872).

2 This latter period could be called the 'Period of the first accurate hunebed plans and registration of their pottery (1871-1910)'. A.E. van Giffen continued this work (1919; 1924; 1925-27; 1943a-b; 1944a-d) and surpassed everything previously accomplished in quantity and quality.

3 There are 53 extant hunebeds in The Netherlands (Figure 57 and Appendix 1): one (G1) in the province of Groningen, the others in the province of Drenthe (D1-D32, D34-D47, D49-D54). The stones of the heavily damaged hunebed D33-Valthe were used by Van Giffen for the reconstruction of D49-Papeloze Kerk and 'D48-Noordbarge' is a huge stone, not a hunebed. Twenty-four sites of demolished hunebeds have been excavated (including the site of D33); an additional four supposed sites of demolished hunebeds have not yet been excavated.
   The extant Stone of Lage Vuursche (U1), province of Utrecht, may or may not represent a former TRB dolmen or passage grave; the demolished hunebeds F1-Riis and D31b-Exloo were actually cists, hunebed D13c-Eext was a passage grave or a cist, and hunebed G5-Heveskesklooster (Figure 59) was a rectangular dolmen (Appendix 1).

graves on Fehmarn (Appendix 2B). Appendix 3 presents additional notes to the description of the Figures. They are followed by an Index of Dutch hunebeds and an Index of persons.

A1. What hunebeds are

Hunebedden is the Dutch name for the megalithic burial chambers of the Funnel Beaker or TRB culture in The Netherlands, dating to about 3350-2700 BC.[4] It is also written *hunebeds* in English,[5] which I shall use here. The TRB culture[6] represents one of the first settled horticultural societies in the North European Plain and southern Scandinavia. Agriculture and stock-breeding began about 10,000 years ago in the Near East from where it gradually expanded to western Europe. About 5300 BC, the horticultural Bandkeramik culture or Linear Pottery culture colonised the fertile central European loess soils along the southern fringes of the North European Plain, almost as far as Paris. It also covered the southeasternmost part of The Netherlands, the loess-covered southern part of the Limburg province, near Maastricht.

Some fifteen hundred or two thousand years later, the much less fertile sandy regions north of the Rhine in The Netherlands, northern Germany and southern Scandinavia were occupied by the West and North Groups of the TRB culture, which built megalithic tombs to the west of the river Oder (Figure 1).[7] Basically, these groups were horticulturalists, keeping domestic animals and cultivating grain and vegetables in small plots, which they had cleared within the primeval oak-and-lime forest. They used the *ard*-plough and wagons with two or four massive wooden disc wheels. To effect fertility for men, beasts and crops, people, objects, and pottery with food and drink were offered to the gods in lakes, rivers, wetlands and drier places.[8]

---

4   The 'calendar years' or 'solar years' BC ('cal BC') of this study are estimates based on available calibrated radiocarbon dates and on Anna L. Brindley's (1986b, 2003) estimates based on the average number of pots of each TRB 'horizon' in hunebeds. Erik Drenth & Albert E. Lanting (1991) estimated the calendar years of a four stages subdivision of the Single Grave / *Einzelgrab* culture (EGK). The review by Jan N. Lanting & Hans [J.J.] van der Plicht (2000) of the relevant radiocarbon dates for both cultures resulted in shifts of 50 years (see, for instance, Figure 2). It is therefore clear that despite seeming precision these estimates may still be some 50-100 years off the mark.

5   For instance. by Augustus Franks (1872) and James Fergusson (1872, 318-24).

6   'TRB' derives from Danish *Tragtbeager* and German *Trichter[rand]becher*, cf. Dutch *trechterbeker*, meaning 'funnel beaker' in English [less common: 'funnel-beaker' or 'funnelbeaker']. The name refers to one of the most general forms that occurs almost throughout the TRB culture. In the West and North Groups, it is container with a roundish body and a chalice- or funnel-like neck, the profile of which changed with time. Its form often resembles a baroque garden vase without the foot.

7   The TRB culture was preceded by the Swifterbant culture, between ca. 4900 and 3400 BC. It was a culture of hunter-fishers-horticulturalists in the wetlands and on the Pleistocene sandy soils of The Netherlands.

8   Becker 1947; Rech 1979, Karsten 1994 (cf. my review in *Varia Neolithica*.2, 2002, 193-200); Koch 1998.

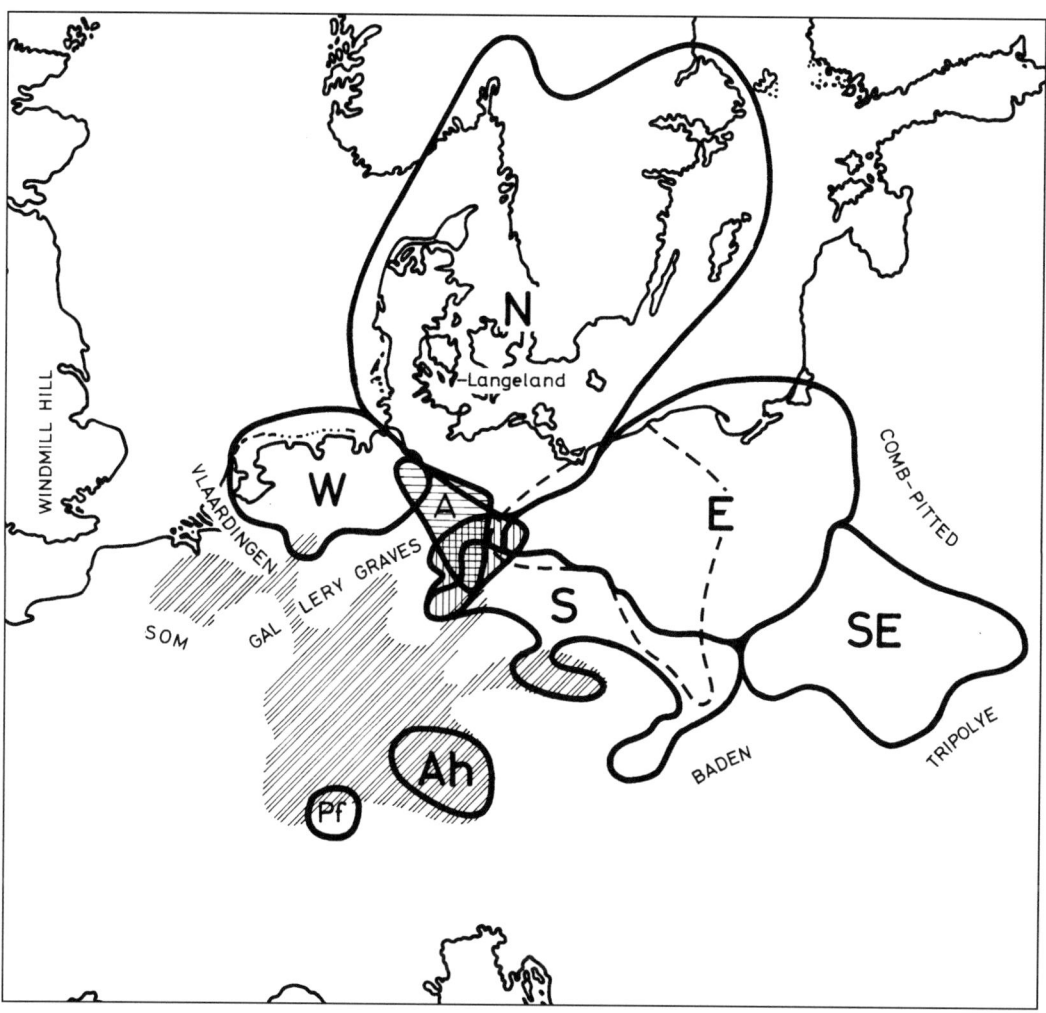

Figure 1. The regional groups of the TRB culture (Bakker 1979a, fig. 1). W = West group, N = North Group, E = East Group, S = South Group, SE = Southeast Group, Ah = Altheim Group or Culture, Pf = Pfyn Group, A and horizontally hatched = Altmark Group, vertically hatched = Walternienburg-Bernburg Group. The broken line indicates the occurrence of the Luboń decoration of three-strand cord impressions.Diagonal hatching indicates the related Michelsberg culture. SOM = the Seine-Oise-Marne culture.

The TRB culture as a whole, consisting of a number of sub-groups, occupied the North European Plain between Amsterdam, Utrecht, Bratislava, Lviv, Kaliningrad, Uppsala and Oslo (Figure 1).[9] Erratic boulders transported from Fenno-Scandia and the eastern Baltic to the North European Plain and southern Scandinavia by the Saalian or Weichselian glaciers of the Pleistocene Ice Age were the building material for megalithic tombs, together with sand and loam.

Megalithic tombs were built in the TRB North Group in southern Scandinavia and northern and northeastern Germany, in the Altmark and Walternienburg-Bernburg Groups in central Germany, and in the TRB West Group. This West Group occurred to the west of the Elbe, between Hamburg-Lüneburg, Hanover, Utrecht and the North Sea. Almost all Dutch megaliths are in the northeastern part of the country, mainly in the province of Drenthe, with a few in the provinces of Groningen and Overijssel; a stone cist was found in Friesland (Figure 57). In addition, a possible hunebed remnant is in Lage Vuursche, province of Utrecht in the centre of The Netherlands.[10] Six hunebeds directly east of the Dutch border in Westphalia suggest that others may have existed in the Dutch province of Gelderland in places where enough large erratic boulders were available.

Elsewhere in the TRB area genuine megalithic chambers are absent, or were built by the Globular Amphorae culture (KAK), a direct TRB descendant in central and eastern Germany, Poland, the Ukraine and Moldavia-Romania, which is partly contemporary to and partly later than the period in which hunebeds were built and used in the TRB West and North Groups.

The TRB North Group interred its deceased in flat earth graves, flat stone-packed graves, earthen long barrows, megalithic tombs or stone cists. Pottery with provisions accompanied them. Male graves often had bows and arrows, axes and perforated battle axes with them, of which only the non-organic parts remain. Neither single nor collective interments of men, women and children are marked by specific grave goods indicating rank or prestige, and it is unclear why a person was selected to become interred in a megalith, in another type of grave, or not at all. The megalithic tombs of the North Group consist of different types of *dol-*

9   The West and North Groups of the TRB culture are discussed by Midgley (1992), Bakker (1979a, 1992), and a great number of South-Scandinavian publications. In the western Ukraine, the TRB culture actually extended 75 km southeast of Lviv to Iwano Frankowsk / Stanisławów and Halicz on the river Dnister, and north of these towns to the Styr and Goryn basins. The TRB culture may even have extended down the Dnister as far as 150 km from Lviv (at Żwaniec, although it is unclear whether or not this was a pure TRB settlement) (Pelisiak 2007, 27-29, 32; I thank Kamil Adamczak, Warsaw, for having sent me this publication).

10   A.E. van Giffen (1925) coded the Dutch hunebeds using a capital letter for the province, a dot and a Roman serial number (e.g. D. XXVI, G.I, O.I, U.I). The dots were later omitted and the numerals changed to Arabic ones (e.g. D26, G1, O1, U1).

mens[11] and *passage graves*.[12] The first dolmens were slightly earlier than the earliest passage graves. Their earliest form, the *Urdolmen* or 'primeval dolmen', was a small square or rectangular grave chamber covered by one heavy capstone, which had to be shifted aside for secondary interments. The sidestones under the capstone usually lay on one of the longer sides. Later dolmens had more capstones and an entrance in one narrow side made them more easily accessible; eventually their sidestones were placed upright. All these tombs had flat inner walls. The large boulders were selected for natural flat surfaces or occasionally they were split. The North Group passage graves usually had a circular kerb of large standing boulders and because of this the entrance passage was much longer than those of the West Group passage graves.

In the TRB West Group, only later types of dolmens occurred.[13] This later type was not recognised The Netherlands until 1983, in the example of dolmen G5-Heveskesklooster (Figure 59; Bakker 1994), and they are left out of consideration in the following historical study. The 'Kuyavian' long barrows, which are up to 120 m long and are found in the earlier Polish East and Southeast TRB Groups (Libera & Tunia 2006) and other tomb types, are absent. The dead of the West Group, like those of the North Group, were interred in megaliths, flat earth graves

---

11 For the TRB culture, the term *dolmen* is used for a specific type of megalithic tomb, see the following description. In the French language and archaeology, 'dolmen' means a 'megalithic chamber' of every possible type and culture.

12 A thorough description of the megalithic tombs of the TRB North and West Groups has been written by Magdalena S. Midgley (2008), who had previously provided a synopsis of the TRB culture as a whole (Midgley 1992). Rainer Kossian (2005) compiled the data of the 'non-megalithic graves' in Germany and The Netherlands and later (2007) the results of Hans Reinerth's excellent investigations of the TRB and later Neolithic settlement site 'Huntedorf' near Lake Dümmer, Germany in 1938-1941 (cf. Reinerth 1939).

13 See Laux 1990, Abb. 1: 1-3 and Abb. 3-5 and Laux 1991 for Germany; for G5-Heveskesklooster (Figure 59), see Appendix 1.

or stone cists.[14] Grave goods for both sexes were provisions in beautifully decorated pottery; only men were provided with arrowheads, battle-axes and axes.[15] The diversity of grave goods of the TRB culture in The Netherlands was 'a custom not seen before in these regions' (Louwe Kooijmans 2007, 467). The Dutch hunebeds are notable for their incredible masses of sherds, the processing of which may take several years. Materials from the flat graves indicate that about 2950 BC (Middle and Late Havelte style period, i.e. Brindley 6-7, see Figure 2) the West Group be-

---

14   The total number of presumed earth graves in the Netherlands is probably 130-136 at 58 dryland sites (Kossian 2005, 454-501, sites 291-352, pls. 188-234; Lanting & Brindley 2004; cf. Van Beek 2009). Cists and "earth grave or ritual deposit"s below the original ground surface were included. The number of earth graves at Hooghalen-3 was estimated as 2-4. Flat grave cemeteries usually consisted of up to ten graves, although 20 graves were found at Heek-Averbeck in Germany (Finke 1983; Kossian 2005, no. 192) and probably also at Hardenberg (Kossian 2005, no. 351). There were no barrows above these graves (although Van Giffen thought so and Kossian left this possibility open).

The 10.5 cm high decorated funnel beaker, probably from a Brindley 2-4 flat grave (Kossian 2005, no. 350), was found 'in Denekamp', years before 1968, by a farmer in Beuningen, Gem. Losser; the actual findspot is unknown (pers. comm. A.D. Verlinde, May 24-25, 2010). Verlinde's surmise that the pot derived from the site Denekamp-Klokkenberg, which was discovered in 1963 (Bakker & Van der Waals 1973; Bakker 2004, 90-7; Kossian 2005 no. 349), may or may not be correct. The Klokkenberg grave to Brindley 7. Although the Hardenberg cemetery comprises a relatively long period, Brindley 4-5 according to Kossian, the occurrence of a Brindley 2-4 grave together with a Brindley 7 grave in one cemetery seems unusual. Eastern Overijssel (Twente) was relatively densely occupied by the TRB population and another burial site may also be concerned.

F1-Riis, which was formerly considered as Friesland's only hunebed, was actually a cist, which stood upon the old land surface and had a low barrow (Lanting 1997; Kossian 2005, no. 333).

In northern and western Jutland, Denmark, at least 282 stone-packed graves (*stendyngegraver*) are known from 50 localities. They date from MNA III-Vb (Fabricius & Becker 1996, 185, 257-9, 364. I thank Svend Illum Hansen for pointing out this publication). From EN till MNA III, they were preceded by flat earth graves without stone packing (*fladmarksgraver*, ibid. 238-9, fig. 329; Ebbesen 1992). Elsewhere in Denmark, flat graves occurred from EN to MN V. Camilla Haarby Hansen, of Copenhagen, recorded approximately 70 Danish EN earth graves without mounds (but at least six of these may have been covered by a barrow, which left no traces). I thank her for this information (March 25, 2010). Numeric data for other regions and periods in southern Scandinavia are not yet available.

15   Only three body silhouettes have been exposed in earth graves of the TRB West Group. (1) A silhouette of a child's body on its right side was found in the entrance of hunebed G1-Noordlaren, in front of entrance stones P2 and P2' – was it an offering? Apart from a few small sherds and chips of flint, the grave contained no artefacts. The sherds date from Brindley 3-4 and are a *terminus post quem* for this grave (Bakker 1983, 147, 174, figs. 9, 14, 16a-b, 29). Two clear silhouettes were found in earth graves in Germany near the Dutch border. (2) One was grave F4 at Heek-Averbeck, which was a flexed body on the left side accompanied by three pots belonging to Brindley 5 / Early Havelte. The grave had a wooden lining (Bakker 1992, 93-4, fig. 32; Finke 1983). (3) The other was found at Geeste on the eastern bank of the River Ems. A flexed body was lying on its right side, oriented east-west and looking south, with one Brindley 4 bowl at its feet, in an oval wooden coffin, measuring 1.10 x 0.82 m, and placed in an oval pit of 1.88 x 1.10 x 0.64 m (Kaltofen 2008, with photograph of bowl, not of silhouette).

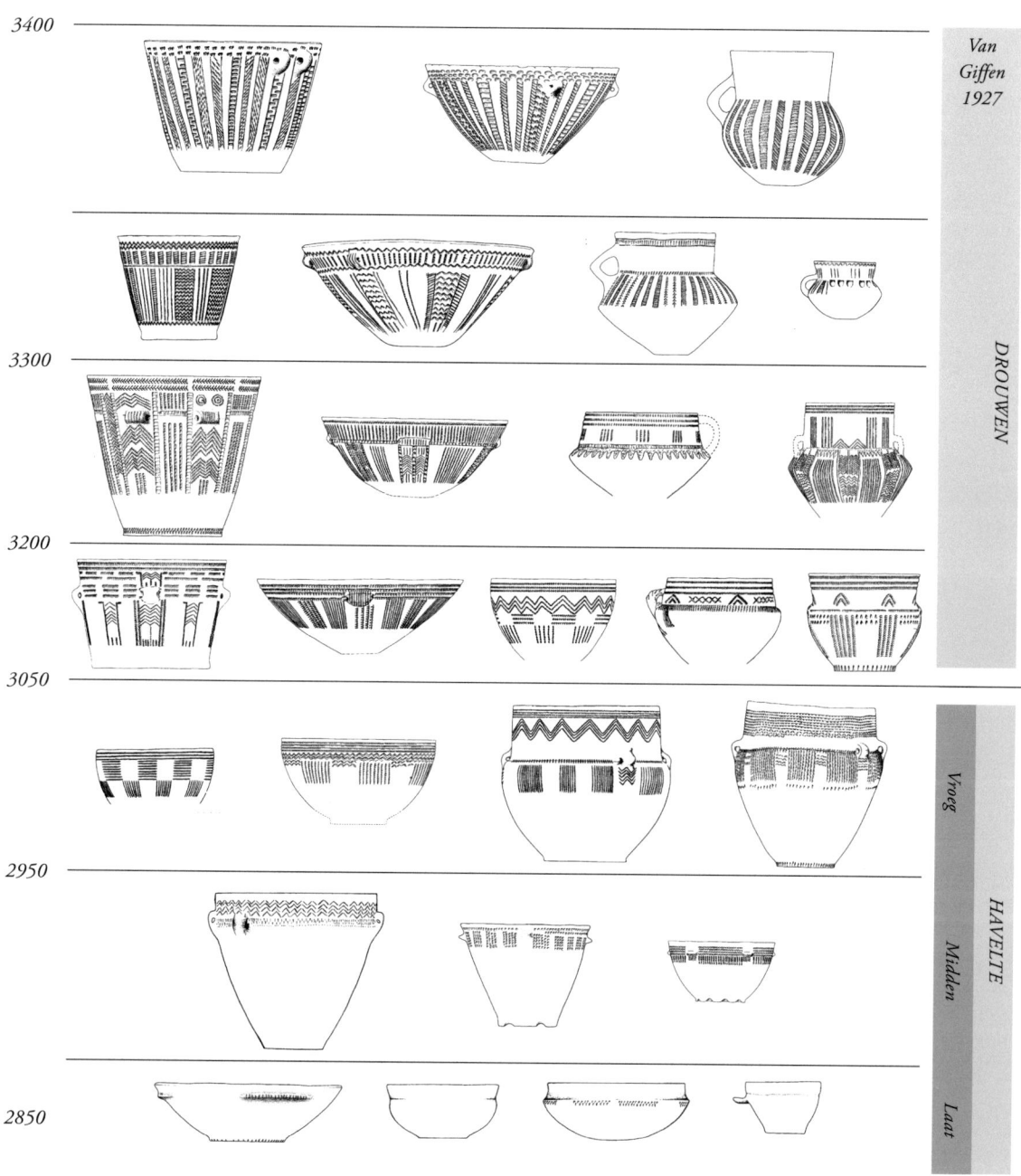

Figure 2. Brindley's typochronological subdivision of pilot types of TRB pottery from hunebeds (1986b) into seven 'horizons' (Van Ginkel et al. 1999, p. 41). See further Appendix 3.

gan to cremate its dead in Drenthe and along the Ems River in Germany.[16] In flat graves, the cremations were deposited in the earth next to one or more pots with food and drink. Such depositions would also have taken place in the hunebeds, as indicated by the types of pottery and the scattered remnants of cremations in the chambers.[17] The grave goods in the chambers seem to have been subjected to a kind of poorly-understood 'Brownian motion', which in several cases resulted in the sherds of one pot being dispersed throughout the entire chamber floor. In the West and North Group we cannot explain why a specific burial type was chosen for the deceased.

---

16 Late Havelte pottery is often difficult to recognise in Germany. See Knöll 1959, p. 168, lists 104-106 and the map in Knöll 1952. An additional site, Leer-Westerhammrich, is near Knöll's 1959 findspot 20 (Bakker 1979d). This flat grave was part of the Late Havelte cemetery with 26 cremation graves, which was later excavated by Wolfgang Schwarz and Ralf Bärenfänger, but has not yet been published (cf. Lanting & Van der Plicht 2000). In addition, a few 'new' Middle and Late Havelte sites were found in Drenthe after Knöll had compiled his list. These were the Gellenerdeich settlement further east in Germany, along the River Hunte, where two Late Havelte pots were found (Pätzold 1955, figs. 5i and 5m) and the Hunte 1 settlement containing several Late Havelte pots (Reinerth 1939; Bakker & Van der Waals 1973; Kossian 2007). Bakker & Van der Waals discussed a few other Late Havelte sites found between the Rivers Elbe and Ems. Louwe Kooijmans (2007, 468) refutes the idea of most other colleagues and myself (e.g. Bakker 1992, 93-4) that cremation replaced inhumation completely during Late Havelte / Brindley 7: 'It seems more likely just an additional, infrequently practised option.' He added (n. 71) 'Only a few examples of Funnel Beaker cremations are known (e.g. Angelslo, Westrup, Leer, not Denekamp!) in spite of the fact that cremated bone is well-preserved and easily recognised. Cf. also Kossian 2005, 64-66.' At Denekamp, province of Overijssel, a Brindley 7 decorated *Halsrillengefäss* was found together with two undecorated collared flasks, a heavy flint axe of Buren type and 3 flint blades, long 3.6-3.7 cm, two of which are endscrapers (Museum Natura Docet, Denekamp, nos. 18, 206, 218). There was *no* cremation in the original pit – as I mistakenly thought for a long time –, so that it probably was an inhumation grave (Bakker 2004, K11; 1979a, fig. B21; Bakker & Van der Waals 1973). The original pit was not completely exposed in the house building trench where it was found, but its exposed diameter of 1-1½ m matches those of the known Brindley 2-5 flat inhumation graves of the West Group (cf. Bakker 1992, 117, n. 54).

17 There is a problem with this generalisation. The 157 TRB pots in the chamber of hunebed D26-Drouwenerveld show that it was used for TRB interments during about 230-250 years, between ca. 3245-25 and 2995 BC (from late Brindley 2/early 3 to early 5). About 150 tiny pieces of burnt human bones, rather equally dispersed through the chamber, were identified by Elisabeth Smits; an additional 11 burnt animal bones were identified by Louise H. van Wijngaarden-Bakker. Middle and Late Havelte pots, which are usually associated with cremations, are completely absent. This leads to several questions: Did TRB cremation start earlier here? (see Kossian 2005, 64-66 about earlier cremations in the TRB West and North Groups in Germany). Or were later cremations placed in the chamber without pottery? Or do the burnt human remains represent food, as is probable for the 11 burnt teeth or bones of cattle, pig and sheep/goat? W. Arentzen (pers. comm., November, 2009) stresses the possibility of anthropophagy, which is rarely considered in studies of the TRB culture or the Neolithic. It is a generally neglected subject in archaeology, but see Boulestin et al.'s article (2009) on 'Mass cannibalism in the Linear Pottery Culture at Herxheim (Palatinate, Germany)'. Another form of anthropogy, the eating of deceased ancestors, which is known from cutural anthropological studies, may also have occurred in prehistoric societies. Or do the bits of human cremated bone in the D26 chamber derive from the following Single Grave period, when two amphorae and two battle-axes, roughly datable between about 2700 and 2550 BC according to Albert E. Lanting, were placed in the chamber? (see Bakker in prep.).

The bulk of the megalithic tombs of the West Group, and a considerable number in the North Group were *passage graves*, the hunebeds. Their main building element is a *capstone* resting on two *sidestones*, in the form of a house of cards or the Greek letter *pi*, which is called a *yoke* or *trilithon*. Two or (many) more of these yokes were positioned in a row behind each other. If exceptionally large capstones were available, the number and position of the carrying sidestones was adapted accordingly. At the narrow ends there were one or two *endstones*. Sidestones and endstones were placed in a pit in the ground, about half a metre deep. Ideally, the sidestones had the form of an obliquely cut hardboiled egg and once placed in their foundation pit with their flat side slightly inclined to the interior of the chamber they were in a perfect balance. This position was usually consolidated by a nest of foundation stones at the bottom of the pit.

Hunebeds are usually oriented E-W with deviations to NE and SSW (González-Garcia and Costa-Ferrer 2007). The *entrance* or *passage* was in the middle of the southern or eastern long side. The entrance for short tombs was just a gap between sidestones, but the entrance for longer hunebeds was made of one or two, in one case three, yokes of heavy boulders, so that the ground-plan had the form of a short-stemmed T. Dutch hunebed chambers had 2 to 10 yokes and interior lengths ranging from 3 to 20 m. Much longer were the German passage graves

980-Damme and 830-Werlte, with interior lengths of 32 m or more and 27.5 m, respectively, with about 19-20 yokes and an interior chamber length of 28 m, respectively.[18] The extremely long passage graves are a peculiarity of the TRB West Group – in the North Group they do not exceed 16 m.[19]

The hunebed *chamber floor* was made by excavating down to the base of the sidestones and placing a layer of local erratic stones not larger than 45 cm, many of them broken, on top; this, in turn, was covered by a thin layer of burnt granite grit on which the deceased were laid. As mentioned previously, the sidestones and capstones usually have a flat inner side. The spaces between the orthostats were filled with a dry walling of broken local erratic stones. Sand was used to fill the spaces in the dry walling, but, curiously, loam does not seem to have been used. In some large hunebeds, shorter intermediary vertical stones between the orthostats were used to fill and consolidate the dry walling.

The tops of the sidestones were placed so that the flat undersides of the capstones would make a flat ceiling. The gaps between the capstones were carefully filled with smaller stones and covered with a sand layer. The exterior of the sidestones, endstones and dry walling of the sides and at least the lowest parts of the clefts between the capstones were covered with sod and earth. The tops of the larger capstones would have stuck out of these hunebed barrows.

---

18 Knöll (1983, 3). The greatly damaged *Hünengrab* 980-Damme had an interior chamber length of 32-34 m (Sprockhoff 1975, atlas-pl. 178, text-p. 145). The longest passage graves did not follow the regular 'yokes' / trilithons building principle. *Hünengrab* 830-Werlte-de hoogen Steener, with an interior chamber length of 27.5 m, had 17 sidestones on its northern side and 21 sidestones on its southern side, supporting 15 capstones, a narrow kerb and just one pair of entrance sidestones (Sprockhoff 1975, atlas-pls. 98-9, text-p. 94). Other examples are: D27-Borger, with an interior chamber length of 20.0 m, 9 capstones supported by 11 stones (10 sidestones and 1 intermediary shorter stone) on the northern side and 13 stones on the southern side (10 sidestones, 3 shorter intermediary stones); almost all kerbstones are missing (Van Giffen 1927, atlas-pl. 58; cf. Figure 52); D53-Havelte, with an interior chamber length of 16.95 m, has 10 yokes, but 1 short intermediary stone in the southern side, two pairs of entrance sidestones, one eastern endstone and *three* western endstones; D45-Emmerdennen, with an interior chamber length of 16.75-16.9 m, originally had 9 yokes (3 capstones are now missing), 2 endstones, 2 pairs of entrance sidestones and a kerb; the construction took advantage of the extreme size of capstone D6 to widen the chamber with a recess (Figure 67), using an extra sidestone next to the entrance. The tomb was restored in 1870. Van Giffen (1925, atlas-pl. 96) shows the situation in 1918. See Bakker (1992, fig. 7, p. 112-3, n. 30) for a discussion of the situation after Van Giffen's restorations of 1957 and 1968.

19 Sprockhoff's word (1938) can be relied on for the North Group passage graves in Germany. Svend Illum Hansen, of Kulturarv, Copenhagen, has kindly sent me a list of the longest Danish passage graves (letter of February 10, 2010): Nørre Ørslev on Falster: 16 m, 8-9 (?) chamber capstones; Vestenskov on Lolland: 12 m, 8 chamber capstones; Roholte on Zealand: 12 m; Græse on Zealand: 12 m; Vesterborg on Lolland: 11 m, 7 chamber capstones; Damsholte on Møn: 10 m, 7 chamber capstones. Plural or very long 'twin chambers' on Zealand are longer than 15 m. Hansen referred to his reports on the passage graves from Bornholm (1986), Samsø (1986), Gl. Holbæk amt (1986), Gl. Sorø amt (1987), København og Roskilde (1987), Frederiksborg amt (1988), Gl. Præstø amt (1990), Lollånd (1995), Falster (1995), Fyn (1997) and to his book *Jættestuer i Danmark* (Copenhagen 1993).
    As Poul Kjærum [who died in 2010] explained to me, in 1961, the Danish passage graves have a round, kerbed barrow, with a passage about half as long as the chamber and consist of a row of megalithic yokes.

Large hunebeds were surrounded by an oval or kidney-shaped *kerb* or *peristalith* of standing stones, which surrounded the earthen barrow, directly around its foot or at some distance from it. Most of the barrow and the dry walling are now gone from extant hunebeds leaving a bare skeleton of large boulders.[20]

The weight of the capstones of Dutch hunebed skeletons varies from one to about twenty tons, far less than the largest capstone of the former Surbolds Grab in the German Hümmling, which weighed almost 33.5 metric tons (see notes 105, 110 and 127). This was probably the maximum weight that could be managed.[21] As will be discussed below,[22] the building boulders were brought on a sledge from the eroded patches of moraine till where they were lying at the surface. The hunebeds were constructed on nearby dry 'coversands', not on the moist till soils. These sands contained no calcium or loam and were later heavily podzolised.

The Dutch hunebeds were built between about 3350 BC and 3050 BC (Lanting & Van der Plicht 2000; Brindley 1986b, 2003; Bakker 2005b). They were used for TRB interments up to 2800-2700 BC, when the TRB culture was succeeded by the Single Grave (*Einzelgrab*) culture, i.e. Corded Ware and Bell Beaker cultures (2800-2000 BC), which, given that their pottery and stone weaponry were deposited in the chambers, probably also interred some of their dead there. This practice continued till the end of the Barbed-Wire Beaker period (the Early Bronze Age), about 1800 BC.

After that the Dutch hunebed chambers were incidentally used for interments or at least depositions of artefacts. A flat piece of copper, about 3.5 x 4.5 cm, was found together with two complete Bell Beakers in the entrance of D15-Loon, in 1974; a Middle Bronze Age leaf-shaped and double-edged bronze razor, dated to 1400-1200 BC, was found in the spoil heaps of Van Giffen's excavations of hunebed D42-Westenes and its surroundings, in 1965; a *kerbschnitt*-decorated Bronze-Iron Age pot was found in hunebed D54b/c-Hooghalen; a Harpstedt pot from the Iron Age was the most recent deposit in the chamber of hunebed D26-Drouwenerveld (Bakker in prep.); a silver *denarius* of triumvir Antonius Augustus – the later Emperor Augustus – was allegedly found in an urn alongside the outer side of a kerbstone of hunebed D14-Eexterhalte[23]; finally, a golden *solidus* of the Roman Emperor Valentinianus I, coined AD 364-7, was found *near* hunebed D10-Gasteren (Van Ginkel et al. 1999, 120-2, 171; Bakker in prep.). But no general re-utilisation of the hunebeds took place during the Iron Age, as occurred with some megalithic tombs in Brittany, or during the Middle Ages, as in Mecklenburg.

---

20 Therefore it is difficult to prove that the barrow foot actually reached as far as the kerb.
21 A 62.5 ton boulder at Helpman, Groningen, was demolished in 1772 and a 55.5 ton boulder near Kalenkote, Overijssel, was demolished around 1732. The pieces were used for dike reinforcement (cf. section '1730-1734'). Apparently these boulders were much too unwieldy for hunebed building. And so was stone 'D48' near Noordbarge, Drenthe, which was left intact thanks to government protection (Appendix 1).
22 See section 'How was a hunebed constructed?'.
23 Van Lier 1760, 190-2; Bakker 1992, 59; see section '1756-1760'.

The later podsolization of the dry and non-calciferous coversand, on which the hunebeds were built, led to the almost complete disappearance of the unburnt bones of the interred persons and bones of animals that had been their ritual food. The artefacts preserved are (the sherds of) the numerous delicate and meticulously decorated ceramics, which probably had contained the victuals for the hereafter, dozens of transversal arrowheads, a few stone and flint axes and an occasional stone battle-axe. Also found were dozens of perforated beads, mainly of amber, although exceptionally of arsenical copper,[24] jet, quartz or other stone, one pierced fragment of a fossil ammonite with a spot of red ochre (Brongers 2006)[25], strips of arsenical copper (Schlicht 1973; Bakker 1979a, 127-31) and a few flint scrapers, sickle knives and other flint artefacts.[26]

The pottery had many standardised forms – for the first time in these regions – and displayed a gradual stylistic change, which has enabled us to distinguish a number of successive pottery phases (Bakker 1979a; Brindley 1986b; Van Ginkel et al. 1999, 40), as shown in Figure 2. The pot form and phase can even be identified from small decorated sherds.[27]

A2. Modern hunebed research began in 1912

Precise surveying of the Dutch hunebeds began with the works of W.C. Lukis and H. Dryden in 1878 and W.J. de Wilde in 1904-1910. The work of Lukis and Dryden actually represents a transition from 'antiquarian' to 'modern' hunebed research, but because their drawings and observations were not published, their impact on Dutch archaeology was negligible at the time.[28] After his intensive studies of the exterior of the hunebeds, De Wilde concluded, in 1905:

---

24 Hunebed D28-Buinen contained two 'cocoon-shaped' cylindric beads of spirally wound copper strips. The interpretation of the analyses of their metal composition is problematic (Butler & Van der Waals 1967, 76; Bakker 1979a, 127-30).

25 In the TRB settlement site Laren, province Noord-Holland, I found two fragmentary sea urchin fossils of flint, illustrating man's general interest in curious objects (Bakker 1979a, 192). Ten amber beads from hunebed D19-Drouwen are illustrated by Van Ginkel & Verhart 2009, photo 4.14 (see frontispiece).

26 A.L. van Gijn stated (lecture on February 6, 2010, *Steentijddag*, Leiden) that the flint axes, scrapers and sickle blades from hunebeds are used and resharpened, but that the tranversal arrowheads bear no signs of use.

27 General introductions to the TRB culture and the hunebeds in The Netherlands appeared in Louwe Kooijmans et al. 2005, *The Prehistory of The Netherlands* (Bakker & Van Gijn 2005; Bakker 2005b).

28 See note 2.

'our Hunebeds are a completely neglected part of our archaeology; so that, in fact, we do not even know the simplest things about them. It is more than high time to finally put the hands, or rather the minds into action.' [29]

Dryden and Lukis and De Wilde drew precise plans and made descriptions of the Dutch hunebeds. Lukis dug test pits in chambers and entrances, sieved the soil and drew potsherds recovered from TRB and other prehistoric periods, which are now in the Assen and Leiden museums of Antiquities[30] and the British Museum. Although the thorough studies of these three investigators are still a match for those of modern researchers, they restricted themselves to the outer appearance of the tombs and did not undertake any complete excavations of the chambers.

De Wilde's call to action was carried out twelve years later, in 1912, when Dr. Jan Hendrik Holwerda [1873-1951], curator of the National Museum of Antiquities in Leiden,[31] excavated the pair of hunebeds at Drouwen, D19 and D20, in a systematic, modern way. He documented the architecture, the stratigraphy of the chamberfills and what was left of the barrows. For the first time it became clear what bewildering masses of meticulously decorated pottery could be found in western hunebeds (Frontispiece).[32] They presumably contained provisions for the journey to the hereafter of those interred. Holwerda managed to have a greater part of the pottery restored – rather crudely – from sherds dispersed throughout the chambers and to publish his well-illustrated report within a year (Holwerda 1913a); publication in the German *Prähistorische Zeitschrift* (Holwerda 1913b) gained him and the Dutch hunebeds a considerable reputation abroad. Hardly any remains of the dead themselves were preserved. A few stone and flint axes suggested that the tombs were built in the Neolithic, or rather during a

---

29 De Wilde's letter to J.A.R. Kymmell, curator of the Drenthe Museum of Antiquities in Assen, December 10, 1905. In 1904, Beatrix Jungman, basing herself perhaps on the *Baedeker*, wrote in her book *Holland*: 'On our journey home we made a detour which gave us a sight of the Hunnebedden, old Roman remains for which Drenthe is famous. Where these enormous masses of granite were quarried, and by what means they were brought thither, are secrets buried with the wonders of the mechanism that raised the Pyramids and constructed the waterways of ancient Rome.' (p. 147).

30 Most provincial and local museums in The Netherlands were founded as 'Museum of Antiquities', in the 19th and early 20th century. They paid much attention to regional archaeology, but after 1945, they developed into regional museums for all possible aspects of nature, art and human life. The 'antiquities' character, especially 'archaeology' was often suppressed and neglected by the curators, who had been trained in art or biology, not archaeology.

31 The National Museum of Antiquities (*Rijksmuseum van Oudheden*) in Leiden is here further called 'the Leiden Museum'.

32 The Frontispiece gives a good impression of the rich finds in hunebed D19-Drouwen. Ninety-three reconstructed pots are shown (only a small part of the original number of ca. 400, see Staal-Lugten 1976a, b – which may be somewhat too high). Thirteen flint axes were found in the chamber, one axe of quartzite was found in the entrance. Among the flint axes was a heavy axe of the 'old type', FN:C–MNA:I, which is not shown. Ten amber beads are also shown.

Copper Age, because ornamental arsenical copper strips and spiral beads were also found. Other preserved ornaments were amber beads. D19 had nine pairs of side-stones and no kerb. D20 had six pairs of sidestones and a kidney-shaped kerb.[33]

In 1913, Holwerda excavated the only Dutch *langbett*, D43 at Emmen, which consisted of two hunebed chambers within a narrow kerb (Holwerda 1914, in *Prähistorische Zeitschrift*; see Figure 65). The contents of both chambers had been badly disturbed by recent digging.

Five years later, in 1918, Dr. Albert Egges van Giffen [1884-1973], of Groningen University, wrote a meticulous description of the present state of the Dutch hunebeds. That same year he also managed to excavate *five* hunebeds – D53-Havelte, D40-Emmerveld, D30-Exloo, D21-Bronneger and D22-Bronneger – and the site of a former hunebed, O1-De Eese. His magnificent publication of 1925-1927, *De Hunebedden in Nederland*, consists of two text volumes and an atlas. Volume 1 contains the updated 1918 report about the present state of the extant Dutch hunebeds (138 pages), a discussion of their architecture and orientation, a systematic geographical review of existing and lost hunebeds per *gemeente* and province (32 p.), a list of the available official reports on Dutch hunebeds (19 p.), an almost complete bibliography of more than 150 publications about Dutch hunebeds published up to 1920 and indices (vol. 1: 26 x 18.5 x 3 cm, 244 p.). Volume 2 contains a very complete and thorough analysis of the earlier literature published since 1685 (72 pages), a summary of Holwerda's and his own hunebed excavations in 1912, 1913 and 1918, and a well-illustrated description and discussion of the artefacts in these tombs (379 p.), remarks about the choice of terrain and orientation of hunebeds elsewhere in comparison with the Dutch ones (30 p.), a summary and final conclusions (23 p.), and a bibliography of more than 980 titles on megalithic tombs in Europe and elsewhere in the world (vol. 2: 26 x 20 x 6.5 cm, 580 p.). The atlas (51 x 33 x 5 cm) contains plans of all extant hunebeds on scale of 1:50 and Van Giffen's own photographs of each, the sideviews of several hunebeds by Dryden (1878), a distribution map, the plans, vertical sections and selected photographs of his own hunebed excavations and a plate with much reduced pottery illustrations (in addition to other pottery illustrations in vol.2). Van Giffen's choice of a 1:50 scale for the hunebed plans was clearly inspired by the Assen set of Dryden's plans drawn on scale 1:48 (¼ inch to 1 foot, cf. Bakker 1979c). In this work, Van Giffen developed a three-part typochronology for hunebed pottery (partly based on Holwerda's earlier research), which nicely paralleled the South-Scandinavian pottery typochronology.[34] He also compared the Dutch hunebeds to almost all other published hunebed excavations elsewhere. With Holwerda's publications and these three tomes, with their fine linen binding, Dutch hunebed archaeology had genuinely come of age.

---

33 In 1961-2, Van Giffen discovered the kerbstones, which had been pulled down sometime in prehistory. See Appendix 1.

34 As stated above, presently seven pottery 'horizons', Brindley 1-7, are discerned in the West Group (Figure 2).

In 1927, Van Giffen excavated hunebeds D14-Eexterhalte, D13-Eext and the sites of the demolished hunebeds D13b-Eext and D13c-Eext. He also investigated the sites of the demolished hunebeds D54b and D54c in 1946 and that of D54a-Spier in 1949.

Between 1957 and 1985, other hunebeds or sites of demolished hunebeds in the northeastern Netherlands were excavated by Cornelus Coenraad Willem Jan Hijszeler [1902-1982] (Lanting & Brindley 2004), myself (Bakker 1983), but principally by Jan Nanning Lanting.

In 1983, Lanting found that the hunebed G5-Heveskesklooster – an enlarged dolmen (Figure 59) – and a directly adjacent stone cist had been partly demolished before they were overgrown by peat, around 2000 cal BC. A few capstones, orthostats and – possibly – the dry-walling stones were removed, probably by Corded Ware, Bell Beaker or Early Bronze Age people. Until then it was generally assumed that all damage to Dutch hunebeds was done in recent history. The hunebed was never entirely covered by its barrow, which at most had reached up to the shoulder of the uprights and the lower parts of the clefts between the three capstones.

Meanwhile, between 1952 and 1972, Van Giffen restored almost all hunebeds with only two technical assistants. He improved the state of the ruined hunebeds considerably. The 'extraction holes' (my term) of missing orthostats were located by excavation and indicated by concrete markers at the surface called *plomben* ('plugs'), and the often damaged capstones were brought back in their original position, if possible.[35]

As an exhibition for visitors, he rebuilt the badly damaged hunebed D49-Papeloze Kerk. One half was restored to its supposed original condition and covered by an earthen barrow, while the other half was left without dry walling and earth cover, allowing comparison between the ruin and the original (Van Giffen 1961; 1969). Van Giffen placed a few copies of hunebed pottery in the restored chamber half, but these were immediately stolen.[36] Hunebed D49-Papeloze Kerk is easily accessible from the N376 road, halfway between Noordsleen and Schoonoord and worth a visit.

Van Giffen's idea that most of the capstones of the hunebeds were covered with earth is now heavily contested. Jan N. Lanting was the first post-war archaeologist in our country to argue that many West Group hunebeds were never completely

---

35 Unfortunately Van Giffen's reports of these restorations are brief or absent. Several extraction holes (my term) of missing uprights were traced under the turf and were indicated by placing *plombes* at the surface, but he probably interpolated the positions of others.

36 D. Versloot, expert restorer of the Leiden Museum, made these copies of existing pots using coloured synthetic material, according to Van Giffen's instructions. They were sufficiently realistic that the Harderwijk Museum bought most of them from the thieves or their buyers. A lady in Hoorn used a copy of a small decorated amphora, which her husband had bought on the market, as a vase to hold spoons, until it reached the Amsterdam Institute for Prae- and Protohistory (thanks to T.Y. van de Walle-van der Woude), where I used it to test the students during lectures on prehistoric pottery. To inexpert persons these pots looked perhaps original, but their stabbed-and-dragged decoration was a bad imitation of the originals.

covered by an earthen barrow, as were several hunebeds in Denmark, contrary to what I thought before (Bakker 1992). Much earlier, James Fergusson (1872, 321-2) wrote about hunebeds in Drenthe:

> 'it seems impossible to believe that on a tract of wretched barren heath, where the fee-simple of the land is not worth ten shillings an acre, any one could, at any time, have taken the trouble to dig down and cart away such enormous mounds as would have been required to cover these monuments.'

Indeed, Figures 6 and 8 demonstrate that larger hunebeds were neither entirely nor partially covered by earthen barrows in 1659, and Figure 28 shows that hunebed D6-Tynaarlo, with 3 yokes of large boulders, had no remains of a barrow in 1790. On the other hand, Figures 40 and 46 show that hunebed D15-Loon, with 5 yokes of boulders, was originally covered by a barrow that did not cover the upper parts of the capstones – before the barrow was taken away in 1870, during 'restoration' (Figure 60 gives its plan after this denudation).[37]

Van Giffen's restorations – including digging in and around most tombs – were executed without sieving and with little attention paid to sherds and other artefacts. Most were thrown back with the soil, although some arrived in the Assen Museum in his sandwich bags. The grand old man, who yearly reported to the Ministry of Education, was never checked by his pupils who had succeeded him in office. It is ironical that we are better informed about the relatively few sherds collected by Lukis and Dryden in 1878 than about those collected by Van Giffen in his later life (cf. Bakker & Waterbolk 1980).

Hunebeds in the adjacent part of Germany, to the west of the River Ems, near the Dutch provinces Drenthe and Overijssel were excavated by Elisabeth Schlicht, in 1955, and by Mahmoun Fansa, in 1981 (these tombs are listed in Bakker 1992, 6-7).

Anna L. Brindley analysed and published no less than four complete hunebed inventories: G3-Glimmen (Brindley 1983); G2-Glimmen (Brindley 1986a); D6a-Tynaarlo (formerly 'D6e', see Brindley et al. 2002 and Appendix 1); O2-Mander with adjacent flat graves (Lanting & Brindley 2004). She is now preparing catalogues of the inventories of hunebeds D14-Eexterhalte, D49-Papeloze Kerk and D54b- and D54c-Hooghalen, which Van Giffen excavated in 1927, 1938 and 1958, and 1946, respectively.[38] I published the inventory of hunebed G1-Noordlaren, excavated in 1957 (Bakker 1983) and am preparing that of D26-Drouwenerveld, excavated in 1968 and 1970.

---

37 West Group examples of German *Hünengräber*, which are not covered by an earthen barrow, are rendered by the following illustrations: 608-Bülzenbett-Sievern (W. Dilich 1604; Gummel 1938, pl. 3); a five-yoke *Hünengrab* near Heiden, Westphalia, which is not 985-Düvelsteene (J.H. Nunningh 1713; Gummel 1938, pl. 6). Nor are covering barrows shown on 909-Karlsteine (1726), 920-Gretesch (1726), and 806-810-Sieben Steinhäuser (1744) (Gummel 1938, pl. 7; Sprockhoff 1975, pl. 24).

38 Pers. comm. A.L. Brindley, 2009. It is hoped that funding for these publications will soon be found. Once that occurs almost all of Van Giffen's TRB pottery in systematically excavated hunebeds will finally be published.

Between 1908 and 1911, Holwerda excavated a TRB settlement and flat graves in and around the Hunneschans, a medieval enclosure on Lake Uddel, province Gelderland.[39] Half a century later, modern investigations of TRB settlements began with the excavation of the small palisaded TRB settlement of Anloo in Drenthe, in 1957-8 (Waterbolk 1960). Several other TRB settlements sites and flat graves have been excavated since then, but no house plans have been recovered in The Netherlands. Most settlements have been found on the presently dry 'coversands' of the eastern, Pleistocene part of the country north of the Rhine and Lek rivers, but the sites of Slootdorp-Bouwlust and Slootdorp-Kreukelhof, *gemeente* Wieringermeerpolder, 50 km north of Amsterdam, excavated by Willem Jan [J.W.H.] Hogestijn, lay in a wetter context of silts and clays, where organic materials, such as animal bones, wood and seeds, are well-preserved. These sites were probably seasonally occupied by inhabitants of permanent settlements on the coversand flanks of the former island of Wieringen, which have not yet been discovered.[40]

A fragmentary TRB canoe, almost 8 m long and 80 cm wide, was found in Dijkgatsweide, Wieringermeerpolder, in 2007, and is now in the process of being preserved in PEG (poly ethylene glycol).[41]

The 'wet' outskirts of a Neolithic settlement and cemetery site on a sand dune attached to a small push moraine ridge on Lot P14 in the Noordoostpolder, 65 km northeast of Amsterdam, were excavated in several campaigns by Willem Jan Hogestijn, Theo [T.J.] ten Anscher and Eli [E.F.] Gehasse, between 1982 and 1992. This sandy outcrop in the bank of the River Vecht(e) was occupied from the Swifterbant culture up to the Early Bronze Age. The ecology of this site and the surrounding landscape were studied by Wouter Gotjé (1993) and Eli Gehasse (1995). The site stratigraphy, the artefacts recovered and the surrounding landscape are comprehensively discussed by Theo ten Anscher (in prep.).

Dry 'coversands' as a preferred location for the other Dutch hunebed, flat grave and settlement sites have been dealt with by Wieringa (1968), Bakker (1982) and Bakker & Groenman-van Waateringe (1988).

---

39 few additional minor observations were made in the 1960s (see Bakker 1979a, 194-6).
40 Hogestijn & Drenth 2001.
41 Preservation by RCE-Lelystad. The canoe is made of oak; one transverse rib, about 7 cm in height, and a rudimentary rib are carved out in the interior. C14-date GrN-30113: 4500 ± 30 BP or 3343-3096 cal BC (2 sigma). It was found in a creek, more than 10 m wide, lying at 4.52-4.64 below NAP (Dutch Ordnance Datum, i.e. about sea level) between higher coversand ridges (surfaces 3.9-6.6 below NAP). On top of a sandy rise, at 3.9 below NAP, less than 25 m from the canoe, a piece of flint refuse was recovered from a bore hole, which suggests the presence of a contemporary settlement, according to Mr. Yannick Henk of RAAP West (pers. comm., 2009), who surveyed the local geology, and the CD *Een 5000 jaar oude kano in de Wieringermeer* (Prov. Noord-Holland / Studio John Meijer 2008). A complete publication with the reconstructed form of the canoe, the local vegetation, and the salinity and possible tidal character of the creek is in preparation. Van Ginkel & Verhart 2009, photograph 4.12. De findspot lies ca. 62 km north of Amsterdam.

In 1959, Johan Herman Isings [1884-1977] drew his school picture[42] of the 'Hunebed Builders' on a cloudy, but dry winter day (Figure 3). He consulted prehistoric archaeologists – Albert Egges van Giffen [1884-1973], Harm Tjalling Waterbolk [1924], Willem Glasbergen [1923-1979] and Hendrik Brunsting [1902-1997] – about every detail.[43] After fifty years, this composition of diagonally arranged elements showing what a Neolithic settlement looked like on a winter day without snow or rain is still quite inspiring.[44]

Also in 1959, the idea occurred to Van Giffen and the writer Evert Zandstra [1897-1974] that a museum devoted to the hunebeds and the Hunebed Builders should be created at Borger, a village in the midst of the Drenthe hunebeds. Zandstra (1959, 99-100) thought the museum should be placed next to D27-Borger, the longest hunebed in the country. But the exposition, made by Johan Diderik van der Waals and Wiek Röhling, which was opened in 1967, found place in a restored ancient wooden farmhouse in the village. It burned down, was re-installed by the same men, burned down again and was ultimately moved to the former Workhouse, Bronnegerstraat 12, Borger, which was near D27. The present 'Hunebedcentrum' was opened in 2005 opposite the Workhouse and next to hunebed D27 – Zandstra's ideal – in an elegant stone museum designed by the architects Aldo E. van Eyck [1918-1999], Hannie van Eyck-van Roojen and Abel Blom. The archaeologist Evert van Ginkel designed the exposition within. This Hunebed Centre is a modern museum presenting an all-round picture of what is presently known and thought about the hunebeds and the TRB culture in The Netherlands. Much attention is given to the pottery,[45] ritual deposits and research history. A visit is worth-while both for the general public and specialists, and can be combined with visits to neighbouring hunebeds. There are 100,000 visitors a year.

---

42 'School pictures' are large coloured illustrations mounted on cardboard (86 x 67 cm, 107 x 77 cm, etc.), illustrating historical scenes, geographical views, plants or animals, etc., which were used for education in primary schools, where they often hang on the walls of school classes. They were accompanied by instruction booklets for the teachers. Most of the Dutch ones were published by Wolters and Noordhoff, Groningen. They were generally used in Dutch, German, Danish (Bakker 1990a) and Swedish (Mankell 2010, 176) schools.

43 See Isings's own description of the school picture (reprinted as Isings 1975) and my extensive comments (Bakker 1990a, 49-60).

44 The clothes known from Danish Bronze Age finds are cut at the waistline, as are these in Isings's picture and on the puppets in the Hunebed Centre at Borger. But the 'Ice Man' or 'Oetzi', whose frozen body was found at the Italian-Austrian border in the Oetztal Alps, in 1991, had a dress without waistline and belt, not unlike the former Tierra del Fuegans. Because Oetzi's northern Italian culture differed considerably from the TRB culture, and the Dutch hunebed region remained part of the northern German and southern Scandinavian 'Nordic' *Kulturkreis* throughout the prehistoric period, the TRB Drenthians probably had clothes that foreshadowed the Danish ones.

45 An ample selection of the pottery and other artefacts from hunebed D26-Drouwenerveld, which Van Giffen, Glasbergen and I excavated in 1968 and 1970 (Bakker in prep.) is a prominent element in the exposition.

Figure 3. Hunebed Builders on a cloudy November day, a now famous school picture by J.H. Isings, from 1959 (photograph Onderwijsmuseum, Rotterdam). See further Appendix 3.

A splendid book by Wijnand A.B. van der Sanden (2007) is devoted to hunebeds D17 and D18 at Rolde, Drenthe. It exemplifies the ample attention paid to Drenthe hunebeds in modern times. Although these two hunebeds have not been systematically excavated, the book presents their architecture, their preservation and legal protection, regional context, and most records and pictures made between 1642 and the present day.

Finally, Evert van Ginkel, Sake Jager and Wijnand van der Sanden (Van Ginkel et al. 1999; 2nd edition 2005) have compiled most of what is known about the Dutch hunebeds, their makers and the research history in a beautifully illustrated book.

Let us now turn to the main subject of this book, the research of the Dutch hunebeds before 1912. As far as written records go, it began as early as 1547, but the generic term *hunnebedden* has medieval roots.

B. Research of Dutch hunebeds before 1912

Chaque période possède ses questionnements et ses moyens, parmi lesquels les facultés intellectuelles et les techniques pour tenter d'y répondre.

P. GOULETQUER 2009, 465

B1. General remarks

The general history of antiquarian archaeology in northwestern Europe is described by a great number of authors, with due emphasis on the early research of megalithic monuments.[46] For unknown reasons – language barriers? –, they have paid no attention, however, to the antiquarian history of The Netherlands, apart from Picardt's illustration of giant hunebed builders published in 1660 (Figure 8). Eminent Dutch researchers, such as Van Lier (1760), Westendorp (1815, 1822) and Janssen (1848, 1853a), have remained out of sight. I will try to fill in this hiatus in this book.

In *The Testimony of the Spade*, Geoffrey Bibby (1957, 241) made this statement about megalithic monuments:

'*These varied monuments of gigantic stones were never "discovered" – they had, in fact never been unknown.*'[47]

The generic name *Hunnebedden* ('Giant's Beds' or 'Giants' Beds') reveals their medieval explanation.[48] It took considerable time before megalithic tombs were "discovered" by the learned European world, however. This discovery happened particularly beyond the Roman frontiers in northern Europe, where no ruins of Roman buildings or other constructions were readily visible.

The mention of a hunebed near Rolde in Drenthe by Schonhovius, AD 1547, is the earliest specific record known of hunebeds west of Hamburg. Despite the questions these megaliths posed by their size and origin of the huge boulders with

---

46 Gummel 1938; Stemmermann 1934; Daniel 1938, 1941, 1958, 1960, 1970; Schnapp 1993; Wollf 1994; Trigger 2006.

47 As quoted by Magdalena Midgley in her opening speech of the 'Borger Meeting', at Borger in Drenthe, which was devoted to the TRB culture and its megaliths, November 25-28, 2009.

48 For regional variants and other use of this and related terms, see below.

which they were constructed; it would take more than a century before Picardt (1660) studied them more closely; the number and the quality of publications about them increased only gradually in the course of time.[49]

In the northern Netherlands, megalith research did not develop much differently than that in surrounding countries, although the tempo and impact varied from country to country. The concepts of that research changed with the prevailing opinions of each time – the Epilogue touches briefly on the succession of these in The Netherlands. Before the late 18th century, discourse about hunebeds took place mainly in studies of Drenthe – their main distribution area – and not in the general historiographies of the Dutch Republic.

In contrast to earlier studies, the present study is not restricted to old observations and considerations which conform with or contribute to our current ideas,[50] but it also deals with views that may now seem strange, but were perfectly logical or at least acceptable at their time. Van Giffen, who laid a firm basis for the study of the history of Dutch hunebed research (1925, IIb, 212-29, 243-4; 1927, 3-78, 526) and who I follow here in many respects, omitted, for example, an analysis of Schonhovius's discussion, in 1547, of one or two hunebeds near Rolde, 'a few irrelevant quotations from classical authors' in the excavation report of D17-Rolde from 1706,[51] and the more general theories of Van Lier (1760) and Westendorp (1815, 1822). Van Giffen (1927) often quoted his sources at length, but his primary aim was not writing a history of Dutch hunebed research. He omitted 'incorrect ideas' found in early sources and used the earlier sources on stratigraphy in hunebed chambers primarily to refute Holwerda's opinion (1913a; b) that the TRB deposits consisted of only one layer and were therefore without chronostratigraphical significance. To detect stratigraphies so that typochronological successions of TRB pottery found therein could be established was a main aim of his hunebed research (1927). Later research (Van Giffen 1943b and later investigations) showed, to his dismay, that Holwerda was right, after all. No typochronological order in the superposition of artefacts has been found in any hunebed chamber west of the Elbe – despite Knöll's interpretation (1959, pls. 43-4) of Van Giffen's record of the chamberfill of hunebed D21-Bronneger (Van Giffen 1927,

---

49 About 109 titles, written between 1547 and 1910, listed in the 'References' of this study concern the Dutch hunebeds directly. One fourth appeared before 1812, between 1610 and 1810, at an average rate of 1.3-1.4 per decade. Since 1810, 8 publications on average appeared per decade.

50 These approaches could be called 'utilitarian', followed by what Arentzen (2007) calls 'the veneration of success' or 'progress' (e.g. Atkinson 1956; Daniel 1981; Trigger 2006). 'Presentism' is a comparable term (internet). Earlier, Jan Romein (1932, xxii-xxiv) pleaded for an objective rendering of the opinions of medieval authors and their arguments, whether correct or not.

51 Van Giffen 1927, 9. Actually the only quotation he omitted was from Alessandro Alessandri (1522); see section '1706'.

231-71). In retrospect, the presence of (later) Zigzag Beakers and Pot Beakers in the middle of the three layers and the TRB pot types in the lower and middle layers show that both were mixed together during or after Beaker times.[52]

The 53 extant hunebeds and the 24-28 known or assumed sites of demolished hunebeds lie in the three northeastern provinces of The Netherlands, Groningen, Drenthe and Overijssel. According to J.N. Lanting (1994 and 1997), the 'hunebeds' F1-Riis and D31b-Exloo were not normal passage graves, but large cists. This may also have been the case with the supposed hunebed D39a-Emmerveld (see Appendix 1). The remnants of another possible megalithic tomb, U1-Lage Vuursche, are found in the province of Utrecht (Bakker 2004; 2005a). The vast majority of hunebeds are in Drenthe, however.

For brevity's sake, I will generalise here that the Dutch hunebeds are oriented E-W, with an entrance in the middle of the southern side, and will designate them using the code number given by Van Giffen (1925), for example D27, D13, G1, and their present locality name. The extant German *Hünengräber* have a locality name preceded by the number given by Sprockhoff (1966, 1967, 1975).

I use such period or culture designations as 'Stone Age', 'Metal Age', 'TRB*' and 'Bell Beaker*' etc. anachronistically, and an asterisk (*) is used if the period / culture was not yet recognised or had not yet acquired the name. [Cal] BC belongs to the same category – in theory all C14-dates designated in years BC are calibrated, viz. identical to genuine solar or historical years.

Publications which I did not study myself, at least not recently, are indicated by #, because a major difficulty in studying the history of archaeology is not knowing if observations described in recent and older publications are first hand. This problem is encountered in the impressive work by Bruce Trigger (2006), who apparently read few German publications himself. Hans Gummel (1938), on the other hand, was extremely careful to indicate his secondary sources as such. To find the full titles of older publications, I was greatly helped by Wout Arentzen and by information available on the internet. Dates of the life of most persons discussed are given within square brackets, [ ]; the year of publication of their studies within round brackets, ( ).

During most of its history as part of The Netherlands, Drenthe has been the poorest, most backward and most unknown region of the country. Until 1814, its government was left to decide more or less independently on internal matters and the hunebeds remained strictly a Drenthe affair until about 1870. Until 1795, Drenthe was a 'Landscape', not a Province of the Dutch Republic, was led by a *Drost* or '*Land-Drost*' (Bailiff), paid very little taxes and had no vote in the General States government of the Republic in The Hague. After the French oc-

---

52 W. Glasbergen and I started, together with Van Giffen, the excavation of hunebed D26-Drouwenerveld in 1968 in the hope that we could record a stratigraphy in typochronological order in the chamber by carefully recording the positions of each sherd, but in vain. Van Giffen, who was convinced of the impossibility of our aim, would have preferred us to excavate in successive horizontal planes, to see if body silhouettes were still visible, a method he had just successfully applied in his excavations of *Hünengräber* at Oldendorf an der Luhe in Germany (cf. Körner & Laux 1980). But we did not comply.

cupation of 1795, the Landscape of Drenthe and the provinces constituting the Republic of the United Netherlands were reorganised in *Departements* under a more centralised government in The Hague. After the political 'Restoration' in 1813, they became 'Provinces' under a 'King's Governor', later retitled 'King's' or 'Queen's Commissioner'.

Drenthe, now a province in the northeastern part of The Netherlands, which is surrounded by the Dutch provinces Friesland, Groningen, Overijssel, and the Land Niedersachsen (Lower Saxony) in Germany, was many travel hours away from The Hague until the 1860s. According to De Leth's table of distances (ca.1765), in which the walking rate used is no less than 5.6 km per hour, Drenthe would have been 40 hours away by foot from The Hague in the 18th century. Lonsain (1915) calculated comparable travel times by land in the 17th century, including the changing of post coaches etc. The railway stretches completed between Utrecht and Zwolle (1864), Zwolle and Meppel (1867) and Meppel-Assen-Groningen (1870) ultimately reduced the travel time to The Hague ultimately to five or six hours.

The uncivilised backwardness of Drenthe is illustrated by the fact that in 1808 the Danish philologist and classical historian B.G. Niebuhr was hooted at and pelted with dirt in Meppel, a small, but yet the largest town in Drenthe (Fuchs & Simons 1977, 131, citing from Niebuhr's *Circularbriefe aus Holland*, 1808 #).

The word hunebed

The Dutch word *hunebed*, formerly *hunnebed, hunnenbed, hunenbed* or *huinebed*,[53] consists of *bed*, meaning 'bed' or 'grave' (cf. German *Hünengrab*), and *hun / huyn / hiun*, plural and genitive singular *hunnen*, meaning giant, giant's, or giants' in the Middle Ages.[54]

Hun ('giant') may sometimes have been confused with the notorious nomadic Huns, who, under Attila (AD 433-53), formed an empire that covered Europe north of the Roman Empire and reached as far as the Frisian and Frank territories in the present-day Netherlands and Belgium.[55] Westendorp (1815, 1822) demon-

---

53 If rendered in German phonetic spelling, these Dutch words are pronounced *hünebed, *hünebedden, formerly *hö: ne(n)bett, *hö: ne(n)bedden. The spelling *huinebed*, probably also pronounced as *hünebett, was used by the editor of the 3rd ed. (1774) of Smids (1711).

54 Verdam 1911. Several dictionaries of Medieval Dutch and Medieval Lower or High German present no other explanations of these words than those discussed here. Most rely on Jacob Grimm (1844, 433 #, pers. comm. W. Arentzen). F. KLUGE, *Etymologisches Wörterbuch der Deutschen Sprache*, 19th ed., revised by W. Mitzka. Berlin, 1963, 320-1, tells that *Hüne, heune, hiune* meaning 'Riese' is documented since the 13th century, but that the root *Hūn-* in Germanic personal names meant 'young animal' esp. 'young bear'– I thank professor W.P. Gerritsen, Utrecht, for this reference.

55 McEvedy 1961, 20-1. Barraclough (1994, 32-3, 1) indicates the extension of the raids of the Huns and Avars. The latter, who were also called White Huns, and later Bulgars, founded the Avar Khanate in the 6th to 8th centuries AD, which covered at its maximum extension former Eastern Germany in the west (McEvedy 1961, 30-4, 44-5).

strated that the Huns could not have built hunebeds and pleaded that *hunebed* be written with one *n*, a spelling which only became completely accepted in Dutch academic circles about 1950.

The medieval definition of *hun* to mean 'giant' had been common knowledge in Middle Lower German and Middle Dutch (e.g. Jacob van Maerlant, 13th century). But it was forgotten before the end of the 16th century, even though it occurs throughout the Dutch-German language area in the names of gigantic earthworks, such as *Hunneschans* and *Hunnenborg* in The Netherlands and the famous *Heuneburg* on the Danube, south of Stuttgart in Germany. That the word *hun* for 'giant' has got out of use before 1590 is shown by the explanation that *hune* means '*riese oder gigant*' by Jonkheer Sweder Schele van Welevelt [1569-1639], written shortly after 1591 in his *Hausbuch* (manuscript, 1591-1637).

Schele wrote shortly after 1591 about *der Hunen greber* (*der Hünen Gräber*, viz. 'graves of the Giants, *Hünengräber* in High German) in the wider surroundings of Osnabrück-Minden-Lake Dümmer, Germany, which he considered as tombs and altars:

> '*Diesen* [Abgöttern] *haben zie* [die Germanen] *hin und here die busche und grossen walde geweihet und mit besonderen ceremoniën darin verehret ohn zweiffell bei ihren begrebnussen, und daher, halt ich, sein ubrig hin und wider in Westphalen die grossen stein-hauffen, deren viel in den buschen umb der Schelenburg, dem hause zu Raden und anderswo. Es sagen auch die bauren und inwoner des lands, das dieselbigen stein-hauffen der Hunen greber sein. Hune ist aber so viel gesagt als ein riese oder gigant, wie dan auch Berosus diese ertzvetter giganten nömet. Diese stein-hauffen liggen uber malkanderen gleich wie altaren, also das es scheinet, das sie ihr opfferhande darauff mussen gethan haben.*' (Schele 1591-1637, 1: 18-9).[56]

Berosus, a Chaldean (Babylonian) priest [3rd century BC], was the alleged author of a history of the world from the Flood to the foundation of Troy, to which a commentary was added by Annius of Viterbo (1498 #). Actually the whole work was invented by Annius himself. In addition to the classical sources, the book was welcomed for providing information about the earliest inhabitants of Europe and was faithfully cited by Schele and Picardt (1660) and several other early historians. 'Berosus' said that Noah and his sons were giants and he presented a pedigree from them to Germanic tribes.

---

56 In 1630, Schele described a 'stone heap' (*Steinhauffen*) in detail, probably hunebed 897 near Ueffeln and Bramsche, Germany, which is still extant and unaltered. While there, he heard that there were 'many more' in the nearby Giersfeld, which is still true (889-896). He also mentioned hunebeds in the neighbourhood of Schledehausen (for instance: 906-7, 917-8, 922-3) and one large stone heap ('altar') directly opposite Rahden House near Espelkamp and others nearby (Recke, now destroyed?: Sprockhoff 1975, 149) (Schele 1591-1630, I, 18-9, 164, 223-4). Although he knew the eastern Netherlands quite well, he did not mention Dutch hunebeds.

The terms *hu(n)ne(n)bedden* / *Hünengräber* were originally used for barrows in general, as they still were in 19th-century Dutch Gelderland, Overijssel and Limburg (also *hunnenbelten, hunnenbergen*).[57] In the adjacent German County of Bentheim, barrows were called *Hünenpölle*[58] and cremation urns *Hünenpötte* (Schlicht 1962). According to Von Estorff (1846, 9-10), the term *Hünengrab* was used for both megalithic tombs and earthen barrows in German Hanover. He listed 28 specific or general names of hunebeds (Richter 2002, 150). Picardt (1660, 32-3; 44) used *Hune-bedden* and *Hune-bergen* in Drenthe and surroundings for the few earthen barrows in which he supposed that giants were buried.

In Germany, between 1320 and 1475, placenames, such as *under Hyne grebern, ze Hünengreber(n), an Hununggreberweg* and *zen haidengrebern*, were used for non-megalithic barrows near Frankfurt am Main and in the Breisgau, where hunebeds were absent (Sippel 1980, 145; cf. also J. Grimm 1844, 433 #, quoted in Arentzen 2006). Rarer variants were *Heldenbetten* ('heroes' beds', in the 16th to 19th-century Altmark and Brandenburg,[59] *heroum sepulchra*,[60] *Riesen- oder Heldenbette*' in the Mark Brandenburg),[61] *Heidenbetten* and *Wendensteine* ('heathen's beds' and 'Wendish Stones').[62]

The word *Steenhoop*, 'stone heap(s)', was used by Schele in present-day Westphalia-Lower Saxony shortly after 1591 (*stein-hauffen*, see above) and shortly after 1630 (*steenhopen* – the plural form used for a single hunebed). The term *Steinhaufen* remained in use in 20th-century Lower German dialects in Geramany (e.g. in Hanum, at the border of the Altmark and Hanover, in the 1940s: Bock 2008, 147-8).

In Drenthe, Schonhovius (1547), Kempius (1588) and Emmius (1596) did not yet have a specific term for hunebeds (Bakker 2002). The word *hunnebedden* and its variants specifically used for hunebeds in Drenthe first appeared in print in the 17th century. Martinus Hamconius [Maarten Hamkema] (1609, 33v-34) wrote *Hunnebedden*, probably referring to hunebeds, not barrows. A manuscript map drawn by Cornelis Danckerts and Pieter Serwouters, from shortly after 1648, denotes D52-Diever as *'t hunnebet* (Coert 1991, fig. 32). Simon van Leeuwen (1685, 230) wrote *Hunen ofte reusen bedden* (Huns' or Giants' Beds').[63] He wrote

---

57 Pleyte (1877-79, 118; 1885, 17, 20) referred to the following cases where the word *hunebed* was applied to other phenomena than hunebeds: earthen barrows at Ellersinghuizen, gemeente Vlagtwedde (province of Groningen); Nutter, Gemeente Tubbergen (Overijssel); two rectangular fields within embankments, perhaps former sheep-folds, at Kootwijk (Gelderland); *Wievenbelten* or *Hunenbelten* at Weerselo (Overijssel). In his opinion *hunebed* was a scientific term, whereas the local word was *steenhoop* or *dikke steenen*. *Hunneveld* was the name of an unreclaimed field near Oldenzaal (Gallée 1901). The Dutch *Topographical Maps* indicate several other locality names with the prefix *Hun-* or *Huin-* on the Dutch sandy soils north of the Rhine.

58 Gallée (1901) recorded the term *hunnepollen* for urnfields on the Tankenberg near Oldenzaal. The Dutch town of Oldenzaal borders on German Bentheim.

59 Entzelt 1579 #; Von Bombeck (1741 #, cited by Fritsch & Mittag 2006, 14).

60 Schaten 1690 #, cf. Gummel 1938, 25 n. 7; 69.

61 Pallas 1771, 673-4, cf. Wetzel 2002, 18-34.

62 Bekmann & Bekmann 1751 #, cf. Fritsch & Mittag 2006, 15; Mittag 2006, 8-9.

63 But in note *m*, p. 293, Van Leeuwen spelled *Hunne ofte Reusen bedden* and on p. 253, note *k*, 'Hunne or Hune is misprinted as Hume.

that these were the local names for the hunebeds in Drenthe, which he had visited himself (1685, 230, 293 n.1). Titia Brongersma (1686, 8) wrote a poem 'LOF OP 'T HUNNE-BED, of de ongemeene, opgestapelde Steenhoop tot BORGER IN DRENTHE' ('Laudation of the Hunne-Bed, or the extraordinary, piled Stoneheap at Borger in Drenthe').

Thus *Hunnebedden*, *huinebedden* and *hunebedden* became the general terms used for hunebeds in Drenthe in the course of the 17th century.[64] But the synonym *steenhoopen* was also used in print for Dutch hunebeds from 1660 (Picardt), 1685 (Brongersma) and 1711 (Smids) to 1724 (H. van Rijn).

Picardt (1660, 32) used the term *groote Steen-Hoopen* ('large Stone-heaps') for hunebeds in Drenthe[65] and called round earthen barrows *Hune-bergen* ('Giant's mounds'). Only once he used the term *Hune-Bedden* (p. 32-3) specifically for hunebeds, however.[66] This may show, perhaps, that he was aware of the more specific use of the word for [megalithic] hunebeds and considered using the term throughout in this sense, but did not after all.

Earlier terms were *stienberch*, *steenberch* (1642)[67], *steenhoop* (both meaning 'heap [or mound] of [large] stones'), and *reusenstien* (1642, 'giant stone(s)' or 'giant's stone(s)').[68] *Steenberch* / *steenberg* was a much more common placename than *Steenhoop*; it was used eleven times to designate a hunebed and was the most common placename for a hunebed in Drenthe and Groningen (Huiskes 1985, 1990). The Drenthe village of Steenbergen derives its name from the nearby hunebed (D1-Steenbergen).

The only place where *Hunnebed* was used as a placename was for the cluster of hunebeds at Borger (Huiskes 1985, 1990); on a map from shortly after 1648, hunebed D52-Diever is named *'t hunnebet* (Coert 1999, see above) and in the course of the 17th century *hunnebedden* became the generic name for hunebeds among scholars (see above). Yet *Steenhoop* was the local name for the hunebeds D19 and D20 at Drouwen near Borger. In print, the name was also used for D27-Borger and perhaps for D23, D24 and D25 at Bronneger, however (Brongersma 1685; Smids 1694, 1711).

---

64 Van Slichtenhorst, historian of Gelderland (where no hunebeds were found), wrote '*Huynen ... graven*' under German influence (1654, 77-8).
65 About Picardt, see section '1660'.
66 '*Sommige* [Reusen] *zijn begraven op een effen grondt / en de levendighe hebben ronde Berghjes t'samen ghedragen van aerde / op de graven / en die heeft men genaemt* Hune-Bergen , *dat zijn* Reusen-Bergen. *In Drenth vint men seer weynigh Steenen / of zy zijn aen dese* Hune-Bedden *geimployeert. Ergo / daer zijn meer ghestorven en begraven / als zy met Steenen hebben konnen ver-eeren; of 't en waer dat men sustineren wilde / dat de groote Vlinten en* Reusen *te ghelijck een eynde souden hebben : 't welck dan wat vreemts soude zijn.*' (Picardt 1660, 32-3).
    This (not completely clear) passage means, literally: 'Some [*Giants*] are buried on a flat ground / and the living have carried earth together on the graves / and these were called *Hune-Bergen*, which are *Giant's mounds*. Only very few [large] stones are found in Drenthe, which are not employed in these *Hune-Bedden*. Ergo / more [*Giants*] have died and were buried than they could honour with [large] stones; or it could be sustained, on the other hand, that the heavy boulders and *Giants* had run out simultaneously; but this would seem somewhat strange.'
67 *Berch* is presently spelled *berg*, as Picardt did, see note 66.
68 Van der Sanden 2007, 4, 17, 57-8, 200 n. 2; Bakker 2004, 201.

Dikke Steen or *Dikke Stenen*, meaning 'Thick Stone(s)', was used for the hunebeds D14-Eexterhalte, D15-Loon and possibly D53 and D54 at Havelte. *Bruin Steen*, meaning 'Brown Stone(s)', was used for the *langbett* of D43-Emmen. *Steenakker* ('Field at the Stones') is linked to 22 known hunebed sites in Drenthe-Groningen; *Hunnesteenakker* ('Field at the Hun's Stones') is linked to the hunebeds D36 and D37 at Valthe (Huiskes 1985, 1990).

The suggestion that *hunne* means *henne* ('corpse') (Liebers 1986, 37-8), made by Hamconius (1609, 33v-34), is unconvincing, because it does not account for *hunne / heune* in the names of the mentioned gigantic earthworks. He wrote:

> '*Vulgo Hunnebedden hunne mortuum sonabat Frisiis unde Vestes defunctorum Gronengae adhuc Hunnecleden appellantur.*'[69]

Nunningh (1714, 85) referred to Waraeus[70] as giving the same meaning. Van Lier (1760, 24), without citing anyone, defended 'corpse' as the meaning of *hunne*. Westendorp (1822, 6), referring to both above sources, rejected the idea, but Janssen (1848, 166-84) quoted Hamconius's lines and accepted it (p. 166). Gallée (1901) wrote that *hennekleed* and variants were used by occupants of the northern Dutch sandy soils east of the Zuider sea and River IJssel north of the Rhine. Similar words for 'shroud' were widely current in Germany: *hen klod* (Saterland), *hunnekled* (Lower German), *Henenkleid* (Emsland), *hennekleed* (1828, Emsbühren) and also in 'Dutch West-Friesland', viz. the Dutch province of Friesland: *hin kled* (Liebers 1986, 37).

A totally different suggestion, made by W. Arentzen (letter of January 30, 2007), is that *henne* may have been the predecessor of the modern Dutch word 'heen', meaning 'away'. Thus *heengaan* (Dutch) or *hennegoan* (western Saxon dialect) would mean 'going / passing away, to die'. This conforms with the Dutch word *hennekleed*, meaning 'the shroud of a deceased', and *verhennekleden*, 'laying out, shrouding a corpse', which was a current expression in the Saxon dialect of Overijssel in 1874.[71] The idea that *hunebedden* meant 'beds or graves of the dead' was therefore correctly rejected by Westendorp.[72]

The Dutch theologian Stephaan Adriaan Buddingh [1811-1869] suggested, presumably,[73] that the word *hune* in the *Codex Aureus* by Ulfilas meant 'offering', but this unconvincing idea was not followed or mentioned by others.

---

69   A translation is complicated by lack of punctuation. I venture: 'General term *Hunnebedden*; *hunne* means *dead bodies* among the Frisians, therefore the garments of the dead (shrouds) are called *hunnecleden* in Groningen, moreover'. Cf. Janssen 1848, 176-7

70   Sir James Ware / Jacobus Waraeus [1594-1666], mentioned in *Republyk der Geleerden*, May-June, 1713 #.

71   About *verhennekleden*, see Ter Gouw (1874, 251, 253) and Gallée (1901) (W. Arentzen, pers. comm.).

72   This since long outdated definition was still being used by the leading *Woordenboek der Nederlandsche Taal* (Dictionary of the Dutch language), vol. 6 (1912), 1319 *s.v.* 'Hunnebed'. I thank professor W.P. Gerritsen, Utrecht, for this reference.

73   According to the relatively unreliable T. Pluim (1896, 287-8), who wrote 'One of our historians, presumably Dr. Buddingh, ...' without any further reference (W. Arentzen, pers. comm., 2010).

Mohen's translation (1997) of the name '*Hühnenbetten*', as spelled by Wedel 1812 (Appendix 2A) and by Bödiker (1828, only on p. 174), as 'chicken's bed'[74] is utter nonsense, of course.

'*Giants*' *become* '*devils and demons*'

The names *hunebedden* in Dutch, meaning 'giant's beds' or 'giants' beds', and *Hünengräber* in German, meaning 'giants' graves', demonstrate the general, probably pre- and early Christian belief that only giants could have built hunebeds. This idea was still defended by the Danish historian Saxo Grammaticus, who died in 1208 (Fritsch & Mittag 2006, 13).

But under Christian influence, giants were later regarded as the Devil and his demons (Liebers 1986, 66).[75] This may have occurred in the 14th and 15th century in The Netherlands (and northwestern Germany), when a genuine '*demono-mania*' was manifest, according to the historians Johan Huizinga (1919, 411) and Jan Romein (1932, 155). It may have continued here into the 16th century. In eastern German Silesia, replacement of giants by the Devil in legends was still going on in the early 20th century:

> '*V. Höttges* [1937] *mentions Silesia as an example of a region where the Devil is quickly replacing the giant. The giant could hold his own completely in Siebenbürgen* [Transylvania in present-day Rumania]. *In other landscapes, such as northwestern Germany, both legendary figures occur side by side, but in connection with megalithic tombs, we find here* [*a dominance of*] *legends with giants*' (Liebers 1986, 66).

Whereas the *Duvel* or *Duyvel* (Devil) occurred only once as element of a hunebed name in The Netherlands (see section '1574') and is since long forgotten locally, it is much less rare among northern German *Hünengrab* names (*Düvel, Teufel,* see Sprockhoff 1966, 1967, 1975).

The role of the devil in folk tales may have originated more or less independently from the official teaching of the Roman Catholic church and the 'science' of Demonology (cf. Gielis 1994).

After the Reformation, between 1660 and 1720, Protestant authors Picardt (1660), Smids (1711) and others abroad revived the idea that giants were the builders.

---

74 Mohen 1997, 21. Although German *Huhn, Hühner* means 'chicken, chickens', the (phonetic) spelling was *Hühnengräber*, not **Hühnergräber*. What would chickens be doing in hunebeds in the middle of nowhere? Mohen's beautifully illustrated booklet about megaliths (1997) made a few mistakes concerning the Dutch-German *hunebedden-Hünengräber*: the current spelling and interpretation of the word (p. 21), the statement that the megaliths were made of *sandstone* boulders (rather than of erratic boulders of granite, gneiss, etc., p. 105) and the statement that a 'witty wife' (one of the *Witte Wijven*) in a hollow *earthen barrow* (Picardt 1660, ill. facing p. 47; reproduced, for instance, by Michell 1982, 45) would have been sitting in a *megalithic dolmen* (p. 16).

75 In section '1547', below, the name 'Devil's Cunt' (*Duvels kutte*) for a hunebed 'near Rolde' in Drenthe will be discussed; in contrast to northern Germany, it is the only Dutch hunebed name referring to the Devil.

Proper names for Dutch hunebeds

In contrast to other hunebed regions of the TRB West and North Groups, proper names for Dutch hunebeds are extremely rare. Only *Papeloze Kerk*, *Calsteenen*, *'s Duvels kut* or *Duyffelskutte* ('The Devil's Cunt', see section '1547') and perhaps *Stemberg* stand out.

The name *Papeloze Kerk* for D49-Schoonoord ('Church without a Roman-Catholic priest', or (?) 'without the Papal doctrine'),[76] about halfway between Noord-Sleen and Schoonoord, reputedly indicates that there, in the middle of the immense treeless heath Ellertsveld, Calvinist open air conventicles were held by the Reverend Menso Alting. The church reformer Jean Calvin [Jehan Cauvin, 1509-1564] had called his own open air conventicles in northern France, '*Église sans pape*', which expression had become almost proverbial. Unfortunately there is no written evidence that such conventicles were actually held near hunebed D49. The name *De Papeloze Kerk* was first mentioned in Drenthe by N. Westendorp, who connected (1812) this name to a *heuvel* ['hill' or 'barrow'] in the Ellertsveld heath, between Rolde and Sleen.[77] Boom et al. (1842-1847) did not mention the hunebed D49, but connected the name *Papeloze Kerk* to a sandy ridge in the Ellertsveld, presumably because they understood Westendorp's *heuvel* as a natural hillock. But at least since Janssen (1848, table) recorded that D49, '45 minutes north of Noordsleen, … is named *papelooze kerk*', this name was generally ap-

76 K. ter Laan (1949, 293) gives another interpretation of the name: 'Tradition has it that the name recalls the conventicles of the Protestants, who had no priest (*paap*) after Menso Alting was compelled to flee from Sleen.' The wall of earth around the tomb site noted by him was probably the dump Van Giffen's excavation.

77 In Westendorp's days the immense Ellertsveld heath to the north of Noord-Sleen had not yet been brought under cultivation. He visited the Drenthe hunebeds in August, 1811 and wrote (1812, 52): 'The following day, we travelled early to Sleen. There are two hunebeds between Noord- en Zuid-Sleen, which are demolished. The ghost, who is haunting on the Ellertveld, in the *heuvel* ['hill' or 'barrow'] called de *papelooze kerk*, has made [*heeft gelegd*] the hunebed at Noordsleen.' He thus mislocated the hunebeds D50 and D51, which are directly northwest of Noord-Sleen (both are shown as isolated clumps of trees in the arable field (*esch*) on the Hottinger Map from 1788-92: Versfelt 2003, map pl. 15). In a study about barrows, Westendorp (1819) wrote: 'Between Rolde and Sleen, I noted [in 1811] no other *heuvel* than the so-called Papelooze Kerk on the Ellertsveld, where the notorious ghost is haunting, who made the Hunebed of Noordsleen.' He said more or less the same in the two printed versions of his treatise about the hunebeds (1815, 1822).

Presently hunebed D49-Papeloze Kerk lies about halfway between Noord-Sleen and Schoonoord (the latter small village was founded in 1854). D49 is now usually indicated as being 'near Schoonoord', but in 1811-12, when that village did not yet exist, Westendorp meant D49, when he wrote about 'the hunebed of Noordsleen', but it is also clear that he did not inspect it. Schultus (mayor) L. Abramy reported, in 1818, about the outer appearance of D49, which report Westendorp inserted in his 1822 treatise about the hunebedden (p. 54-5): 'Half an hour from [Noord-Sleen], along the road to Schoonloo, there is one [hunebed] of the same width and orientation, thirty feet long; there are seven [should be: six] stones on each side, apart from the endstones. This tomb stands on a small rise'. But he was not aware that this passage overlapped with what he had written in the preceding paragraph about the Papelooze Kerk.

plied to hunebed D49. And documents from 1861-2[78] state that not far from Schoonoord 'there is a hunnebed, which is known by the name of Papelooze Kerk, within living memory.'[79]

The enigmatic name *Calsteenen* for D1-Steenbergen is only mentioned in a letter to Janssen, dated November 4, 1859, with an illegible signature (Arentzen 2006, 81-82). Etymologists have not yet studied this now forgotten name. *Ste(e)nen* means 'stones'. Verdam's 'Concise Dictionary of Middle Dutch' (1911, 279) records the medieval word *caelliau, caliau*, which meant '*keisteen*' (pebble), and was clearly related to *caillou* in French. If '*cal*' in '*Calsteenen*' is derived from this word, it would mean, illogically, 'Pebble Stones'. Further, *Callen* meant 'speaking', 'talking', 'chatting', 'babbling', 'giving away' [cf. English 'to call'] and *calle* was 'the name of various birds', and also meant a 'gossip', 'darling' or even 'tart' (Verdam 1911, 280). If *Cal* derived from *Calumme*, meaning 'column' (Verdam 1911, 280), it would mean 'Column Stones', which reminds one of the *Columnae Herculis* near Rolde (see section '1547'), but seems literally far-fetched, because Rolde is 21 km away.

The name *Calsteenen* is mentioned nowhere else, however, and the present-day name *Steenbergen* ('Stone-heaps') of the tomb (D1-Steenbergen) and the neighbouring hamlet seems to have been prevailing.

Hunebed D13-Eext was reputedly called *Stemberg* ('Barrow with a voice'), because of the rumbling noise heard when the capstones were probed with an iron rod when they were still covered by an earthen barrow, about 1735 (Van Lier 1760). But in my opinion this idea may also be due to misreading of the general term *Steenberg* by Van Lier (see section '1756-1760').

Hunebeds D3 and D4 at Midlaren were named *Hunenborg*, according to 'HotspotHolland' on internet. I cannot remember to have heard or read this name before. *Hunenborg / Heuneburg* is typically a name for defensive earthworks in The Netherlands and Germany. Have visitors of the Hunnenborg at Denekamp, Province of Overijssel, erroneously introduced the name to Midlaren? D3 and D4 are situated on the *Steenakkers* ('arable fields with [hunebed] stones') and hunebed D42-Westenes-N lies *op den Stien Camp* ('on the field with the [hunebed] stone[s]').

The terms 'altar' and 'dolmen'

Whether the hunebeds were tombs or altars, or both, was discussed for a long time in Germany, but not in The Netherlands. The medieval names *hunebedden* etc. show that they were regarded as tombs. Schonhovius (see section '1547') thought that they were altars, and Schele, shortly after 1591 (Schele 1591-1637, 1: 18-9),

---

78 *Provinciale Drentsche en Asser Courant*, November 19, 1861; *Algemeen Handelsblad*, December 27, 1862.

79 The preceding paragraph tries to improve my discussion of this subject in Gerding et al. 2003, 710-11 (for which I was much helped by J.N. Lanting). Cf. Van Giffen (1925, 124n), who mistakenly concluded that Westendorp (1822, 54) had called hunebed D50, not D49, 'Papelooze kerk'.

thought that they were simultaneously graves and altars (see section 'The word hunebed'). He would have been influenced by the current ideas in Germany. The idea that they were altars was soon rejected once and for all in The Netherlands by Van Slichtenhorst (1654, 77-8) and subsequent authors, because the curved capstones were obviously unsuitable – in contrast to the flat capstones of most TRB dolmens. Thus hunebed D13-Eext with its flat capstones, because it was discovered much later, in 1735/1756, was never considered an altar. Primeval dolmens with flat capstones had never been found in The Netherlands, which is perhaps another reason that Dutch scholars rejected the idea that hunebeds were altars, unlike their colleagues in northern Germany and southern Scandinavia.

The 'Stone' U1 of Lage Vuursche occurs in illustrations beginning about 1781. Perhaps it was unearthed from a sandy rise that was levelled, about 1640 (Bakker 2005a). It was interpreted it as a prehistoric monument for the first time, by Jacques Scheltema (1833) in his study '*Berigt over een oud altaar, (Dolmin)* [80] *of een naar een Hunebed zweemend overblijfsel van de eerste bewoners dezer landen*' ('A Note on an Ancient Altar, (Dolmin), or Remnant bearing a slight likeness to a Hunebed, from the first Inhabitants of these Regions'). In 1833, the current Scandinavian, German and French literature still considered dolmens to be altars. Ten years later, the Danish archaeologist Jens Jacob Asmussen Worsaae [1821-1885] demonstrated (1843) that dolmens were burial chambers, and this was generally accepted for the TRB North and West Group dolmens.

G5-Heveskesklooster, excavated in the early 1980s, turned out to be a 'rectangular dolmen', the first genuine dolmen in The Netherlands. The idea of J. Hoika (1993, 308), that hunebed G3-Glimmen was a dolmen instead of a short passage grave, has not been accepted by the excavator (J.N. Lanting, pers. comm., 1995).

B2. From Schonhovius (1547) to De Wilde (1904-1910)

1547: Schonhovius [81]

The first known treatise written about hunebeds in Drenthe and northwestern Germany is a 1547 manuscript by Schonhovius, in which it is argued that a hunebed at Rolde in Drenthe represented the Pillars of Hercules in Germania, which were mentioned by Tacitus in *Germania* 34:

---

80 The spelling *dolmin* was introduced in 1796 in Brittany by La Tour d'Auvergne, but it competed with the more correct spelling *dolmen*, which was introduced in 1805-7 and definitively replaced it about 1885 (Le Menn 1990, 374-5; Chaigneau et al. 2009, 400-2).

81 I discussed the contents of the following paragraph *in extenso* in Bakker 2002. Hermanus Hartogh Heijs van Zouteveen [1841-1891] discussed Schonhovius's text about the Pillars of Hercules in Germania briefly in the first volume of the *Nieuwe Drentsche Volksalmanak* (1883), the publication of which he had initiated. L.O. Gratama reacted in the second volume (Gratama 1884b).

'Common is a rumour [among the Frisians] *that the Pillars of Hercules are still preserved on the spot, either indicating that Hercules has been there or because we are used to ascribing magnificent things wherever to his fame'.*

Anthonius Schonhovius Batavus (Antony van Schoonhove) [ca.1500-1557] was a canon of St Donatian in Brugge / Bruges, Flanders, and born in that city.[82] He studied classical languages, antiquities, law and history in the humanistic tradition. In 1546, for instance, his editions of the *Historiae Romanae* by Flavius Eutropius (Basle, 1546 #) and the *Annales AD 379-534* of Marcellinus Comes (Paris, 1546 #) were published. In 1547, he finished a Latin treatise about the location of the Germanic tribes mentioned by the classical authors, particularly Tacitus, whose *Germania* had been found and printed in the 15th century.

Schonhovius argued that the *Columnae Herculis* of Tacitus were represented by a hunebed in (or near) the village Rolde in Drenthe. He added a local legend and some other information, but disregarded the explanation, given by Tacitus, that 'we are accustomed to ascribe magnificent things' to the fame of Hercules. He did not question why Germanicus would have had to sail over the Germanic Ocean to see the (northern) Pillars of Hercules while he could easily have visited them by going over land, to Drenthe (see below). Did Germanicus suppose he would find the Pillars on Heligoland, perhaps? I translate freely, with abridgements:[83]

'The Pillars of Hercules can still be seen at Rolde in Drenthe, not far from Coevorden. They are greatly admired by visitors, because the stones, which form an enormous heap, are so large that no cart or ship could have conveyed them. And there are no stone quarries because the region is marshy. So, it is surmised that they were brought in by demons, who are venerated under the name of Hercules.

---

82 Why Van Schoonhove called himself 'Batavus' is unclear. He himself was not born in the small town of Schoonhoven at the border of Holland and Utrecht in 'Batavia', i.e. Holland, Utrecht and Gelderland in the northern Netherlands, but in Bruges in Flanders in the southern Netherlands, one of the wealthiest and largest cities of Europe at the time.

83 Schonhovius's original text (1547, in Matthaeus vol. I, 1698, 63-4) is '*Sane non possum hic præterire Columnas illas Herculis, quas Tacitus* in Frisiis fuisse magna celebritate commemorat, quarum reliquiæ hoc tractu Trenterorum, hoc est in Drenta, adhuc visuntur, vico Roelden, haud procul a Coevordia, non sine spectantium admiratione. Sunt enim singuli lapides (quorum non parvus acervus est) tantæ magnetudinis, ut nullos currus, nullasque naves admittere posse videantur neque ibi fodinæ lapidum sunt, ut loco paludoso, quare suspicio est, eos illuc a dæmonibus, qui Herculis nomine ibi colebantur, adductos fuisse. Stabant enim super columnas aræ, (saxa vocant Itali, ut quidam** inquit Poëta) quas ad aras incolae vivos immolabant, maximeque advenas, quos prius quam mactarent, cogebant transire angustum foramen, quod sub aris erat, transeuntemque stercoribus infectabantur, ac petebant. Quod & hodie faciunt, præsertim si Brabantum nacti fuerint, unde sæpe cædes oriuntur. Foramen ipsum ob ignominiam 's Duvels Kut, hoc est, Dæmonis cunnus, appellatur. Sed immolationem sustulit D. Bonifacius. Hujus monumenti videndi causa, Drusus Germanicus fama excitus, auspiciis Augusti, primus Romanorum Septentrionalem Oceanum navigavit, teste Plinio, lib. vv. Sed, ut refert Tacitus, obstitit Oceanus in se simul & Herculem inquiri. Haec eo paulo latius retuli, ut eximatur Commentariis Althameri error; qui hunc Taciti locum explicans, has Herculis columnas pro iis accipit, quas in Gadibus ille statuit.*' The notes are '* *Lib. De morib. Germanor.*' and '** *Virgil. Aeneid. Lib. I. v. 109.*' The 2nd edition of Matthaeus, The Hague 1738, has minor changes in the punctuation. '*Cap. 34*' was added to note * and note ** was added; but '*vv.*' of '*teste Plinio lib. vv*' was not filled in.

On the pillars rest altar stones – Italians call rocks altars, as a renowned poet states [Virgil, Aeneis, lib. I: 109] – on which the inhabitants formerly sacrificed living people, especially foreigners. Before the victims were slaughtered, they were compelled to crawl through a small passage under the altar stones, during which they were soiled by faeces and then caught.

This is still done nowadays, especially with native Brabanders, and murder frequently ensues. The passage itself is called 's Duvels Kut, which means Daemonis Cunnus [Devil's Cunt]. Saint Boniface has put an end to the sacrifices, however.

According to Pliny, Drusus Germanicus, incited by its fame, tried to visit this monument and was the first Roman to sail over the North Sea in the name of Augustus. But, as Tacitus tells us, [stormy weather] prevented him from investigating the sea and Hercules. I digress on these matters to correct an error in the Commentaries by Althamer, who in his explanation of these lines of Tacitus took these to be the Pillars of Hercules at Cadiz.'[84]

Rolde was the best known village in central Drenthe in the 16th century. At the time, the towns of the southern Netherlands (the present-day Belgium) were the administrative and intellectual centres of all The Netherlands under King and Emperor Charles V of Hapsburg. The Rolde legend may have reached Schonhovius in Bruges through the Frisians Joachim Hopper ('Hopperus') [1523-1576] and Viglius (Wigle) van Aytta [1507-1577], who were prominent advisers to the Emperor.

Presumably under influence of Van Aytta and Hopper, the *Duuels kutte* appeared on maps made by the imperial cartographers Jacob van Deventer and Christiaan sGroten, from 1568 onwards. It occurred on maps of Drenthe until 1636 (Bakker 2002, 78).

Some of Van Deventer's maps were published in *Theatrum Orbis Terrarum* by Abraham Ortelius, including the first palaeogeographic map, first printed in 1570, of the northern Netherlands, as it was during the reign of the Roman Emperor Augustus (Figure 4). This map, which was designed by Hopper, shows two pillars at Rolde, with the legend 'COLUMNAE HERCULIS, *Duuels Cutz hodie*'.[85] The two

---

84 Andreas Althamer (ca.1500-ca.1539) published (1529), the first long antiquarian commentary to *Germania* by Tacitus, cf. Langereis 2001. Actually, 'Cadiz' should be read as Gibraltar / Tarifa – Ceuta / Tanger.

85 *Cut / Kut* is the current word for 'cunt' in Dutch. *Cutz* is unusual if not unique, however. It does not look like a plural form and may have been influenced by the German word *Fotze*.
'Devil's Cunt' was initially part of the title for this book (similar to that of Bakker 2009b). In the *Encyclopedie voor Drenthe* (Gerding et al. 2003, 255-6: *Duvelskut*), I summarised Schonhovius's Devil's Cunt story and precisely this element was applauded by the journalist Atte Jongstra in his review of the encyclopaedia in *NRC Handelsblad*. The early-19th-century French/Breton archaeologist Joseph Mahé protested vehemently against Emmius's (1596) 'indecent' version of the story. It is, however, popular among present-day Dutch archaeologists. But the editors of the present book considered 'Devil's Cunt' in the title out of the question, because the indecent name would prevent the distribution of the book in the English-speaking world. Apparently there are striking differences in the prudery of various nations…

pillars are similar to the two Pillars of Hercules at Gibraltar in having the coat of arms of the Emperor Charles Vth of Hapsburg, whose heraldic device 'plus ultra' indicated that he reigned the world widely beyond the Strait of Gibraltar.

Figure 4. One or two hunebeds in the village of Rolde denoted as 'COLUMNAE HERCULIS, Duvels Cutz hodie' on the first palaeographic map of the northern Netherlands (Ortelius 1579) (photograph Amsterdam University Library). See further Appendix 3.

It is obvious that manuscript copies of Schonhovius's story circulated widely in the 16th century, because Hadrianus Junius (Adriaan de Jonghe) [1511-1576] and Cornelius Kempius (Cornelis Kemp) [ca.1520-1589] both quoted parts of the *duyffelskutte* story in 1588, more than a century before it was printed (1698, vol. 1) by Antonius Matthaeus [1635-1710]. Where the original manuscripts are kept is unknown to me. The story was also briefly referred to (1596) by Ubbo Emmius [1547-1625], Arend van Slichtenhorst (1654) [1616-1657], Johan Picardt (1660, 25, 27, 33-4) [1600-1670], Joan Blaeu (1662) [1571-1638] and Martin Mushard (1754) [1699-1770].[86] That Schonhovius's story was repeated for so long shows how rare studies on hunebeds still were at the time.[87]

Interestingly, Schonhovius spoke of only *one* stone-heap (hunebed) representing the Pillars of Hercules. And he described the entrance passage of *one* hunebed. Schonhovius may have been referring to hunebed D16-Balloo (Bakker 2002, 78-9). Perhaps hunebed D10-Gasteren is another possibility, because it is located where the *Duuels kutte* was roughly placed on the maps made by Jacob van Deventer.

Hopper, on the other hand, may have based the depiction of *two* Pillars on his map on the two hunebeds at Rolde, D17 and D18, which lie parallel, 70 m apart, about 200 m east of the church of Rolde.[88] There were, of course, many more hunebeds in Drenthe, but the public servants Hopper and Van Aytta may only have known those at Rolde, where the assemblies of Drenthe convened.

After Schonhovius (1547), it took more than 110 years before original observations on hunebeds were made, by Picardt (1660).

1660: Picardt

Johan Picardt [1600-1670] (Figure 5) was the eldest son of the Dutch Reformed (Calvinistic) clergyman of the Count of Bentheim. The family name Picardt (or Piccardt) derives from a farm named Pickhart in the County of Bentheim, just east of the Dutch Republic (and has nothing to do with Picardie in northwestern France). He was born in Neuenhaus or Schüttorf, County of Bentheim, and studied at the protestant Gymnasium Arnoldinum in nearby Steinfurt, and at the universities of Franeker and Leiden in The Netherlands. He was a clergyman in

---

86   Martin Mushard, a German antiquarian who worked in the Bremen-Stade region, cited the Devil's Cunt story anonymously and in general terms in his manuscript of 1754 (Mushard 1762, cf. Liebers 1986, 46-7, Bakker 2002, 82).

87   Claudia Liebers (1986, 22-6) left out Schonhovius's text in her excellent study of the role of folk tales in German and Dutch studies of hunebeds from the time of Humanism and the Renaissance until the early 18th century. Further details about and possible explanations for this rather enigmatic text are in Bakker (2002). Several studies on Hopper and Van Aytta by Edzo H. Waterbolk that I overlooked in 2002 are cited in Bakker 2004, 197-202. In northwestern Germany, several hunebeds are named *Düvelsteene* ('Devil's Stones') etc. (Sprockhoff 1975).

88   The close proximity of the two hunebeds D17 and D18 to the late medieval church of Rolde and the intact *Hünengrab* a few metres from the old church and presbytery of Winterfeld, Kr. Salzwedel in the German Altmark, show that the common idea that Christian priests urged their flock to destroy such heathen monuments does not hold water.

Egmond aan Zee in Holland (1623), and in Rolde (1643) and Coevorden (1648), both in Drenthe. Picardt took the degree of Doctor of Medicine in Leiden in 1628 and was inscribed in the Album of Groningen University in 1647. He had a special interest in reclaiming waste lands for cultivation. The Count of Bentheim appointed him, in 1648, director of the reclamation of a peaty region to the south of the Drenthe-Bentheim boundary, in Germany, where he founded the villages Alte Piccardie and Georgsdorf.

Picardt's *Antiquiteten* (1660) gave Drenthe its first history.[89] This history of Drenthe and surrounding Dutch and German regions, consisted of three 'books' in the same volume, of which 125 copies were made.[90] His first 'book', *A Short Description of some Forgotten and Hidden Antiquities of the Provinces and Lands between the North Sea, [and the rivers] Yssel, Ems and Lippe* was followed by two other 'books', one about the history of Drenthe and the other about the Drenthian town of Coevorden. He integrated folk tales, constructive imagination, historic sources and archaeological monuments. He was the first field archaeologist of The Netherlands and paid attention to prehistoric landmarks and discussed hunebeds, barrows, Celtic Fields,[91] mottes, ring forts, hoards of Roman *denarii*, etc. in detail. Jacob-Friesen (1954) called him 'the first researcher of Lower Saxon prehistory', which he also was for the northeastern Netherlands.

Picardt argued that the hunebeds were burial chambers for giants, the first inhabitants of Drenthe, who had come from Scandinavia and ultimately from the Near East, basing himself on the *Old Testament*,[92] the *Historia de gentis sep-*

---

89   Gerding 1997; Gerding in Gerding et al. 2003, 723-5: 'Picardt'; Minderhoudt (1981) and H.H. Bechtluft on the internet.
90   My own copy of Picardt (1660) is numbered 20 (in ink in the left lower corner of the first side of the last endpaper) and has no handwritten dedication. Marginal notes in ink show a special interest in Rutger van den Boitzelaer, Bailiff of Coevorden and the Landscape of Drenthe, to whom the text pays ample attention (p. 255; portrait fol. 255; p. 266; dedication on p. 278) and who acted as Picardt's protector in Drenthe. Presumably this copy was once Van Boitzelaer's. The book is very popular among Dutch archaeologists; W. Glasbergen even gave a 1660 copy to each of his six children (letter from Kaj Glasbergen, 19 April, 2010)!
91   'Celtic Fields' are systems of walled rectangular fields (each ca. 400-1600 m²), which occur on the sandy soils of The Netherlands, northern Germany, southern Scandinavia and Britain and date, perhaps, from about 800-100 BC (Brongers 1976). The name 'Celtic Field' for these field systems was once used in England, but is there now replaced by 'walled fieldsystems'. It stuck in The Netherlands, however. The Danish term is *porsehaver*.
      Although Cornelius Kempius (Kemp) [ca.1516-1589] mentioned 'Roman *castra*' (Roman camps / lairs, viz. *'Romeynsche Legerplaetsen'*, viz. Celtic Fields) in Friesland-Drenthe in his *De origine, situ, qualitate et quntitate Frisiae, et rebus Frisiis olim praeclare gestis, libri tres* (1588, 29-30; cf. Bakker 2002, 64-8), he didn't describe them. Picardt (1660, 41-3), on the other hand, described Celtic Fields in detail. Before Tonkens's discussion of a Celtic Field (1795, 39-45), Picardt's was the only accurate description on the continent.
92   Picardt (1660, 27-8, 55) referred to giants (*Reusen, Huynen, Giganten*, children Enakim, Emim, Nephilim, Rephaim) mentioned in Genesis 6: 4, Sapientia [Wisdom] 14: 16, Numbers 13: 22 and Deuteronomy 3: 11 in the *Old Testament*. Moses mentioned giants who ultimately perished in the Flood (Genesis 6: 4). But there were also giants after the Deluge, because the spies of Moses saw giants in the Land of Canaan (Numeri 13). According to 'Berosus', they descended from Noah and his sons (Picardt 1660, 27, 31).

IOHAN PICARDT, THEOLOGUS,
*Ecclesiæ Covordiensis Pastor primus,
et Doctor Medicus.*

Goedesberg Excudit.   P. Holsteijn schulp.   H. Nijhoff. Pii.

*Figure 5. Johan Picardt (print by P. Holsteijn II after a painting by H. Nijhoff) and the title page of
Picardt (1660) (photograph Sidestone Press). See further Appendix 3.*

KORTE BESCHRYVINGE

Van eenige Vergetene en Verborgene

ANTIQUITETEN

Der Provintien en Landen

Gelegen tuffchen de Noord-Zee, de
Yffel, Emfe en Lippe.

Waer by geboeght zijn

ANNALES DRENTHIÆ,

Dat zijn

Eenige Aenteyckeninghen en Memorien, van
fommige gedenckwaerdige Gefchiedeniffen, gepaffeert
in het Antiquiteet-rijcke Landfchap DRENTH,
van de Geboorte CHRISTI af, tot
op defen tijdt.

Mitsgaders een korte Befchrijbinge der Stadt,
des Cafteels, en der Heerlickheyt COVORDEN.

t'Samen vergadert, en aen 't licht gebracht, door

JOHAN PICARDT,

*Theologum, Paftorem Covordienfem primum, & Docto-
rem Medicum.*

Met koopere Platen verçiert.

t'Amfterdam, *Gedruckt by* Tymon Houthaak,

Voor Gerrit van Goedesbergh, Boeckverkoper op 't Water/
aen de Nieuwe-brugh/ in de Delffe Bybel/ Anno 1 6 6 0.

Figure 6. Giants and a hunebed; one giant is munching a bearded man. Print facing p. 23 in Picardt (1660), probably by P. Holsteijn II. Figures 6 and 8 are the first pictures of Dutch hunebeds, but not very faithful renditions. Giants and men are clad like Hercules or Wild Men (photograph Sidestone Press).

tentrionalibus by the Swedish bishop Olavs Magnus (1555),[93] and a great number of gigantic bones found throughout the world.[94] One of Picardt's plates of these giant hunebed builders (Figure 8) is now found in many books on the history of archaeology. Picardt (1660, 33-4, 55) argued that the giants were formerly called Herculeses;[95] the minimal attire and the clubs of the giants in Figures 6-

---

93   Olavs Magnus's ideas about giants (1555 #) were inspired by the *Gesta Danorum* # written by the Danish historian Saxo Grammaticus (who died in 1208). Saxo thought that most of the stone monuments had been built before the Flood (K.-G. Sjögren, pers. comm., 2007), but Olavs also stated: '*Too little is known to us to decide whether these* [megaliths] *were not built after the Flood by giants or people with extreme physical strength*' (Wollf 1994, 193, citing the German translation by Jantzen, 1900, xvii).

94   A giant's tooth from the Utican beach, in present-day Tunisia, was described by Saint Augustine (354-430) in *City of God*, 15.9 (#). Emperor Maximilian of Austria possessed the weaponry of a giant, found in Roomburg near Leiden. Dutch sailors found remains of giants in Tierra del Fuego. A giant's skeleton was found in a round barrow, the Topbergh at Westerbork in Drenthe; others were found on the beach of Terschelling, and on Crete (Picardt 1660, 28-9).

95   Picardt referred to Tacitus, but not explicitly to Schonhovius (see section '1547'), from whom he borrowed the idea that the 'Herculeses' were builders of hunebeds (Picardt 1660, 34, 55): '*There is hardly a country in Europe with no stories about Hercules* ... [This is incredible, but these stories contain] *the naked truth* [that] *these "Herculeses" were actually giants clad in skins of wild animals and armed with clubs, who ransacked everywhere and tore all other tyrants to pieces like lions and tigers.*'

Figure 7. Giants wailing during a cremation of a deceased giant (Picardt 1660, print facing p. 33, probably by P. Holsteijn II) (photograph Sidestone Press). See further Appendix 3.

8 were taken from illustrations of Wildmen that were reproduced from the late Middle Ages to the 16th century,[96] from folk theatre[97] and heraldry, and pictures and sculptures of Hercules.[98] The normally sized prehistoric Drenthians also have similar Herculean attires and clubs in Picardt's plates (opp. fol. 33 (twice), 42, 47, 67).[99]

---

96   The naked or almost naked Wildmen always carried a wooden club like Picardt's giants and were associated both with the primeval forests before the Fall and with unrestrained abandonment to dancing, drinking and sex. They were first depicted in the art of the mid-thirteenth century and became very popular in the second half of the fourteenth century (Moser 1998, 48-52). Ostkamp (2007) discussed Wildmen on 16th-century Rhineland stoneware and referred to the catalogue *Die wilden Leute des Mittelalters*, Hamburg: Museum für Kunst und Gewerbe 1963 #. Hendrik van de Waal [1910-1972] (1952) and S. Moser (1998, 90-96, W. Arentzen, pers. comm.) pointed out similarities in dress etc. between the people on the pictures in Picardt's book and those on the plates in Cluverius (1616).

97   See the woodcut after Pieter Brueg(h)el, 'The Wild Man' or 'The masquerade of Orson and Valentine' at Shrovetide, from 1566 (Orenstein 2001, 241).

98   One of numerous examples is the portrait of a well-fed, naked burgher painted as a triumphant Hercules in 'Hercules and Caius' by Hendrik Goltzius, 1613 (Frans Hals Museum, Haarlem).

99   For ideas about the giants and other large ancestors in Scandinavian history, see Klindt-Jensen 1975, 9-10. Picardt (1660) did not discuss them in detail. In 1647, Johannes Loccenius, the Holstein-born professor at Uppsala, had argued that megalithic tombs near Skara, Sweden, could only have been built by giants (Sjögren 2003, 62 and additional information from him and from the internet). Loccenius (1647) is not cited by Picardt.

Figure 8. Giants building a hunebed, while normally sized men are contemplatively looking on (Picardt 1660, print facing p. 33, probably by P. Holsteijn II) (photograph Sidestone Press). See further Appendix 3.

Picardt (1660, 25) dated the Drenthe hunebeds after the Flood, because many similar megaliths were found in Scandia, most with Gothic [runic] inscriptions, according to Olavs Magnus (1555), whereas Hebrew was the only language spoken before the Flood.[100]

Previously, several German scholars had written that normally proportioned men had built the megalithic tombs of the TRB culture. In the early 16th century, Nicolaus Marschalk [ca.1460/70-1525] and Thomas Kantzow [ca.1505-1542]

---

100 That Hebrew was the only language spoken before the Flood was not always considered as an irrefutable truth. In 1569, the learned scholar Johannes Goropius Becanus [Jan van Gorp from [Hilvaren-]Beek, 1519-1572] had concluded from etymological speculations that Dutch was the most ancient and most perfect language in the world, which was spoken in paradise itself, the *lingua adamica* (Frijhoff 2010, 6). Becanus published this in a book of ca. 1100 pages (1569), in which he also mentioned for the first time, and published samples from, Ulfilas's Gothic *Codex Argenteus*. The *lingua adamica* was discussed by Umberto Eco, in 1993, and by Allison P. Coudert et al., in 1999 (Frijhoff l.c.) and several others, among whom (1967) the Antwerp novelist Hubert Lampo [1920-2006]. See Frijhoff (l.c.) about the discussions evoked by Becanus's statement. About at that time, Scandinavian scholars tried to prove that the Finnish language was related to Hebrew.

wrote about the megalithic tombs in Mecklenburg and Pomerania.[101] In 1579, Christoph Entzelt [1517-1583] wrote that the ancient Lords of Zera in the German Altmark were buried at 'a particular spot where large high stones are erected in a circle and neatly ordered, which the farmers call the *steinbette* (quasi lectum lapideum, vel lapidum) or the *Helden bette* (quasi lectum heroum)', near the village of Stapel[102] near Ballenstedt.[103] In 1604, the German geographer Wilhelm Dilich [1597-1622] attributed the megalithic 'monumenta' in the region of Bederkesa to giants as well as to the Chauci and Saxones, ancient Germanic tribes.[104] In 1613, Johann von Velen, sexton of the cathedral of Münster, who investigated Surbolds Grab, the immense megalithic grave at Börger in the Hümmling, did not say which tribe had built this tomb, but apparently did not think of giants (Gummel 1938, 16-7, 68 n. 4; see notes 105, 110 and 127). Neither did the cartographer Johannes Gigas [1587-1637], in an inscription on his map of the Lower Bishopric of Münster, Germany, from 1620.[105]

In 1630, Jonkheer Sweder Schele van Welevelt visited and described a 'stone heap' (*Steinhauffen*), probably hunebed 897 near Ueffeln and Bramsche, Germany, which is still extant and unaltered. While there, he heard that there were 'many

---

101 Stemmermann 1934, 20-2; Gummel 1938, 18-9, 441. The chronicles of Kantzow and Marschalk were probably handwritten, and not published at the time. Marschalk assigned the megalithic graves to the Germanic Heruli. He seems to have been the first German scholar who excavated megalithic graves and urnfields for scientific purposes (Gummel 1938, 10).

102 Dutch *stapelen* and German *stapeln* mean 'piling up'. The locality name Stapel refers to the 'piled' stones of a hunebed; cf. Stapelstein, a small hunebed at Etzel-Stapelstein in Ostfriesland, Germany. Another Stapelstein was a small hunebed near Friedeburg, Ostfriesland (Friedrich Arents in *De Vriend des Vaderlands* 1829, 581 #, see Arentzen 2009, 26); the distance from Etzel to Friedeburg makes it improbable that Arents, who was usually quite accurate, was referring to the Stapelstein at Etzel.

103 '*darbey nicht fern / ligt ein Dorff / heist Stapel /* quasi stabulum, *darbey findet man einen sonderlichen ort / da grosse hohe steine auffgericht sein / in einem kreyse und feiner ordnung / das nennen die bawren das steinbette /* quasi lectum lapideum, vel lapidum, *oder das Helden bette /* quasi lectum heroum, *da sollen die alten Herrn von der Zera begraben sein / wie vorzeiten grosse Herrn sich also in die Hügel im felde begraben lassen.*' (Entzelt 1579, Jiii; Fritsch & Mittag 2006, 14; Wetzel 2002).

104 '*In hac [praefectura Bederkesa] etiam visuntur multa monumenta gigantum et veterum Chaucorum Saxonumque eximiae molis lapididibus congesta. Illorum forma in tabula sequenti* [the map mentioned below] *manifestatur.*' (Dilich 1604, 26, cited by Gummel 1938, 18).
   Dilich's naturalistic picture of a megalithic grave, 'Monumenta Chaucorum', in the corner of his map of the Amt Bederkesa was 'the first depiction of a [*Hünengrab*] in German literature' (Gummel 1938, 18; pl. 3). It shows the chamber of the Bülzenbett at Sievern, 608, without a covering barrow, viewed from the northeast. The two gentlemen climbing on it are, however, much too small in relation to the monument, just like the students on George Hoefnagel's print of the Pierre Levée near Poitiers, France, from which Dilich clearly got his inspiration (in G. Braun, *Civitates orbis terrarum*, vol. v, 1598, often reproduced, e.g., in Michell 1982, 41). Hoefnagel attributed the Pierre Levée to the Picts, 'the founders of Poitiers', not to the famous giant Pantagruel, known from François Rabelais (whose real name was Alcobifras Nasier: Giot 1985, 8).
   According to Piggott (1976, 15), Olaus Wormius (Ole Worm) published the earliest illustrations of megalithic graves of the TRB North Group in Denmark (Wormius 1643 # or 1651/1636 #).

105 Gigas inscribed on this map, near the location of *Hünengrab* 'Surbolds Grab' in the Hümmling (see note 110): '*plurima ... antiquitatis monumenta ex congestis inusitatae magnitudinis lapidibus*' (Gummel 1938, 18), with no mention of who had made them.

more' in the nearby Giersfeld, which is still true (889-896). He also mentioned hunebeds in the neighbourhood of Schledehausen (cf. 906-7, 917-8, 922-3) and a large stone heap ('altar') directly opposite Rahden House (Schele 1591-1630, I, 18-9, 164, 223-4).[106] He ascribed these tombs to the ancient Saxons, not to giants.

On the other hand, the 'universal scholar' Hermann C. Conring [1606-1681], professor of law and medicine at the Lutheran Helmstedt University in Germany, argued, in 1665, that the megalithic tombs 'Lübbensteine' near Helmstedt were built by giants before the Deluge – fossil bones from the Baumann's cave convinced him of their former existence (Gummel 1938, 25). Johann Daniel Major [1634-1693], who wrote about the archaeology of Jutland and Schleswig-Holstein (*Bevölkertes Cimbrien*, 1692 #), also believed that giants built the megaliths (Gummel 1938, 32).[107] It has been suggested that the giants theory was particularly popular in Protestant circles, because of reference to giants in the Bible.

Picardt (1660, 33) wrote:

> 'These Pagan Giant-Sepulchres and Stone-heaps were frightfully haunted in ancient times. The Devil played here his tricks in a surprising way[108] and strange and unbelievable things are said to have been heard and seen there about. Few people were found to be so bold and undaunted that they dared to pass them by night. But the more Jesus Christ dominated our region, and the more that the light of the Holy Gospel broke through, the less the Devil could have his way and the more this Egyptian darkness waned. Therefore this manifestation (pracherije) is no longer experienced.'

Picardt (p. 22-3) provided a good general description of the hunebeds in general, but did not mention their locations:

---

106 It is uncertain if the now demolished tomb at Recke (Sprockhoff 1975, 149) was among those mentioned by Schele.

107 The question whether giants existed elsewhere in the world was frequently discussed in the 17th century. In 1615, the Dutch navigator Jacob LeMaire / Jacques Lemaire [ca. 1585-1616] described skeletons of 10-11 feet tall people (which is 3.1-3.5 m tall if the 'Rhineland foot' equalling 31.4 cm is used) under heaps of stones on an island near the coast of Patagonia (Chaigneau, in prep.). Although Picardt (1660, 30) was well aware that all giants 'were exterminated in all parts of the world by God's hand', the Amsterdam patrician Nicolaes Witsen, known for his books about Tartarye (inner Russia) and ship building (Peters 2010), expected that his skipper would find giants in Terra Australis on his 1696 voyage (Naarden 2006, 87). Even in 1785, the French chemist and pharmacist Antoine Beaumé [1728-1804] thought that the Giants' Causeway in County Antrim, Ireland, actually a natural basalt formation, was constructed by men who were 15¼ m tall! (letter from A.G. Camper to P. Camper, Paris, July 10, 1785: Bots & Visser 2001, 48). And as late as 1868, F. Focke (1868, p. 3n) wrote that hunebeds contained 'human skeletons of gigantic sizes' (Liebers 1986, 63 n. 264).

108 '*By dese oude Heydensche* Reusen-Begraffenisen *en Steen-hoopen heeft 'et in ouden tijden schrickelijck gespoockt; en den Duyvel heeft omtrent de selve wonderlijck sijne personagie gespeelt*'. The devil was not a metaphor for 17th-century Calvinists, but an actual person, as he still was in a widely used mid-20th-century Dutch Roman Catholic religious manual for children (Br. Bertilo [H. Randag], *Luistert naar Hem*, Bois-le-Duc 1949, cited by Caspers 1994, 286, ills. p. 270, 303). He was still active in 20th-century Dutch folklore (Sinninghe 1975; Heupers 1979, 1981).

'These Stone-heaps are mostly sixteen steps long, some twenty and more. They are four, five or six steps wide.[109] All lie east-west in length. The smallest stones lie underneath, planted in the ground, and serve as pillars and foundation stones. The largest lie on top, some of which are nine man's fathoms[110] in circumference. Some are forty feet in circumference, others 36, 30, 25, 20 etc.[111] And, as a venerable gentleman[112] has told me, on the Hummelinck in the Bishopric of Munster, one stone placed on other stones was of such a [large] size that one hundred sheep could take shelter under it from storm and rain. In most and in the largest Stone-heaps three stones are found at the western side, which are placed such that they have the shape of a window-frame or door, so that someone, slightly bending himself, may enter and take shelter. … All round these oblong Stone-heaps, at about three steps distance, stands another row of stones, set into the ground and each 4, 5, 6 feet tall and usually spaced two feet apart,[113] standing upright, encircling the principal

---

109 A step (*tred*) had no fixed size. The cartographer Jacob van Deventer [ca.1505-1575], however, took single steps of exactly 75 cm, which is known because after ten single steps (7.5 m) he placed a dot on his town maps (Ahlers 2005; Koeman 1983, 122-3). If we assume an equivalent of 0.75 m for Picardt's steps, most hunebeds were, according to him, usually 12 m long, sometimes 15 m and more, and 3, 3¾ or 4.5 m wide (which is correct). If we assume a slightly smaller equivalent of 70 cm, most hunebeds were, according to Picardt, about 11 m long, whereas others were 14 m or more long and the widths were 2.8, 3.5 and 4.2 m (which is also correct).

110 A fathom was about six feet; one Drenthian foot equalled 0.294 m (see note 111) and nine fathoms would have equalled 15.9 m. As H.T. Waterbolk observed (letter Dec. 6, 2006), such large capstones are absent in Drenthe (Van Giffen 1925, Atlas). He suggested that Picardt was referring to one or more hunebeds on the Hümmling in adjacent Germany, because his following sentence told of the sheltering of one hundred sheep in a hunebed in that region. This suggestion is confirmed by other sources, which assign Picardt's reference to the gigantic 'Surbolds Grab' ('Surbolds Hus', 'Surbolds Ruhehaus', 'grosses Hünenhaus'), near Börger in the Hümmling; it was demolished about 1800 (Veltman 1886, 253-5; Gummel 1938, 16-7; 69; Schlicht 1963).
According to Von Velen's report of 1613 (Veltman 1886; Laux 1989, 126-7), its largest, westernmost capstone was 22 feet long, 10 feet wide and 4 feet thick. The exact length of the '*plump Westphalian*' foot of Von Velen is unknown. Schlicht (1963, cited by Sprockhoff 1975, 90) and Laux (1989), using the Rhineland foot of 31.4 cm, calculated that the dimensions of this huge capstone were 6.90 x 3.14 x 1.26 m. According to I. Pelster, Stadtarchiv Münster, no record is known about the foot which Von Velen may have used, but 'often 2 feet were defined as 1 *Elle*. One *Münster Elle* was 57.6 cm'. If so, Von Velen's foot would have been 28.8 cm and the capstone's dimensions 6.34 x 2.88 x 1.15 m. If the formula of Huisman and Van der Sanden (2003) and the specific gravity of 2.65 for granite are applied (cf. Bakker 2004, 147-8), it would have weighed about 0.6 x 6.34 x 2.88 x 1.15 x 2650 = about 33.38 metric tons.
Laux (1989, fig. 1) estimated that the original outer length of the chamber was about 20 m (which would have been about 18.3 m if the Münster foot of 28.8 cm was used). In German Lower Saxony, the current feet were between 28.5 and 32.5 cm long (Engel 1965, 65-6), but I have no list of the different feet used in Westphalian Münsterland.

111 The Frisian *hout* was 29.6 cm, the Groningen *houtvoet* was 29.2 cm (Van Swinden 1812, 152-4, 158, 172, 188-90). A Drenthian foot was 29.4 cm (Brood 2003). Which one Picardt used is unknown, but if it is assumed that he used the Drenthian foot, which was the average of the Frisian and the Groningen *houtvoet*, the circumferences of the largest capstones would be 11.8, 10.6, 8.8, 7.4 and 5.9 m and their lengths between more than 3.8 m and more than 1.9 m (which is plausible). The *Rijnlandse voet* (Rhineland foot) was 12 *duymen* (thumbs). One *Rijnlandse voet* was 31.4 cm, 1 *Rijnlandse duym* was 2.61 cm. [The Prussian *Fuss* of 12 *Zoll* was identical with the *Rijnlandse voet* – actually it was borrowed from the Holland surveyors.]

112 Picardt's informant was probably Georg Brabeck, later provost of Meppen (Veltman 1886, 253-4; Gummel 1938, 69).

113 Viz. 1.18, 1.47 and 1.76 m tall, usually 0.6 m apart.

*Stone-heaps ... I have heard that on some of these stones letters and strange charac-
ters were found; I looked for these with great diligence, but couldn't find the least
trace of them. Any letters that may have been there, or any that may be discovered,
would be Gothic letters.'*

That the entrances of the hunebeds are found in the 'western side' is perhaps a
slip of the pen, because Picardt gave an otherwise quite accurate description of the
entrance porches, which are in the middle of the long southern side of the larger
hunebeds.[114] Alternatively, could this have been another example of Picardt's ad-
aptation of facts to theory? (cf. Bakker 1993). In arguing for a close similarity
between the hunebeds in Scandinavia and Drenthe, Picardt wrote:

*'[the Drenthe hunebeds] have the same structure, length, width, height as the
Giants' sepulchres in the mentioned Nordic countries: they all lie also east-west;
have a similarly made square hole in the western side, under which one can take
shelter; lie also on hillocks or somewhat elevated grounds; are also scattered on wild
terrain, on public roads, in bushes, on arable fields. Creditable men who have seen
them in Scandia as well as in Drenthe state that they are one and the same work.
The illustrations made of them testify to this.'* (Picardt 1660, 32).

Picardt (1660, 33) mentioned *potten of kannen* (pots or jugs) in which the cremated bones of giants were placed in hunebeds, which suggests some knowledge
of the ceramic contents of hunebeds (acquired by excavation?).

Displaying insight remarkable for his time, Picardt stated:

*'that the [time between the building of the] strange giants' tombs and the Roman
buildings built around the birth of Christ is longer than the time between the
Roman buildings until the present time',* i.e. earlier than 1660 BC.[115]

Picardt's appraisal that the hunebeds were among the rarest antiquities internationally and were perhaps the most valuable property of Drenthe made a lasting
impression on subsequent Drenthe government officials and intellectuals.

---

114 This slip would mislead Westendorp (1815; 1822), who also wrote that the entrance was in
the western end of the hunebeds. Tonkens (1795, 48) even reported that the entrances were in
the eastern end. These erroneous statements may reflect the ruined state of the hunebeds at the
time.

115 Freely translated from '*aengesien de vreemde* Reusen-Sepultuyren ... *ouder zijn voor de Geboorte*
Christi*, als der* Romeynen *Gebouwen oudt zijn van de Geboorte* Christi *tot op desen tijdt.'* (Picardt
1660, 131).

Somewhere between 1642 or 1648 and April, 1659, Picardt undertook the first documented intentional excavation of non-Roman antiquities in The Netherlands. He recorded that he had dug in a walled lot (*perckje*) of a *Heydensche Leger-Plaets*, i.e. a Celtic Field*, viz. a cluster of rectangular walled fields from the Bronze-Iron Ages:[116]

> '*I once let dig here and there in the earth in one of these [Celtic Fields*] / to investigate if something could be found in the ground / and I found a place in the middle of one of these lots / of the size of a cart-wheel / which was paved with small pebbles; from which I deduced / that it had been a fire-place or hearth / on which a fire had been made: for which reason it is believable / that formerly there were similar hearths in every lot / within a small hut.*'

He described (1660, 41-3) the Celtic Fields* with a sharp eye and compared them to a 17th-century window with hundreds of lead-framed glass panes, the lead frames being the straight earthen walls separating the fields. His illustration shows that he was aware that these walls were lower in the middle than at the corners (Brongers 1976).[117] He argued that the fields were former camps of nomadic *Sueven* (Suebi or Swabians), who had come from Brandenburg, Mecklenburg, etc. east of the River Elbe, and had stayed for only three years in Drenthe.

Picardt (1660, 34-6) also described first-hand the stratigraphy and composition of peat bogs, and of the objects found therein (among which were 'potsherds'). One hundred years later, this would induce Van Lier (1760) to discuss peat bog formation in Drenthe at length (see section '1756-1760').

1685: Van Leeuwen

The jurist and historian Simon van Leeuwen [1626-1682] in Leiden and The Hague devoted some space to the hunebeds in his *Batavia Illustrata* (1685).[118] He had seen these himself when he travelled through Drenthe and was convinced that Picardt's description (1660) of the hunebeds was correct. Because he could not understand how they could have been constructed by normally sized men, he considered Picardt's giant hunebed builders theory 'not so very unlikely'.[119] He thought that the builders were the Cimbri and Celts. As the earliest known

---

116 '*In een van dese heb ick een reys hier en daer in de aerde laten graven / om t'ondersoecken of men yet in de grondt soude vinden / en hebbe in 't midden van een deser perckjes gevonden een plaets / soo groot als een wagen-radt / bestraet en geplaveyt met kleyne keselingen; waer uyt ick gepresumeert heb / dat 'et een vyer-stede of haert geweest zy / waer op vyer gestoockt is geworden : waerom gelooflijck is / dat in een yegelijck perckjen voortijds een soodanigen haert-stede geweest zy / leggende binnen een hutjen.*' (Picardt 1660, 42). About Celtic Fields, see note 91.
117 Plate fol. 42, which, however, does not show a hut in each walled lot.
118 Van Leeuwen had become deputy clerk (*subtituut-griffier*) of the *Hoge Raad* (High Council) in The Hague in 1681. He died in January, 1682, when he was still working on *Batavia Illustrata*. It is sometimes supposed that he only started writing *Batavia Illustrata* when he acquired access to the national archives, in 1681, but this is impossible. Considerable parts of this voluminous book, including his ideas about Picardt, hunebeds and giants, must have been written earlier.
119 '*Het welk so heel onwaarschijnlijk niet en is*' (Van Leeuwen 1685, 293, notes *l-m*).

people they preceded the Germani. In note *m*, p. 253-4, he wrote that he had seen 'the excavated bones of a very large person, a giant' in the Land of Kleve (Cleves), Germany. He mentioned giants in the *Old Testament* and concluded that the Germani were strong hefty men. Even in the present-day Netherlands, he noted, there was a contrast between the large and strong Frisians and the short and slender Brabanders and Flemish. Van Leeuwen apparently did not know that the 'Cimbric Peninsula', comprising Jutland and Schleswig-Holstein, is very rich in megalithic tombs.

Apart from Ludolph Smids (1711), who had visited the Drenthe hunebeds from nearby Groningen, where he lived, before he moved to Amsterdam (see section '1685-1694'), no other historian from the western parts of the country would pay attention to the hunebeds until Andries Schoemaker in 1732, who would then be followed by Arnout Vosmaer, in 1756, and Engelbertus Engelberts, in 1790.

1685: excavation of a megalithic tomb at Cocherel, France

In July, 1685, the same year that the religiously tolerant Edict of Nantes was revoked, an entrenched *allée couverte* at Cocherel near Évreux, west of Paris,[120] was demolished so that its stones could be reused in a lock. Before this occurred, Robert le Prévôt de Cocherel, on whose property it stood, carefully excavated the monument and supervised the writing of a detailed report.[121] It was 'the first really scientific excavation of a prehistoric grave' (Chaigneau, in prep.). About twenty intact skeletons were found. It was reported that one skull had a deliberately made hole, which is now known to be the first description of a trepanation. The skeletons were accompanied by what Le Prévôt recognised as stone axes, several mounted in antler sleeves. Flint arrowheads and daggers, a pierced pendant of jade and handmade pottery were also found. A layer of cremated human bones lay under the skeletons. Le Prévôt concluded that the cremations belonged to the ancient Gauls, who practised cremation of their dead according to classical sources. He thought that the skeletons, on the other hand, belonged to a barbaric people who were vanquished, slaughtered and then interred by the Gauls. 'It seems that these barbarians used neither iron nor copper, nor any other metal'. Obviously no Christian graves were involved and the ecclesiastical and profane authorities, who had been invited to the investigation, authorised Le Prévôt to deal with the excavated objects as he saw fit. His report was printed almost in full in English, in London (Le Prévôt 1686), but, apart from a few summaries, it remained un-

---

120 On Cocherel: Daniel 1960, 14-15 and frontispiece; Masset 1997, 5-7; Schnapp 1993, 237, 268-9; Giot 1985, 10 (ascribing the report to the parish priest M. Devin). The history of documentation and publication is very complex. See the detailed study by Cyrille Chaigneau (in prep.), on which most of my summary is based.

121 On July 11, 1685, a legal document, which extensively describes the situation, was drawn up by the notary Ollivier-Estienne. Chaigneau (in prep.: Annexe) and http://giverny.org.archeos/cochergb.htm present a modern translation from the old French.

published in France till 1722.[122] Bernard de Montfaucon [1655-1741] discussed the grave and artefacts in detail, in 1719,[123] as did Pierre le Brasseur, in 1722, and Jacques Martin, in 1727.[124] Montfaucon was puzzled by the remark about a people without knowledge of any metals and asked the opinion of Jacob Christoph Iselin [1681-1737], an antiquarian in Basel, Switzerland, who had been professor in history, eloquence and theology in Marburg from 1705 to 1717. Iselin responded that this observation was to be expected, because it tallied with the surmise of Lucretius and Hesiod that there was a succession of stone, copper and iron used for weapons and tools in prehistory.[125] Moreover, older graves of the ancient Germani contained copper, and those that were younger, iron. Iselin's letter was published by Montfaucon (1719, 5 (1), p. 199).[126] [127]

122 Guillaume-Etienne le Prévôt, Robert's brother, published the original report, with three plates, for the first time in France as an appendix to Le Brasseur 1722 #.

123 Montfaucon 1719, vol. 5: 1, p. 195-9 # (pers. comm. W. Arentzen).

124 Martin 1727. For his illustrations of the skeletons in the tomb in Cocherel and of hafted flint axes, a stone axe, a pot and other objects from the tomb, see Schnapp 1993, 269, ill.

125 See section '1756-1760'. See Schnapp (1993, 332-3) for an English translation of these lines by Lucretius.

126 Stemmermann (1934, 125ff., cited by Gummel 1938, 95 n. 3) and Schnapp (1993, 269) noted that Montfaucon and Iselin did not yet grasp the fundamental importance of this sequence for prehistoric chronology. Through the studies by Alexandre-Yves Goguet (1758 #) [1716-1758], Piere Jean-Baptiste Legrand d'Aussy (1799) [1737-1800] and others, the former existence of successive Stone and Metal Ages (and sometimes of Bronze and Iron Ages) would ultimately become generally known. See Laming-Emperaire (1964, 99-103 #) about Legrand d'Aussy 1799 (pers. comm. W. Arentzen).

127 On the internet, the *Syndicat d'Initiatives* calls this find the 'First archaeological discovery in the world', which is not true, even if this statement is restricted to megalithic tombs. For instance, Johann von Velen wrote a detailed report of his excavation in Surbolds Grab in Germany, in 1613 (see note 110) Admittedly, Von Velen did not describe the artefacts from this tomb, which he sent to elector Ferdinand of Bavaria in a cask together with those from nearby tombs outside Börgerwald, except to say that they were only 'pieces of old pots or pans':
'*Ich hab auch woll negst dabei ausserhalb den Burgerwalt under etlichen grossen steinen alss nur under einen stein etwas eingraben lassen, aber In eil nicht finden konnen, alss stucke von alten potten oder duppen, gleich In dem fesslein auch eingepackt ...*' (Veltman 1886, 250; Gummel 1938, 17n; Laux 1989, 127). And: '*... ob Ich woll bedenckens gehabt von denselben, wass In der erden gefunden, als geringscheszig Ew. Curf. Durchlaucht zuzusenden, So hab Ich doch zu bezeigung meines fleisses und dass die historici und Antiquarii darauff zu speculieren haben mugen, von allen ettwas In ein fesslein gepacket, dasselbig einen Fuhrmann auffgeben ... und muss dass fesslein an dem end, dah es mit H verzeichnet, eroffnet werden ...*' (Veltman 1886, 247).
He did not further specify '*vom allen ettwas*'. Moreover, Picardt excavated in a Celtic Field in Drenthe, between 1642 and 1659 (see section '1660').

1685-1694: excavation in D27-Borger (Brongersma, Smids)

On June 11, 1685, Titia Brongersma, born about 1648, a poetess from Groningen, called 'Sappho, musarum certe decima'[128] by her admirers, spent the Whitsuntide with her family in Borger in Drenthe. At the request of Ludolph Smids [1649-1720], her Groningen friend, who was a medical doctor, antiquarian and playwright,[129] she and her cousin Jan Laurens Lentinck organised an excavation in the chamber of the Great Hunebed D27-Borger (Figure 9). This was the second documented excavation of non-Roman antiquities in The Netherlands.[130] Afterwards she wrote a poem (in Brongersma 1686, 8) about this tomb, referring to the 'ninefold lintel' (*neegentalge drempel*) of D27, viz. its nine capstones, but not about her excavation. In this poem she rejected the idea that this Stoneheap was a memorial of the gallant Huns [*het dappre Hunnenschap*], or that it were [*sic*] uplifted pyramids [*getorste pieramyden*] or tombs, because its vault contained offerings of holy ashes from prehistoric times, and that the hunebed had been built by giants.[131] She concluded that it was a marble temple dedicated to the goddess Nature, who should be venerated there. Therefore she laid a wreath of flowers and oak leaves on the tomb.[132]

While this poem did not directly increase the knowledge of hunebeds, Titia's finds in the chamber were critical for the study of megaliths. Smids, who did not assist with the excavation, but received what she recovered, published (1694) her description that a street-like cobble stone layer was in the chamber under which were pottery, 'breaking to pieces', 'ash'[133] and 'petrified' bones.[134] Shortly after 1685, Smids corresponded in Latin with the antiquary, numismatist and librarian

---

128 Sappho was called the Tenth Muse by Plato. About Titia Brongersma, one of the earliest poetesses from Friesland-Groningen, see R. Brongers (1996) and Eilskov Jensen & Nijboer (1998). The actions and poems of Brongersma and Smids concerning hunebed D27 and hunebeds in general were discussed in more detail in Van Giffen (1927, 3-9) and Bakker (1984), R. Brongers (1996) and Eilskov Jensen & Nijboer (1998). Nijkeuter (2001, 2005) added little.

129 Smids was born in Groningen, in 1649, where he soon became an orphan. His Roman Catholic education began in Antwerp, in 1665, and continued in a Westphalian monastery, in 1667. In 1670, he studied at Groningen University. Thereupon he studied in Leiden, where he took his doctor's degree in medicine, in 1673, and returned to Groningen, where he married in 1674. His wife died in 1692. He remarried a Calvinist woman and was converted to her faith. The couple moved to Amsterdam, in 1695, because his Groningen friends were hostile to this conversion. There he practiced as a medical doctor and wrote books and stageplays and earned fame for his antiquarian studies (Smids 1711).

130 Picardt preceded her, see section '1660'.

131 *Of 't syn alleen getorste Pieramyden, / Of Tomben, want dit grove berggewas / Besluyt in haar gewelfsel, van voor tyden / Nog tot een blyk, geheylgde offer-ass.* 'From pre historic times' (*van voor tyden*) is an early instance of the use of this term (in a poetic context).

132 It takes some time to understand this poem. In it, Titia (1686, 8) gave D27-Borger the following names: *Hunne-bed* ('Hunnebed'); *de ongemeene, opgestapelde Steenhoop* ('this exceptional, piled up Stoneheap'); *dees Steenmyt* ('this Pile of Stones'); *dit grove berggewas* ('this crude mountain-growth'); *Steen-Paleys* ('Palace of Boulders'); *Grott* ('Cave') and *Keye-slott* ('Boulder-palace').

133 In antiquarian texts, 'ash' and 'ashes' in relation to 'urns' usually refer to bones powdered during cremation, in contrast to larger pieces of [cremated] bone. Charcoal was not explicitly mentioned.

134 Smids (1694) and (1711, 326-8).

De HUINEBEDDEN, of
Groote Steen hoopen ; in Drenth en Weſtfalen .

Figure 9. Titia Brongersma, dressed as Sappho, supervises the excavation of hunebed D27-Borger by her nephew Lentinck and workmen, in 1685. Print by J. Schijnvoet in Smids (1711). See further Appendix 3.

Christian Schlegel [1667-1722] in Arnstadt and Gotha in Germany. To Schlegel's question 'If the hunebeds are really graves, have bones of giants ever been found in them?'[135] Smids replied 'I know what nonsense farmers and shepherds tell, but listen to the observations made in 1685', and briefly told the story of Titia Brongersma's excavation. He enclosed some of the sherds, which displayed 'the uncivilised simplicity of that ancient time', and some of the bones, which showed a 'hard petrification'.[136] These bones were apparently from persons of normal size, although Smids did not state that explicitly. Elsewhere he stated that Titia's digging (*gewroed*) in a hunebed was the first such action he knew of.

---

135 This not documented question is implied by the reply of Smids.
136 The 'petrification' of the human bones (which would have fitted in embryonic ideas about fossils in geological layers) seems to have interested Smids more than their normal size. As we know now, this hardening of the bones was mainly due to the cremation itself. See Part A1, above.

Smids also wrote a poem about Titia's excavation, to which Titia replied with another poem with the same rhyme-words (both published in Smids 1694, 58-61 and 1711, 327-8; Titia's poem was also published in Brongersma 1686, 9). After these three poems from 1685-1686 and a lost one written by Johannes Mensinga,[137] no other poems concerning Dutch hunebeds appeared until 1844. Between then and the year 2000 more than forty were written.[138]

Smids (1694) suggested that Swabians, Saxons and Danes may have been interred in this hunebed in urns (after cremation?), which confirms that he considered the bones to be from normally sized people. He did not speak about giants.

The implicit conclusion that the hunebeds were built by normally sized men, not giants, in his correspondence with Schlegel shortly after 1685, was published in 1701 (#) by the Germans Johann Christoph Olearius [1668-1747] and in 1713 by Jodocus Hermann Nunningh [1675-1753]. This observation led to the rejection of the theory that giants were the builders by Olearius, in 1701, Nunningh and Johann Heinrich Cohausen [1665-1750], in 1713-14, and Johann Georg Keysler [1693-1743], in 1720.[139] Cohausen and Nunningh thought that the hunebeds were built by ancient Germani of normal stature, who were more robust than modern-day Germans and would have been able to move the heavy boulders on wooden rollers or sticks, while using their own arms as levers. In 1724, Hendrik van Rijn (or Henricus van Rhijn) [?-1732] dismissed Picardt's (1660) theory that giants had once lived in Drenthe (Van Rijn 1724). He mentioned the terms *Hunebedden* and *Hunebergen* for tumuli, and that *Huine* meant 'giant', but did not discuss the hunebeds themselves – which is not surprising in a book on ecclesiastical history.[140] Although there remained a few objectors to the rejection of the giant hunebed builders until the early 19th century, it was accepted by most scholars.

---

137 *Saxa agri Trentini, carmen*, printed in 1687, cited by Smids (1711). Gratama (1886, 25) and the Koninklijke Bibliotheek, The Hague, in the 1980s and 1990s, could not find this work. Johannes Mensinga [1635-1698] was a professor of Eloquence and History at Groningen University. An undated manuscript *Joh. Mensinga in Terentii sex Comoedias Dictata* is or was in the University Library of Giessen (Catalogue Adrian 1840).

138 A poem of four stanzas by 'Extempore' (1844, cf. Arentzen 2006, 93) and a poem of forty-eight stanzas by Willem Seymour Mulder [1820-1896], written in 1852, are excellent (see Klompmaker, Nijkeuter & Tissing 1996, also with a selection of later poems). About Seymour Mulder, see Nijkeuter, *Waardeel* 27, 2007 (3), 10-4. In 1801, the German clergyman J.G.T. Lamprecht published a poem of seventeen stanzas with the legend of the *langbetten* Visbeker Braut and Visbeker Bräutigam in Oldenburg (952 and 936) in the hope that by increasing their fame, their demolition would be prevented (Liebers 1986, 49 and her Appendix 7).

139 Keysler (1720, 5-9, 583). He recorded the megalithic graves he knew from Drenthe, northern Germany and southern Scandinavia and copied the list of Smids (with its errors).

140 This book was a translation of the study or studies from 1719 [#] and / or 1714 [#] by Hugo Franciscus van Heussen [1654-1719], but I do not know if this note of Van Rijn is based on the Latin original or is his own addition.

1687 and 1700: Tollius's trip through Germany and Von Hennin's giant hunebed builders

In two letters, written in 1687, the Dutch learned philologist Jacob Tollius [1633-1696][141] described megalithic *langbetten* (megalithic long barrows) near Magdeburg, Germany, which he saw on his way to Potsdam. In his opinion, they contained the remains of ancient Germani, and he obviously did not believe in giant megalith builders himself. In Potsdam he met the 'Great Elector' of Brandenburg, Friedrich Wilhelm of Hohenzollern [1620-1688, who ruled from 1640 to 1688] and told him of these monuments. In response, the Elector stated that he had once organised the excavation of such a megalithic tomb in Holstein with the expectation of finding the bones of giants, but that only ancient coins were discovered (Schulz 1959).[142]

Heinrich Christian von Hennin [1658-1703], cousin of Tollius and professor at the University of Duisburg in Germany, published Tollius's 1687 letters posthumously as *Epistolae itinerariae* (1700). In contrast to Tollius, Von Hennin still believed that only giants could have built the hubebeds. Picardt (1660) is referred to in the notes and there is a plate of giants building a hunebed (Figure 10), which is clearly based on Picardt's illustrations (Figures 6 and 8).[143]

1706: excavation in hunebed D17-Rolde

On August 12, 1706, Johannes Hofstede [1685-1736] and Abraham Rudolph Kymmell [1683-1725] dug a pit in the chamber of hunebed D17-Rolde. Hofstede described the excavated 'Roman' pottery and its stratigraphical position between different layers of stones in detail; he mentioned 'ash', but no stone or flint arte-

---

141 About Tollius, see Peters 2010, 485 n. 50.
142 The second wife of the Elector, Dorothea von Holstein-Sonderburg-Glücksburg, may have enabled this excavation, as Schulz (1959) suggested. Krause & Schoetensack (1893, 117n) discussed this publication and referred to [G.H.] Handelmann, *Zeitschrift für Ethnologie* 1882, 22 #. That no bones were found may be due to negligence of the excavators, to the absence of cremated remains, or to an earlier clearance of the chamber. See Part A1, above, about coin finds in megalithic graves.
143 Even later than Smids (1711; see section '1711'), the belief that giants built the megaliths in Denmark can be found in a report of 1727 and in a study by P. Syv in 1787 (Klindt-Jensen 1975, 35-6). A certain Boymans defended this idea even later in *Gazette van West-Vlaandren en Brugge*, 1819, no. 119 (Westendorp 1822, 6, 77-8, 166). He was one of the last to do so before the present-day 'New Age'.

Figure 10. Giants constructing a Hünengrab *near Magdeburg, Germany, according to H.C. von Hennin in Tollius (1700). The picture is clearly inspired by Picardt's prints (Figures 6 and 8) (photograph University Library Amsterdam OTM O61 5504).*

facts.[144] With a reference to Alexander ab Alexandro (1522, lib. 3, cap. 12),[145] he inferred that pots situated higher up on a flat stone in the chamberfill had contained food and drink brought to the deceased whose ashes were buried in funeral urns deeper in the chamber.[146] This is also the present interpretation of the function of most pottery in hunebeds, although collared flasks and a few other small pots may have contained medicine or incense. Hofstede's 1706 report was the first to present this modern explanation for (part of) the mass of pottery in Dutch hunebeds. Giants were not mentioned. This objective and detailed report was not published until 1848[147] and had no notable influence on subsequent studies.

1711: Smids returns to the giants

Amazingly, in his 1711 encyclopaedia of Dutch castles, towns and antiquities, published twenty-six years after Titia Brongersma's excavation in hunebed D27-Borger (1685), Smids reverted to the theory that giants had built the hunebeds (1711, 136, 275-7, 326). To attribute this acceptance of Picardt's theory to Smids's conversion from Roman Catholicism to Calvinism in 1685, and his moving from Groningen to Amsterdam in 1695, may seem far-fetched, but orthodox Calvinism took – and takes – God's Word literally.[148] Thus Smids (1711, 136) reproached Hadrianus Junius (1588, see section '1547') that he had not taken Schonhovius's story seriously, because if he had seen the hunebeds at Rolde, Drouwen, Tynaarlo etc. himself, he would not call Schonhovius's story that giants had built them 'a

---

144 Hofstede's report, known from two copies, is cited in full and discussed by Van Giffen (1927, 9-12), Bakker (1979b, 145-7, 166-7; in prep.; cf. 1992, 4-5) and Van der Sanden (2007, 59-61 and n. 5 on p. 203). Both copies of the manuscript, which were obviously copied from the lost original by uneducated clerks, denote Hofstede's first name with the initial S., but J. is probably more correct, because no S. Hofstede was found in the Drenthe archives, according to Van der Sanden. And Abraham Rudolph Kymmell, the new sheriff of Rolde, was written 'Kymmel' instead of Kymmell. In 1707, Johannes Hofstede became the protestant minister at Ruinerwold (Van der Sanden 2007, 60-1, 203, n. 5-9; see also Arentzen 2006, 140-1). Several other (younger) members of the prominent Groningen-Drenthe family Hofstede figure in the present study.

145 Alessandro Alessandri ('Alexander ab Alexandro') was an Italian humanist and jurist [1461-1523]. He wrote *Dies Geniales* (1522), see 'References'.

146 That the majority of the pots in megalithic tombs were 'urns' filled with burnt human bones was a common, but mistaken, conviction in Europe until the early 20th century – therefore I disagree with Gummel (1938, 15, n. 6), who thought that the 'urns' that were dug up in 1588 from a *Hünengrab* northeast of Schleswig, Germany (Cypraeus 1634, 17), were later burials dating from the Bronze-Iron Ages; they were TRB ware, in my opinion.

147 The report was published by Petrus Speckman van der Scheer [1820-1858], *Kronyk van het Historisch Gezelschap te Utrecht* 1848, 190-2. It was cited and dicussed by Van Giffen 1927, 9-12.

148 In January, 2010, an inventory of the archaeological sites in the Dutch municipality of Staphorst, Province of Overijssel, was presented to the municipal council of this strictly orthodox-Calvinistic village. The earliest known artefacts from Staphorst date from the Middle Ages, but a standard timescale was added to the report, because much earlier finds could be expected here. The timescale triggered a vehement discussion in the municipal council about the dates for the Palaeolithic period. An alderman demanded that a statement saying that according to the Bible the world was created less than 6000 years ago would be inserted in the report (which, according to Dutch law, was paid for by the municipality).

nice fairy-tale or just a vision in a dream' (*een aartigh sprookje, of een enkel droom-gesicht*). Smids's giants were, however, the earliest humans, who had a taller and larger body, or were much stronger than present men ('*het menschdom is in de aller-eerste tyden grooter en onbesuisder van lichaam, of sterker en geweldiger van krachten geweest*': 1711, 303).

Smids's later avowal that giants built the hunebeds may have been more apparent than real. In the first place, Smids himself never explicitly wrote that normally sized men had built the hunebeds; he only stated that the bones found in the chamber of D27 were those of normally sized men. Secondly, it is conceivable that only after 1686, when he speculated that Swabians, Saxons or Danes constructed the hunebeds, he came to think about how such heavy capstones could have been positioned. Consideration of this feat had prompted his contemporaries Van Leeuwen (1685) and Von Hennin (1700) to accept Picardt's (1660) theory that only giants had been able to do this (see sections '1685: Van Leeuwen' and '1687 and 1700'). Apparently, none of these authors consulted engineers.

The idea that normally sized men could have done this with levers, rollers, etc. was developed in German Westphalia by Nunningh and Cohausen, in 1713 and 1714, just after the appearance of Smids's book (1711), in which hunebed building was a marginal topic.

Smids published the first list of extant hunebeds in The Netherlands and adjacent parts of Germany in his encyclopaedia (1711, 324-8). This list, partly a compilation of hunebeds mentioned by Picardt, was inaccurate because it also included several non-megalithic barrows, but the existence of a large number of tombs in the northeastern Netherlands and adjacent parts of Germany was communicated to a wider audience.[149]

1730-1734: the shipworm and the legal protection of the hunebeds in Drenthe

In 1730-3, the dikes and sluices along the sea in The Netherlands and Ostfriesland and Jever in northwestern Germany became endangered with the arrival of the shipworm, *Teredo navalis* (Dutch: *paalworm*, German: *Pfahlwurm* or *Schiffsbohrmuschel*), a wormlike bivalve mollusc, up to 30 cm long, inadvertently brought in from Asia in the hulls of ships, which attacked wood in salty waters (Figure 11). The sea side of most dikes along the North Sea and the Zuyder Sea consisted of 1.5-2 m wide dams of compact, non-putrefying seaweed[150] behind vertical wooden fences, made of oak and pine beams, which acted as surf break-

---

149 Apart from better known authors, Smids (1711, 326-8) referred to 'Joh. Rist, in *Colloq. Junior.*, who wrote about megalithic graves in Scania (Skåne) and elsewhere in Denmark', and to 'Schildius, *De Cauchis*, lib. 2, cap. 11, p. 302ff.' Schild's study was reprinted, in 1742, in Aurich as *De Cauchis, nobilissimo Germaniae populo* by JOH. SCHILD [# internet; I found no mention of the first edition, nor did I find the full title of the study by JOH. RIST [1607-1667].

150 *Zostera nana* and *Zostera maritima*, Dutch: *zeegras*, German: *Seegras, Meergras*.

Figure 11. A pamphlet of 1732 by Elias Baeck à H. gives a good impression of the dangers and panic caused by the shipworm catastrophe in Holland, Zeeland, Flanders and German Ost-Friesland (photograph Atlas van Stolk, Rotterdam). See Appendix 3 for the German text.

ers. These wooden fences were rapidly tunnelled by the shipworm and broke like matchsticks. General panic ensued, because if the dikes broke half of the country could easily be flooded![151]

Fortunately, the modern type of dike with a sloping profile and consisting of stone-covered earth and clay was invented soon afterwards by Pieter Straat and Pieter van der Deure, mayors of Bovencarspel in West-Friesland, north of Amsterdam (Figure 12).[152] The result was that the erratic boulders in Drenthe and parts of Germany and Scandinavia along the North Sea suddenly became valuable as building materials.[153] Everywhere in Drenthe and abroad the erratic boulders were blasted and carried away, and hunebeds were dismantled and their stones removed. The removal of such boulders used to mark boundaries, however, prompted the Drenthe government to pass a Resolution (*Resolutie*), on July 21, 1734, prohibiting this activity, which also protected 'the so-called Hunebeds, which, as venerable monuments and time-honoured memorials, were to be preserved everywhere'.[154] I have no doubt that this was due to Picardt's laudation of the hunebeds as one of the most valuable assets of Drenthe in his 1660 book: that it was reprinted in 1731 and 1745 can hardly be accidental.

This 1734 Resolution in Drenthe was the third law in the world enacted to protect antiquities. The first law was proclaimed by King Christian IV of Denmark, in 1620, and, in 1630, King Gustav Adolph of Sweden gave legal protection to

---

151 That German Ostfriesland was also affected (Figure 11) seems to be little known in Germany; at least a recent study (Endlich 2005) does not mention the shipworm catastrophe.

152 Straat & Van der Deure, 1733; Schilstra 1974, 60-95; De Waal 2008. Three drawings by Rembrandt at the Diemen sea dike show the heads of the vertical beams of the old wooden dike fences (cf. Figure 12): Benesch 1358 and 1172; HdG 844 (B. Bakker et al. 1998, 228-9; Lugt 1915, 140-2; figs. 90-3).
When Lady Portland, née Jane Martha Temple [1672-1752], asked her son Willem Bentinck [1704-1774] in 1737 about the condition of the dikes in Holland., he answered, from The Hague, 'Everyone here is convinced that dikes, instead of being laid behind driven piles, should have upwardly slanting slopes which are covered by heaps of huge stones!' (W. Bentinck, letter of March 5, 1737). See Hella S. Haasse (1978), whose paraphrase shows that she misunderstood Bentinck's technical explanation and thought that the dikes were 'first laid *on* driven piles and later *on* heaps of stones (*Iedereen is er hier van overtuigd, dat die* [dijken] *in plaats van op in de grond geslagen palen op schuin oplopende stapels van grote stenen aangelegd moeten worden!*).

153 Current prices of stone were given by Straat & Van der Deure, 1733. Nordic erratic boulders were used from 1732 until 1860, when basalt from the Rhineland became used instead. During the French occupation, 1806-1813, Tournay stones were used. The quantities used and costs were enormous: between 1732 and 1802, 1.2 million tons of stone were brought to West-Friesland (north of Amsterdam) alone, which comprised only a small part of the coast line where the dikes were renewed with stone in the same way (Schilstra 1974, 84-7).

154 An exception was granted by the Resolution of Nobles and Commoners in the General Assembly of Drenthe, passed on March 15, 1735, allowing hunebed D52a-Wapse to be demolished, because 'the beauty of the view was not harmed' and, probably and more importantly, because this work had been planned weeks before the Resolution of July 21, 1734, was passed. Otherwise, the 1734 Resolution protecting the hunebeds was reconfirmed (text in Bakker 1979b).

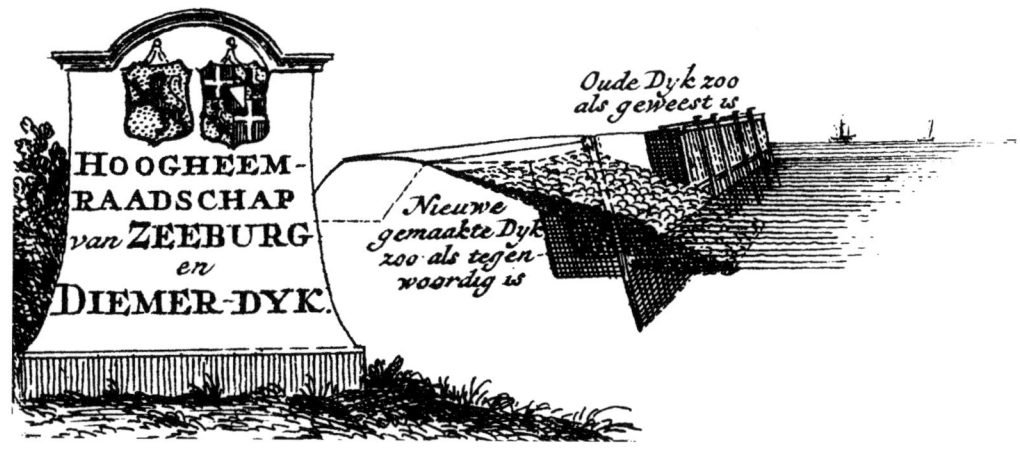

Figure 12. The Zuyder Sea dike at Diemen before and after the shipworm catastrophe of the early 1730s. The new stone-covered dike is in the front. Behind it is the former dike, which consisted of a fence of wooden beams protecting a dam of compacted seaweed (De Leth ca. 1765, detail of map 34).

castles, forts, dolmens, rune-stones, graves and barrows in his wide realm.[155] The legal protection of the hunebeds in Drenthe was restated in 1790. In 1809, Petrus Hofstede [1755-1839], acting as the Bailiff (*Land-Drost*) of Drenthe, prohibited smashing and transporting of stones from the hunebeds and the probing and digging for stones in tumuli. In 1818, as governor, he extended the Resolution of 1734 by ordering the local authorities 'to keep a vigilant eye on the strict compliance of this [decree] ... . Excavation or investigation of antiquities or monuments remains forbidden without demonstrable advance knowledge of the proper authority.'[156] The law protecting hunebeds was proclaimed again in 1846 and 1854.[157] From 1818 and 1819 onwards, the *schultessen* (mayors) of municipalities in Drenthe with hunebeds were obliged to report each year in writing about the condition of these hunebeds, which resulted in much paper work.[158] The first systematic survey of 1818-9 is very useful (Van Giffen 1925, 217-8, No. 36, so-called *Schultesrapporten*).[159]

---

155 Schnapp 1993, 176; Klindt-Jensen 1975, 27 (who called a proclamation of 1666 'the first law for the protection of monuments of Sweden and Finland'). Most of the former is dealt with in Bakker 1979b. In present-day Germany, the first monument protection laws in regions with *Hünengräber* were proclaimed in the Duchy of Mecklenburg, in 1804 (Jacob-Friesen 1928), and the Duchy of Oldenburg, in 1819 (Rosenow 1961). In France, only 'from about 1825 onwards, [did] a concern about the preservation and description [of megalithic monuments] manifest itself, at least in the Morbihan' (Giot 1985, 15).

156 Full texts of these proclamations, in Dutch and translated into English, are in Bakker 1979b, 166-70, 174-5.

157 Van Giffen 1927, 38 (but see Bakker in prep., ch. 2). The proclamation of 1846 was perhaps connected with the refusal of Janssen's request for permission to excavate hunebeds in 1846 and 1847 (see section '1840-1868').

158 Van Giffen (1925, 194-211) listed the reports of the mayors and the correspondence and deeds concerning the hunebeds in Drenthe, between 1809 and 1878, in the Provincial Archives of Drenthe, but even this long and useful list is not complete.

159 L.O. Gratama (1887) was the first to point out the importance of these reports.

1732: Schoemaker, Pronk and De Haen visit hunebeds

The Amsterdam wealthy textile merchant Andries Schoemaker [1660-1735] had a passion for topography and history. He travelled through large parts of the northern Netherlands to document ancient buildings, mansions, churches and the like. At seventy-one years, he visited Drenthe, Friesland and Overijssel between June 28 and July 9, 1732, with the topographical draughtsman Cornelis Pronk [1671-1759] and his pupil Abraham de Haen [1707-1748], who drew many topographical views for him. His maidservant Geesie Arens accompanied them (and was shown sitting on a capstone in one of the drawings),

Half a century after Simon van Leeuwen (1685), Schoemaker was the first known visitor from the western Netherlands with an active interest in hunebeds. Thanks to Schoemaker's initiative, Pronk drew the first realistic views of Dutch hunebeds, D53-Havelte and D54-Havelte (Gevers & Mensema 1985, figs. 34-35).[160] Directly related, but later in time are the drawings of D53-Havelte (Figure 13), dated September 17, 1737, and D3-Midlaren (Figure 14), dated July 30, 1754. Probably Abraham de Haen drew the one that is reproduced in Figure 13.[161] Its style is quite different from that of the 1732 drawings by Pronk and that of Figure 14, which is dated after De Haen's death and ascribed to Pronk. That the pictures of Figures 13 and 14 are dated seven and twenty-two years, respectively, after the trip with Schoemaker, shows that Pronk and De Haen also drew hunebeds on later trips to Drenthe[162] – Schoemaker had apparently convinced them of their topographical interest. Van Giffen concluded from Pronk's [and De Haen's] drawings that the position of the large boulders of D53 and D54 was almost the same as in 1918, whereas the oak coppice mentioned by Schoemaker and shown in Figure 13 had disappeared and [barrow] sand had been taken away (Van Giffen 1927, 126).

Schoemaker described both Havelte hunebeds extensively in 1732.[163] He was astonished that the Havelte tombs were not as large as Picardt (1660) had suggested. But he was told that much larger hunebeds could be found near Zuidlaren.[164]

---

160 Van Giffen (1927, atlas-plate 123) reproduced, on a very small scale, Pronk's 1732 drawing of D53 and [De Haen's] 1737 drawing of D53 (my Figure 13), in which he indicated his code numbers of each stone. He discussed these drawings in detail (1927, 124-6, 136, 143).

161 The drawings by Abraham de Haen are often so similar in style and manner of execution to those by Cornelis Pronk that even experts have great difficulty telling them apart. Schoemaker stated that Pronk drew D53 and D54 in 1732, i.e. those reproduced by Gevers & Mensema. This suggested to me that the 1737 drawing of D53, in a different style (Figure 13), was made by De Haen.

162 The precise dates of both drawings (Figures 13-14) show that they were not updated finished drawings copied from dated sketches made earlier.

163 Manuscript from 1735: Van Giffen 1927, 124-6; Gevers & Mensema 1985, 91. Cf. Van Kuik 1897.

164 This is not true: only D27-Borger is longer than D53-Havelte. Schoemaker was presumably impressed by Picardt's story that a flock of sheep could be sheltered under a capstone, but Picardt was referring to a different hunebed, Surbolds Grab in Germany (see section '1660' and note 110). Moreover, the loose stones of a destroyed large hunebed usually make a smaller impression than the original tomb – this is a well-known optical illusion.

Figure 13. Hunebed D53-Havelte viewed from ESE, in 1737. Washed pen drawing, probably made by Abraham de Haen [1707-1748], September 16, 1737 (Drents Museum Assen, negative 194511). See further Appendix 3.

Figure 14. Hunebed D3-Midlaren drawn by Cornelis Pronk [1671-1759], Tuesday July 30, 1754 (Groninger Museum, photograph Marten de Leeuw). See further Appendix 3.

'One heap [D53-Havelte] *consisted of 20 to 22 small and large stones, among which some are as tall as I am.*[165] *The smallest are standing upright and they are covered by large stones. Under them is a hollow* [viz. the chamber]. *Formerly, this hollow was dug in and urns were found containing dead men's bones, ash and Roman coins* [penningen]. *These stones were artificially placed upon each other [by men] and not by Giants, as often is claimed. I think that, although Giants existed, they lacked the strength to place these astounding stones upon each other, but I cannot find out the real truth.*

The second heap [D54-Havelte] *had fewer stones, but the underlying stones* [leggers] *were still larger than in the first heap. These stones looked bluish on the outside and some were covered with a mossy slime, but seen from inside they resembled red marble with white and brown veins and sparkled like very small pieces of rock-crystal. I took a piece as a curio with me, which was almost as red in colour as red brick.*

There was an oak coppice around these stone-heaps [cf. Figure 13] *and at a shot's distance away peat was dug from the heath, although it is not as good as our bog-peat is. Having satisfied our curiosity, we brought our guide* [the schoolmaster] *back to Havelte and drove to Steenwyk. We saw many stones of this kind on the way, but they were much smaller and more numerous until we were close to Steenwyk.'*[166]

Schoemaker also related reports from 1735 about the shipworm catastrophe and the resulting stone trade (Van Giffen 1925, 163-6).

---

165 Van Giffen 1925, 131-3 counted 64 large boulders, from which it can be inferred that several were covered in sand, in 1732. The boulders that were Schoemaker's size were capstones.

166 Schoemaker's original text is: '*De eene hoop bestond uyt 20 à 22 soo klyne als groote steenen, waaronder eenige waren soo hoog als ik ben. Synde de klynste die overynde staan door de groote gedeckt en daaronder is dan een holte, welke holte weleer syn opgegraven en wierden daar urnes in gevonden daar doodsbeenderen, assche en Romynse penningen in gevonden wierden. Na myn oordeel syn dese steenen door konst op malkanderen gebraght en niet door Reusen als er voorgegeven word, immers het kompt myn soo voor want het schynt myn, schoon er Reusen geweest waren, dat die geen kragten gehad hebben om dese soo verbaasde steenen op den anderen te brengen, hoe 't sy de regte waarhyt daarvan te weten kan ik niet navorssen.*
De tweede hoop waren sooveel steenen niet, maar de leggers waren noch grooter als van de eerste hoop, dese steenen vertoonde haar buyten aan de blaauwe kant en eenige met een mosachtig slym bedeckt, doch wanneer men die van binnen besagh soo vertoonden se sich als een rood marmer met witte en bruyne aaren vol glinsterende [steentjes] als een soort van bergchristal doch seer klyn. Ik braght om de rarityt een stuckie mede, het rood was haast van coleur als de roode gebacke steenen. Rondom deze steenhoopen was kreupelbosch van Ekenhout, een scheutweegs van daar groef men in de hey turf, doch die was lang soo goet niet als onse veenturf is. Onse nieuwsgierighyt als daar voldaan synde bragten wy onse lydsman weder te Havelte en wy reden na Steenwyk, onder wegen vonden we veel van die soort van steenen doch in lang niet van die groote maar wel een groote menigte tot dicht onder Steenwyk toe.' (Van Giffen 1927, 124-6; Gevers & Mensema 1985, 91).

1756-1760: Van Noorde's drawing and Van Lier's investigation of hunebed D13-Eext, and Vosmaer

As a consequence of the protection law of 1734, Joannes van Lier [1726-1799] (Figure 16), deputy (alderman) of the Landscape of Drenthe, who had studied classical languages and law in Leiden,[167] was instructed, in 1756, by the Drenthe government to restore D13, a small hunebed at Eext that was found under a barrow, ca.1736 (Figure 18). From his detailed discussion of this discovery (Van Lier 1760, see Figure 17), a broad outline of the course of events can be reconstructed. D13 was first discovered, around 1736, by a 'stone seeker',[168] who was probing a barrow for stones to sell as reinforcement for sea dikes. When his iron rod hit a capstone, a 'thundering and hollow noise' caused him to flee. After that, the barrow was called *Stemberg* ('Speaking Barrow' or 'Barrow with a Voice'). Nevertheless, the capstones were removed, although the rest of the chamber was left intact (Van Lier 1760, p. 12-13).[169] The chamber, which had been filled in by the sand from the barrow top, was rediscovered shortly before April 18, 1756, by local stone seekers. Between two floors of stones, less than one foot apart, they found stone axes and pots, which were sold to amateur collectors of national antiquities (Figure 19).[170] Sherds were not collected. Van Lier, who lived in the village of Annen, 4-5 km away, and had a keen interest in nature and antiquities, was apparently soon aware of this discovery. I assume that he forbade further digging and removal of the stones, according to the 1734 protection law, after consultation with the bailiff, whose secretary he was, and the two other deputies of the

---

167 About Van Lier's study, career and family, see Mulder 1942; Foorthuis & Van Dijk 1987; Niemeijer 1989; Pieters 2002; *Drentse Biografieën* 3 #. Van Lier was baptised Joannes Henricus Petrus van Lier and wrote his first name successively as Jan, Joannes (Van Lier 1760) and Johannes (Van Lier 1773, 1781). He was born in Rotterdam, was the son of a wine merchant and studied in Leiden from 1743 to 1748. Petrus Hofstede [1716-1803], an orthodox Calvinistic clergyman and Orangist born in Groningen, was his parson in Rotterdam. In 1750, Van Lier went to Drenthe, where he married Rolin(d)a Johanna Hofstede [1730-1796], Petrus Hofstede's sister, the following year, and made a career in the Drenthe government. The couple got fifteen children.

168 *Stenenzoeker* in Dutch. A stone seeker collected erratic stones, which he sold for the building of sea dikes and, in the 19th century, also for macadam road pavements.

169 This story of the discovery of D13 about 1736, as related by Van Lier (1760, 12), may have been embellished, because the word *Stemberg* could be a misspelled variant of *Steenberg* (Stoneheap), a current denomination for hunebeds in Drenthe. One capstone, which had covered a culvert since about 1736, was replaced in 1976. Rumour has it that one of the two other capstones lies somewhere near the old church; the third may have been shattered and the pieces sold for reinforcing sea dikes (Van Lier 1760, p. 13 and pers. comm. J.N. Lanting).

170 'Liefhebbers van vaderlandsche oudheden'. One collector, in Groningen, remained anonymous. Others were Mr. Alberda tot Vennebroek and Van Lier himself (p. 199-206). Van Lier's book reveals that the hunebeds were being exploited not only by locals probing for stones, but also by several gentlemen who rummaged for artefacts in hunebeds, barrows and urnfields at the time.

daily government of Drenthe, who backed him.[171] He restored the chamber floor – in the manner of a modern cobblestone street – and the steps, on April 18, using the same stones, but 'did not forget to dig in and beside the damaged chamber' (p. 15-6). Within two days he published a detailed anonymous report about the discovery, construction, investigation and restoration of the tomb, with no illustrations, in the *Groninger Courant* of April 20, 1756 (Van Lier 1760, p. 6-8).[172] The *Leidsche Courant* of April 28, 1756 paraphrased this report.

Less than a month after the publication in the newspapers, Cornelis van Noorde [1731-1795], a draughtsman from Haarlem, began an expedition to draw topographic features in the northeastern parts of the Republic and the bordering German regions around Bentheim, Rees and Wesel (Sliggers 1982).[173] He sketched D13 in black chalk, enhanced in white, on blue paper, '*May 26, burial chamber of the Romans discovered between Eeks and Rolde*' (Sliggers 1982, 35).[174] This sketch from 1756 and the finished drawing based on it (Figure 15) show some of the same details as my Figure 18, but the steps are not visible from the viewpoint chosen. The church in Eext is outlined on the horizon. On the same leaf he drew to scale a plan and sideview of a small flat flint axe with a straight cutting edge that had been found in the chamber.[175] That day he also drew the nearby hunebed D14-Eexterhalte, in which one gentleman seems to be excavating and another is standing on one of the capstones (Sliggers 1982, 33). Van Noorde's washed pen drawings of both tombs were generally faithful to these sketches, but he added more gentlemen (who are too small) and omitted the flint axe and the

---

171 Van Lier is vague about the exact date and circumstances of the rediscovery, in 1756, making it seem that the rediscovery, his deliberations with bailiff and deputies, and the restoration all occurred in one day, April 18, 1756. The decision would have been made orally, which was easy, because Van Lier was the private secretary of the bailiff. No mention is made of D13 in the *Correspondentie Registers R and E of Drost en Gedeputeerden* for 1756 in the Assen archive (letter from H. Luning and W.A.B. van der Sanden, July 19, 2007). The sequence of events in 1756 is my reconstruction; the reality may have been slightly different. In Van Lier's seventeen letters to Arnout Vosmaer, written between 1750 and 1757 (University Library Leiden BPL 246), I found no mention of D13. The last page of an undated letter from the winter 1756-7 has been cut away and Van Lier's original 'antiquarian letters' from 1758-9 are not preserved, probably because they were used as copy for the printing of the 1760 book. One of the two handwritten autobiographies of Vosmaer briefly mentions his own editorship of the book (National Archives, The Hague, No. 2.21.271-57; cf. Pieters 2002). Later letters from Van Lier to Vosmaer and copies of Vosmaer's own letters to Van Lier are also absent from the files.

172 Earlier on I translated Van Lier's term *Grafkelder*, burial chamber, for D13 as 'burial vault'. This term is deceptive, because the ceiling of D13 consisted of three flat capstones and was not a barrel vault or corbelled. Van Lier (1760, 12, 57) explicitly rejected Cannegieter's misconception (1757, 11) that D13 had had a vaulting (*verwelfsel*), according to *Nederlandsche Jaarboeken* 1756 (5), 560-2.

173 His first and last views drawn on this trip are dated Assen, May 24 and Almelo, June 18, 1756 (Sliggers 1982, 27-9, 64).

174 '*den 26 Meij 1756. tussen Eeks en Rolde ontdekte grafkelder der Romeinen*'.

175 '*dit bijteltje van vuursteen in de Grafkelder gevonden, levensgroote*'. This may have been the axe illustrated by Van Lier (1760, pl. II: 3*), although its size seems slightly different. This drawing on blue paper cannot be satisfactorily reproduced.

ROMEINSE GRAFKELDER,
Gelegen in 't Landschap Drent, tusfen Eeks en Rolde, Ondekt in 't Jaar 1756.

Figure 15. Hunebed D13-Eext drawn by Cornelis van Noorde, based on a pencil sketch from May 26, 1756: 'Roman Burial Chamber, located in the Landscape of Drent, between Eeks and Rolde, Discovered in the Year 1756. C. V. Noorde, ad Vivum del. 1756' (Gemeentearchief Haarlem: Van Ginkel et al. 1999, ill. on p. 121).

church (Sliggers 1982, 33-4; Van Ginkel et al. 1999, 121). Van Noorde's trip seems to have been directly related to the discovery of D13, perhaps instigated by an unknown principal.

Soon after, during the summer of 1756,[176] Arnout Vosmaer [1720-1799] paid a visit to Van Lier and D13. Vosmaer, a self-taught, renowned collector of zoological, geological and ethnographical objects and topographical drawings, had been a close friend of Van Lier since their youth in Rotterdam.[177] After Van Lier moved to Drenthe, in 1750, they were regular correspondents. Van Lier improved Vosmaer's

---

176 Van Lier 1760, viii, 2. The [meteorological] summer is June-August.
177 Both were sons of wealthy wine merchants in Rotterdam. Before his marriage and his move to Drenthe, in 1751, Van Lier shared a house with Vosmaer in Rotterdam for more than a year (Pieters 2002, 21; Niemeijer 1989). From 1751 to 1773, Van Lier was the private secretary of the bailiff of Drenthe, A.C. baron van Heiden (Okken 2004). From 1753 to 1758, he was also a member of *Gedeputeerde Staten* (county alderman), a member of the highest court in Drenthe (*Etstoel*), from 1754 to 1784, and, from 1758 onwards, general tax-collector in Drenthe.

Den Heere
Arnout Vosmaer

De Vriendschap noople my U uw Van Lier te schenken,
't Zien van dees' eenen Vriend doe U aan twee steeds denken.

Rotterdam 1751   *B. Bruyninx*
                                                      ob. 17 .

Figure 16. Joannes van Lier in 1751, five years before his investigation of hunebed D13-Eext in Drenthe. Pencil and brush in grey and light brown by Daniël Bruyninx [1724-1787] in Arnout Vosmaer's Album Amicorum (Niemeijer 1989, 150). The small portrait of 1773 (frontispiece of Van Lier 1781) depicts the same open, inquisitive look.

poems and treatises and translated French publications, such as Réaumur, and works in other languages for him, because Vosmaer did not know foreign languages. Vosmaer bought books for Van Lier in The Hague.

During his visit, Van Lier gave a perforated axe to Vosmaer to add to the Prince's Cabinet (Figure 19; Van Lier 1760, p. 17, 203, pl. IV: 3). The axe very probably 'had lain in the chamber, because it was later found in sand, most of which had been excavated from the chamber.' This axe was found after Alexander Carel baron van Heiden [1709-1776], the bailiff of Drenthe and Van Lier's employer, had presented all artefacts from D13 to H.R.H. Princess Anna of Hanover [1709-1757], widow of Prince William IV of Orange [1711-1751] and regent of her eight year-old son, Prince William V [1748-1806], to place them in his cabinet. She had been collecting natural curiosities and apparently also objects of historical importance for the young Prince since 1751. On September 28, 1756,

OUDHEIDKUNDIGE
BRIEVEN,

BEVATTENDE

Eene verhandeling over de manier van BEGRA-
VEN, en over de LYKBUSSCHEN, WAPENEN,
VELD- en EERTEKENS, der

OUDE GERMANEN,

En in het byzonder de befchryving van eenen alouden Steenen
Grafkelder, *met de daarin gevondene* Lykbuffchen,
Donderkeilen en Donderbylen, *enz.*

By het BOERSCHAP EEXT, in het Landfchap
DRENTHE, ontdekt,

In welke befchryvinge zekere BRIEF, over byzondere
NEDERLANDSCHE OUDHEDEN, zo op-
gehelderd als wederlegd word,

DOOR

Mr. JOANNES VAN LIER,

*Oud Gedeputeerde Staate, thans Ontfanger Generaal
en Medelid van den Loffelyken Etftoel
des Landfchaps Drenthe.*

Met noodige afbeeldingen opgehelderd.

Uitgegeeven en met een Voorreden en Aantekeningen
vermeerderd door

A. VOSMAER.

IN 'SGRAVENHAGE,
By PIETER VAN THOL, in de Veeneftraat
M. DCC. LX.

Figure 17. Title page of Van Lier's 'Antiquarian Letters' (1760).

she appointed the 36 year-old Vosmaer as Director of this Cabinet of natural and artificially made curiosities.[178]

Meanwhile, another version of Van Lier's press report appeared in the *Nederlandsche Jaarboeken* of 1756, part 5 (May), p. 560-2. On the basis of this and the report in the *Leidsche Courant* of April 28, 1756, Dr. Henrik Cannegieter [1691-1770] wrote a learned treatise on D13, in 1756 (Cannegieter 1757), without ever having seen the tomb or the artefacts, or having discussed it with its investigator. Cannegieter was rector of the Latin School (grammar-school) in Arnhem and a well-known antiquary, with an expertise in Roman objects from Nijmegen and Domburg (Brongers & Wynia 2005, 15). In this treatise he also spoke about the interpretation of 'thunderstones' (stone axes), the distribution and contents of tumuli (Cannegieter 1757, 9-10), and about 'Jacoba's jugs' (Cannegieter 1757, 19-26). Since several of these medieval jugs (which are white stoneware from Siegburg in the German Rhineland) were found in the moat of Teylingen Castle, they were generally considered at the time to have been made by the Holland Countess Jacoba of Bavaria ('Jacoba van Beieren') [1401-1436], when she was imprisoned in that castle [!].[179] Cannegieter, however, thought they were earlier, because sherds of this type of pottery had been found in a hillock in the park of Rozendaal Castle near Arnhem, which he thought was an ancient tumulus. The 'thunderstones' from D13 were unsuitable for use as battle-axes in his opinion, and he thought they were probably ritual tools made by the Germanic priests for drumming on planks to chase the thunder away; they would have been interred in graves in tumuli and elsewhere until Charlemagne forbade this pagan ritual (Cannegieter 1757, 26-32). He cleverly noted that the steps leading into the chamber of D13 were too small to accommodate giants and his opinion was that the builders were ancient Germani or Nordic peoples (Cannegieter 1757, 46-7). He also questioned whether the discoverers had not stolen precious objects from D13 'which are sometimes preserved in many graves and a few Urns' (Cannegieter 1757, 18). Although Cannegieter cited authors like Trogillus Arnkiel [ca.1639-1712] (1691), Johann Daniel Major [1634-1693] (1692 #), Bernard Montfaucon [1655-1741] and Jacques Martin [1684-1751],[180] he had no clue about the former existence of a Stone Age* and could only date D13 before Charlemagne's interdic-

---

178 Van Campen 2000, 202-22; Pieters 2002; Pieters & Rookmaker 1994; Pieters 1994. Vosmaer sold his own collection soon after this appointment to the Prince. It consisted of 'an incredible number of quadrupeds, snakes, fishes and reptiles preserved in alcohol; (2) a multitude of stuffed birds; (3) insects; (4) minerals, stones [..] and fossils; (5) corals, …, sponges and other zoophytes; (6) a rich collection of conches and sea-shells; (7) simplicia, or other objects [used in] medicine; (8) bird's nests with their eggs; (9) a few artificially made rarities.' (Pieters & Rookmaker 1994, 17-9).

179 These jugs are still called *Jacobakan* in The Netherlands.

180 Cannegieter (1757) referred to Picardt (1660); Martin (1727 #); Montfaucon (1719 #); Nunningh (1713); Keysler (1720); Major (1692 #); Smids (1711); Arnkiel (1691 #); T. BARTOLIN, *Antiq. Dan.*; Eckhard (1734 #); Harkenroth (1712 #); Liebknecht (1730 #); Von Mellen (1679 #); J. Martin (1727 #) and to classical authors and the *Bible*. For the 'Jacoba's jugs' Cannegieter referred to Van Alkemade & Van der Schelling (1732-1735 #).

tion of cremating the dead (Cannegieter 1757, 74). Cannegieter wrote his treatise in the form of a 'First letter about particular Dutch antiquities' to an unknown gentleman. It was anonymously published, in 1757, and had no sequel.

When Vosmaer found several errors in this booklet, he sent it together with his remarks to Van Lier and asked him for a critical review (Van Lier 1760, viii). Van Lier, who was then thirty-two, wrote his comments and observations about the tomb and its contents *in extenso* in four letters to Vosmaer, between January 31 and April 10, 1758. They were followed by a fifth letter on September 1, 1759. These letters (or essays) were very well edited and published by Vosmaer in a book (Van Lier 1760), which had 206 pages and five folded plates. Vosmaer's critical remarks were added in a preface and extensive footnotes. The book was dedicated by Vosmaer to H.S.R. Lodewyk, Hertog van Brunswyk-Lunenburg, i.e. Ludwig Ernst, Duke of Brunswick-Wolfenbuttel (Braunschweig-Wolfenbüttel) [1718-1788], who reorganised the Dutch army in 1750 and following years, and was tutor and adviser to Prince William, becoming his regent after the death of Princess Anna, in 1757.[181]

Cannegieter's learned study and Vosmaer's stimulation were the springboard Van Lier needed for writing the letters, which constituted an excellent first monograph of a Dutch hunebed. He composed it as a juridical treatise, with many citations from classical and a few from contemporary authors.[182] Every supposition or objection he knew or could think of is carefully dealt with in an agreeable style, but it demands slow and careful reading, also because the meaning of several words differs from that of today.

---

181 The five plates in Van Lier (1760) were etched by Abraham Delfos [1731-1820], whose signature 'A. Delfos Sculp' is on pl. 1. In letters written to Vosmaer on November 24, 1759, and January 23, 1760 (University Library Leiden, BPL 246), Delfos complained about the bad quality of the drawings sent to him and the time consuming corrections of his plates that were needed, including those to the contours of the illustrated artefacts. The drawings for pls. I-V, especially pl. I, sent by Van Lier to Vosmaer (Van Lier 1760, 16), may have been Van Lier's own. The artefacts from D13 were dispersed over pls. III-V (they are rearranged in Figure 19).

182 Pertinent passages from Latin and Greek poems were quoted at length and also translated into Dutch. Cannegieter's texts were also quoted verbatim and at length, but since his name was not known, he was referred to as the unknown author. The texts were adapted to the orthography of Van Lier and Vosmaer (or, perhaps, the publisher's, Pieter van Thol), including names of books and authors. Cannegieter's ideas about the Jacoba's jugs were considered irrelevant by Van Lier (1760, 98).

Figure 18. Hunebed D13-Eext with its three-stepped entrance and closely set sidestones, drawn after the capstones and the top of the barrow were taken away, in 1756, looking southward across the heath (Van Lier 1760, pl. I, etched by Abraham Delfos). See further Appendix 3.

The burial chamber of D13 is described as consisting of three pairs of sidestones and two endstones, 3 feet (88 cm) thick[183] and with flat inner sides. The interior measured 12 x 6 x 5 feet (3.50 x 1.75 x 1.45 m). Its orientation was E-W and there was a 2 feet (58 cm) wide entrance on the southern side with stairs of five steps, each step composed of one to three stones. The stones of the stairs, the pavements (*straten*) and those between the larger sidestones were 'usually somewhat larger than the normal paving-stones in towns'. Two pavements formed the base of the chamber; they were less than 1 foot (29 cm) apart and the space between them was filled with sand. They had remained intact until the tomb's partial disturbance in 1756. The artefacts supposedly were found between the two floors, although some may have come from above the upper one; below the lower

---

183 The Groningen *voet* (foot), used by Van Lier (p. 9), was 29.2 cm and consisted of 12 *duimen* (thumbs, 2.43 cm each). According to Van Lier's estimates (1760, 8-9), D13 was about 500 *passen* west of the village Eext and almost 45 minutes south of Anloo. According to him, 4000 *passen* equalled one hour's walk. According to the modern *Topographical Map 1:25,000*, the distance between D13 and the late medieval church of Eext is 875 m and the distance between D13 and the medieval church of Anloo 4375 m. Van Lier's *pas* would thus have been about 1.75 m (based on the distance from D13 to the church of Eext) or 1.5 m (based on the distance from D13 to the church of Anloo which would equal ¾ x 4000 *passen* = 3000 *passen*; 1 *pas* would thus be 1.458 m, actually two steps, one stride for each leg). 'One hour's walk' of 4000 *passen* would be 5.83-7.00 km. 1.5 m for a *pas* and a walking rate of 5.8 km/hr seem acceptable. Jacob van Deventer's *pas* was also 1.5 m (cf. note 109). Van Lier may have been taller, but a *pas* of 1.75 m and 'an hour's walk' of 7 km seem unrealistic, which means that Van Lier either underestimated the distance from D13 to [the church of] Eext, or estimated the distance from D13 to the perimeter of the village.

one Van Lier found nothing but sand and small pebbles. The surrounding earthen barrow had a diameter of 33.5 feet (9.8 m) and was still more than 8 feet (2.3 m) high after the removal of its top (Van Lier 1760, 7-12, 96).[184]

The pottery found between both pavements consisted of three intact and three damaged 'urns', which found their way into different collections. They had diverse forms, were less than half a foot (14.5 cm) high[185] and some were differently coloured from one another. Many intact urns were 'filled with burnt bones (some of which were still recognisable) or ash' (p. 7). Later on Van Lier wrote, however, that the urns contained 'very few' bones and that even twelve of such small pots would not suffice to hold all bones of one body (p. 65). A few urns were found upside down (p. 77). A sepulchral lamp (*Graflamp*)[186] was found in the sand fill of the chamber and perhaps came from above the upper pavement (Figure 19). Vosmaer (p. 66n) thought that instead it was a sacrificial vessel filled with oil and thrown into the fire. He also suggested that it, together with some of the other pots, could have served in the household of the deceased. Many other urns had been broken by the stone seekers. The sherds lay in different places in the sand. Some of the pottery 'had an entirely plain surface, other [sherds] were marked by incised stripes or other figures and coloured grey, yellow, brown, or ashy; they had four, two or no small handles; some were wider at the top, others had narrow necks. They were fired from a coarse and sandy material, mixed with grit and tiny stones, in which many glittering yellow particles are visible' (p. 18-9). 'The stripes are rather deeply impressed' (p. 202). Unfortunately, because these sherds comprised most of the pottery in the chamber, they were considered insufficiently important to collect and to illustrate. It was advised that, 'to excavate an urn undamaged, one should remove the sand around it with the fingers and have it gradually dry in the air so that it regains a certain degree of hardness' (p. 16).[187] Despite the apparently large number of sherds from different vessels, Van Lier estimated that, apart from the 'lamp', fewer than twelve urns had been in D13 (p. 65-6). Urns from tumuli differed very much from those found in D13 (p. 97).

---

184 As J.N. Lanting pointed out to me, D13 has a unique chamber, because the sidestones are so closely fitted that only very few dry walling stones had to be inserted in the narrow gaps between them. Only four other tombs to the west of the Elbe have steps (Bakker 1992, 22). De Wilde saw that the steps and the floor were being reconstructed by workmen in 1906 or 1907 (letter to J.H. Holwerda of February 19, 1913 in Arentzen 2010). D13 was re-excavated by Van Giffen, in 1927 (Van Giffen 1943a), and by J.N. Lanting, in 1934. Van Giffen detected two phases in the barrow, both of which he assigned to the TRB period. Lanting (pers. comm. in Bakker 1992, 22) assigned the first phase, which has no stone packing and reached only halfway up the orthostats, to the TRB period, but thought that the top layers and the steps probably dated to Bell Beaker times. A stone hammer-axe of 'Emmen type' and a barbed-and-tanged flint arrowhead (both shown in Figure 19: IV:2 and III:8), which were found out of context, but would have come from D13, are Bell Beaker artefacts (Lanting, *ibid.*).

185 The pots pl. II: 1-2 in Figure 19 from D13 were more than 7.3 cm and more than 9.8 cm high, respectively, and both were more than 9.8 cm wide; the collared flask from D12 in Figure 19, pl. III: 5, is more than 9.8 cm high and 8.6 cm wide.

186 Now usually considered as a *biberon*, a sucking vessel for small children (Van Giffen 1943a).

187 This advice is also in Nunningh (1713). Both may be based on a similar advice given by M. Gotthilf Treuer (1688) # (Gummel 1938, 28-32).

The 'five or six' flint flat axes from D13 were 1 *duim* (2.45 cm) wide and 20 *duim* (49 cm) long (p. 7, 15; Figure 19).[188] Van Lier considered that 'it is not diffi-cult to imagine how the Germani fitted these sharply polished stones to the cloven end of a stick and fastened them by braiding wiry twigs', as had been suggested by others, but he rejected this idea (p. 149). Nor did he think that they were projec-tiles for a sling (p. 154). Instead, Van Lier thought that the axes had been fitted onto the head of a club (p. 154-6, pl. III: 7; Figure 19). Another flint object from D13 was a narrow flint chisel, which was ¾ foot (22 cm) long and ½ *duim* (1.2 cm) wide (p. 7, 15; Figure 19).

An 'iron ball' from D13, the size of a marble and almost flat on one side, was, in Van Lier's opinion, either a cast bullet made sometime after the invention of gun powder[189] and shot into the barrow during recent wars, or a piece of ore (p. 15; 160-3; Figure 19). Initially, Vosmaer (p. 15n) thought that the bullet was made of iron, which was 'no small impediment' to Van Lier's ideas about the stone chisels:[190] why use stone if iron was available? But Vosmaer identified the material later, 'after repeated experiments', as iron ore 'such as found in great quantities in large and small lumps in the soil near Deventer etc. ', which he considered to be marine deposits (p. 163-4n, 200).[191]

A perforated stone hammer-axe, 14 cm long (pl. IV: 3; Figure 19),[192] was found, sometime after April 28, 1756, in sand that 'for the greater part' came from the chamber [and the top of the barrow – B.] of D13 (p. 17, 203). A rather thick,

---

188 Van Lier, p. 18, wrote: 'At a distance of about 25 passes [37.5-43.75 m] from the centre of [D13], on diverse places around it, just below the surface, a few stones and boulders were found, which probably came from another place, along with five or six chisels [flat axes] and a few sherds of urns.' Van Lier did not say so, but appears to have thought that sand from the top of the barrow and the chamber of D13 had been thrown down around the foot of the barrow. It is not clear if some of the aforementioned 5 or 6 axes were the same as those (pls. II: 3-5 and IV: 1, see Figure 19) found in the chamber (p. 200-1; 203). A confirmation that sand from D13 actually had been tossed outside is that sherds were found there 'just below the surface'; if they had been there in their original position, acid podzol soil formation over the centuries would have destroyed them. Perhaps the surrounding area was levelled after the excavations in the chamber and barrow, in or after 1726 or 1756 (a distance up to 37.5-43.75 m from the barrow centre seems extremely far for the spoil to have been spread, though). Due to the filling in of sandpits and the levelling of the surrounding terrain, the barrow of D13 seems higher now than it originally was.

189 Gun powder was introduced here in AD 1339-40, according to Picardt (1660, 200).

190 According to Van Lier, the presence of exclusively stone tools implied that D13 dated from a Stone Age* which preceded a Metal Age*, although he did not use these terms, see below.

191 Van Giffen found a similar ball, in 1929, in a TRB cist at Diever, Drenthe, which P. Kruizinga identified as a natural marcasite concretion from the Upper Cretaceous period (Cenomanian, Turonian), which is found near Bentheim among other places (Van Giffen 1930; 1943a, 109-10; 1944d, 433-4; Bakker 1979a, 110). Beuker (2008) identified this ball and a new one from hunebed D42-Westenes-N as a pyrite concretion, both with traces of having been struck, prob-ably by a flint strike-a-light (such as those found in TRB contexts; Beuker 2010, fig. 256; Van Gijn 2010 Figs. 6.10 and 8.1; Friedrich 2007). He remained uncertain if they are pyrite or marcasite (but supposed that they are pyrite). Later on, Beuker (2010, 6-10) discussed pyrite / markasite balls and their distribution. His statement that they did not naturally occur in the northern Netherlands is refuted by Vomaer's records (Van Lier 1760, p. 15n). The where-abouts of the ball from D13 are unknown (perhaps in the Quaestius collection in Fries Museum, Leeuwarden, see note 231).

Figure 19. Artefacts from hunebed D13-Eext and a collared flask from hunebed D12-Eext (Van Lier 1760, etched by A. Delfos). See further Appendix 3.

long stick was stuck through the perforation as with a halberd; it may have served as weapon, a mark of distinction (*eerteken*) or a standard (*veldteken*) (p. 120-46).

Finally, a barbed and tanged flint arrowhead (pl. III: 8, Figure 19), now considered typical for the Bell Beaker culture, was found in the sand excavated from D13. Van Lier acquired it between March 15 and April 10, 1758, and recognised it as a '*Flits* or arrowhead' (p. 164-5).[193]

Van Giffen (1927, 12-25) compiled an excellent summary of most of the preceding observational data, but omitted most of the more general observations and deductions, a selection of which follows here. Van Lier noted that the Drenthe hunebeds were usually oriented W-E, like D13, but that there were exceptions. For instance D12-Eext Es was oriented S-N and D11-Anloo-Evertsbos SE-NW, according to compass measurements (p. 68).[194] He did not find it strange that, according to Arnkiel (1691, Lib. 2, cap. 3 and 12), in Schleswig-Jutland megalithic graves of kings and commanders were oriented E-W and those of common people N-S (p. 69). The translation of *Huinebedden* into *giant's beds*, although erroneous in his opinion,[195] could derive from the tradition of calling not only tall persons but also rich or high-ranking people '*giants*' (p. 70, 176-7). Many hunebeds were not precisely oriented E-W due to seasonal differences in the locations of the rising and setting sun on the horizon (p. 71). Hunebeds were not altars (p. 25, ref. to Van Slichtenhorst 1654), although human sacrifices undeniably occurred (p. 25-30), nor were they cenotaphs (p. 31). 'As far as known, nobody has found anything other than axes and urns in intact hunebeds in Drenthe. Precious [metal] ornaments of dress or furniture do not occur' (p. 96, loosely translated).

Hunebed D11-Anloo is 32 feet (9.4 m) long (p. 68). An undecorated funnel beaker (pl. III: 1) from 'a hunebed between Anlo and Zuidlaaren',[196] now in possession of an amateur in Groningen (p. 201), may have come from it. Hunebed D14-Eexterhalte, 'one of the largest and most regular built hunebeds' and oriented E-W, consisted of seven heavy [cap]stones 'resting on' 32 other stones. The middle capstones measured 13 x 9 x (nearly) 5 feet (3.80 x 2.65 x about 1.45 m)

---

193 The now forgotten Dutch word *flits* was derived from French *flèche*. Vosmaer and Van Lier recognised from the description that several of Cannegieter's curiously formed stone artefacts were *echinites*, fossil sea urchins, and *belemnites* (p. 102; 158). Vosmaer (p. 127n) subdivided the 'natural thunder and lightning stones' into *cerauniae*, viz. petrified sea urchins, and belemnites, which he considered as points or spines from different sorts of echinids. Van Lier's idea that belemnites were probably used as arrowheads (p. 127) was not adopted by Vosmaer (p. 127n). Vosmaer (p. 128n) subdivided man-made, 'artificial' stone *cerauniae* into thunder-chisels (*Donder-beitels*, flat axes), thunder-hammers (*Donder-hamers*, battle-axes) and thunder-arrows (*Donder-pylen*, viz. spear- and arrowheads, referring to Mercatus (#, see note 211), the *Museum Wormianum* and Kilian Stobaeus. Metal artificial *cerauniae* were 'thunder-shovels' (*Donderschopjes*), e.g. the long chisel-like metal tools with a widening, sharp cutting edge from Ambon, Indonesia, 'see Rumphius, pl. L' (i.e. Rumphius 1705, pl. 50 #), axes and chisels, therefore.

194 Van Giffen (1925) recorded the following orientations: D11 ESE-WNW (67° west of N), D12 SSE-WNW (ca. 24° 30' west of N), D13 ENE-WSW (115° 30' west of N), D14 E-W (83° 30' west of N).

195 Van Lier's interpretation appears incorrect, see the previous section.

196 This was D8-Anloo-Kniphorstbos (Pleyte 1877-1902: Drente, 1880-2, pl. LIII).

(p. 8).[197] A 'careful hand' had excavated intact pots, some of which were upside down 'even between stones of pavements' in hunebed D12-Eext Es (p. 77). An intact lachrymatory or tear-flask (*lacrimatory* or *traanflesch*) from this tomb (p. 77-8, pl. III: 5, viz. a collared flask; Figure 19)[198] was in the collection of Mr. Alberda tot Vennebroek (p. 202). Its illustration, the first ever of a decorated TRB pot from Drenthe, is not very good. The flask is now in the Leiden Museum (see Knöll 1959, pl. 32: 5; Bakker 2004, 166-7). In 1750, 'a certain young gentleman' found a silver coin of *triumvir* Antonius Augustus in a broken urn buried one foot deep next to the exterior of one of the westernmost (kerb) stones of hunebed D14-Eexterhalte. Van Lier thought that the Roman coin, which he described in detail, was later than the hunebeds (p. 190-2).

Van Lier stated that giants were not the builders of the hunebeds, because the steps of D13 were much too small (*pace* Cannegieter) and because the identifiable burnt bones[199] from D13 were within a normal size range (p. 167, 171). According to him, Roman legionaries were 5½ *pedes* (1.7 m) tall,[200] whereas 'our ancient ancestors' were more than 7 feet (2-2.10 m) tall! (p. 172). Although Van Lier mentioned that heroes were also called giants (p. 176-7), he did not wish to deny that giants had existed in different times and at different places, but stated that these were exceptional and that a race* of giants had never existed (p. 172-5).

That normally sized people are capable of building with gigantic stones without machinery he thought evident from the walls of Cuzco, Peru, built by the Indians before the arrival of the Spaniards. Boulders of 30 x 18 x 6 feet (8.82 x 5.29 x 1.76 m, i.e. about 82 m³), much larger than hunebed stones, were transported across rivers and used to construct a wall with barely visible joints (p. 168).[201] Van Lier does not speculate about how exactly the capstones and other boulders of the hunebeds were transported and positioned. He did think that the builders dressed the stones used for constructing D13 (p. 58).

The geological* origin of the hunebed stones was not understood at the time. Van Lier thought that they were concretions of local sands and gravels that formed in Drenthe's soil (p. 10). But Vosmaer argued that the stones were various types

---

197 Van Giffen (1925, 41-2) counted 39 stones: 7 capstones, 18 sidestones, 2 endstones, 2 passage sidestones, 1 possible passage capstone, 8 kerbstones, and 1 loose boulder with traces of cleaving with wedges.

198 A lachrymatory is a 'phial of [a] kind found in ancient-Roman tombs & conjectured to be tear-bottles' (*Concise Oxford Dictionary of Current English*, 5th edition, Oxford: Clarendon Press 1964, 673-4).

199 Van Lier actually wrote 'unburnt bones' (p. 171), which is what he called bone fragments that had been burnt, but not completely to ashes.

200 Citing *Cujacius, Observat. Lib. 2, Cap. 5* (p. 172). # (Jacques Cujas [1522-1590]).

201 Van Lier referred to Keysler 1720, 226-7, to De Acosta, *Historia natural y moral de las Indias* (1590, lib. 6, cap. 14 #, reference taken from Keysler) and to 'Colonne, Histoire Nat., vol. 2, ch.3', viz. Francesco Maria Pompeo Colonna, *Histoire naturelle de l'univers dans laquelle on rapporte des Raisons Physiques, sur les Effets ... de la Nature. Enrichie de Figures en Taille-douce par Colonne*. Paris: Cailleau, 1739. #

of granite and other rocks, broken from mountains somewhere and rounded off during their transport to Drenthe by an enormous flood, either the Deluge, the Cimbrian Flood,[202] or an unknown flood (p. xiii-xix, 10n).

Vosmaer's explanation for the presence of erratic boulders in Drenthe and elsewhere in the northeastern Netherlands was accepted (1769-1811 #) by Johannes le Francq van Berkhey [1729-1812] and, in 1777-79 (#), by Johannes Florentinus Martinet [1729-1795]. In 1792, Van Lier and his sons (1792, 355-6) accepted Vosmaer's identification of the hunebed stones as granite, but insisted correctly (p. 365-8) that the North Sea, even when stormy, lacked the power to transport such heavy boulders (Van der Woud 1998, 91-2). And transport by the sea from Scandinavia to Drenthe would not account for their roundness. Moreover, such rounded stones occurred in Norway itself (Van Lier et al. 1792, 368, ref. to Olavs Magnus 1555). Vosmaer (in Van Lier 1760, p. xviii-xix) could not explain why Drenthe did not have as many rocks as nearby Bentheim and why the sorts of stones in the two regions were so different.[203]

Van Lier's chronological perspective regarding the Stone Age* was progressive for its time (p. 120ff.). According to classical authors, weapons had been developed in stages (*trapsgewyze*, p. 122). Horace (lib. 1: *Satyr*. 3, vs. 99ff.) had written that primitive man had defended himself first with fingernails and fists, and sticks, but then had developed weapons by wit and experience. Lucretius (*De Rerum Natura*, lib. V: 1283-95) had described successive stages of weaponry, at first using hands, fingernails, teeth, stones, sticks from trees, flames and then, after a long time, when fire was used, weapons made of copper, and finally weapons made of iron. Pausanias, citing Hesiod, had confirmed that weapons of copper were made before iron was known (lib. I: 50).[204]

---

202 The Cimbrian Flood of the North Sea prompted the Cimbrians, who lived in the North of Jutland ('*Himmer*land'), and the Teutones to migrate to southern Europe in the 2nd century BC.

203 Vosmaer was referring to the sandstone bedrock at Bentheim and Gildehaus in Germany, which was used for stone buildings in The Netherlands, including the Town Hall / Royal Palace in Amsterdam, and, in the eastern Netherlands, for the parapets of wells, water-troughs, foundation stones of brick or wood-and-loam buildings, and medieval baptismal fonts and coffins.

204 Van Lier (1760, 120-2) cited Lucretius, *De Rerum Natura*, lib. 5, vs 1284ff:

  '*Arma antiqua, manus, ungues, dentesque fuerunt*
  Et lapides & idem; Silvarum fragmina, rami:
  Et flammae, atque ignes, postquam sunt cognita primum
  Posterius ferri vi est, aerisque reperta:
  Et prior aeris erat, quam ferri, cognitus Usus'

  Schnapp (1993, 332-3) presented an English translation of these lines. Van Lier also cited Hesiod, *Works & Days* (ca. 720-700 BC), lib. I, vs 150-259; Horace, lib. I, *Satyr*. 3 vs 99ff. and Pausanias, *Description of Greece*, lib. I, vs 150. Van Lier (*ibid.*) translated these lines into Dutch. Lucretius lived 99-55 BC, Hesiod about 740-670 BC, Horace 65-8 BC and Pausanias about AD 115-180.

Van Lier pointed out that perforated stone hammer-axes like the one from D13 (pl. IV: 3; Figure 19) also had been found at Annen, close to hunebed D9 (pl. IV: 4, in his own collection), another 'in Drenthe' (illustrated by Alstorphius 1722);[205] one near Potsdam in Brandenburg, Germany in 1728 (pl. IV: 5);[206] and one in the 'Toppelberg in Saxony',[207] Germany (pl. IV: 6). This latter one and a flint axe from the same locality (pl. II: 7, p. 103n) were in the Cabinet of the Prince of Orange (p. 203-4).[208] Van Lier also knew from traveller's reports that many savage (*wild*) peoples, when they were discovered still used stone weapons, for instance on the

205 The Latin booklet (1722) by Johannes Alstorphius [ca. 1680-1719] has the first illustration and discussion of a perforated stone battle-axe or hammer-axe found in Drenthe. The original battle-axe presumably belonged successively to the collections of Wolther van Doeveren [1730-1783], Petrus Camper [1722-1789], Adriaan G. Camper [1759-1820] and, certainly, Johan G.S. van Breda [1788-1867]. A.W. Franks bought it at the auction of the latter's estate, in 1871, for the British Museum, where it is registered as being found at 'Doeverden', Christy collection, Holl. 5. See Smith (1926) *A Guide to the Antiquities of the Stone Age ... British Museum* (3rd ed.), fig. 168: '*Perforated axe-hammer, Doeverden, Holland*' and p. 154: '*found in 1721 at Doeverden, Drenthe*'. According to Alstorphius (1722), the axe was found in the field of Deputy J. Nisinck at Diever during ploughing ('*in arendum, in agro tuo Dieverensi reperto*'). Alstorphius saw a small part of an urn that had been found nearby, which had contained burnt bones and which had 'certain characters' on its surface that he could not decipher (p. 1-2). He thought that a man had been burned by lightning on the spot and buried there with the thunderstone (battle-axe) in the urn (p. 16; cf. Van Lier 1760, 105). Alstorphius's illustration of the battle-axe is a quite reasonable rendition. In the administration of the British Museum the name of a former owner, W. van Doeveren, was used for the artefact location, viz. 'Doeverden', instead of Diever or Dieverden. According to A.E. Lanting (pers. comm., ca.1980), the battle-axe, which is 20.0 cm long, is assignable to the Single Grave or early Bell Beaker culture. The sherd, which is now lost, may have come from a Bell Beaker and the illegible 'letters' suggest that it was of the Veluwe type, which is just too late to be associated with the battle-axe. It is not known whether the assertion that the sherd came from a cremation urn was based on observation or on the assumption, common at the time, that all pots in graves contained cremations. Bell Beakers sometimes do contain cremations, however.

206 Copied from Treverus (1728) #.

207 The text mentions '*Toppelberg in Saxony*' twice (p. 103n, 203) and '*Troppelberg in Saxony*' once (p. 204). The Töppelberg ('Pottery Mountain') at Massel / Masłów, Silesia (not Saxony), is known for the 10,000 urns excavated there by the local priest L.D. Hermann, who published *Maslographia oder Beschreibung des Schlesischen Massel im Oels-Bernstädischen Fürstentum ...* Brieg 1711 #, see Gummel 1938, 33-4, 424 and further refs.

208 The perforated axe from Masłów, Pl. IV: 6, seems to be a 'Danubian' perforated axe (perforated *Breitkeil*), cf. Brandt 1967, 11-9 and Van der Waals 1972).

island of Guam, on one of the Ladrones (Marianes in Micronesia) and on another unnamed island, both discovered by Dampier.[209] Until the Spaniards arrived, the American Indians had never seen iron and used polished stone (p. 122).[210]

The *Old Testament* depicted quite a different picture, however. Tubal-cain was a master in the working of copper and iron before the Flood (Genesis 4: 22) and, in Van Lier's opinion, Noah's Ark could not have been built without using iron and copper (p. 123). He entertained the idea that delay in iron use among certain peoples was due to its prohibition by tyrannical despots, but was more compelled by Colonne's explanation that iron technology went into disuse and was soon forgotten after the Flood. Then, according to the oldest Histories, iron was re-invented in Asia, several centuries later, from where it dispersed into Europe and the rest of the Old World,[211] but remained unknown to the Americans until the arrival of the Spaniards (p. 123-6). Cannegieter had cited Le Prévôt's report on the *allée couverte* at Cocherel in Normandy, investigated in 1685,[212] which contained human bones and stone axes fitted into deer antler, and Van Lier concluded that 'probably iron was not used at that time'. Thus it was clear that in simpler times (*eenvoudiger tyden*) stone weapons were used (p. 129).

He also noted that Tacitus wrote about the Germani using iron spears and swords (p. 129-30), but made no mention of stone axes or other stone weapons (p. 131). Among the Germani, stone rather than copper would have been the predecessor to iron for making weapons, because copper was absent in their regions. Stone weapons and the hunebeds – in which the stone axes occurred – were therefore much older than the time when Tacitus lived (p. 130). After iron and copper were introduced, the use of stone was abandoned and forgotten.

---

209 Van Lier (p. 120) does not give a more specific reference, but may have used the Dutch translations of *New Voyage around the World* (1697 #) and *Voyage Descriptions* (1699 #) by William Dampier [1652-1715]: Dampier (The Hague, 1698 #) and Wafer (The Hague, 1700 #), pers. comm. W. Arentzen). Arentzen could not find any mention of stone axes used on Guam or any other island in Dampier's first book. Probably Van Lier had no access to these books in Drenthe and quoted from memory what was generally known. Vosmaer (p. 110-1n) refers to stone axes used 'for the cutting of trees and the hollowing out of their canoes' by 'the Americans' mentioned in the first book (1698) by Dampier, p. 61 – which is correct – 'and by other travellers'. Dampier (*l.c.*) described the perforated stone hammer-axes, which were 10 x 4 x 3 inches in size and fixed to the top of a four feet long stick, used by [Nicaraguan] indians, and also mentions the stone arrowheads of the Patagonians. Neither Van Lier nor Vosmaer cited these details.

210 Rumphius (1705) mentioned several stone axes found in trees on the island of Ambon, Indonesia (Vosmaer, p. 110-1n). Van Lier did not know that the Incas were using both copper and stone implements when discovered by Europeans (Von Hagen 1956, 167-73).

211 Van Lier (1760, 126n) referred to '*Colonne Hist. Nat. lib. 34, cap. 14; vol. 2, cap. 3*', viz. Colonna's comment to Lucretius, *De rerum naturae, l.c.* (#). He did not cite Alexandre-Yves Goguet (1758 #) [1716-1758], Michele Mercatus [1541-1593], whose study, *Metallotheca Vaticana*, was not published until 1717 in Rome #, Antoine de Jussieu (1723) [1686-1758] and others, who asserted the same (excerpts in Heizer 1962a, 11-21, 61-9; Trigger 2006, 93; Wollf 1994, 209). In the 16th century, Mercatus had recognised that thunderstones (see above) were human tools used before metals were known.

212 '*Hist. Reg. Acad. Scient. Lib. 3, cap. 1*' , viz. Le Prévôt (1685 #), see Cocherel, in section '1685'.

Drenthe's most ancient inhabitants had brought the custom of constructing hunebeds with them from the northernmost regions of the earth (p. 36). The hunebed builders were 'our earliest ancestors' (title and p. 3). But Vosmaer (p. 3-4n) doubted that they were 'our ancestors', because many hunebeds would then also have occurred in other parts of The Netherlands. Moreover, they were also found in England, Germany, Saxony and elsewhere. He suggested that military tribes had built them when passing through Drenthe and did not concern himself further with the identity of the builders.

Van Lier thought that 'stone-less' tumuli or barrows containing urns with burnt human bones dated from the time when the Germani had learned from the Romans to use iron. Such a barrow lay near D13 (LETT. A: 4 in Figure 18). In January, 1758, two similar urns made of 'grey earth' were excavated from another earthen barrow, half an hour's walk [2.9-3.5 km] north of D13, one 23.5 cm high and the other 27 cm (p. 19-20, 201, pl. III: 3-4). The shorter urn was half filled with bones. In February, 1758, Van Lier heard that a large urn had once been found somewhere in Drenthe, 'together with a small hook of copper, similar to the hook on the strap of a contemporary dagger (*porte d'épée*), which made unclasping unnecessary (p. 97-8).

Van Lier dispatched the fourth of his *Antiquarian Letters* (1760, 160-85) on April 10, 1758. Lieutenant Meursinge and the surveyor Meursinge, his cousin, had excavated five 'low and flattish hillocks' in the heath (*markte*) of Gasteren, 'not long before'. This is in the large urnfield dating to the Late Bronze and Iron Age that Van Giffen excavated in 1939 (Van Giffen 1945; De Wit 1998), which we know now was exceptionally rich in grave goods for Drenthe. The lieutenant's accurate description of his findings was related almost verbatim and commented on by Van Lier in an Appendix to that fourth letter (p. 186-92). Three of the artefacts, which Van Lier had received from the excavators, were illustrated (pl. V: 3-5, p. 205-6). The first excavated hillock was 75 cm high. Two red copper decorated metal bracelets (pl. V: 3-4) were found in it underneath a few bone fragments at a depth of 37 cm. The largest bracelet was pseudo-torded and open, both ends having been torn off (pl. V: 3, diameter 16.75 cm). The other bracelet (pl. V: 4, p. 187, 205) had an outer diameter of somewhat more than 8 cm, an inner diameter of somewhat more than 7 cm, a cross-section in the shape of a D or C and was cut through at one place. Van Lier (p. 190) noted that it was too small for an adult male and he thought that it had been worn by an adolescent boy, a hero perhaps, although such bracelets were normally women's ornaments. The second hillock produced an intact urn full of ashes and placed upside down (pl. V: 5).[213] In the third hillock a bronze bracelet of similar shape and size as that shown in pl. V: 4, small metal fragments, probably from a finger-ring, a larger ring and one object in the form of the letter H were found (p. 188). The fourth hillock con-

---

213 According to the measurements given by Van Lier (1760, 205-6), the urn's foot was 4.7 cm wide in diameter, its body 14.8 cm, and its upper rim 10.9 cm. In the illustration (pl. V: 5) the foot is too wide, which accords with Delfos's complaints about the bad quality of the drawings, see note 181.

tained many small bones, concentrated 'within ¾ foot [22 cm] in the earth, as if they had been buried in an urn that had subsequently disintegrated' (Meursinge). The fifth hillock contained only pieces of charcoal (p. 188).

In his fifth and last letter, dated September 1, 1759, Van Lier told of an excavation by two or three amateurs of several 'stone-less tumuli which lay in the Eexterveld almost one hour's walk east of Rolde' (p. 193-5; see De Wit 1998, fig. 24, for their location). This too was an urnfield consisting of small, low hillocks. These gentlemen found 'a few' iron spearheads, 14.7 cm long, with a 2.5 cm wide hollow pipe at the lower end, 'very suitable for inserting a wooden shaft'. They also found a few pieces of beaten brass and a few iron chainlets (*kettinkjes*). These objects were given to Van Lier, who suggested that they were the remains of a kind of breastplate (*Borstwapen*) or helmet, and that the chainlets were used as fasteners. Such barrows without stone constructions [that is, the low hillocks] 'were made by the Romans, or at least after their arrival', when they taught the Germani to make and use iron weaponry.[214]

Thus Van Lier's archaeological chronology for Drenthe consisted of a very ancient Germanic Stone Age*, during which the hunebeds were constructed, followed by a Germanic Iron Age* after the arrival of the Romans.

Van Lier did not include an intermediate Bronze Age*, because of the absence of copper ore in the region, and, moreover, in his opinion, bronze artefacts were made exclusively by the Romans. He was well aware that the transition from the Stone Age* to the Metal Age* took place at differing times around the world.

Van Lier (p. 178-85) also discussed *disci*, i.e. thick, centrally perforated ceramic discs, about 12 cm in diameter, which had circular stamped impressions; a few had a stamped impression of a cross in a circle (pl. V: 1-2). One was found on the surface of the sandy subsoil of a peat layer in eastern Drenthe, the other was in the possession of Deputy C.S. Nysing. Van Lier thought they were used for disc throwing, but actually they are Carolingian loom-weights.[215]

Van Lier ended his treatise with a critical remark (p. 195-8) about the common opinion, which had been expressed in a popular book,[216] that fir and pine trees (*Vuuren, Dennen of Sparreboomen*), the trunks of which were found lying in

---

214 De Wit (1998, 357-9) dated these graves with bronze and iron artefacts, urns and cremated bones in urnfields to the Early and early Middle Iron Age (ca. 800-300 or 250 BC). She considered them to be elite graves. Although the artefacts predated the Romans, Van Lier guessed right about some of their other aspects and he had certainly a flair for finding artefacts!

215 See section '1790'.

216 *Antiquitates Belgicae*. Amsterdam: G. Bos, 1756, 5th impression (*druk*). # This was a very popular book on archaeology, early history and ancient geography of The Netherlands. Originally it was an adapted version of Richard Verstegen's, *Nederlantsche Antiquiteiten* (Antwerp 1618) by the publisher J. van Royen, *Antiquitates Belgicae of Nederlandsche outheeden, zynde d'eerste opkomst van Holland, Zeeland, 't Sticht Utrecht, Overyzel, Vriesland, Brabant, Vlaanderen enz ...* Amsterdam: J. van Royen, 1700 #. It was reprinted many times, for instance in 1701, 1715, 1717, 1733 ('5th impression Amsterdam: G. Bos'), 1733 ('5th impression, Amsterdam: G. Tielenburg'), 1756 ('5th impression, Amsterdam: G. Tielenburg'), 1756 ('5th impression, Amsterdam: G. Bos'). A final edition appeared in Gent: C.J. Fernand, 1809 #. Curiously, it is seldom or never mentioned in present works about the history of archaeology.

a SW-NE orientation at the base of peat bogs in Brabant, Drenthe and elsewhere, could never have grown in such wet soils at lower elevations. These trees, it was assumed, could only have grown in higher and more mountainous countries, such as Germany up the Rhine closer to the Alps and Norway. Accordingly, they must have been uprooted by heavy storms, and transported by enormous floods, such as the Cimbrian Flood of about 860 BC, to their present locations, where they sank to the bottom of peaty or silty deposits. Van Lier objected that although this could explain hundreds of horizontal, uprooted trees, it could not account for many others, whose lower trunks were still rooted, standing two to more than three feet high (60-90 cm), in the surface of the sands lying below the peat bogs and mosses of Drenthe and Groningen. He concluded that the peat, not the trees had drifted thereto. Vosmaer objected (p. xi-xiii), correctly, that the peat originated locally from plant remains and through successive inundations, decay and accumulation had overgrown local woods.[217]

Van Lier's book was path breaking for the Dutch scholarly community and in line with what was internationally produced. It did not surpass, however, certain German archaeological studies, especially *Cimbrisch-Hollsteinische Antiquitäten Remarques* (Hamburg 1719, 1720) written by Christian Detlev Rhode [1653-1717] and his son Andreas Albert Rhode forty years earlier.[218] Despite his moderate command of the international literature, which was difficult to obtain in Drenthe, Van Lier's *Oudheidkundige Brieven* (1760) is quite an original achievement, which undeniably filled a scientific hiatus concerning the Dutch hunebeds. The originality of the book by a self-taught archaeologist was perhaps even due to the difficult availability of pertinent publications (and the exchange of ideas with Vosmaer).[219]

In 1758, Van Lier became fiscal-general of Drenthe and moved into the *Ontvangershuis* ('Fiscal's House') in Assen.[220] In 1777-8, he built there Overcingel, a delightful country house. He wrote about an article of the ancient law of Drenthe

---

217 See Arentzen (2009a, 35-9) and Van der Woud (1990 or 1998) for overviews of the theories about peat formation in The Netherlands, from the late 16th to early 19th centuries.

218 Rhode & Rhode (1719) seems to be a first version of Rhode & Rhode (1720; see Gummel's 67-page analysis of this work (1938, 34-100). Van Lier (1760) briefly mentioned this study twice (1760, p. 69 [via Cannegieter] and 108), but his work bears no resemblance to it.

219 The anonymous author of an article about D13 in *Byvoegsels op de Nederlandsche Jaerboeken, April 1756*, vol. 1, 876-80 (written in or after 1770) identified H. Cannegieter as the 'great man' who wrote the anonymous treatise about its discovery (1757). Basing himself on Van Lier (1760), the author in *Byvoegsels* briefly discussed the discovery, the form and contents of D13, but expressed doubt that the tomb was built long before the Romans for two reasons: (1) Keysler (1720) and De Rhoer (1770) had dated the hunebeds to the time of the Viking raids, and (2) Van Lier described a tear-flask from hunebed D12-Eext Es [pl. III:2, a collared flask*; Figure 19], which, according to Conyers Middleton (1745), were used as containers for ointments, oils or spices in the Classical Period. Instead of concluding that the flask had also been used for such purposes, presently quite an acceptable explanation, the lachrymatory was used as argument for a Roman or post-Roman date of the hunebeds, because it was supposedly copied from Roman examples. [Actually, Keysler assigned the hunebeds to the Anglo-Saxons, not to the Vikings.]

220 Strikingly, *Wikipedia* describes Van Lier in the first place as 'a Dutch politician, jurist, tax collector and depute in Drenthe' and only briefly mentions his scientific publications.

(Van Lier 1773) when he became a member of the society 'Pro Excolendo Jure Patrio' in Groningen. In 1774, he suggested to the Maatschappij der Nederlandsche Letterkunde ('Society of Dutch Literature'), of which he was an 'active member', that he write a treatise about 'some words and expressions in the common local language of Drenthe, which are unknown from elsewhere, and a collection of terms used by the peat-cutters regarding their work'. Nothing further is known about this proposal (Nijkeuter 2001, 68 n. 294). In the 1780s, Van Lier corresponded with Wolther van Doeveren [1730-1783] about the geology of Drenthe. Probably such a correspondence could have led to a publication entitled, e.g., *Geological Letters*, but Van Doeveren's untimely death precluded this from happening. Van Lier's best known later work is his magnificent book on the snakes and adders of Drenthe (Van Lier 1781).[221]

---

221 Van Lier worked long on his 1781 book. The adder, and two 'snakes' were drawn *ad vivum* by Wibrand Veltman [1744-1800], Groningen, in 1772 (reproductions: Sliggers 2002, 62-3), Veltman drew the frontispiece in 1773 and all four plates were engraved by Jan Caspar Philips, who died in 1775 [he was born before 1700]. The frontispiece has a small portrait of Van Lier and is bordered by objects representing his hobbies: archaeology, music, peat and heath exploitation, and snakes. These objects were the subject of an explanatory poem in the book by his daughter, the poetess Barbara Maria van Lier [1751-1778]. The 'snakes and adders' were the grass-snake (*Natrix natrix*, Dutch: *ringslang*), the adder (*Vipera berus*, Dutch: *adder*) and the slowworm (*Anguis fragilis*, Dutch: *hazelworm*, actually a lizard with no legs). Van Lier did not yet recognise the smooth snake (*Coronella austriaca*, Dutch: *gladde slang*), which was first described by J.N. Laurenti in France, in 1768. Van Lier kept his snakes in glass boxes. In 1752, he had planned to send snakes to Vosmaer, for his Cabinet, but because of the extremely wet year, he could hardly find any. Moreover, 'the farmers caught them by beating them to death with a stick on the head' and could not be taught to do otherwise (letter of September 26, 1752, to Vosmaer, University Library Leiden, BPL 246). In 1772, Van Lier became a member of the Hollandsche Maatschappij der Wetenschappen (Holland Society of Letters and Sciences) in Haarlem and presented the three Drenthian 'snakes and adders' in stuffed form (Sliggers 2002, 60, 62-3, 132).

His scientific interests preoccupied Van Lier so much,[222] however, that his administration of Drenthe's finances resulted in a large deficit, in 1785[223] and he absconded to Kleve (Cleves) in Germany, just outside the Republic.[224] There he wrote the most of the volume about Drenthe in the series *De Tegenwoordige Staat* ('The Present State and Histories of the different parts of the Dutch Republic': Van Lier et al. 1792). In it, the archaeological relics visible in Drenthe are summarily described, based on his 1760 book and no new elements were added. Cook's *Voyages*, which described the use of stone axes on islands in the Pacific Ocean, took its place among Dampier, Fresier, Forster, Robertson and 'Scheloocke' (?) who described their use in other parts of the world. The Celtic Fields* in Drenthe had never much interested Van Lier and he did not say much about them. Contrary to local tradition, these were certainly no Roman encampments.[225]

As an example of what could be achieved in Drenthe, Van Lier gave a thorough description of the land reclamation at Pfalzdorf and elsewhere in the Gocherheide, a large heath between Goch and Kleve (Cleves) in Germany (p. 245-63). This heath had been colonised by Lutheran and Calvinist emigrants from the German Palatinate (Pfalz) who were headed towards Pennsylvania via the Dutch Republic When the sea captain who organised the travel cheated the first twenty families, in 1741, out of their fares to America, they were not admitted to the Dutch Republic and were stranded along the border. Emperor Frederic the Great of Prussia allowed

---

Arnout Vosmaer filed no letters from Van Lier after 1757, but this does not necessarily imply that the friends had fallen out; any later correspondence may just not have been worth filing. In the 1780-90s, Vosmaer wrote on the last page of one of his two hand-written autobiographies (*Memorie*): 'that this [after my death] should be dealt with at will / whereas much should have to be added. It is the best to speak about this with Mr. van Doeveren, ... [illegible] van Lier [this sentence scratched is out]. This to be given to Mr. ... [scratched out] or rather to Mr. Martinet Clergyman in Zutphen? Better? [Scratched out] Deceased' (National Archives, The Hague, 2.21.271-257). Wolther van Doeveren died in 1783, J. van Lier absconded in 1785, J.F. Martinet died in 1795 and Vosmaer himself in 1799.

222 After 1778, Van Lier neglected his accountancy as Fiscal-General for Drenthe (Foorthuis & Van Dijk 1987), perhaps because he was working hard on his *Snakes and Adders* (1781). As early as 1766, his brother-in-law Rev. Petrus Hofstede (in Rotterdam) wrote: 'because he is closely related to me I would not dare to say otherwise than that he esteems wisdom and scholarship endlessly higher than the prominent duties that are entrusted to him by the fatherland' (Hofstede 1766, 341; cf. Mulder 1942).

223 A main reason for the fiasco was perhaps that Van Lier could not cope with the problematic system of hiring persons to collect taxes whose fee was supposedly a percentage of the levied tax (Mulder 1942; Foorthuis & Van Dijk 1987).

224 Soon his wife followed him there. She died in Kleve in 1796 and was buried in Assen.

225 Tonkens (1795, 39-45), however, described the walled fieldsystems of the Celtic Field in the Noordsche Veld heath near Zeijen in some detail (R.D. Mulder 1942 identified the Noordsche Veld near Zeijen as the locality of the Celtic Field, that Tonkens discussed). Tonkens was first asked by the publisher to write the volume Drenthe of *Tegenwoordige Staat*, but when he died in 1790, he left a short, unfinished text. Only then his publisher asked Van Lier to write this work. When this appeared successful, the publisher added Tonkens's text as 'Introduction', and bound it with Van Lier's text in one volume.

them to settle on the Gocherheide, and other settlers arrived in due course. Their first Reformed pastor, Rev. Johann Wilhelm Janssen [1738-1822], was praised by Van Lier for his good work.[226] Van Lier died in Kleve in 1799.[227]

Roelof Daniël Mulder [1910-1974] called (1942) Van Lier 'Drenthe's first scientific researcher of Nature'. That he certainly was, but in fact he investigated much more. His plans for studies of geology and the Drenthe dialect were not fulfilled, but his books about the archaeological prehistory (1760) and the history (1795) of Drenthe show how multifarious his investigations were. This inquisitive and thorough researcher of so many subjects is one of the best representatives of Dutch 18th-century Enlightment. Strikingly he stuck to Drenthian subjects – which restriction may have incited his precise observations.

It is quite remarkable that so many artefacts from the hunebeds D13-Eext and D12-Eext in the princely collection survived until the present day despite their complicated history after 1756. Van Lier's friend and editor in 1760, Arnout Vosmaer, prepared the skeletons of the animals who died in Prince William V's zoological garden for the princely collection and museum (*cabinet*); he even wrote that the animals had 'the laudable habit' of dying soon after their arrival (Pieters 2002, 34). Many animals from the East and West Indies, Asia and Africa were shown there for the first time in Europe. The *cabinet* also displayed objects from primitive peoples, corals, fishes and butterflies (Van Campen 2000, 202-15). François Hemsterhuis [1721-1790] was curator of the numismatics and antiquities at the time, and enormous sums were spent on acquisitions to augment these collections. Vosmaer became renowned for his directorship of both collections and his publications about several of the animals.[228]

When the French invaded the country and triggered a revolution, in 1795, Prince William V fled to England and his collections and zoo were confiscated and taken to Paris, where Georges Cuvier [1767-1832] and other researchers would benefit from them. The French *citoyens* who collected the loot (217 packing cases containing the collections, the Indian elephants Hans and Parkie (or Margueritte), and all the other animals from the zoo, several of which were eaten during the six months *en route*), the botanist André Thouin [1747-1814] and the geologist Barthélemy Faujas de Saint-Fond [1741-1819] permitted the aged and

---

226 Rev. J.W. Janssen was grandfather of the Dutch archaeologist L.J.F. Janssen [1806-1869] – who will be discussed in section '1840-1868' and who did most of his first excavations in the surroundings of his grandfather's house in Pfalzdorf – and also grandfather of the philanthropist and antiquarian Rev. Ottho Gerhard Heldring [1804-1876]. An elder, more distant cousin of L.J.F. Janssen was the archaeologist Caspar Jacob Christiaan Reuvens [1793-1835], who was succeeded by Janssen in the Leiden Museum (Arentzen 2005, 7-9; 51ff).

227 The whereabouts of Van Lier's own archaeological collection is unknown, which was auctioned after his bankruptcy; it was not added to that of J. Hofstede (see below)

228 See Pieters 2002; Pieters & Rookmaker 1994; Pieters 1994 and Van Campen 2000, 202-22 about Vosmaer's directorships of the Stadholder's Cabinet in The Hague from 1756 to 1795 (which was housed in the Princely quarters in the Buitenhof until 1766 and thereafter in the Kneuterdijk palace) and of the Prince's Zoo at the Kleyne Loo in Voorburg from 1771 to 1786. The Cabinet was sometimes called 'the Museum' and could be visited three days a week by the educated.

famous Vosmaer to keep a number of objects (Van Campen 2000, 34-8, 282-6). Among these were two cases with *animalia in liquor* that had been prepared by Albert Seba [1665-1736], the famous 'sword of Claudius Civilis',[229] who was the Batavian leader of the rebellion against the Romans in AD 79 (Tacitus), cloths, weapons and other ancient objects considered as regalia of the House of Orange, and perhaps also the artefacts from D13 and a collection of jewels. In 1796, before he died in 1799, Vosmaer entrusted the collector Jean Théodore Royer [1737-1808] with these objects. Most of them were taken, in 1803, to Prince William V who was living in Brunswick (Braunschweig), Germany. After his death, his widow sold what was left of the famous collection, in 1806-7, *pecuniae causa* (Van Meerkerk 2009, 200).

There is no mention of the artefacts from hunebed D13-Eext in the administration of these collections.[230] Eventually most of them were accessed by the Museum Meermanno-Westreenianum in The Hague (Bijvanck 1912; Bakker 2004, 120-1). They may have been bought by Johan Meerman [1753-1815] at the auction of Vosmaer's personal collection in 1800 (which lasted fourteen days!). At that time, Meerman was Director-General for Public Education and Letters and Sciences

---

229 This was an iron Merovingian ULFBERHT (?) sword, type H, according to J. Petersen. It was donated, in 1766, by Maximilien Henri marquis de Saint Simon [1720-1790] to the Prince's Cabinet, together with a winged iron spearhead and an iron bodkin (Van Campen 2000, ills 6-8, 34-8; 246-7). Saint Simon, who studied ancient river courses in The Netherlands, did not mention it in his *Histoire de la guerre des Bataves et des Romains* (1770). A copy of his note to Vosmaer reports that the objects were found 10-12 feet (2.9-3.5 m) deep in a 'terrain where the ancient Rhine once passed through', but did not name the locality. Saint Simon thought that this terrain, in which the two other weapons were also found, was an ancient battlefield. 'At about one mile (*lieue*) distance, still on the same ancient course of the Rhine, the General Hardenbroek had found a ship's anchor at the same depth.' My guess is that both sites are along the Kromme Rijn, formerly course of the main Rhine, from Wijk bij Duurstede to Utrecht. Hardenbroek House lies on the Kromme Rijn about 5 km downstream and northwest from Wijk bij Duurstede. The possible association of three weapons from about AD 850-925 in the same field might seem to indicate that they came from a grave rather than river deposits, although river deposits of swords and spearheads were rather common at the time. But their depth, 3-3.5 m below surface, and the anchor confirms their discovery in an ancient Rhine course, as Vosmaer's note indicates. Nothing is further known about dredging of or along the Kromme Rijn during the mid-18th century. Royer, who had received the 'sword of Claudius Civilis' and both other weapons from Vosmaer, returned them, in 1803, to the Prince of Orange, William v, who resided in Brunswick. They were delivered by Willem Carel Vosmaer [1749-1818], nephew of Arnout Vosmaer. Sometime after 1813, they entered the Royal Cabinet of Rarities in Amsterdam. They are now in the Legermuseum (Army Museum) in Delft, inv. no. 015.414 (Ypey 1961; 1982, 265, no. 31; Van Campen 2000, *l.c.*; Swinkels 2004; pers. comm., 2001 from Dr. J. van Campen, Amsterdam, J.P. Puype, Legermuseum Delft and J. van Heel, Museum Meermanno-Westreenianum, The Hague).

230 Princess Anna, who died in 1757, kept her own small collection of coins and *naturalia* more or less separate from the Prince's collection. Her collection was sold at auction in 1797 (Van Campen 2000, 210). The chance that the artefacts from hunebed D13-Eext were among these objects is very small, because Van Lier and Vosmaer (1760) stated expressly that the D13 artefacts belonged to the Prince's cabinet. Whether or not the artefacts from D13 were part of the Prince's collection of – mostly classical – antiquities and numismatics, of which François Hemsterhuis was curator, and then transferred to Vosmaer's care after Hemsterhuis's death, in 1790, is unknown but not very probable. Knowledge about the Prince's collections is still fragmentary and incomplete (Van Campen 2000).

(*Openbaar Onderwijs en Wetenschappen*) under King Lodewijk of Holland (Louis Napoléon Bonaparte, who reigned from 1806 until 1810). A considerable part of Meerman's collection of incunabulae, ancient books and archaeological objects was bought by Willem Jan Hendrik baron van Westreenen van Tiellandt [1783-1848]. After Meerman's death, his house, along with the small archaeological museum and the extraordinarily important collection of medieval manuscripts and books, became the Museum Meermanno-Westreenianum in The Hague.[231]

1768-1769: De Pauw

Cornelius de Pauw [1739-1799] was a philosopher, geographer and diplomat at the court of Frederick the Great of Prussia. Born in Amsterdam and a Roman Catholic, he spent most of his life in Kleve (Cleves) just outside the Dutch Republic. He discerned (1768-9) four orders or classes of increasing primitivism of humankind in his book: (1) cultivators, (2) herdsmen, (3) gatherers, (4) hunters (Rodden 1981).

He also wrote (1768-9) about 'les haches de pierre qu'on déterre en Suède, et en Allemagne, à des très grandes profondeurs, et qui doivent être extrèmement anciennes, ayant été employées avant l'invention du fer et de cuivre' and that the contemporary savages of the New World made use of such primitive artefacts (Rodden 1981, 63).

De Pauw's remark illustrates the theoretical climate of the time. Whereas Van Lier (1760) developed a Two Age system and did not concern himself with the appearance of 'copper' (bronze) objects, De Pauw's statement shows that the general idea of a Three Age system that Lucretius generated had currency in this period.[232] His statement that stone axes had been excavated in Sweden and Germany *at very great depths*, displays an early notion of associating stratigraphy with time, although in this case, it was incorrect.

---

231 In the early 19th century, Reuvens thought that the objects from D13-Eext that were not in the Meerman-Westreenen collection in The Hague, were 'probably later acquired by surgeon Quaestius in Leeuwarden. After his death dispersed by auction' (Leiden Museum, MS CII.39). This was Johannes Wybrandus Quaestius [1766-1827]. His son, Assuerus Quaestius [1815-1887], gave 29 ancient objects from the remnants of this collection to the Fries Museum, Leeuwarden (pers. comm. E. Kramer, curator, August 25, 2007). Apart from an 'unglazed marble from Friesland', inventory no. 87A-68, which could have come from D13, but is presently lost, few or no Neolithic objects seem to have been among the donated artefacts.

232 See sections '1685' and '1756-1760'. De Pauw does not mention Van Lier's 1760 book.

1768-1781: Petrus Camper's hunebed drawings

According to Goethe, the natural scientist Petrus Camper [1722-1789] was 'a meteor of spirit, science, talent and diligence'.[233] His interests, ranging across a wide variety of subjects, included obstetrics, surgery, anatomy, palaeontology, mineralogy, botany, draughtsmanship, physical features of different contemporary peoples and those portrayed by classical sculptures (he invented the facial angle which would be crucial for measuring skulls in the 19th and 20th centuries),[234] gems, cabinet-making and correctly formed shoes. He was also interested in hunebeds. Between 1768 and 1781, when he was professor at Groningen University (1763-1773) and lived at Klein Lankum near Franeker in Friesland, he drew eight hunebeds (Figures 20-27), showing entrances on the southern side of D8-Anloo-Kniphorstbos (Figure 23), D13-Eext (Figure 20) and, less clearly, O1-De Eese (Figure 27). He erroneously suspected that D14-Eexterhalte (Figures 21-22) represented two hunebeds, like D3 and D4 at Midlaren ('N. Laren', Figures 25-26). He had a special interest in hunebed dimensions and the volume, weight and availability of the largest stones, but almost none in the identity of the hunebed builders. Five of his drawings were published by the Russian ambassador Gallitzin (1789).[235] In the quire with the original drawings[236] Camper also excerpt-

---

233 Quotation in *Wikipedia* ('P. Camper'), no further reference given. Dr. M. Niedermeier, Goethe-Wörterbuch, Berlin, kindly informed me that it is from Goethe, 'Zur Morphologie' (*Goethes Werke, hg. im Auftrage der Grossherzogin Sophie von Sachsen*. Weimar, 1887-1920, II. Abteilung, vol. 6, p. 18). Goethe wrote once more about Camper's excellent qualities as a scientist (*Ibid*. II. Abt., vol. 7, p. 188). About Petrus Camper and his son Adriaan (section '1796-1808'), see Bots & Visser 2001; Schuller tot Peursum-Meijer & Koops 1989.

234 Although he studied the skull forms of apes and various human peoples, Camper did *expressis verbis* not attach any racist or moral values to differences among them.

235 Anonymous publication by Dimitri Alexewitsch Prince de Gallitzin / Golitsin [1738-1803], who was the ambassador to Paris of the Russian Empress Catherine the Great from 1763 to 1770, after which he became her ambassador to The Hague until 1782-3. He dwelled in The Netherlands until the arrival of the French and the foundation of the Batavian Republic, in 1795, when he moved to Brunswick, Germany. Because Gallitzin's draughtsman drew only the outlines of the stones, these prints are inferior to Camper's drawings.

236 *De hunnen bedde[n] van Drenthe Getekend door P. Camper* ('De hunnen bedde[n] of Drenthe Drawn by Petrus Camper') [1768, 1769, 1781], a quire with manuscript notes by P. and A.G. Camper, from 1768 to 1811, and drawings of 8 hunebeds (and a few megalithic constructions elsewhere), University Library Amsterdam, MS II G 53 (KNMG). For a further discussion of this 'hunebeds quire', see Bakker 1978; 1989; 2004, 148-9.

Figure 20. Hunebeds D9-Annen on May 27, 1769, 9 AM (above) and D13-Eext on May 1, 1768, 7 AM, drawn by Petrus Camper (photograph University Library Amsterdam MS II G53-KNMG). See further Appendix 3.

ed publications about megaliths in France (Caylus,[237] Montfaucon) and England (Edwards), again with special attention to the volume and origin of the stones. He argued that much heavier stones than those used for building the hunebeds were available in the countryside, but had been too heavy for the hunebed builders to transport. He offered no opinion about the origin of the boulders or the ethnicity of the hunebed builders and noted that Van Lier's drawings of D13 (1760) were imprecise, but paid no attention to his theories.

Camper presented his rather general ideas about hunebeds comprehensively in a letter written, in 1780, to Prince Henry of Prussia (Friedrich Heinrich Ludwig Prinz von Preussen) [1726-1802], whom he advised to build a hunebed in his Rheinsberg estate, 100 km northwest of Berlin:[238]

---

237 Anne-Claude-Philippe de Turbières-Grimoard de Pestels de Lévis, comte de Caylus [1692-1765], wrote about his reflections on the megaliths of Brittany, which he never had visited, in vol. VI (1764) of his *Recueil d'Antiquités Égytiennes, Grecques,Étrusques et Romains* (pers. comm. W. Arentzen). Pierre-Roland Giot [1919-2002] found his remarks important enough to quote them at length in his brief history of megalithic research in Brittany (1985, 10-11). Caylus did not attribute the megaliths to the ancient Gauls. 'Did not this nation, whatever it was, and which could not write', he asked himself, 'want to leave proof to posterity of its existence and ability to move the stones?'

> '... *elle en indique beaucoup* [de preuves] *sur les forces mouvantes, ou du moins sur l'accord et l'emploi d'une bien grande quantité de bras, comme on le voit dans l'Histoire des Incas, qui ont taillé, remué et placé de pierres d'une volume et par conséquent d'un poids énorme ... La quantité de ces pierres placées sur la côte de Bretagne, constate la longueur du séjour fait dans cette partie de Gaule par des peuples dont la façon de penser était uniforme, au moins sur cet article; mais il est plus simple et de plus dans l'ordre des vraisemblances, de convenir que ce genre de monument est l'ouvrage du même Peuple.*
> *Ces réflexions augmentent la singularité du silence absolu que la tradition même a gardé sur un usage si répété; on peut en inférer une Antiquité d'autant plus reculée, que du temps des Romains la trace en étoit perdue; César auroit parlé de ces monumens singuliers, ils les méritoient par eux-mêmes; ils faisoient preuve de l'ancienne habitation du pays. On peut appyer sur ces monumens ces probabilités; car personne ne voudra soutenir que ces monumens et ceux de l'Angleterre ayent été depuis la construction de l'Empire Romain. Il faut donc convenir qu'on ne peut rien dire de positif à cet égard; on voit seulement que la disposition de ces pierres, constante et elle-même, est l'ouvrage d'un Peuple et la suite de sa superstition; le rapport des opérations certifie que ce Peuple a successivement débarqué en Gaule et en Angleterre; tout le reste est et sera toujours ignoré, mais ne perdra rien de sa singularité.'*

P. Camper did not quote these lines and ideas directly, but several ideas would be repeated in Westendorp (1815, 1822, see section '1811-1822'). Late in the 19th century and in the 20th century, ideas similar to these of Caylus, but much more elaborated, would return in the guise of definitions of prehistoric 'cultures' by G. Kossinna and V.G. Childe (see section 'Regional Groups and the concept of a 'TRB culture'').

238 Draft dated '*Hambourg, le 10 de Juillet 1780*' in P. Camper's diary of his journey, made together with his sons Adriaan and Jacob, *Reyze over Hanover en Brunswyck naar Berlin en over Hamburg, en Bremen naar Kl. Lankum. 1780* ('Journey by Hanover and Brunswick to Berlin and by Hamburg and Bremen [back] to Klein Lankum'), University Library Amsterdam, MS II F37 (KNMG), p. 99-100. This letter may have been copied by Adriaan Camper, but it is difficult to tell the handwritings apart. The Campers had been the Prince's guest in Rheinsberg on July 2 and 3, 1780.

Figure 21. Hunebed D14-Eexterhalte viewed from the south, drawn by Petrus Camper on May 29, 1769 (photograph University Library Amsterdam MS II G53-KNMG). See further Appendix 3.

'Le dessein du monument des Huns,[239] *et plus probablement d'un peuple plus ancien encore, puisque l'histoire en est perdue, prouvera à V. Alt. R.*[240] *que j'ai pensé au goût decidé de V. Alt. R. pour se répresenter les plus anciens, et les plus precieux monumens de la terre. Il n'a certainement aucun attrait pour plaire à ces amateurs des beaux arts, qui ne recherchent que l'imitation de la belle nature, et des objets brillants. Celuy ci ne peut attirer les egards que des Grands Hommes, qui sçavent apprécier ces anciens objets de valeur, et des grandes entreprises d'un peuple oublié, qui ne connoissant pas encore l'usage du fer*[241] *a pourtans scu êlever des pierres immenses à une hauteur prodigieuse par des machines probablement fort simples, mais aussi inconnues aujourdhuy que la nation qui s'en servoit.*

On trouve des pierres sur ce monument, qui ont 40 pieds de circonference,[242] *ils les ont du non seulement transporter mais élever; ce que nous ne saurions faire sans les fendre en plusieurs pieces, ou par des machines extrêmement coûtentes.*

---

239 Which drawing was concerned, is unknown. Perhaps it was a drawing of *Hünengrab* 630-Osterholz-Scharmbeck near Bremen, Germany, a copy of which is reproduced in Bakker 1978, or one of Camper's drawings of Dutch hunebeds.

240 '*V. Alt. R.*' is *Vôtre Altesse Royale.*

241 Cf. Van Lier 1760.

242 This is again the circumference, 40 feet or 11.8 m, of the largest capstone of the German hunebed Surbolds Grab (see note 110).

Figure 22. Hunebed D14-Eexterhalte viewed from the northwest, drawn by Petrus Camper, 'Hu[NNEN] BED outside EEXT from the NW side, drawn May 28, 1769' (photograph University Library Amsterdam MS II G53-KNMG). See further Appendix 3.

Les urnes disposées sous le pavé prouvent que cette nation bruloit les corps morts; et la hauteur de la pierre occidentale, qu'ils adoroient le soleil. Ces monumens me representent l'idée primordiale d'une église, et la grosse pierre l'origine du clocher, que les Chrêtiens du moyen age ont constamment placé à l'occident de leurs temples.

Le terrein de Reinsberg fournira aisément à V. Alt. R. des pierres semblables. Un monument pareille [sic] sera sans contredit un tres bon effet dans cette delicieuse retraite, plus encore s'il est placé sous quelques arbres dont l'ombre rendra ce monument simple encore plus majestueux … .

Le souvenir de ces deux jours, les plus agreables que j'ai passé dans ma vie me rendra le plus heureux du monde, et me representera un des grands princes dont j'ai l'honneur d'être avec le plus profond respect … .'[243]

---

243 The Prince answered on July 20, 1780: '*Je tacherai de mettre votre dessein en execution, et je serois alors très charmé de vous le montrer dans ma solitude comme un objet digne de votre attention, et d'entendre vos remarques et réflexions sur d'autres objets aussi interessans.*' (University Library Amsterdam, MS X118, KNMG). But a hunebed was never constructed in Rheinsberg.

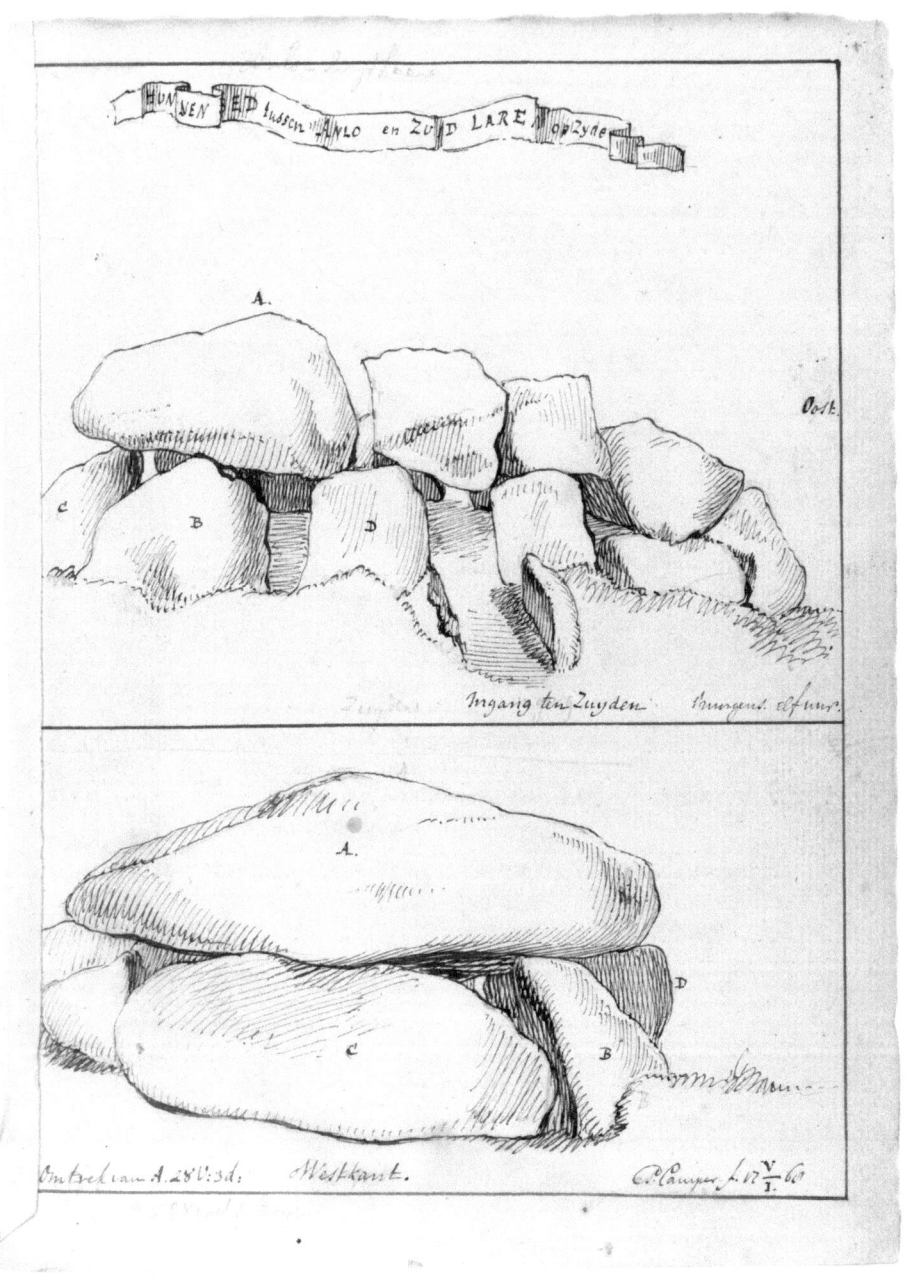

Figure 23. Hunebed D8-Anloo-Kniphorstbos viewed from the south (above) and from the west (below), drawn by Petrus Camper on May 1, 1768: 'Hunnen Bed between Anlo and Zuid Laren from the side' (photograph University Library Amsterdam MS II G53-KNMG).

Figure 24. Hunebed G1-Noordlaren drawn from the northeast by Petrus Camper on May 1, 1768 (photograph University Library Amsterdam MS II G53-KNMG). See further Appendix 3.

Figure 25. Hunebed D3-Midlaren drawn by Petrus Camper (photograph University Library Amsterdam MS II G53-KNMG). See further Appendix 3.

Figure 26. Hunebed D4-Midlaren drawn by Petrus Camper. This drawing can be fitted to the right of Figure 25, using the trees sketched in pencil as a reference (photograph University Library Amsterdam MS II G53-KNMG). See further Appendix 3.

Figure 27. Hunebed O1-De Eese viewed from the south, drawn by Petrus Camper on August 11, 1781 (photograph University Library Amsterdam MS II G53-KNMG). See further Appendix 3.

1774: Van Brussel

In 1774, a third edition of L. Smids's 1711 encyclopaedia[244] was published with several new additions by Theodorus van Brussel [ca. 1730-after 1783]. His additions to the term 'Steenhoopen' were extensive (1774, 360-5). According to him, hunebeds could not be the work of men, because the stones were much to unwieldy. The study of De Buffon's Natural History (1749-1804, vol. I, 105)[245] had convinced him that the hunebeds were formed in situ on the seabed and that their present shape was completely due to marine, and atmospherical erosion after they had fallen dry. This was also the case with the stones of the Giant's Causeway in Ireland. The uppermost hunebed stones were the largest because they had risen out of the water before the lower stones, which were longer exposed to the breakers of the sea. It is evident that Van Brussel had neither seen hunebeds nor read Van Lier (1760). As discussed in section '1756-1760', there was no unanimous opinion at the time about how the heavy boulders in Drenthe had originated. Not surprisingly, Van Brussel's foolish ideas were left unmentioned in later studies.

1790: Engelberts

Engelbertus Matthias Engelberts [1731-1807], a clergyman at Hoorn, 30 km north of Amsterdam, devoted considerable attention to hunebeds in volume 3 (1790, 160-82) of his history book for the general public, *De Aloude Staat en Geschiedenissen der Vereenigde Nederlanden* ('The Ancient State and Histories of the United Netherlands', 1784-1799). This is exceptional for a historian in the western part of the country, and he was the second, after Simon van Leeuwen (1685), to do so in print.[246] Engelberts was, however, born in Noordlaren in Groningen, near hunebed G1-Noordlaren and the Drenthe hunebeds, which would have attracted his attention during his youth and later sojourns to the region. He presented the existing knowledge about the hunebeds in a sensible way, mainly based on Van Lier (1760), Picardt (1660) and Smids (1711), and added two pictures of the Tynaarlo hunebed D6 (Figure 28), which he drew himself. Besides D6-Tynaarlo, he visited the hunebeds D3 and D4 at Midlaren (which he thought were one), D13-Eext, D14-Eexterhalte, D16-Balloo and D17 and D18 at Rolde. Curiously, he did not mention the hunebed G1-Noordlaren at his place of birth. Was it perhaps too incomplete for didactic purposes in his eyes? He noted that the flat sides of the hunebed capstones were always on the bottom side, which proved to him that hunebeds were not meant to be altars.

---

244 See section '1711'. W. Arentzen discovered this addition about July 1, 2010.
245 Georges-Louis Leclerc, comte de Buffon [1707-1788] *Histoire Naturelle générale et particulière, avec le description du Cabinet du Roy* (1749-1788, 36 vols. and 8 posthumous vols.1789-1804).
246 Thirty years later, De Koning (1810) did not mention the hunebeds in his book about 'The ancestral way of life and habits in this country, from the earliest times till the end of the sixteenth century'.

Figure 28. Hunebed D6-Tynaarlo viewed from SSW and from SW (Engelberts (1790, vol. 3, p. 162). Drawn by E.M. Engelberts, print by N. van der Meer, Jun. (photograph University Library Amsterdam OTM O 80-744). See further Appendix 3.

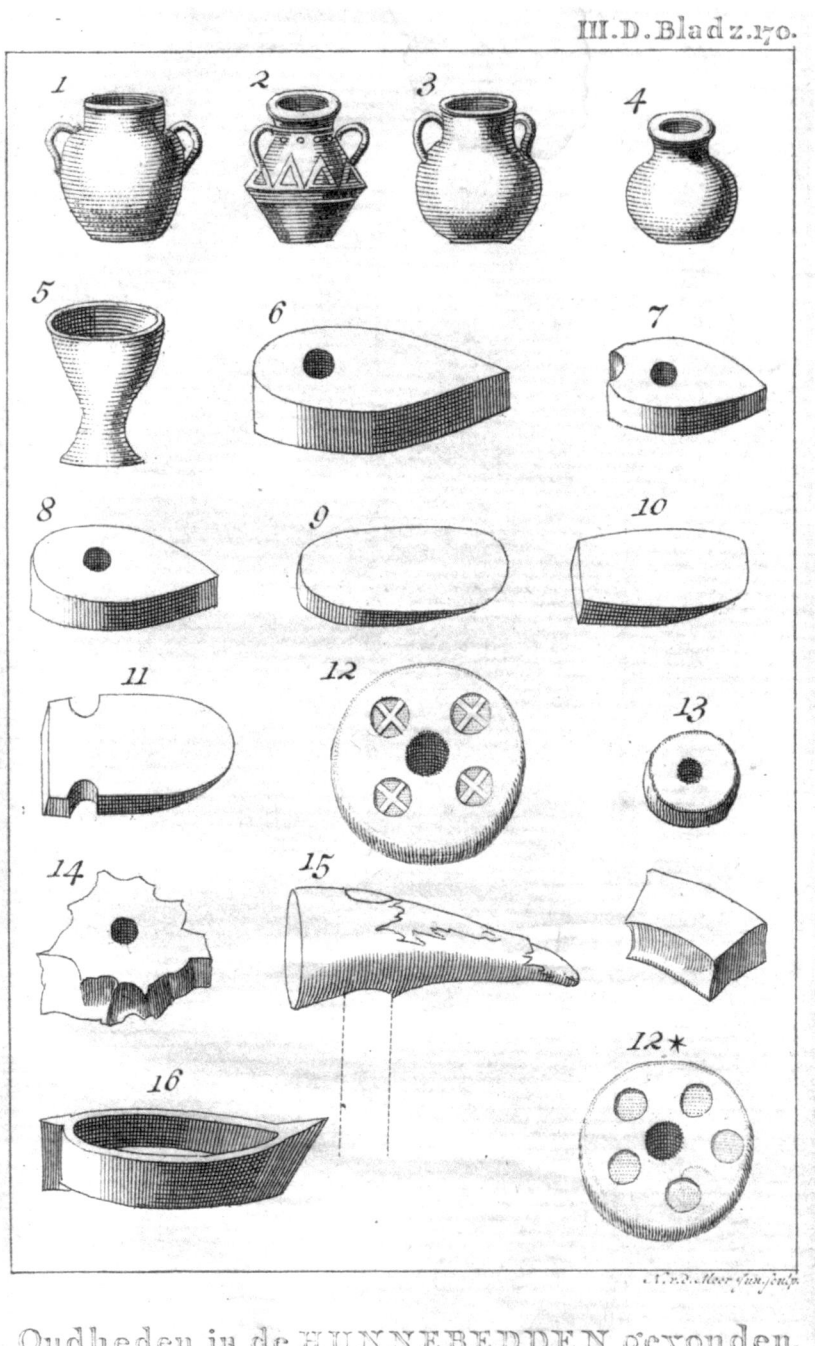

Oudheden in de HUNNEBEDDEN gevonden.

Figure 29. 'Antiquities found in the HUNNEBEDDEN'. *Print by N. van der Meer, Jun. after sketches by E.M. Engelberts (Engelberts 1790, vol. 3, p. 170). See further Appendix 3.*

Furthermore Engelberts illustrated seventeen 'Antiquities found in the HUN-NEBEDDEN' (Figure 29), which he drew with the help of a '*voetmaat*'[247] (p. 171), and he listed several measures of each object (p. 170-1). Although Engelberts was a good draughtsman by reputation, his drawings, or at least the engravings based on them by Noach van der Meer, Jun. [1741-1822], are clumsy. Moreover, several of these objects were not recovered from the hunebeds at all, since the *entire* collection of antiquities of Johannes Hofstede [1765-1848], chief clerk of the 'Landscape' of Drenthe (Gerding et al. 2003, 408), in Assen, appears to have been drawn.[248]

Engelberts's exceptional digression into prehistoric archaeology* (vol. 3, 1790, 160-82) was not mentioned by the anonymous reviewer of this third volume in a leading periodical.[249, 250]

1796-1808: Adriaan Camper and the prize contest about the ethnicity and date of the builders of the hunebeds

Adriaan Gilles Camper [1759-1820], the son of Petrus Camper, followed in his father's footsteps and published several of his unfinished manuscripts. He went on to write abstracts in the hunebeds quire until 1811. Among these was one from Jean Potocki's *Fragmens historiques et géographiques sur la Scythie, la Sarmatie et les Slaves* (Brunswick 1796 #),[251] which discussed the presence of Slavs to the west of the Elbe and attributed the hunebeds in that region, the Duchy of Bremen, to them. Adriaan was not aware of the crucial fact that Van Lier had found only stone weapons and implements in D13, because he looked through Van Lier's book only superficially and ascribed the illustrated bronze objects from Iron Age* graves in the urnfields of Gasteren and Rolde to the hunebeds.[252]

---

247 In pre-decimal times, a [Rhineland] *voetmaat* was a one *voet* (foot) long ruler, which was sub-divided into 12 *duimen* (inches). A [Rhineland] *voet* measured 31.4 cm. Engelberts, who lived in Hoorn in Holland, would have used a Rhineland *voetmaat*, although the Groningen *voet* equivalent to 29.1 cm, was probably current in Noordlaren, where he grew up.

248 Three discs and a ceramic model boat were presented by J. Hofstede to King Louis Napoleon in 1809. These objects were nos. 12, 12*, 13 and 18 in Figure 29, as Hofstede's drawings in his Catalogue show. See section '1809'.

249 *Algemeene Vaderlandsche Letter-Oefeningen*, vol. 1791 (1791), 438-41.

250 Engelberts was perhaps the first to write about 'the Hunneschansen', viz. the category of me-dieval round earthworks surrounded by an earthen wall and moat (Hunneschans and Duno in Gelderland, one on Grebbeberg in Utrecht, and Hunneborg in Overijssel). Smids (1711, 148) adduced the '*Huine schanssen* near Doorewaart [i.e. Duno at Doorwerth]' as proof of the former presence of giants, but did not discuss this type of earthwork as a category.

251 The talented Polish count Jan Potocki [1761-1815] is still famous for his *Manuscrit trouvé à Saragosse* (complete edition by R. Radrizzani. Paris: J. Corti, 1990 #. Dutch translation by J. Versteeg, Amsterdam 1992: Wereldbibliotheek). Potocki also wrote several works on geography, history and political systems of other countries (including The Netherlands, which he visited in 1785). See Lech 2008 (who does not mention the 1796 publication).

252 A.G. Camper wrote in the *Hunne*[n] *Bedden* quire: 'Van Lier [1760] described an intact hun-nenbed [D13-Eext] and what was found in it: stone chisels, copper rings, urns, etc.' (p. 8, abbreviated).

Unlike his father, Adriaan Camper – possibly influenced by Potocki – took the ethnic identification of the hunebed builders very seriously and he even became the instigator and author of the text for the 1808 competition conducted by the Hollandsche Maatschappij der Wetenschappen (Holland Society of Letters and Sciences) in Haarlem:

'Because there is no reasoned description of the ancient burial places in the Department of Drenthe and the Duchy of Bremen known by the name of Hunnebedden, the Society has approved the following [question]: *"Which peoples built the so-called hunnebedden in Drenthe and the Duchy of Bremen? In which times can it be supposed that they lived in these regions?"'*

The explanatory note reveals his wide international views on the matter:

'Because the Histories about these Monuments do not give a sufficient clarification, the Society requires 1°. That these Monuments be compared with similar monuments present in Great Britain, Denmark, Norway, Germany, France and Russia. 2°. That the Coffins, Urns, Weapons, Ornaments, Offering tools, etc. from the hunnebedden be compared with similar Coffins, Urns, Weapons, etc. from the burial places of the ancient Germani, Gauls, Slavs, Huns, and other Nordic Peoples about whom Pallas[253] *has noted different peculiarities.'* (De Bruijn 1977, 111-2).[254]

The text for this competition was published in Dutch and French and also advertised by other Academies. It may have inspired the text for the 1862 competition conducted by the *Académie des Inscriptions et Belles-Lettres* at Paris, which was won by Alexandre Bertrand in 1864 (#; cf. Daniel 1960, 20; Cartailhac 1889).

---

253 The Berlin-born anatomist Peter Simon Pallas [1741-1811] studied in Leiden, between 1763 and 1767, and published illustrated descriptions of new zoological specimens from the Stadholder's zoological cabinet in The Hague, where he was acquainted with A. Vosmaer and P. Camper. In 1767, he received an appointment in St Petersburg and travelled throughout the Russian Empire. He exchanged fossils and minerals with P. Camper. A.G. Camper's reference may refer to Pallas (1771, 673-4 #). When Pallas saw megalithic kerbs around tumuli or flat spaces in the Upper Jenissei-Altai region, he was 'always reminded of the ancient Riesen- or Heldenbetten, which are found in some regions of Germany, particularly in the Mark Brandenburg, which have the same shape' [pers. comm. W. Arentzen]. The Campers probably owned Pallas's tomes.

254 A.G. Camper's draft for the text for this competition was too long (archives Hollandsche Maatschappij der Wetenschappen in Noord-Holland Archives in Haarlem) and a shorter version, probably edited by Marinus van Marum [1750-1837], secretary of the Society, after discussions in the meeting of the Hollandsche Maatschappij der Wetenschappen, was used for the published version. Camper's draft had asked for drawings of the monument and objects found therein, but this request was left out in the shorter version.

1809: discovery of hunebed D41-Emmen under a barrow

On April 19, 1809, an intact four-yoke hunebed (D41-Emmen) was discovered under a barrow at Emmen by a stone seeker. Within three days detailed cross-sections were drawn by the government surveyor P.A.C. Buwama Aardenburg (Figures 30 and 34) and details of the construction were recorded by Johannes Hofstede [1765-1848], who was fiscal-general of Drenthe and brother of the governor (*Land-Drost*), Petrus Hofstede [1755-1839].[255] The extensive report by J. Hofstede, from April 30, 1809, which was addressed to *Mijn Heer de Land-Drost van het Departement Drenthe*, his brother, was published by Van Giffen (1927, 32-39).[256] The barrow was removed and the chamber – especially the layer between two irregular stone floors – was explored 'with bare hands'. A 'broken urn' was found in the small recess between two orthostats at the southern side. Sherds of fourteen or fifteen urns 'of different forms, sizes, colours, and variously decorated with foliage, stripes and pits along the rim' are described, but they and the 'broken urn' are not illustrated in the manuscript report, and are now lost. These sherds, along with a decorated collared flask, a tureen and a small globular pot, the latter two without decoration (Figure 31),[257] were found between the first and second floors. No flint or stone artefacts and no remains of later burials on top of the second floor in the open chamber were recorded.[258] The tomb and its contents were considered to have been made '*bien longtemps avant que le métal fût connu*'[259]. The three complete pots were presented to King Lodewijk Napoleon, following J. Hofstede's collection of antiquities, which had been sent several weeks before

---

255 Johannes Hofstede [1765-1848] was also an active collector of and expert in archaeological objects from Drenthe. He was dominated by his authoritarian and ambitious brother Piet or Petrus Hofstede [1755-1839], who was ten years older. They were nephews of Joannes van Lier (see section '1756-1760'). Petrus was first the Bailiff (*Land-Drost*) and then the Governor (*Gouverneur*) of Drenthe. Cornelis Pothoff [1766-1844], mayor of Emmen and L. Oortwijn, attorney-general (Gratama 1886, 33n), may also have taken an active part in the excavation.

256 W. Arentzen found it in the Leiden Museum in Pleyte archives, box C257, file Cd Drente. This file also contains a brown drawing in ink-and-watercolour of the three pots mentioned below (Figure 31). L. Amkreutz, curator of the Leiden Museum, could not yet trace the three pots (e-mail June 2, 2010).

257 That Buwama Aardenburg drew the three pots is recorded in the documents from 1809 (Van Giffen 1927, 29, n. 1; 36), but this drawing can now be published for the first time since W. Arentzen found it in the Leiden Museum, attached to J. Hofstede's original report (see the preceding footnote).

258 The anonymous 'first discoverer' of the hunebed told that 'he had found already a few small pieces of an Urn and bones when he dug the sand' (report J. Hofstede in Van Giffen 1927, 33, 34) may or may not concern TRB or other pottery higher up in the hunebed barrow or in the chamber. It is lost.

259 P. Hofstede followed Van Lier's prehistoric Two Age system (1760) in his letter of May 16, 1809, to King Louis Napoleon Bonaparte of Holland (Van Giffen 1927, 29n).

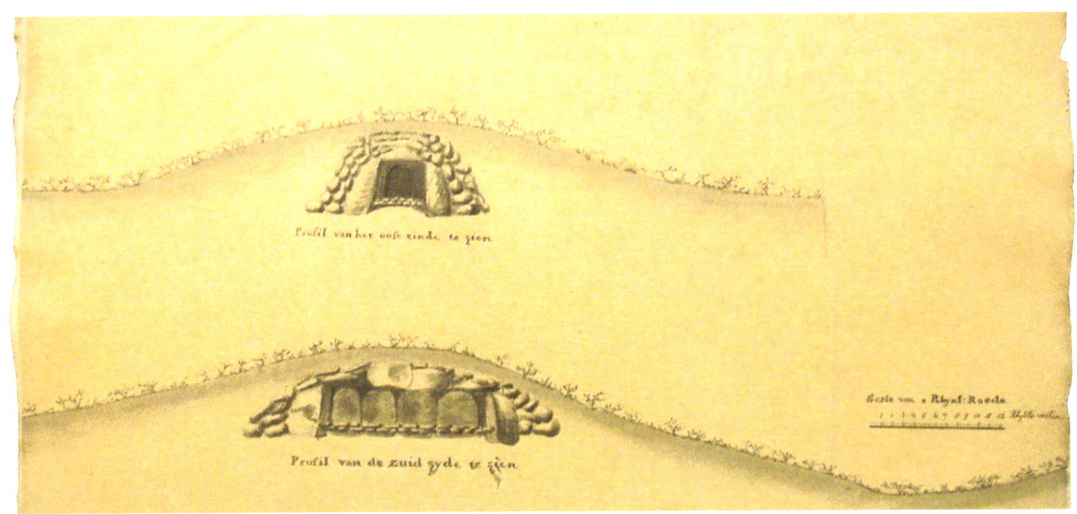

Figure 30. Sections through hunebed D41-Emmen, three days after its discovery under a barrow on April 22, 1809. Scale in Rhynlandse Roeden and Voeten. Grey watercolour (34.5 x 17.5 cm) by P.A.C. Buwama Aardenburg, attached to J. Hofstede's report to the King (National Museum of Antiquities at Leiden, Pleyte archives C257; photograph Wout Arentzen). Cf. Figure 34.

Figure 31. Undecorated tureen, decorated collared flask and small bowl from hunebed D41-Emmen, drawn by P.A.C. Buwama Aardenburg (picture attached to J. Hofstede's report to the King (National Museum of Antiquities at Leiden, Pleyte archives C257; photograph Wout Arentzen). See further Appendix 3 and Figures 30 and 34.

to the Royal Museum in Amsterdam.[260] The Governor of Drenthe renewed and extended the Protection Law of 1734 on this occasion. Both Hofstedes were convinced that all hunebeds originally had been covered by a barrow.

The flat capstones of D41 were overlain with flat stones and earth, probably in order to divert rainwater and keep the chamber dry, like several megalithic tombs in Denmark (Dehn and Hansen 2006; Midgley 2008, 89-93).[261] The barrow covering most other passage graves seems not to have been higher than the base of the capstones. The capstones of D41 were flat and relatively thin, whereas the capstones of most other hunebeds were bulky and extended beyond the supporting stones and the barrow.[262]

The discovery of hunebed D41 under a barrow, in 1809, was reported in at least two newspapers (*Opregte Haarlemsche Courant,* July 15, 1809 and *Ommelander Courant,* July 21, 1809). The active Amsterdam publisher E. Maaskamp included a few pages of text and an aquatint print of it in his travel guide for The Netherlands (ca.1812; see fig. 16 in Bakker 1992).[263]

Petrus Hofstede decreed, on April 21, 1809, that his brother Johannes was the only person allowed to excavate antiquities in Drenthe[264] and on May 16, 1809, he asked the King of Holland '*de vouloir bien ordonner qu'on mette entre les mains de Mr. J. Hofstede, à charge d'en render compte, une certaine somme, pour fournir aux frais des recherches des antiquités de ce Département, conformément à la volonté que votre Majesté a daigné me faire connoître verbalement.*' (Van Giffen 1927, 29n). By royal decree (1809, no. 22, of September 26, 1809), this reimbursement was granted by the King (Van Giffen 1927, 28). Van Giffen concluded that 'a sort of excavation service was created in this way!' (ibid.).

---

260 The draft reports by J. Hofstede and P. Hofstede in the Assen archives were reprinted and analysed by Van Giffen (1927, 28-42). A version by P. Hofstede appeared as an Appendix in Westendorp's publications (1815 and 1822, pl. ii, see Figure 34). Cf. the letters from Louis Apol, director of the Royal Museum, to J. Hofstede (7.4.1809) and J. Meerman (8.4.1809 and 13.3.1810) in his Letterbook of Outward Letters, Rijksmuseum Amsterdam, inv. no. 35, pp. 1-2, 3, 26-7 (information from E. Bergvelt, September 7, 1995). The artefacts from the Royal Museum have been in the Leiden Museum since 1825-6. The inventories of the Hofstede collection, 2nd consignment of December 18, 1809, in the Pleyte archives (C82: C33-54) were copied by Governor Van Ewijck for Reuvens from the Assen archives. Cf. also Van Giffen (1927, 37n). Hofstede's two lists of objects sent to Amsterdam, dating from April 4 and December 18, 1809, are in the Reuvens or Pleyte archives, CII 22-36, Leiden Museum. Unfortunately, Hofstede's catalogues and Janssen's drawings of objects in this collection were cut up and re-arranged in geographical order by Pleyte for the preparation of his tome *Drente* (1880-82).

261 Although clay and loam were often used to make Danish megalith chambers waterproof (Midgley 2008, 91-3) and loam was available in Drenthe, where it was used for pottery production, no loam was recorded in the barrow of D41 or in barrow remnants of other hunebeds. Perhaps the transport of sufficient loam to the hunebeds was too difficult.

262 See Bakker (2009a), referring to an unpublished study by J. N. Lanting. Early illustrations show large hunebeds without covering barrows (see notes 37 and 104). But see the discussion of this problem by Midgley (2008, 84-93).

263 My late colleague Ben L. van Beek [1938-2005] gave me this aquatint in 1973.

264 Complete text of this *Bekendmaking*: Van Giffen 1927, 27. This Announcement is clearly related to J. Hofstede's investigation of the newly discovered hunebed D41-Emmen on the next day.

That year, Johannes Hofstede excavated the chambers of no less than four hunebeds: D15-Loon (before April 4, 1809),[265] D41-Emmen (April 22, 1803),[266] D46-Angelslo (May 1, 1809),[267] and D5-Zeijen (September 28, 1809),[268] but no details of the architecture were recorded. No drawings of hunebeds or pottery were made, as was the case when his brother Petrus Hofstede saw to – or even participated in – the writing of the excellent D41-Emmen report.

1811-1822: Westendorp

Although he did not have a library comparable to that of the Campers at his disposal, Nicolaus Westendorp [1773-1836], the Protestant minister in Sebaldeburen in the Groningen countryside, managed to write a treatise for the 1808 Haarlem competition.[269] The librarian of Groningen University library and others helped him locate primary and secondary sources, but he was greatly hampered by the slow arrival of the books and it took him three years to complete his manuscript. The closing date for contributions to the contest was shifted from January 1, 1813, to January 1, 1815, for Westendorp's sake. He won the gold medal prize and 150 guilders[270] and his contribution was published in a much reduced form by the Society in its new periodical (Westendorp 1815).[271] He became famous and published his unabridged and extended study seven years later as a book (Westendorp 1822[2], see Figure 33).[272]

Westendorp inspected and summarily described the hunebeds of Drenthe, in August, 1811, and seven others in Germany to the west of Bremen and the artefacts found in them that were in Dutch and German private collections.[273] Unfortunately, he was a poor draughtsman and did not make sketches or plans of

---

265 Van Giffen 1927, 25-8; no report is known.

266 This section and Van Giffen 1927, 28-42.

267 Van Giffen 1927, 43-4.

268 Van Giffen 1927, 44-52.

269 A study about Nicolaus Westendorp by W. Arentzen appeared during the preparation of this book (Arentzen 2009a; see also Arentzen 2009b).

270 Or 'twenty-five golden ducats' (Westendorp 1822, title-page: Figure 33).

271 Additional evidence published by Westendorp in *Algemeene Konst- en Letter-Bode* (1817, 137-9; 189-90; 190-1) was later incorporated in Westendorp (1822) [pers. comm. W. Arentzen].

272 Westendorp's book (1822), including the Notes, Addenda, and the Appendix on hunebed D41-Emmen by P. Hofstede (which is identical to that of 1815 and counts ca. 1.645 words), is some 69.500 words long, i.e. almost 2.5 times as long as the 1815 version of ca. 28.200 words. The 1812-1813 manuscript version counts ca. 31.750 words. In 1822, about 655 references were cited.

A second contributor of the contest was Georg Wolfgang Ulrich Wedel, '*Erbherr auf Freudenholm bey Preetz in Holstein*' (Wedel 1812). His treatise, dated July 1, 1812 discusses several archaeological finds and megalithic tombs in Holstein and their contents. It argues that the Vikings built the hunebeds. Composition, argument and scope were second-rate compared to Westendorp's contribution and the work was not printed. It is filed in the Hollandsche Maatschappij der Wetenschappen archives in the Noord-Holland Archives in Haarlem. Some of his data, for example a description of *langbetten* and dolmens on Fehmarn, are important for the research in Holstein. An abstract, in German, of Wedel's study is given in Appendix 2A.

273 Bakker 1978; the correct date of the trips through Drenthe (in 1811) and Germany (in 1813) are in Bakker 2004, 130-1; Bakker, in prep. and Arentzen 2010.

Figure 32a. 'Tombe des Huns (Hunebed) duquel on en voit en Drenthe'; on a loose bit of paper is added, in primitive handwriting, 'Een Hunnenbed in Drenthe (1817)'. Artist unknown (photograph Drents Museum, Assen, E32, No. 14, negative 199907). This pencil drawing is incompletely retraced in ink, cf. Figure 32b.

Figure 32b. The drawing of Figure 32a in which all pencil lines have now been retraced in ink. This large hunebed, which probably had 7-10 capstones. is not yet identified.

hunebeds or artefacts.[274] His 'mental image' of the hunebeds and their contents were mainly based on the descriptions by Picardt and Van Lier and he was not a keen observer himself. He did not even recognise entrances on the south side of the tombs, although Petrus Camper (1768-1769, 1781) had recorded them from the hunebeds D8-Anloo, D13-Eext and O1-Eese (Figures 23, 20, 27) and Engelberts (1790, 181) also had recorded the southern entrance of D8-Anloo.[275] In Westendorp's opinion, a genuine hunebed did not have a covering barrow; those which did were transitional to the later earthen tumuli. The artefacts recovered by Van Lier in hunebed D13-Eext were similar to those in other megalithic tombs and were ascribed to a Stone Age*, which preceded a Metal Age*. At Westendorp's request, the Governor of Drenthe ordered all mayors in the province to answer a questionnaire about the hunebeds, barrows, mottes and Celtic fields in their municipalities, in 1818-9.[276] The information collected about the hunebeds was incorporated in Westendorp's second edition (1822).

Westendorp regarded all free-standing megalithic burial chambers from Iberia to Scandinavia as 'hunebedden' and dated them all to the Stone Age* on the basis of the artefacts within them. His detailed description of their locations allowed me to make a distribution map (Figure 36). He described a line drawn from Swedish Lapland to Nystadt [Uusikaupunki] in Finland, past the mouth of the Oder, Bohemia, Bavaria and Savoy to the Rhone Delta, east of which no hunebeds occurred.[277] 'Hunebeds' occurred in Ireland and Scotland, except the Orkneys, and parts of France and the Iberian Peninsula. The Dutch hunebeds were part of a subgroup clustered north of a line drawn from Kampen in The Netherlands to Wesel, Kassel, Dessau, Berlin and the mouth of the Oder in Germany.

---

274 Westendorp's personal papers seem to have been lost and no portrait of him is known. A photograph of his tombstone in the Losdorp churchyard is in Van der Sanden (2007, 64).

275 Engelberts may have known Camper's drawing from Gallitzin (1789). Westendorp knew this publication also, and, moreover, copied P. Camper's original drawings in A.G. Camper's house in Klein Lankum near Franeker, most of which had been published earlier by Gallitzin (1789). The Society considered Westendorp's clumsy copies unsuitable. Instead it published J. Hofstede's report, re-edited by P. Hofstede, who was one of the 'directors' of the Hollandsche Maatschappij der Wetenschappen, about the investigation of hunebed D41-Emmen, with its drawings by P.A.C. Buwama Aardenburg (see section '1809').

276 This is the first known survey (enquête) of archaeological phenomena in The Netherlands. In Britain, Scandinavia and France such surveys began in the 17th and 18th centuries. Although Westendorp (1822) made a few mistakes when he combined his own hunebed descriptions with those from the survey, I do not agree with Van Giffen's statement (1943a, 103n) that the 1815 edition is 'much better' than the 1822 edition (although '1815' is topographically more accurate). But the not abbreviated and updated edition of 1822 is otherwise much more informative. Westendorp appears to have been adding fresh details until the book was printed.

277 Alexandre Bertrand drew a comparable line between Arles-Lyon-Troyes-Châlons-Brussels-Cologne-Magdeburg on his map in Revue archéologique 1864, in part following the Rhone, to the east of which supposedly no megalithic graves were found (Daniel 1960, fig. 3, p. 20-1). Bertrand's line lay slightly more to the west in France than Westendorp's line (Figure 36). Actually, there are also megalithic tombs to the east of the Rhône in France (Daniel 1960, figs. 4-5, viz. distribution maps of A. de Mortillet 1901 and Arnal and Burnez 1957).

VERHANDELING

TER BEANTWOORDING DER

VRAGE:

WELKE VOLKEREN HEBBEN DE ZOOGENOEMDE HUNEBEDDEN GESTICHT? IN WELKE TIJDEN KAN MEN ONDERSTELLEN, DAT ZIJ DEZE OORDEN HEBBEN BEWOOND?

DOOR

NICOLAUS WESTENDORP,

Predikant bij de Hervormde Gemeente te Losdorp, en Lid der Commisfie van Onderwijs in de Provincie Groningen,

aan wien, door de algemeene jaarlijksche Vergadering van de Hollandsche Maatschappij der Wetenschappen te Haarlem, op den 20 Mei 1815, de gouden eerprijs benevens eene premie van vijf en twintig gouden dukaten is toegewezen.

TWEEDE DRUK.

TE GRONINGEN, BIJ
J. OOMKENS,
1822.

Figure 33. Title page of Nicolaus Westendorp's 'Treatise' (1822), author's collection.

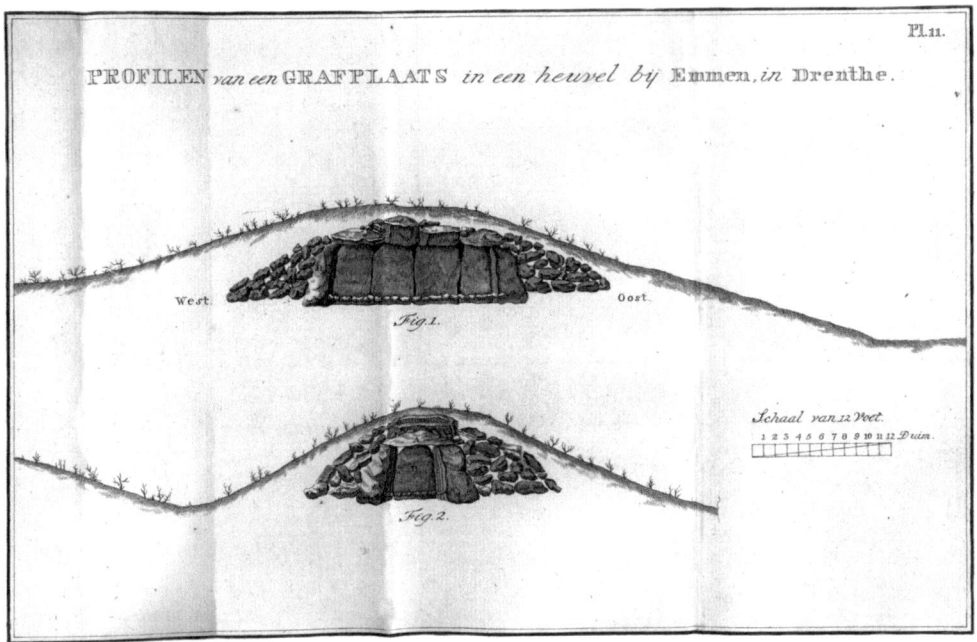

*Figure 34. Sections of hunebed D41-Emmen made three days after its discovery, in 1809
(Westendorp (1815, 1822, pl. II). See further Appendix 3 and Figure 30.*

According to him, all these western European tombs were made by one and
the same people – in contrast to the plural 'peoples' asked for in the Haarlem
competition. He used similarities in the folk tales associated with the 'hunebeds'
throughout western Europe to support this idea. Moreover, his detailed survey of
the world's peoples had shown that each had its own distinctive forms of religion
and religious constructions.[278]

To answer the main question of the competition, he carefully analysed twelve
possible early peoples, including the Huns, Vikings[279] and the Romans, and rejected all but one on the basis of what was known about their artefacts. That the
hunebeds were built by an unknown people was unthinkable, because that 'would
leave the first History of our Fatherland as dark and uncertain [as before], or as a

---

278 See Westendorp's manuscript of 1812. Although such a survey had been asked for by the Society,
    at the advice of the committee this section was omitted in the 1815 edition. The 1822 edition
    contains a much reduced version of it (p. 4).

279 J. de Rhoer (1770) had argued that the Vikings were the builders of the hunebeds. He was fol-
    lowed by J. Tonkens (1795). Given the geographic distribution of megalithic graves in western
    Europe and that their pre-Roman* age was not recognised, this was a reasonable proposition
    under the assumption that all were built by one and the same people. On June 12, 1812, De
    Rhoer suggested this answer in conversation to Westendorp, who pointed out that the objects
    found in the hunebeds were much older than the Viking age (Westendorp 1812, in an abbrevi-
    ated form also in 1815, 299 and 1822, 124-5). G.W.U. Wedel (1812, see Appendix 2A) and
    L.O. Gratama (1884a, 1886) also assigned the hunebeds to the Vikings. The historian J.W. te

hodgepodge of fabricated fables!' (1822, 158). The only known people Westendorp could not reject were the (early) Celts, who according to some older classical sources had also lived in Scandinavia and northern Germany (Cimbri).[280]

De Rhoer[281] had ascribed the hunebeds to the Vikings (1770), which, given the geographic distribution of megalithic graves in western Europe, was a reasonable proposition under the assumption that all were built by one and the same people and as long as their pre-Roman* age was not recognised. This ascription was adopted by several authors between 1770 and 1886,[282] but Westendorp objected to this, maintaining that the hunebeds dated from the Stone Age*.

Westendorp had made an exciting discovery about the absolute age of these Celtic hunebed builders in the *Mémoires de l'Académie Celtique*, vols I and II (1807-8 #), in which Strabo's description of stone altars at Cape St Vincent in southwestern Portugal, in book III of his *Geography*, was discussed.[283] According to Strabo, Artemidorus (1st century BC), rejected Ephorus's mention of a sanctuary for Hercules on the Cape, stating that there was no altar dedicated to him nor to other gods there. 'At several places three or four stones have been placed together; these stones are turned and rearranged by visitors who have come to offer a drink to the gods, following some old traditional custom. Sacrifices are not allowed there, nor is it permitted to visit the place at night – when the gods are there, they say –, but the visitors spend the night in a nearby village and return by daylight, bringing water, which is absent at the spot.' Westendorp argued that these stones were hunebeds and that the idea that the stones were turned overnight was based on a poorly understood, but still extant legend about certain men-

---

Water [1740-1822] wrote in 1815 that he had adhered to the Viking thesis until he had read Westendorp's (1815) study (letter of March 17, 1815 to the Hollandsche Maatschappij der Wetenschappen, files on the hunebedden prize contest in Archives HMW in Noord-Holland Archives, in Haarlem). J. Fergusson (1872, see section '1886-1911') had a similar idea. Megalith specialists in Leiden and abroad did not take the theories of Gratama and Fergusson seriously. In Drenthe, H. Hartogh Heijs van Zouteveen (1886) rejected Gratama's theory.

280   This supposition was not as strange as it may seem now, because early authors, such as Artemidorus and Plutarch, had called the Cimmerians or Cimbri Celts. This idea was generally rejected during the 19th century. It still is, although recently Gerhart Herm (1975), an author who certainly does not refrain from fantastic theories, using the same sources as Westendorp, drew similar, but more extreme conclusions:

> 'the Teutones and Cimbri were Germani, the Germani, however, were not only an element of the large Celtic complex of peoples, as opposed to the Scythian peoples, but even the original core of it. They were the most 'Celtic' of all Celts ...' (1992 edition, 89).

For the geographical extent of the Celtic language and culture, see, e.g. Haywood (2001) and Cunliffe (1999), who disagree with Herm, as do most other specialists.

281   About De Rhoer, see below.
282   About Viking megalith builders, see notes 219, 272, 279.
283   Westendorp 1822, 197-201; STRABO, *Geography* III: 4 (ed. S. Radt, *Strabons Geographika*. Göttingen: Vandenhoeck & Ruprecht, vol. 1, 338-9). I thank professor Stefan Radt, Onnen, for his help and advice.

Pl.1.

Figure 35. Hunebed D6-Tynaarlo as illustrated by Westendorp (1815, pl. I; 1822, pl. I). Print by C.C. Fuchs, draughtsman unknown.

hirs in France.[284] He supposed that Ephorus was referring to these stones when he spoke of a Hercules sanctuary and that they were already extremely old because their original purpose was forgotten when Ephorus wrote about them, before 338 BC.[285]

Because Herodotus recorded hat the Cimmerians / Cimbri, supposed builders of the hunebeds in Jutland and Schleswig-Holstein, were chased away from the Black Sea area by the Scythians around 1500 BC (Herodotus I, cap. 14-5; IV, cap. 11-2),[286] Westendorp reasoned that they should have arrived much earlier in

284 Legends of a *Pierre-qui-tourne* ('Rock that turns'), as Westendorp noted, are about menhirs (not dolmens) in France. Northernmost are two *Pierre-qui-tourne*s in the Belgian provinces of Hainaut and Namur (Mariën 1952, 164; figs. 142-3). 'Three to four stones' in Artemidorus / Ephorus suggests dolmens instead of menhirs, however. That visitors were able to move them is very unlikely, and the present legends tell us that this moving of menhirs happened overnight by supernatural action. Cape St Vincent, the southwesternmost point of Europe (Strabo's Holy Promontory) and the Sierra de Monchique from which it projects, are rich in 'menhirs or cromlechs' and megalithic graves (maps: Kalb 1980, fig. 1; Vortisch 1999, fig. 1).

285 Westendorp dated Ephorus's death to 338 BC. Actually, Ephorus wrote between 330 and 320 BC.

286 The chasing of the Cimmerians from the Black Sea coast actually took place in the 8th century BC (Herodotus, translation by O. Damsté, 3rd edition 1974, 541).

Europe as nomads from Asia, possibly 'a few thousand years after the Flood?' The hunebeds, which were built 'before the first historiography', were certainly not antediluvian (Westendorp 1822, 310).[287]

Westendorp's thoughts concerning the stage of civilisation of the hunebed builders are intriguing:

> *'They still only knew stone weapons such as those now used in Peru, the Pacific area and North America, and had no metals yet (all peoples began at this stage). Their pottery-making was considerably advanced. They hunted and fished, but did not yet farm. They were at no higher stage of civilisation than the Hottentots, but they had a more complex social organisation and religion. Without the well-established authority of chiefs and priests, such as existed on Otaheite [Tahiti], the building of the hunebeds would have been impossible. Their way of life was surely not as nomadic as that of many a North American tribe today. Some trade with other tribes must have taken place, since the materials for some of the battle-axes could only have come from distant regions.'* [288]

The second, enlarged edition of Westendorp's study (1822) was very positively reviewed at length by Wilhelm K. Grimm (1824), writing anonymously, in the *Göttingsche gelehrte Anzeigen*.[289] Christian Jürgensen Thomsen [1788-1865], who was developing his Three Age system as director of the Museum for the Nordic Antiquities in Copenhagen,[290] read this review and immediately wrote to the leading German archaeologist, Johann Gustav Gottlieb Büsching [1783-1829] in Breslau, in 1825, to whom he just had explained his views on relative chronology, expressing his hope 'that you will not take me for a plagiarist', because several of his opinions appeared also in Westendorp's book (Seger 1930). Grimm was convinced that ancient Germani, not Celts, had built the hunebeds and protested Westendorp's comparison of them with nomads such as the Hottentots [Khoikhoi] and the wild American tribes:

> *'... these large megaliths, built with great difficulty in honour of a revered deceased, display a totally different sense of history, which is typical only of peoples of a higher education. Just as they thought to keep the memory of their heroes, leaders or priests for posterity, they honoured the past in monuments and preserved it in*

---

287 Westendorp was more careful in his age estimation than I suggested earlier (Bakker 1979a, 20).

288 Compiled from a number of places in Westendorp 1815 (286-90) and 1822 (99-104, 192-3, 310). The passage about Otaheite was omitted in 1822. The three examples, Hottentots, American Indians and South Sea Islanders, had previously appeared in: *Of the origin and progress of man and languages*. Edinburgh: J. Balfour; T. Cadell, 6 vols., 1773-92, anonymously published by Lord Monboddo (J. Burnett) #, as examples of the 'third stage of development of Man' (pers. comm. W. Arentzen; Piggott 1976, 151-9); Westendorp did not cite this work.

289 That W.K Grimm wrote this review is shown by a manuscript register of all reviewers in the *Anzeigen*, vols. 1819-1830 (Göttingen University Library, Ac. 20; Bakker 1979a, n. 2: 16). Westendorp sent his book to Grimm on July 25, 1822, and asked him to review it (letter in Staatsbibliothek Berlin). The Berlin Staatsbibliothek has the 1815 and 1822 editions, the BVB Bayern library has the 1822 edition (pers. comm. W. Arentzen).

290 This became the National Museum of Antiquities in Copenhagen, in 1892. Grimm's 1824 review was analysed by Arentzen (2009, 211-4).

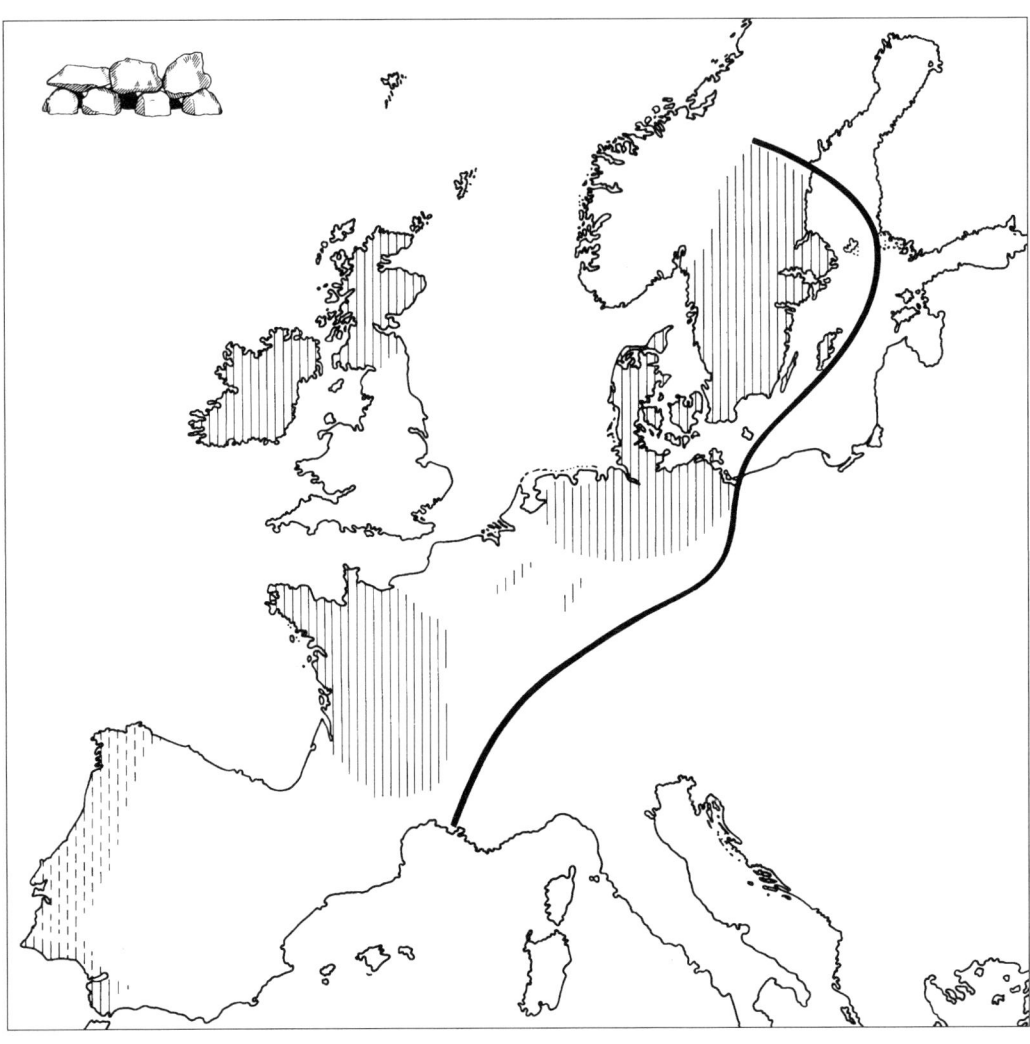

Figure 36. The distribution of 'the hunebedden' in western Europe as described, but not illustrated by Westendorp (1815, 1822), designed by Bakker (1979a, fig. 9). Westendorp thought that 'hunebedden' were absent to the east of the thick line.

legends and songs. What conclusion could be more natural than that the people who made the hunebeds had just as high a mental development as the people whose deeds are celebrated by Ossian[291] and whose monuments and graves equalled theirs in crude simplicity, according to his description.' (Grimm 1824, 697).

Although Westendorp knew the theory of a succession of Stone, Bronze and Iron Ages from Lucretius (as shown by his additions to the 1812 manuscript, made in early 1813), the distinction between the latter two ages was irrelevant for his theme, and, like Van Lier (1760), he argued (1815; 1822) for a Two Age System* consisting of a Stone Age* and a Metal Age* (Arentzen 2006; 2007; 2009a).

Thomsen (1836), on the other hand, adopted the 'Three Age system', Stone*, Bronze* and Iron Age*, and used it to chronologically order the artefacts of the Copenhagen museum. His letter of July 16, 1818, to a Swedish colleague already described an embryonic Three Age system (Klindt-Jensen 1975, 50). Excavations by J.J.A. Worsaae and others would soon demonstrate the reality of this system (Heizer 1962b).

Arentzen (2007, 9-13; 2009a, 214-7) noted that Thomsen's first letter to Büsching (February 19, 1825, quoted by Seger 1930) did not comment on the existence of a Stone Age; only his second letter (March 1, 1825) discussed Westendorp's Stone Age*. Thus, Arentzen remarks, Van Lier (1760), followed by Westendorp (1812; 1815; 1822), was earlier than Thomsen to write about a Stone Age* preceding a Metal Age, based on the context of the artefacts. The artefacts that Van Lier recovered from hunebed D13-Eext and those from the *allée couverte* at Cocherel (see section '1685: Cocherel') had proved the reality of a Stone Age* long before Thomsen's scheme. But Thomsen did not read Dutch.[292]

In addition to the succession of materials of weapons and tools, Thomsen's 1818-1836 chronology used an extensive number of other cultural features (although his absolute age estimates were much too short). One may add that the division of a Metal Age* into a Bronze Age* and an Iron Age*, and their later subdi-

---

291 At the time the *Songs of Ossian* # were still often considered to be authentic (also by Grimm and Westendorp). But actually they were composed, in 1760-5, by James Macpherson [1736-1796], who had exalted ideas about intellectual life in Scotland and Ireland during the 3rd century AD. For a small part, the *Songs* may have been inspired by Scottish folk-songs, but Macpherson added much of own invention. *Ossian* was translated in almost all European languages and greatly inspired Romanticism throughout Europe (it was admired, e.g., by Walter Scott, Goethe, Herder, Bilderdijk, Napoleon and Ingres). The controversy about the authenticity of Macpherson's 'translation's', 'fabrications' or 'forgeries', and his sources continued until the mid-19th century. Samuel Johnson [1709-1784] doubted the authenticity as early as 1762, because the *Songs* appeared not to be familiar to whoever he asked, in Scotland.

292 I bought my own copy of Westendorp (1822) in Lynge's Antikvariat in the Fiolstraede in Copenhagen in 1971. It carries two oval and crowned stamps of ANT.TOPOGR.ARCHIV, which cross each other, meaning: 'removed' and the pages were cut up to page 97, suggesting that Thomsen tried in vain to read this wordy Dutch book, see Figure 33. There were no notes in it. It was for sale together with a great number of reprints from the National Museum (esp. from Hans Kjaer [1873-1932]) and an invitation to J.A.A. Worsaae [1821-1885] to become a member of the Wiltshire Field Club, which I did not buy.

visions, was more natural in countries rich in metal artefacts, such as Scandinavia, than in The Netherlands, where prehistoric metal artefacts are extremely rare (the metal artefacts reported by Van Lier 1760 are rather exceptional).

The speculations of Westendorp and Grimm about the economic stage of development of the hunebed people are remarkable since relatively little was known about them at the time. Westendorp removed the reference to the Kingdom of Tahiti in his 1822 edition, probably considering them too highly developed in comparison to the supposedly nomadic hunebed people. Grimm rejected the idea that the hunebed people were nomadic, because he could not imagine how megalithic tombs could be built without priests and a hierarchical social structure and because the *Songs of Ossian* – which seemed to refer to the hunebed people – attributed a more developed civilization to them.[293] The problem was, of course, that no evidence for dwellings, agriculture or for the raising of domestic animals by the hunebed people had yet been found.

In 1825, Thomsen considered the absolute age estimated by Westendorp much too early. He was opposed to Westendorp's appraisal, who quoted Count Münster from Westphalia, that the pottery from the hunebeds was of much higher quality than later prehistoric* ceramics (Westendorp 1822, Aanteekeningen p. 23, sub a; cf. Bakker 1979a, 20-1), that the pottery from the hunebeds was of high quality in comparison with later pottery. Westendorp and Münster were carried away by the elegant decoration of the pottery and thought that it had been made in moulds and fired as hard as modern table ware. Thomsen, on the other hand, thought that all [prehistoric*] pots were 'coarse', although those from the hunebeds were 'admittedly, sometimes decorated with strokes and provided with rims' (Bakker 1979a, 23).

Although inconsistencies are not difficult to find, Westendorp's compilation of available sources, is impressive, given the early stage of research. His identification of the Celts as hunebed builders was given full credence in the *Handbuch der germanischen Altertumskunde* (1836) by Gustav Friedrich Klemm [1802-1867] – 'a first-rate work for its time', according to Gummel (1938, 430).

Other critics pointed out several inconsistencies in Westendorp's *magnum opus*. Applying his 'Celtomania' to the TRB* area was soon generally repudiated. Westendorp's critics asked why no hunebeds were found in the large area formerly occupied by Celts in central and southeastern Europe and Anatolia to the east of the thick line drawn in Figure 36. Several members of the committee who reviewed Westendorp's manuscript texts, in 1813 and 1815, and Caspar Jacob Christian Reuvens [1793-1835], in an unpublished review of the 1822 edition, asked whether it would not have been wiser to conclude that the hunebed builders could not be identified with any of the peoples known from historical sources.[294] Reuvens's review contained much criticism about details, which was based

---

293 See the preceding note.
294 Reviews of the contest committee of the Hollandsche Maatschappij der Wetenschappen in Noord-Holland Archives, Haarlem. Reuvens's review in Pleyte archives CI 24-5, Leiden Museum; cf. Bakker 1979a, 163.

on careful reading of the classical literature, and it casted doubt on almost all of Westendorp's conclusions. It was written in the years after 1822 (after 1824?) and carries the final note 'not to be published without further revision, June 1832' (p. CI 24; Arentzen 2009a, 218-28). Reuvens was not, like Westendorp, a follower of Van Lier's idea that a Stone Age* preceded a Metal Age*, which started before the arrival of the Romans; actually, as a classicist, he remained very doubtful about the slowly developing *prehistoric* chronology.[295] Reuvens asked, for instance, whether the increasing number of 'hunebeds' in The Netherlands and abroad in which Roman coins were found might not indicate that the latest hunebeds were made in the Roman period.

Westendorp's interest in antiquities in general had been awakened by the lectures in national history and Roman and national antiquities given by professor Jacobus de Rhoer [1722-1813], which he heard when he was studying theology at the University of Groningen.[296] Following in De Rhoer's footsteps, he published, in 1809, a thorough geographical and historical study of Sebaldeburen, his first parish, but seems not to have been actively interested in prehistory before setting himself to write his treatise on the hunebeds. Between 1819 and 1826, he published *Antiquiteiten, een oudheidkundig tijdschrift* ('Antiquities, an antiquarian periodical'), the first of its kind in The Netherlands, which he published together

295 I agree here W. Arentzen (pers. comm.), *vs.* Brunsting (1947), who concluded the opposite.
296 The talented De Rhoer, whose interests were many, lectured on these subjects between 1779 and 1804. On June 17, 1769, he had had his student J. Roldanus in Groningen defend the thesis: "Moles illae sepulchrae in vicina Drentia etc., quae *Hunnebedden* vulgo vocant, neque opus Gigantum censeri debent, neque Silices Mercuriales, neque fuerunt arae, idolorum sacrificiis excitatae" (*Observ. philolog. auct. et praes. J. de Rhoer defens.*, Gron. 1790, p. 48) (see Ali Cohen 1844, 300, n. 5; cf. Van Deursen 1970, 38; Arentzen 2009, 18). Westendorp (1815, 280; 1822, 88), who began his study at Groningen University in September 1789, called him *myn Leermeester* ('my most important teacher'). After Westendorp was shown a beautiful stone battle-axe by De Rhoer in one of these lectures, he 'never forgot antiquities.' He wrote in 1812 that he had seen this artefact more than 18 years earlier (viz. as a student). De Rhoer wrote an historical description of Westerwoldingerland (east Groningen) and several other studies and text editions concerning the history and historical geography of Groningen #. A large manuscript on the geography and history of Drenthe (1774-1790), located in the Drenthe Archives remained unpublished (coll. Gratama 233, see Van Deursen 1970, 105; Nijkeuter 2001, 24); an 'archaeological' abstract from it by Mr. Saïd Mooijman was sent to me by W.A.B. van der Sanden and W. Arentzen. Its passages on the hunebeds D13-Eext and D14-Eexterhalte and on artefacts from low barrows near Gasteren, p. 253-5, are apparently copied from Van Lier (1760, 6-7; 186-8, pl. V 3-5) and the manuscript apparently offers nothing new on prehistory. A reference on p. 255 to *'groote steenen, die des Duivels Cutz genoemd worden'* (large stones called Duvels Cutz; see section '1547'), which were located on the Groningen (viz. northern) side of Gasteren, identifies them with hunebed D10-Gasteren. The location is probably based on Hopper's map (Figure 4) or later maps until 1633.

with Reuvens, who was mentioned before, from 1823 onwards.[297] Hunebeds were not discussed in *Antiquiteiten*. Westendorp's interest moved also to comparing the temples of different religions, mythology, folk tales, folklore, regional history, comparative linguistics and palaeogeography.[298]

Unfortunately, Westendorp's incorrect statement (1815, 1822) that genuine hunebeds had never had a barrow would result in the removal of hunebed barrow remains when restorations were undertaken, about 1870, in Drenthe.

1841: Magnin's attempt to give legal protection to the Drenthe hunebeds and barrows

In 1841, the distribution of the common heath lands to individual inhabitants (*Markenverdeeling*) was expected to take place soon and the hunebeds were in danger of passing into private hands. Johan Samuel Magnin [1796-1888], Province Archivist of Drenthe, petitioned King William II, in November 1841, to proclaim that all hunebeds, tumuli and burial chambers be exempt from the royal permission to divide the common grounds (Van der Sanden 2007, 71). 'These antiquities, which provide Drenthe with an inestimable value in the eyes of researchers of archaeology and history ... should be holy, inviolable, if not the property of the whole learned world, but at least of the Dutch people, because they contain the ashes of their forebears or perhaps preceding inhabitants of these regions, which were driven out by them.' If the existing preservation laws were not sufficient to protect these monuments, private owners should be convinced to give or sell them for a trifle to the state. To demarcate the monument, a dry ditch should be dug around each hunebed, tumulus or burial vault, at a minimal distance of 0.5 to 1 m.

This petition, which was published in the *Provinciale Drentsche en Asser Courant* of December 9, 1842, was not successful (Van der Sanden 2007, 71).[299] But Magnin remained alert and acquired four hunebeds for the Province, and a demarcation ditch was dug around each of them (Van der Sanden 2007, 87). In

---

297 Although there are proofs for Vol. III, issue 2 (1826) in the archives of the Leiden Museum, which were never published (Brunsting 1947, 235), it is worth noting that a prospectus of *Antiquiteiten* from February, 1822, stated that the editors were well aware that this periodical 'should not be continued ad infinitum' (reproduction p. 58-9 in Buijtendorp 2007).

Reputedly, Caspar Jacob Christiaan Reuvens [1793-1835], was the world's first professor in General Archaeology (including Prehistory), at Leiden University, and founder of modern archaeology in The Netherlands. He was founder and first director of the Leiden Museum of Antiquities. Reuvens excavated in Forum Hadriani, a Roman town at Voorburg near The Hague, and excavated prehistoric barrows in a modern, analytical way (Brunsting 1947). This was not continued by his successor Janssen, who excavated little, nor by Janssen's successor Pleyte, who excavated even less. Reuvens did not excavate hunebeds or study their architecture, but he mapped their locations in parts of Drenthe and sketched D27-Borger (see Brunsting 1947; Brongers 1973; 2002; Cordfunke et al. 2007).

298 See Arentzen 2009a about Westendorp's earlier and later studies.

299 A formal answer from the King and government to this petition has not yet been found. The positions taken by Magnin's superiors in Assen and the officials in Leiden and The Hague deserve further study.

1844, the physician Levy Ali Cohen [1818-1889] stressed the necessity of taking measures to protect the hunebeds in a popular article that included a lithograph of six hunebeds (Van der Sanden 2007, ill. p. 75), which was mainly about the geological origin of the hunebed boulders (1844), but again without much success.

1841 and 1849: Arend and Stratingh

In the 1840s, two popularizing history books dealt with the hunebeds and their builders. Dr. Johannes Pieter Arend [1796-1855], from the west of the country, wrote *Algemeene Geschiedenis des Vaderlands* ('General History of the Fatherland'). This work of, ultimately, fourteen volumes (1841-1879, the last volumes were written by others) was richly illustrated with pictures of historical moments, maps and portraits. The Celts were cited as the earliest inhabitants and their way of life was described at length, mainly from classical sources. 'The crude objects, which were found in the hunebeds', showed that the Celts north of the Rhine were 'still in a stage of childlike simplicity'.[300] For his description of the hunebeds (1841, 26-9), Arend leaned heavily on Westendorp (1822) and Engelberts (1790), but he suggested that the hunebed builders were no less than 6-7 feet tall (1.9-2.2 m)! (Arentzen 2009a, 231-2).

The Groningen physician and historian Dr. Gozewinus Acker Stratingh [1804-1876] devoted nearly one hundred pages to the hunebeds and their builders (1849, 1-96) in his three-volume study of the ancient geography and inhabitants of The Netherlands (1847, 1849, 1852). Stratingh summarised the available Dutch literature much more thoroughly than Arend and noted that Ossian's works were not original. He assigned the hunebeds to ancient, *nameless* predecessors of the Celts and Germani (Arentzen 2009a, 236-8; Arentzen 2010). After forty years of attempts to identify the ethnicity of the hunebed builders, still general practice in contemporary Germany and Denmark, this was an original and modern idea![301]

Neither of the two books have illustrations of hunebeds and both are now obsolete and not worth reading for information about them.

1840-1868: Janssen

After completing his study in theology and a short, unsuccessful career as a clergyman and teacher of classical languages, Leonhardt Johannes Friedrich Janssen [1806-1869] (Figure 37) became Second Curator, later First Curator of the collection of Dutch antiquities in the Leiden Museum, in 1835. His first field re-

---

300 Arend 1841, 26: '*De vroegste bewoners onzer gewesten althans, zullen slechts die weinige kunsten gekend hebben welke de dringendste behoefte leert uitvinden en beoefenen, gelijk de kunstlooze voorwerpen getuigen, welke in de zoogenaamde* Hunebedden van Drenthe, *de onmiskenbare sporen van hun verblijf in* Nederland, *gevonden zijn, en die een volk aanduiden, dat nog in den eersten kindschen staat van wetenschappelijke ontwikkeling verkeerde.*'
301 Stratingh could not have known that C.J.C. Reuvens had suggested, in an unpublished review from ca.1822-24 of Westendorp's book (1822), that it would have been wiser to conclude that the name of the people of the hunebed builders could not be found in the sources (see section '1811-1822').

search was devoted to archaeological remains of southeastern Gelderland, where he was born, and the region of Gocherheide in Germany, where he had often stayed with his grandfather in Pfalzdorf and where he undertook his first excavations.[302] In 1840, he published a catalogue of the prehistoric antiquities in the Leiden Museum, '*Germaansche en Noordsche Monumenten in het Museum te Leyden*' (Germanic and Nordic Monuments in the Museum at Leiden, Janssen 1840), which included plates showing samples of decoration and types of forms for reference (Figure 38). This cheap, inventive way of illustrating types makes it very difficult for a reader to visualise them and, fortunately, was not taken up by later Dutch publications.

It took some time before Janssen became actively interested in the hunebeds in far-away Drenthe. In 1843, he commissioned a model of hunebed D6-Tynaarlo for his museum. This hunebed was the only one in Drenthe with all orthostats and capstones still in place, and, for that reason, it was often used for illustration in the 18th and 19th centuries (cf. Figures 28, 35, and 55). He asked Willem Jan Hendrik baron van Westreenen van Tiellandt [1783-1848],[303] Lodewijk Napoleon graaf van Randwijck [1807-1891], Governor of Drenthe, and professor Theodorus van Swinderen [1784-1751], who was the director of the Museum of Natural History of Groningen University, for their help. Van Swinderen sent his laboratory assistant (*amanuensis*), J.O. Karsten, to the hunebed to make a 1:100 scale clay model on the spot (Figure 39).[304] Karsten took also small samples of the stone from the eleven heavy boulders of the tomb, which were sent to the Leiden Muscum with a list of the types of granite that were concerned.[305] He made three other models for 20 guilders each, paid for by the Province of Drenthe, which were sent to Van Westreenen's private museum, the Leiden Museum and the residence of the Drenthe government in Assen.[306] The original model remained in the Germanic Antiquities (*Germaansche Oudheden*) section in the Groningen Museum for Natural History. In November, 1843, L. Ali Cohen used the newly made Groningen model in a lecture to the Genootschap ter Bevordering der Natuur Wetenschappen ('Society for the Advancement of Natural Sciences') in

302 See Arentzen (2005) and note 226 about L.J.F. Janssen's grandfather and the reclamation of the Gocherheide near Pfalzdorf, as described by J. van Lier et al. (1792).

303 Van Westreenen van Tiellandt is also mentioned at the end of section '1756-1760'. He was a member of the *Raad van State* (State Council) and had a small private archaeological museum of his own in The Hague (the present-day Museum Meermanno-Westreenianum). He travelled through Drenthe in 1842, and described and drew D6-Tynaarlo in his diary, on September 23, 1842 (Museum Meermanno-Westreenianum 78/11 and 78/21; pers. comm. W. Arentzen).

304 In a letter, dated July 12, 1843, Van Swinderen informed Janssen what his laboratory aide would do and that it would cost 100 guilders (Arentzen 2006, 79).

305 Karsten's plan indicating the location of the eight supporting stones and the three capstones of D6 from which the samples were taken, along with a description of the type of granite of each (related by Arentzen 2006, 80-1), is in the Leiden Museum in duplicate (one is a copy by Janssen: Pleyte archives C52-6). Karsten's plan was reproduced by D. Lubach (1873, 9-11; 1877, 162-4), cf. Van Giffen (1925, 24, n. 1).

306 Arentzen (2006, 76-84) made a thorough study of the available documentation about these four hunebed models. For an earlier, much less complete discussion of the model in The Hague, see Bakker 2004, 167.

Figure 37. Leonhardt Johannes Friedrich Janssen [1806-1869] (photograph National Museum of Antiquities at Leiden. Courtesy W. Arentzen).

Groningen (Ali Cohen 1844, 356). He described D6-Tynaarlo in detail [based on Karsten's notes] and said that most stones of the hunebed were 'covered by yellow and green moss, through which the colour of the stones can be seen at places'. Presently, most lichens and algae on the hunebed are gone.

The original model (Figure 39) is now kept in the Groningen Museum.[307] It is mounted on a 40 x 80 cm plank and appears quite realistic, with the small natural hollows in some of the capstones. Capstone D3 is now lost. The stones are formed out of dried clay and painted grey. The top of capstone D2 sticks 13 cm out above the clay covered surface of the plank. The plank and three transverse laths for re-

307 Dr. Egge Knol, museum curator, showed the model to Wout Arentzen and me on January 21, 2009. It was the first item concerning hunebeds or TRB in the Museum of Natural History.

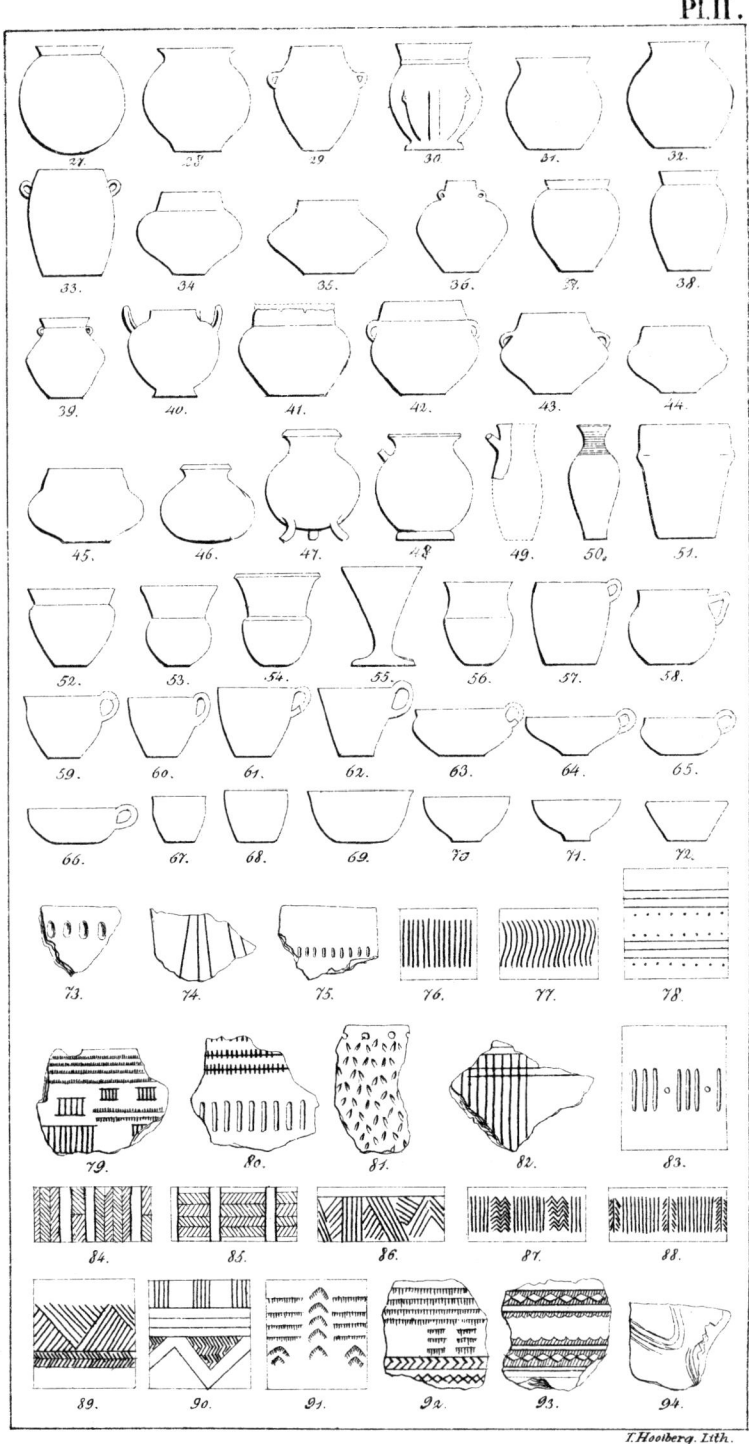

Figure 38. Types of decorations and forms of prehistoric pottery in the Leiden Museum (Janssen 1840, photograph Wout Arentzen).

Figure 39. The 1843 Groningen model of hunebed D6-Tynaarlo (photograph Marten de Leeuw, Groninger Museum). One capstone is now lost.

inforcement, all 2 cm thick, were taken from a packing-case. Its under side shows two addresses, one scratched out and illegible, one '*Keep dry / Rev. J. Bachma*[...] */ Charleston / S. C.* [= South Carolina]'.[308]

Janssen (1848, table of hunebeds) and Pleyte (1877-1902: Drente 1880-1882, 57) explicitly mentioned the four models. Only the models in Groningen and in the Museum Meermanno-Westreenianum in The Hague are still in existence. The very heavy and ugly model in The Hague, on a similar scale, is made of erratic cobbles from the neighbourhood of the hunebed.[309]

From 1846 onwards, Janssen tried to fill in the picture of the hunebed build-ers, which Van Lier and Westendorp had denoted '*our most early ancestors*'.[310] He disagreed with Westendorp that the hunebeds were built by the earliest Celts and

---

308　The Lutheran Rev. John Bachman [1790-1874] was a famous naturalist and social reformer, who argued that blacks and whites are the same species (although the former degenerated later), and in whose honour Bachman's Sparrow and Bachman's Warbler were named (*Wikipedia*). Nothing is known about contacts between Van Swinderen and Bachman nor how the packing case came to Groningen, in or before 1843. Probably Bachman had sent stuffed animals to Van Swinderen's Museum of Natural History, which had a famous collection of them, including two giraffes pictured in the small painting of the interior by Franciscus Hermanus Bachg [1865-1936], now in the Groningen University Museum. The Museum of Natural History burnt down in 1906.

309　Both remaining models are illustrated by Arentzen 2006, 81, 83. Gratama's (1868) record that the model in the Assen Province House, which is now lost, was made of wax, is dubious. The Leiden model, now lost, was also made of granite cobbles. According to a visitor of the museum, '[the model on a small table had] no similarity to the original hunebed, except for the number of stones' (letter with illegible signature 'P.C. ...' , dated November 4, 1859, to Janssen in Arentzen 2006, 81-2). In one of the first Baedeker travel guides, Karl Baedeker (1873, 240) mentioned Karsten's model in the Leiden Museum: 'Dritter Stock. Korknachbildungen antiker Bauwerke; Modelle von Pfahlbauten im Zürcher See; Modell eines Hünengrabes in der Provinz Drenthe ...; germ. Alterthümer aus denselben, germ. Götzen, u.s.w.' [the 'Germanic Idols' are intrigu-ing! – B.]. W. Pleyte (1877-1902: Drente, 1880-82, 57) mentioned the model also. After J.H. Holwerda's reorganisation of the sections Prehistory and Dutch Antiquities in the museum, in 1905-1908, this model is not mentioned again (A.E.J. Holwerda 1906; J.H. Holwerda et al. 1908; J.H. Holwerda 1913c). The stone samples taken by Karsten from the D6-Tynaarlo in the Leiden Museum were also thrown out.

310　See also Arentzen 2006 about Janssen and the hunebeds.

thought instead that they were built by the earliest Germani.[311] He excavated
D31a-Exloo and D44a-Zaalhof, in 1846, and studied the hunebeds and other visible archaeological phenomena in Drenthe more extensively in 1847. During five
weeks,[312] he sketched views of the hunebeds he knew, drew schematic plans and
made a list of them (Janssen 1848, table of hunebeds (Figure 42), and Figures 40-
41).[313] He recognised that the entrance of the hunebeds was in the middle of the
southern or eastern long side. Janssen was no doubt stimulated to write his 1848
synopsis by Georg Otto Carl Freiherr von Estorff's impressive work about the prehistoric tombs near Uelzen in Hanover (1846 #).[314] Von Estorff [1811-1877] had
been chamberlain of the former King William I from 1841 to 1843, had dug in
barrows and surveyed the Hunneschans (a medieval earthwork at Uddelermeer),
in the Royal Domain in the Veluwe, province of Gelderland (Arentzen 2006, 33).
Janssen, who had accompanied him, continued his research, corresponded with
him and called him 'my friend'[315]

Janssen was familiar with publications on megalithic tombs and the Neolithic
by the archaeologists George Christian Friedrich Lisch [1801-1883] in Schwerin,
Christian Jürgensen Thomsen [1788-1865] and Jens Jacob Asmussen Worsaae
[1821-1885] in Copenhagen and Sven Nilsson [1787-1883] in Lund, with
whom he corresponded. But, *pace* Von Estorff and Ludwig Lindenschmit [1809-
1893], founder and director of the Archaeological Museum in Mainz, he rejected Thomsen's Three Age system, ultimately denying the existence of a separate
Bronze Age,[316] and ascribed non-Roman bronzes to the Celts.

---

311 Unlike Westendorp, Janssen did not consider the people who built the Dutch hunebeds to be
identical to the builders of the megalithic tombs in France. Actually, he never discussed French
megaliths, but looked to northern Germany for parallels. According to Cartailhac (1889, 198),
the thesis that all megalithic tombs had been built by one and the same people was generally
rejected in Europe due to the fertile research climate created by the Exposition and the 2nd
session of the Congrès International d'Anthropologie et d'Archéologie Préhistorique of 1867, in
Paris.

312 Janssen's tour through Drenthe lasted from May 23 till June 23, 1847 (Arentzen 2006, 111,
121-2).

313 Janssen's article 'Opmerkingen van een Geldersch reiziger in Drenthe', *Drentsche Volksalmanak*
1848, 1 [#], viz. 'Observations in Drenthe by a Gueldrian traveller', would have had a more
general character.

314 P.B. Richter's analysis (2002, 149ff.) showed the (high) documentary value of Von Estorff's
work.

315 Janssen's renewed proposal of 1860 to have his hunebed drawings of 1847 published by the
Royal Academy of Sciences was accepted, in 1861, at the advice of C. Leemans, L.A.J.W. Sloet
& L.Ph.C. van den Bergh (*Verslagen en Mededeelingen Koninklijke Akademie van Wetenschappen,
Afdeling Letterkunde, 6e deel,* Amsterdam, 1860-64, 137, 173-4, 176-83, 184, 189-98, cf. 201),
but they never reached publication because Leemans objected to a number of points. Janssen's
proposal to have all hunebeds photographed failed as well (*ibid.*), again due to obstruction by his
director.

316 Although Janssen assigned a bronze axe to '*the so-called Bronze Age*', which was later than the
Stone Age and earlier than the Roman Period (1856, 67, pl. X: 1), this happened only once
(Arentzen 2007 and pers. comm.).

Figure 40. Hunebed D15-Loon drawn by L.J.F. Janssen, 1847 (photograph Drents Museum, Assen).

When Janssen stayed in Drenthe in 1847,[317] the Drenthe government would not give him permission to dig in hunebeds, possibly because he was from distant Leiden, and there was a feeling that 'these are our hunebeds' in Drenthe, or maybe because he had not asked permission for his excavations in 1846. That year he had excavated hunebed D44a-Zaalhof, which was very ruined. The Drenthe government was probably not aware that it was a hunebed, even though Reuvens had recognised it as such in 1833 (Reuvens manuscript, ed. Brongers 1973).[318] Picardt (1660, 80) had already noted 'some marked large boulders' (*eenige groote gemerckte Keselingen*), which were the remains of D44a, within the embankments and moats of the Zaalhof, which he considered as remnants of a Frankish palace. One stone was 'marked' by six holes from an unfinished attempt to cleave it with iron wedges. Janssen (1848), who did not know of this technique nor of Reuvens's 1833 description, recognised these round pits as typical features of hunebed stones.[319] He described his findings (1848, 118-20), but did not draw plans, vertical sections or artefacts (cf. Van Giffen 1927, 56-8). The floor of the tomb was covered with small stones, pieces of granite and gravel. It measured 5.5 x 2 m, lay 40 cm below the surface and was oriented NE-SW. Only two orthostats were in place, 3 m from each other in a N-S direction. The original hunebed D44a would have had 4 pairs of sidestones, the most common type of passage grave in Drenthe (cf. Bakker 1992, fig. 9). Janssen noted that, since the hunebed floor continued under the earthen bank of the Zaalhof enclosure, the hunebed was older.

---

317 Apart from hunebeds, he studied many other archaeological features during the month he spent in Drenthe, in 1847 (Janssen 1848).
318 Reuvens copied Petrus Camper's drawings (Figures 20-27) in Adriaan Camper's house, about 1817, and mapped and studied the hunebeds in southeastern Drenthe, in 1833 (Reuvens manuscript, ed. Brongers 1973 and collection Leiden Museum).
319 Arentzen 2006, 128-32.

Figure 41. View of hunebed D17-Rolde in 1847 by L.J.F. Janssen (photograph Drents Museum, Assen).

According to Janssen, the potsherds from this tomb had 'the Germanic character', which was his designation for TRB* pottery. 'Thirteen of these were decorated in different ways.' Janssen did not illustrate them, unfortunately, but referred to nos. 74, 76, 80, 84 and 91 in his previously published chart showing different samples of decoration on prehistoric pottery (Janssen 1840, pl. II, see Figure 38). He noted that some decorations were similar to those illustrated by Georg Christian Friedrich Lisch [1801-1883], which were considered typical for the 'Hunen period or Stone Age' in Mecklenburg, Germany.[320] Some of the pots

---

320 Lisch, *'Jahrbücher des Vereins für Mecklenburgische Geschichte* x, p. 254-5, 256 n. 1, 257 n. 3' (Janssen 1848, 110).

from which the sherds derived appeared to have had the form of nos. 34, 36 and 56 in his chart. One hollow pipe of pottery seemed to be from a small cup like Van Lier had illustrated (1760, pl. III: 6, Figure 19). Presently, it is called a 'biberon' (sucking-cup).

> *'Most of the sherds were from small and rather fine pots and vases [funnel-beakers], rather well finished, coloured light-brown and blackish-brown and similar to the pottery found in Drenthe hunebeds.'* [321]

Flint or stone artefacts were not recorded, but it was 'striking that a small piece of oxidised iron, perhaps from a large knife or a sword, occurred in the stone floor [of D44a], 'which is usually absent from the Hunen Period or Stone Age'. Moreover, 'two pieces of very old and light tuff stone were found next to the 'decorated' stone', 1 m below surface, i.e. 60 cm below the top of the stone floor.[322] Janssen recognised the 'tuff' [tephrite] as coming from Andernach in the German Siebengebirge / Eifel mountains and dated it to the Roman Period, *making this the date when the last hunebeds were built.*[323] But Janssen did not recognise 'recently moved soil', in this case, the darkish top soil, which contrasted with the yellow Neolithic soil and the natural subsoil.

Decorated TRB* pottery from Dutch hunebedden was first illustrated by Van Lier (1760, pl. III: 5, a collared flask, see Figure 19), with a good description (1760, 202) and – hardly recognisable – by Engelberts (1790, see Figure 29: 2). If the reader takes the trouble to look up the decorative patterns and pot forms in Janssen's chart (Figure 38), his description of the TRB sherds from D44a is rather precise. But how many of his readers took the trouble?

---

321 Unfortunately, the site of hunebed D44a-Zaalhof and the surrounding Iron Age embankments of the Zaalhof were built over, in the early 20th century, before any further archaeological investigations were undertaken.

322 The pieces of iron, tuff, flint or other stone, as well as the hollow stem of a ceramic biberon, mentioned by Janssen, are no longer preserved in the Leiden Museum, according to Dr. L.B.M. Verhart, curator, with whom I inspected the artefacts on October 11, 2007. I identified the fragments of about 20 TRB pots, formerly numbered E1-21 in white ink, dating from Brindley 3-5 (the majority are from Brindley 4-5, cf. Brindley 1986b). Several sherds no longer have numbers and numbers E1-E2, E4-E6, E11, E14, E15, E18, and E20 are missing. Some mixing with TRB sherds from other sites had occurred after the 1908 museum catalogue was printed. At least one fragment of a Brindley 7 bowl marked LH.8a comes from hunebed D15-Loon (1871) – actually, Brindley 7 pottery is lacking in D44a. A not very significantly decorated sherd marked WM.49c comes 'from an urn found near a hunebed at Emmen in 1853' (pers. comm. L. Amkreutz, curator, 2008). If 'WM' meant *Wind Molen*, windmill ('near Emmen'), this sherd – together with other objects marked WM.49a-b – may also have come from D44a, which was near a windmill. The sidestone with its five chiselled holes next to hunebed D44-Westenes (Arentzen 2009, 190) is so similar to the sidestone of D44a-Zaalhof drawn by Reuvens (although that one had one hole less), that one is tempted to suppose – incorrectly – that it was actually brought from there to Westenes, some 6 km away. Van Giffen (1925, 113) documented that stone next to D44 in 1918.

323 Bakker 1990b, 76, n. 20. The 'tuff' of querns would now be called 'tephrite' (Kars 1983). Until about 1970, the word tuff was generally used in The Netherlands. Tephrite querns were used in The Netherlands from the Late Bronze Age onwards (Van Heeringen 1989), but not before about 200 BC in Drenthe (J. Beuker, *Werken met steen*. Assen: Drents Museum, 23, 49).

Janssen's text in *Drenthsche Oudheden* ('Drenthe Antiquities', 1848) reviewed and compared the 'fifty' hunebeds in Drenthe and one in Groningen[324] (chapter I, 'Hunebedden', p. 5-17) with the aid of an extremely large lithographed table (Figure 42). The table is 67 cm wide, 102 cm high in neat handwriting; it was folded by the binder so that it could be inserted in the back of the booklet, which measured only 23 x 13.5 cm. The table consists of nine columns which present: alphabetically ordered placenames; the number of hunebeds at each place; the topographical location (e.g. '15´ northeast of Anlo'); a schematic plan of the original state with a north arrow (lost stones stippled); the orientation; the exterior dimensions; the interior width; the size of largest boulder; the ownership; and horizontal dimensions and height of the barrow, and artefacts and other peculiarities published in Smids (1711), Van Lier (1760), Westendorp (1822), Janssen (1840) and J. Boeles (1844). The thirteen pages of text compile these data.

This was the first scientific inventory of the outer appearance of the Dutch hunebeds. It provided the basis for further hunebed studies until Van Giffen's work (1925), in which the tombs were rearranged in geographical order and each was given a capital initial, designating the name of the province, and a sequel number.[325]

Janssen (p. 11) referred indirectly to the curious theory developed by Johann Karl Wächter [1773-1846], in Hanover (1841), that each capstone covered one single transverse interment,[326] so that an entrance passage with several capstones would have lodged as many additional graves (*nevengraven*).[327] Under Von Estorff's influence (1846), Janssen made the hunebed kerbs rectangular, instead of oval, in his schematic plans. Janssen thought (p. 13) that an earthen slope was built to the tops of the orthostats so that the capstones could be moved up to their final position.

Since all hunebeds have the same principal form and architecture and cremated human bones had been found in several of them, he reasoned that the hunebeds could be considered to be *tombs* (p. 13-4). Bored holes in some of the stones suggested a religious function, possibly for use as altars. Lisch, Von Estorff and other researchers abroad were firmly convinced that the holes were *Opferlöcher* and

---

324 Actually Janssen listed 51 hunebeds in Drenthe and G1-Noordlaren in Groningen. He missed D1-Steenbergen, D2-Westervelde, D11-Anloo, D12-Eext Es, and D38-D40-Emmerveld present in Van Giffen's list of extant hunebeds (1925). He also listed the now demolished hunebeds D32a-Odoorn, D35a-Valthe and D43a-Emmen, the cist D31a-Exloo and 'the Stone' of Noordbarge ('D48'). The 'hunebed' [cist] F1-Riis was not discovered until 1849.

325 Other numbering systems by Leemans, in 1879 (see below), and De Wilde (see De Wilde 1910a) remained unpublished and never caught on. Van Giffen's system (1925) did; the roman numerals initially used for the sequel numbers have now been replaced by arabic numerals.

326 This untenable theory, which was never dealt with in any Dutch publication, was expounded by a female Dutch tourist guide at the D52-Diever hunebed in the 1960-70s (pers. comm. W. Glasbergen); an astounding and puzzling survival!

327 Janssen referred here to *4ter Bericht der Königl. Schleswig-Holstein-Lauenburg. Gesellschaft für Vaterl. Alterth*. Kiel, 1839, p. 5 and 12.

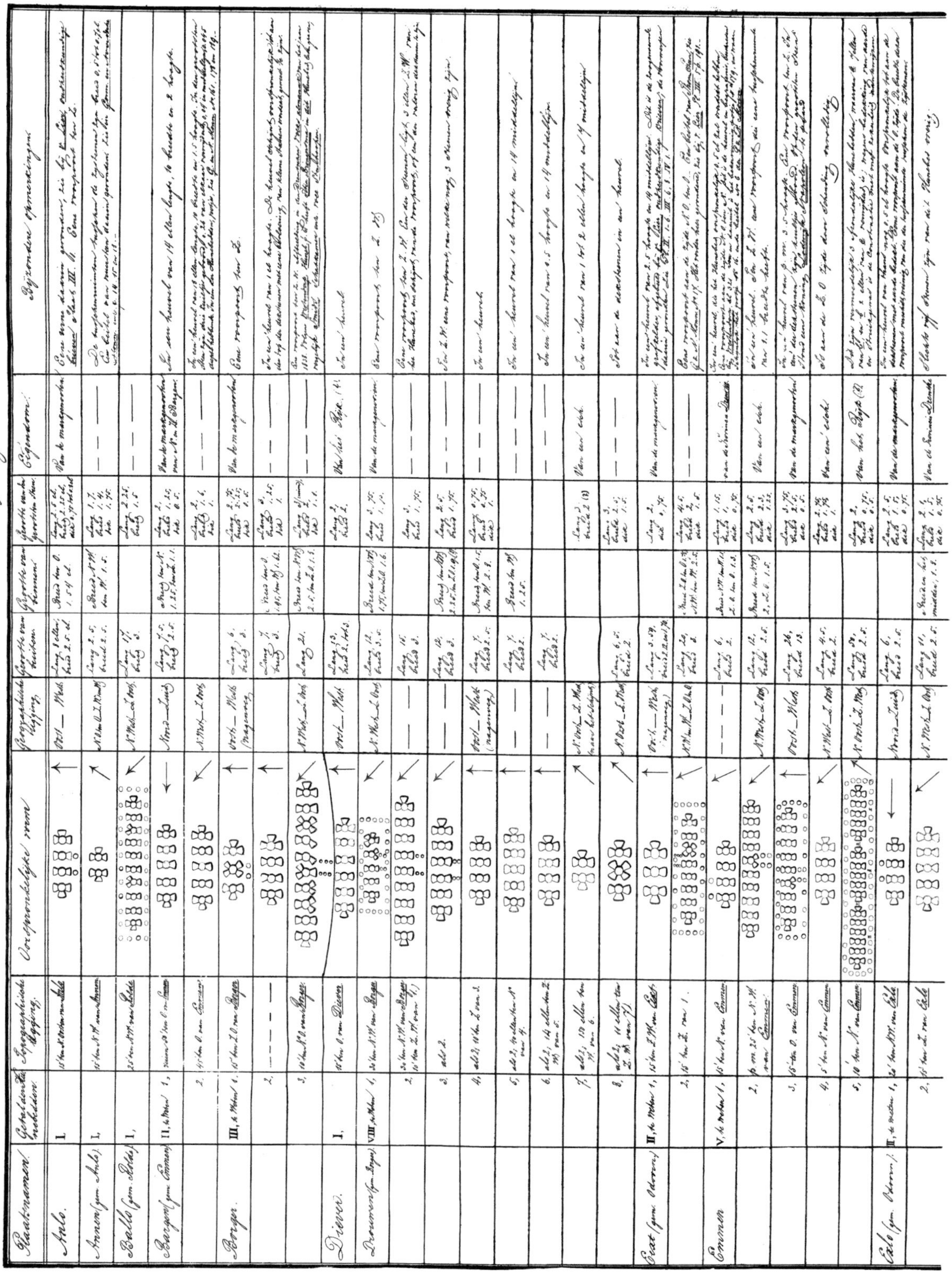

Figure 42. Upper half of Janssen's large table, 67 x 50 cm (photograph W. Arentzen).

Blutlöcher (blood- and offering holes).[328] Countryfolk in Drenthe drilled holes in large boulders to blast them with gunpowder; they told Janssen that the holes in hunebed stones had been made for the same purpose, but he noted that similar holes were in the granite boulders of the oldest walls of the churches of Odoorn and Emmen, which predated gunpowder (p. 15-6).

Janssen confused the two types of recent man-made holes in hunebed boulders and other large erratic stones. Beginning around 1735, deep holes with a diameter less than 2 cm were bored in large stones and filled with gunpowder and a fuse to blast the stone into irregular fragments for macadam roads or dikes. Such a borehole was made, shortly before 1800, in each of the two remaining capstones of hunebed G1-Noordlaren, but a local gentleman prevented the blasting (Bakker 1983, 122-3).[329] The Stone of Noordbarge, 'D48', has seven boreholes of this type (see D48 in Appendix 1). Between about AD 1150 and 1250, large boulders were cleft to form quadrangular boulders with three straight sides (Romanesque *Quadersteine*) by hammering a row of iron wedges into the stone. These boulders can be seen in the walls of the oldest churches of Emmen (tower) and Odoorn (choir and churchyard wall) in Drenthe and many church walls in northwestern Germany. Opposing flat surfaces of the boulders were positioned so that they showed on both faces of the walls, the intermediate space was filled with mortar. This cleaving method had been forgotten in Drenthe in Picardt's time (1660), and he thought that the boulders were *sawn*. East of Bremen in Germany, wedge cleaving was still being practised in 1922, however (Bakker 1992, 3-5). Janssen thought that the older holes used for cleaving, which were 4 cm in diameter, were an original ritual decoration of hunebed stones.[330] The hunebed builders themselves actually used methods for cleaving stone that left almost imperceptible traces (Bakker 1992, 25-6; Körner & Laux 1980).

In discussing the artefacts found in hunebeds and published by Van Lier, Engelberts and Westendorp, Janssen refused to accept that the thick discs and the perforated ox-horn illustrated in Engelberts's plate (Figure 29: 12*, 12-13 and 15) were TRB* artefacts. He noted that Westendorp wrote about an arrowhead of *bone* found in hunebed D13-Eext, but that was clearly an error because Van Lier had not mentioned it (p. 16). The bones Janssen had found, in 1846, in a compact clump in hunebed Exloo-3 (D31a) [actually a cist, according to Lanting (1994)] were analysed by Gerard Sandifort, professor of anatomy at Leiden University [1779-1848], who determined that they were from a person of average size (p. 17). In his 'Appendix I' (1848, 167-84), under the topic 'Something about the name and the origin of the hunebeds', Janssen discussed all possible linguistic

---

328 *Opferlöcher* refer to small holes in the tops of capstones, which date from the Neolithic and Bronze Age and occur in Germany and southern Scandinavia. In The Netherlands, they are only in capstone D6 of hunebed D16-Balloo, where they were recognised in the 1980s (Bakker 1992, 31).

329 The 11 missing orthostats and 3 capstones had been taken away before 1750 and probably even before 1694 (cf. Bakker 1983, 116-9, fig. 7). See Figure 24 (1768).

330 Van Giffen clearly discerned the two types of recent man-made holes for the first time, and professor Willem Glasbergen taught this to his students.

interpretations of the words *hun* and *bed* and ended with the statement that only an excavation of one of the least damaged hunebeds would further enhance our knowledge of them. But that would happen only 64 years later.

In 1849, the TRB cist of Riis [Rijs] was found (and directly destroyed) during the reclamation of a field in Gaasterland, the southwesternmost sandy outcrop of the province of Friesland. Janssen investigated its remains and published his findings in two detailed reports (1853, 1859). He, and after him Van Giffen (1927) and followers, considered this tomb as a genuine hunebed, but J.N. Lanting (1997) identified it as a cist (see Appendix 1).

Ownership, prohibition of destruction and of excavation of the hunebeds

In 1847, Janssen had asked the Minister of Internal Affairs to request permission from the Drenthe government to excavate hunebeds. The Drenthe government refused to grant this permission, although it did allow excavation of tumuli.[331] This refusal spared some hunebeds from Janssen's hand, whose excavation techniques were rudimentary or nonexistent. Meanwhile, however, Drenthe gentlemen continued to dig in hunebeds.

The contemplated selling of hunebeds D17 and D18 at Rolde was announced in the newspapers during Janssen's tour of inspection, on June 14 and 18, 1847. He reacted with a long letter of protest to the Minister on June 24, 1847,[332] and his director Leemans wrote to the King on July 25, 1847. They both stressed the danger of destruction of the tombs. Janssen's letter was sent by the Minister to the Drenthe government. The announcement of the public sale of D17 and D18 together with heath lands and forests by the communal *Marke* of Rolde, to take place in December, was advertised in the *Provinciale Drenthsche en Asser Courant* of November 5, 1847. The provincial government finally reacted, on November 9, 1847, to the Minister on Janssen's letter of eleven weeks earlier. It asked the Minister to state as soon as possible if the publications of 1734 and 1818 from previous governments, which interdicted the destruction of hunebeds and (1818) to dig therein for small stones or – without special permission – for antiquities, were still valid, and, if so, to take legal action on behalf of the State against this sale of hunebeds. On November 11, 1847, a discussion of this sale appeared in the *Algemeene Konst- en Letterbode* and Janssen wrote again to the Minister. The assembly of the Second Class of the Royal Institute of Sciences, Letters and Arts

---

331 Arentzen (2006, 107-8) quotes the following letters in full and their file numbers in the National Archives in The Hague and the Drenthe Archives in Assen: Janssen's letter to the Minister of April 11, 1847; his letter to the referendary of the Minister, dated April 27, 1847; and the letter from the Minister to the Governor of Drenthe, dated April 19, 1847. He also quotes the minutes of the discussion of the last letter in the meetings of the Province aldermen (*Gedeputeeerde Staten*) held on April 29, 1847, and May 11, 1847.

332 This was the day after Janssen's return to Leiden from Drenthe.

in Amsterdam[333] discussed the matter on November 18, 1847, and asked the secretary to do his utmost to try and prevent their destruction. When the collective owners of the communal grounds of Rolde became aware of this general indignation, they informed the *Haarlemmer Courant*, on December 13, 1847, that they had no intention of destroying the tombs, but wanted to sell them to the highest bidder. In a long letter to the *Algemeene Konst en Letterbode*, of December 8, 1847, one of their members asked whether or not they were the legal owners of the hunebeds. Not waiting for an answer, on January 11, 1848, the collective owners decided not to sell D17 and D18. The Drenthe government officially informed the Minister of Internal Affairs of this decision and posed the juridical question of ownership, on February 18, 1848. The juridical question was relayed to the Minister of Justice, who answered, on March 14, that the Protection Law of 1734 was still valid, which was reported to the Drenthe government two days later.[334] Only the Act of 1818 had strictly forbidden the digging in hunebeds, and this Act was not referred to in the Minister's answer. Nevertheless, destruction of the hunebeds remained forbidden and their legal ownership, whether communal or private, remained intact.

In 1848, communal owners donated hunebeds D16-Balloo, D31-Exloo, D41-Emmen and D45-Emmerdennen to the Province. In 1850, however, the Great Hunebed of Borger, D27, was sold to a private person, as were many others.[335]

How was a hunebed constructed?

Ideas of how hunebeds could have been built gradually took form in the 18th and 19th centuries.[336] Cohausen (1714) had written that the Germanic builders, who were very strong due to their primitive way of life, had moved the large stones on wooden rollers and had used their arms as levers. Westendorp (1822, 104-5) thought that the capstones were brought into place with the help of a ramp made of a few fir trees, wooden rollers and levers. He referred to similar previous ideas of 'the Nordic scholars', Scandinavian or north German authors who he did not identify.[337]

---

333 *Koninklijk Instituut van Wetenschappen, Letterkunde en Schone Kunsten*, predecessor of the present Royal Dutch Academy of Arts and Sciences in Amsterdam

334 Arentzen 2006, 115-9; Van der Sanden 2007, 73-9, 205; Okken 1989.

335 Arentzen 2006, 118-9; Van Giffen 1925, 47, 195 (V15: D16, notarial deed of 1871), 85 (D31), 104 (D41, presented and accepted in 1847, but still bought May 28, 1869) and 115 (D45). In 1856, it was announced in the newspapers that hunebed D5-Zeijen would be sold by the *Markegenooten*. This was prevented by Gratama and Magnin (Okken 1990) and the Province bought it for fl. 68.00 (deed of conveyance of July 1857: Van Giffen 1925, 21). In the 1870s, about half of the hunebeds were still collectively owned by *Markegenooten* and half by private persons (see section '1867-1886'). See Van der Sanden (2007, 98-9) and Van Giffen (1925, 194-203) for the correspondence between the provincial government and the local mayors about the attempts to acquire hunebeds, which were rather unsuccessful.

336 Bakker 1999, 151-5, 159-62, but see below about Bödiker.

337 They have not yet been identified.

How hunebeds probably had been built was described in great detail by Hermann Bödiker (1828, 190-1), a lawyer and surveyor at Aschendorf, who investigated them in the Hümmling near Meppen in Germany:

'Those regions where several larger and smaller stones were present, which were used for such monuments, were preferred for their construction; we must therefore assume that such areas were expressly chosen to raise our monuments. After having chosen the building site and levelling the ground, the supporting stones were drawn by horses and oxen across the flattened surface to the site using rollers and levers made of tree trunks. As many stones as needed to support the intended number of capstones were erected at the site, usually three next to each other. Now and then more supporting stones may have been used, or a few capstones (by which I mean any larger stones) may not have had supporting stones.[338] The spaces between the supporting stones were then filled up with small stones and earth to effect greater firmness, like a sort of masonry; finally, a layer of earth was laid on top, so that the construction acquired the appearance of a hillock with gradually rising slopes, from which the tips of the supporting stones stuck out. This construction enabled the capstones to be positioned on the supporting stones. This took more labour than required for the placement of the standing stones, but supernatural or gigantic powers need not be assumed. They were drawn to the top of the hillock on rollers by oxen and were put into place on top of the supporting stones using levers. Where large boulders were abundant, or perhaps for special reasons, the hillock was frequently bordered by a ring of stones.'

This explanation became known in The Netherlands when Heinrich Gottfried Haasloop Werner [1792-1864] published an accurate translation (1845), without, however, providing a full reference to the original.[339]

In 1853, Janssen described the building of a hunebed as follows:

'The simplest way of construction was this. Using a felled tree as a lever and a few truncated trees as rollers, the large boulders, which were lying about, were brought together, as many as were needed for the building of a hunebed. A few people sufficed to move the stones by pushing from behind; others in front may have pulled a rope, made by twisting twigs or strips of animal skin, wound around the boulder. First, the sidestones were erected with the same lever, and mantled with earth and

---

338 Bödiker 1828, fig. 3. From the dilapidated state of the Hümmling hunebeds, he incorrectly concluded that a number of capstones were originally missing. Hunebed demolition was in full swing at the time in the Hümmling, as he described. He did not recognise that the rows of wedge pits in hunebed stones were traces of unfinished wedge-cleaving in the Middle Ages (1828, 185, 187, figs. 1-2) – nor did Picardt recognise these as such in Drenthe (1660, 80), nor Janssen, although the method was still used until about 1920 east of Bremen (Bakker 1992, 4, 25). Van Giffen (1925-27) was the first to explain the wedge-cleaving correctly in The Netherlands, perhaps advised by K.-H. Jacob-Friesen, from Hanover, who participated in some of Van Giffen's excavations in 1918.

339 Haasloop Werner's article (1845) in a popular periodical was signed G.H.W. and only referred to 'Wigand' [viz. '*Wigand's Archiv*'] without mentioning Bödiker's name. Before W. Arentzen recently traced both publications, I was not aware of Bödiker's fundamental study of 1828 (Bakker 1999, 151-4, 159-62). The same is true for P. Eriksen, who cited my 1999 study at length (*Kuml* 2002, 65-103).

thus fixed; then the capstones were pushed upwards along an earthen ramp and then put in place on the sidestones. The few Drenthe hunebeds that are covered by earth as high as the capstones look as if they are just a group of flat large boulders lying in a row on a hillock. Most of our hunebeds appear originally to have been covered by a mantle of earth on the outside to consolidate the construction. It can thus be explained how man, lacking metal technology, without the aid of draught animals and not possessing the strength of giants, could make such gigantic stone constructions ... .' (Janssen 1853a, 11-12).[340]

Bödiker was therefore the first to suggest the use of earthen ramps, and Janssen that of ropes. Perhaps Janssen overstressed the necessity of the earth mantle, with its dual function as counterweight for the uprights and a ramp for placing the capstones, in the construction.

Four years later, in 1857, the Danish King Frederik VII developed an almost identical model of how megalithic tombs were built, which was published in a great number of modern languages.[341] Needless to say, Janssen was not enthusiastic about a Dutch edition of Frederik's study,[342] but a translation was eventually published (1863) by the Frisian historian Montanus de Haan Hettema [1796-1873].

The ideas of Cohausen, Westendorp, Bödiker, Janssen and King Frederik about how hunebeds were built, differ in two respects from the way megalithic monuments are being constructed in present-day pre-industrial societies. On Sumba, an island near Flores and Bali in Indonesia, the megalithic capstones and one-piece hollowed-out chamber boulders are placed on a forked tree about 15 metres long. The tree is then pulled, like a sledge, by a multitude of men over gnarled sticks that have been placed about 1.5 metres apart. Because the sticks are gnarled, they do not roll as the forked tree is drawn over them, but serve to fortify the track. This technique could have been used for hunebed building in the woods of Drenthe, where the terrain is rough and the surface soft. To use the sticks as roll-

---

340 Although Janssen kept contact with Haasloop Werner, who lived at Harderwijk in the Veluwe, there is no documentary proof that he actually read the G.H.W. (1845) or Bödiker (1828) study (W. Arentzen, pers. comm.). Janssen may have read King Frederik's publication of 1853 in *Antiquarisk Tidskrift 1852-4*, 6-8, since he received the German edition of this periodical, but this article arrived after completion of his study, which is dated January, 1853 (pers. comm. W. Arentzen). Moreover, Frederik's 1853 article did not contain the essentials of his 1857 publication (Bakker 1999, 159-62). Janssen added in a note to the 1853a text that although no animal bones had ever been found in a Dutch hunebed, Lisch had found horse bones in Mecklenburg *Hünengräber* [they were probably post-TRB – B.]. The animal bones found shortly afterwards in the Hilversum fireplaces were thus considered extremely important (in the 1930s it was discovered that they were fake, see section '1853-1856').

341 M. Axboe, curator of the Prehistoric Department of the National Museum in Copenhagen, informed W. Arentzen that Janssen sent an offprint of his 1853a study to the '*Königl. Societät für Nord. Altherthümer*' in Copenhagen (of which he was a member) immediately after it was printed. The offprint is stamped ANT. TOPOGR. ARCHIV and cut open, but there are no notes in the margins or other signs that it has been studied, for instance by the King or Worsaae. Frederik's model need not have come from Janssen; it could have been largely taken from Bödiker or created with little outside inspiration.

342 *Verhandelingen Tweede Klasse Koninklijke Akademie van Wetenschappen 1857-1865*, 1862, 191-4.

ers for the forked tree the ground would have to be hard and smooth; this was not the case in Drenthe, except perhaps when the ground was frozen. Neither the use of a forked tree as a sledge nor the use of sticks as track reinforcement (instead of as rollers), has been suggested by 19th- or 20th-century archaeologists in Europe. On Sumba, the capstones are put into place using rather flimsy-looking scaffolds made of bamboo stalks about 15 cm thick, rather than earthen ramps. The scaffold is removed as soon as the capstone is in place. In a cemetery built up by densely spaced tombs, the capstone was lifted, however, by levers on a steadily raised platform of beams – comparable to the way in which the lintels of Stonehenge were presumably raised between 2500 and 2000 BC.[343] Supposition of the Sumba method for hunebed construction, however, would leave unexplained the post hole traces found along the outer sides of hunebed orthostats, which are usually considered to have contained the vertical posts supporting wooden ramps.[344]

The life of the hunebed builders

In January, 1853, just before the discoveries near Hilversum (see below), Janssen (1853a) finished the text of a lecture about the life of the hunebed builders for publication, 'On the civilisation of the very earliest inhabitants of our fatherland, deduced from recovered remains', which includes the passage quoted above on the technique of hunebed construction. By scraping together all the information available, he described the daily life of the hunebed people (p. 13-26). Their main occupation was hunting and fishing. A ceramic model boat, allegedly found in hunebed D15-Loon (Figure 29: 16), was considered primary evidence for navigation. Another model boat was in a private collection, marked 'found in Drenthe'. We now know that J. Hofstede, from whose collection the first boat reached the Royal Museum in Amsterdam, in 1809, and the Leiden Museum, in 1825-6, was ill-informed about its findspot and not aware that it was manufactured in the Middle Ages rather than the Neolithic.[345] Dugouts, which had been found in Swedish bogs, were further evidence. Janssen's passage about how these boats

---

343 Stonehenge's wall and ditch are dated to ca. 2950 BC, its first wooden constructions to 2950-2600 BC, i.e. at or after the end of the TRB culture. Its successive stone constructions are dated to 2600-2500 BC (Blue stone circle), 2500-2000 BC (Sarsen circles, Phases 3ii-v), 2000-1600 BC (Y- and Z-holes, Phase 3vi) (Darvill 2006, fig. 29), i.e. more or less contemporary with the Dutch Late-Neolithic B (Bell Beaker period, 2500-2000 BC), Early Bronze Age (2000-1800 BC) and Middle Bronze Age A (1800-1500 BC) (Louwe Kooijmans et al. 2005, fig. 1.10).

344 The postholes are described in Bakker 1983, fig. 15; 1992, 32, fig. 17; 1999, 151, fig. 4 and 2009a; Midgley 2008, fig. 3.42. Cf. Figures 58 and 60. Megalith construction on Sumba in the 20th century is described by Bakker (1999, 152-4; 2009a) and by R. Adams, lecture Lisbon, september, 2006. On Nias, an island west of Sumatra in Indonesia, huge boulders placed on sledges were hauled up slope over well-rounded poles, which may have pivoted like mechanical rollers (Bakker 1999, 152-4).

345 See section '1790' about how two model boats were considered at the time to be based on the boats of the hunebed builders. Westendorp (1815; 1822, 10), who was not aware that these ceramic model boats had probably not been found in hunebeds, paid some attention to them. In 2007, a genuine canoe from the TRB period was discovered 62 km north of Amsterdam, see note 41.

would have been made was based on Peter Wilhelm Lund's description of how they were cut out with stone axes and fire by contemporary Indians in Brazil.[346] Ancient harpoons and fish-hooks of stone and bone were also known from Sweden (Sven Nilsson 1838-45; 1844). Remnants of the available game and plant foods were preserved in bogs in Sweden and The Netherlands, including hares, rabbits, fox, wild boar, deer, aurochs, acorns, beech-nuts and hazel-nuts.[347] He surmised that excellent beverages could have been made of bilberries, sloe, and, if available, wild honey. Clothing would have been made of animal hides. By analogy with pottery-making among the Mandans, Hidatsa and Arikara in the North American plains of Dakota, described by Prince Maximilian of Wied [1782-1867], Janssen set out in detail how pottery was made without a wheel and elaborately decorated. He also speculated about how the various forms of pottery were used. In Janssen's opinion, the presence of hunebeds indicated that their makers did not lead a no-madic life, but that they had permanent homes, that they knew family life, ap-preciated family ties and upheld property rights. The lack of idols indicated that their religion was not polytheistic. According to him, savage peoples had various stages of religious development. First came fetishism, in which man viewed na-ture as a multitude of separate divinely possessed things, which were feared and venerated. Then followed a belief in an invisible world of spirits and demoniacal natural forces. This evolved into a belief in a great and powerful spirit who ruled like a chief over the other spirits. Some peoples identified the sun as such, and indeed evidence for the practice of cremation found in the hunebedden indicated a veneration of fire (the sun?). He was not certain, however, that this was true for the hunebed builders, because the megalithic graves of northern Europe con-tained unburnt skeletons. Jacob Grimm [1785-1863] had argued that inhumation preceded cremation in megalithic graves, [348] but to Janssen this seemed uncertain and even very improbable because the same types of implements occurred in both types of graves.

1853-1856: the Hilversum hoax

Janssen's late dating of hunebed D44a-Zaalhof seemed to be confirmed by the remains of seventeen stone 'fireplaces' (*haardsteden*) found near Hilversum, 25 km southeast of Amsterdam, in 1853 (Figure 43). These were not only discov-ered, but also fabricated by Dirk Westbroek [ca.1800-1877], a workman who was digging up a parcel of heath for planting trees in the southeastern corner of the province Noord-Holland. He carried on a profitable business selling hun-

---

346 The famous Danish palaeontologist and ethnographer P.W. Lund [1801-1880] was active in Brazil in the first half of the 19th century. He influenced the interpretation of the function of prehistoric artefacts by the Swedish prehistorian Nilsson and his Danish colleague Worsaae. See Klindt-Jensen 1976.

347 The beech tree and the rabbit arrived only much later in The Netherlands, as we know now.

348 J. GRIMM (1850) *Über das Verbrennen der Leichen*. Berlin (#, pers. comm. W. Arentzen).

Figure 43. One of the 'fireplaces' at Hilversum and a few of the stone artefacts found in them in 1853 (lithograph by T. Hooiberg in Janssen 1853b) (photograph Library Amsterdam).

dreds of home-made polished stone tools for 20-50 cents each.[349] Janssen, who had been informed of these finds by the mayor of Maartensdijk, Frans Nicolaas Marius Eyck van Zuylichem [1806-1876], visited Westbroek's excavations several times in 1853 and corresponded about these with Hilversum amateur archaeologist and local historian, notary Albertus Perk [1795-1880], who acted as his local representative and overseer. Janssen thought that he had made a discovery about Stone Age life as important as the Danish shell-middens and the Swiss-German pile-dwellings, which where discovered about the same year. He wrote two exemplarily detailed and well-illustrated publications, which included identifications of the burnt wood, bone particles and rocks by Leiden specialists (Janssen 1853b, 1856).

Westbroek and his son had made a few mistakes, not recognised as such by Janssen. Below the pavement of one 'fireplace', which Janssen excavated himself (which was quite unusual), lay a bone button, 'of a type presently used by labourers'. Janssen, who was unable to discern between natural, anciently moved, and recently moved soil, commented that such things may happen in excavations. Nor was he aware that the depressions on the surface he thought characteristic for the fireplaces were in fact due to compaction of the loose soil with which they had been filled a few days before. The fireplaces were surrounded by low walls of erratic stones from the surrounding heath. One stone among them, however, was a Bentheim sandstone fragment with a cut profile from a medieval or early modern building,[350] which Janssen identified as a Roman building fragment. Combining his Emmen and Hilversum observations, he argued that the fireplaces and last hunebeds dated from the Roman period and that the Stone Age* lasted until the Roman period. Among the bones from the fireplaces were those of a dog, a beaver (sic), sheep/goat and, probably, a calf, whose identification Janssen considered a considerable contribution to the knowledge of the life of the hunebed people – but unfortunately was not.

Janssen's interpretation of the Hilversum complex was fatal for the Leiden concept of prehistoric chronology. The well-known archaeologist Jan Hendrik Holwerda [1873-1951] followed Janssen's views in this respect during his entire career as curator and later director of the Leiden Museum (1904/5[351]-1938). Fortunately, other leading archaeologists, such as Pieter Catharinus Johannes Albertus Boeles [1873-1961] at the Frisian Museum in Leeuwarden and Albert Egges van Giffen [1884-1973] at Groningen University, stuck to the Three Age system, which had been published by Thomsen in 1836. The Hilversum complex

---

349 Westbroek asked 50 cents apiece for these from the mayor of Maartensdijk, but Janssen paid 20-30 cents apiece. This was exorbitant! A workman then earned 30 cents for a 14-hour workday, a painter 40 cents (Arentzen 2006, 36; 2007).

350 Janssen soon altered the date from '15th to 16th century AD' in his original manuscript to 'the Roman Period' (pers. comm. W. Arentzen).

351 See A.E.J. Holwerda 1906.

was finally recognised as a fraud, in 1932, by the amateur archaeologist Hendrik Jan Popping [1885-1950]. The Hilversum artefacts were not removed from the exposition in the Leiden museum until about 1945.[352]

1856-1862: Hofdijk

Willem Jacobsz Hofdijk [1816-1888], a popular writer of gripping historical scenes, carefully studied Janssen's detailed publications (1853a; 1853b; 1856) and other available literature on the hunebed builders.[353] Whereas the other contemporary Dutch 'historical romantic' authors between 1829 and 1880,[354] who were also inspired by the works of Walter Scott [1771-1832][355], devoted their prose to the Christian period, Hofdijk is the only one who ventured into prehistory.[356] His vivid picture of life in the TRB period* developed gradually (Hofdijk 1856a; 1856b; 1857). It reached its best form in *Ons Voorgeslacht* ('Our Ancestors'), which appeared in 1859, with excellent illustrations by Charles Rochussen [1814-1894], Hendrik Dirk Kruseman van Elten [1829-1904], David van der Kellen [1804-1879] and Hofdijk himself (Bakker 1990a, figs. 8-10). The book was reprinted many times and determined the image of the hunebed builders for generations.[357] In his earlier works, Hofdijk dated the hunebeds to about 650 BC, but in 1862 he dated them to about 3000 BC and ascribed them to the Fenes (a backward Germanic people mentioned by Tacitus). For that time, 3000 BC was a very early

352 About the Hilversum hoax, see Bakker 1964, 1990b and Arentzen 2006; 2007. About Popping's exposure, Bakker 2004, 156.
353 See 'Epilogue' and the compilations of Janssen 1853a and Hofdijk's writings about the Hunebed Builders in Bakker 1990a, 41-9; 1990b, 77-9. Cf. the sources given by Hofdijk 1859, viii-ix.
354 Margaretha Jacoba de Neufville [1775-1856]: *De Schildknaap*, 1829; Aernoud Drost [1810-1834]: *Hermingard van de Eikenterpen*, 1832; Jacob van Lennep [1802-1868]: *De Pleegzoon*, 1833; *De Roos van Dekama*, 1836; *Ferdinand Huyck*, 1840; *Elisabeth Musch*, 1850, etc.; Jan Frederik Oltmans [1806-1854]: *Het Slot Loevestijn in 1570*, 1834; *De Schaapherder*, 1838; and Geertruida Bosboom-Toussaint [1812-1886]: *Het Huis Lauernesse*, 1840; *De Delftse Wonderdokter* 1870-1, etc. (#). I thank professor H.A. Heidinga, Edam, for his advice. *Wikipedia* and other internet sites helped me further.
355 *The Lay of the last Minstrel*, 1805; *The Lady of the Lake*, 1810; *The Antiquary*, 1816; *Waverley*, 1814; *Ivanhoe*, 1819; etc. (#).
356 Hofdijk (1859-65) also discussed Germanic barrows. Arnout Drost's *Hermingard* (1832) dealt with Christianisation in the 4th century AD and the others dealt with much later episodes.
357 J.G. Frederiks, 'Levensbericht van Willem Hofdijk Jacobsz', *Jaarboek Maatschappij Nederlandsche Letterkunde* 1889, 197-273, highly praised Hofdijk's imaginative chapter 'Het Hunebed te Rolde' (1857): 'Whoever has not acquired an image of an indeterminate period of our unwritten history after having read 'Het hunebed van Rolde', is missing a feeling (*een orgaan*) for history ...' (p. 218). Cf. also *De Gids* 1888, 167-70. As late as 1959, when J.H. Isings had painted his admirable school picture of the Hunebed Builders (Figure 3), Wijbenga (1960; 1975) could not do better than paraphrase Hofdijk's century old depiction of TRB life in his explanatory booklet for the teachers (Bakker 1990a, b).

Figure 44. Hunebed D6-Tynaarlo drawn by Alexander Ver Huell in 1859 in Tijdspiegel, vol. 3, 1859, p. 337 (Arnhem: D.A. Thieme; lithograph by J.H. Hoffmeister). See further Appendix 3.

date. Although Hofdijk was a careful historian, he did not explain why he selected this early date, which is astonishingly in agreement with present-day dates for the TRB culture and hunebed building (see part A).[358]

After Janssen's attempt to portray the daily life of the TRB culture* to the west of the Elbe, nothing comparable would become available for more than eighty-five years, when Hans Reinerth [1900-1990] published an article on his 1938-41 research of the 'wet' settlement site Hunte 1 or Huntedorf on the River Hunte, north of Lake Dümmer, Germany, using the help of first rate biologists (Reinerth 1939; see Kossian 2007).

---

358 J.J.A. Worsaae (1843) had dated the Danish 'Stone Age' [Neolithic] to at least 1000 BC. At the time, J.K. Wächter (1841) and others in Germany placed the *Hünengräber* around or after the beginning of the Christian area. P.B. Podczaszyńsky (1857: Jażdżewski 1965, 14-5) thought that the Stone Age ended in Poland around 1250 BC and Chr. Petersen (1857: Gummel 1938, 174) and G.C.F. Lisch (1863) thought that this had occurred about 1000 BC in northern Germany. After discovery of the Kjøkkenmøddinger (shell middens) in Denmark, in 1850, Worsaae (1881) estimated the Danish 'Old Stone Age', to which they were assigned, to about 3000 BC or earlier, and the subsequent 'Late Stone Age' [Neolithic] to about 2000-1000 BC (Bakker 1979a, 24).

1856-1887: the origin of the large hunebed stones

As we have seen in section '1756-1760', Van Lier and Vosmaer (1760) could not satisfactorily explain the geological origin of the large boulders from which the hunebeds were made. Seventy years later, Charles Lyell [1797-1875] propagated the 'Drift theory' (1830), hypothesizing that these boulders had been transported from Scandinavia to northern Germany and Drenthe by icebergs floating across a former sea.

The Dutch geologist Winand Carel Hugo Staring [1808-1877], who made the first Geological Map of The Netherlands on a 1:200,000 scale (1856-1867), almost on his own, still adhered to this theory (1858; 1860, 21ff.). Although he looked carefully at the 'boulders of the heath lands', viz. those on the Pleistocene sandy soils, and discerned[359] a Scandinavian and a 'mixed' diluvium[360] north of the Rhine based on the erratic stones, he was not aware that the scratches on the Scandinavian boulders were glacially derived and he did not recognise a periglacial fissure (or an oblique shift in frozen state of the sandy soil) that he observed (1860, 72) as such. No one at the time knew that so much water had been bound in the glacial ice that the Ice Age sea level was 120 m or more below the present-day level (cf. 1858, 107-26). Nor did he know that end moraines, push moraines, and glacial tills in The Netherlands and northwestern Germany were glacial landforms. Staring wrote:

'Although very many boulders and large boulders, which lay on the surface of the diluvium, have been removed by the inhabitants, it may be concluded from what is left that the Scandinavian diluvium contains generally more and larger boulders than the mixed diluvium, and that those boulders in the latter are much more numerous in the eastern parts of Twente [eastern Overijssel] *than on the Veluwe* [central Gelderland] *and in the province of Utrecht. Such a multitude of very heavy granite boulders that were needed for constructing the Hunebeds could only be found in this country in concentrations in Drenthe, where they could be assembled by simply rolling them.*[361] *It is not conceivable that those gigantic boulders were transported in another way* [and] *for long distances. One of the six capstones of the hunebed at Rolde*[362] *near Assen, weighs about 18,000 kilogram. In the regions where the Hunebeds occur, many such huge granite stones are found lying about in the heaths; the grey, moss-grown backs of these monuments from*

---

359 Staring 1858, 79-106, map II (p. 106-7); 1860, 25-47, 305-6, pl. I (map). The first mentioned map is the clearest. Staring (1858) explained more about the supposed mechanisms behind his stone provinces; in 1860, he described the distribution of the stones, the geomorphology*, the wells, and the extremely rare vertical sections that were available.

360 'Diluvium' is now called 'Pleistocene' or Ice Age deposits. The 'mixed diluvium' has a mixture of boulders from Scandinavia and those deposited by the Rivers Rhine and Meuse / Maas. This concept is still used in the present Dutch geological literature.

361 Staring did not explain if he meant transporting the stones on rollers, but this was probably the case. See section 'How was a hunebed constructed?'. Although he did not say so, Staring may have read Janssen (1853a).

362 Staring probably meant hunebed D18-Rolde, which has 7 capstones, not D17-Rolde, which has 8 capstones. Before the 1873 restoration of D18, the exact number of capstones was difficult to discern, because some had fallen between the orthostats.

Figure 45. View on hunebed D18-Rolde and the church of Rolde in 1871, shortly before its resto-
ration. Drawing in black chalk by Johannes Hendrik van West [1803-1881] (photograph Drents
Museum, Assen).

> *the Ice Age are seen time and again sticking out of the surface; in regions such as*
> *between Borger and Exlo, near Noordsleen and to the south of Weerdinge they still*
> *occur in considerable quantities, because they are too far from canals to transport*
> *them economically. This reason for the preservation of these stones will soon cease*
> *to exist, when the Oranjevaart* [Orange Canal] *is dug* (1860, 72-3).[363]

He noted that granites and diorites occurred only north of the Rhine, except
a strip along [Wychen-Nijmegen in The Netherlands and] the surroundings of
Xanthen and Kleve in Germany (1858, 103).[364]

In 1875, the Swedish geologist Otto Martin Torell [1828-1900] convinced the
majority of his colleagues at a conference in Berlin that a thick cover of inland ice
had transported the erratic stones from Scandinavia, Finland and the Baltic Sea

---

363 These were prophetic words! Contractors for the construction of the Orange Canal not only
   collected loose stones, but also began to demolish hunebed D49-Papeloze Kerk until they were
   stopped by the mayor (Van Giffen 1969 and the following section '1861 and 1867').
364 Pleyte (1877-79, 2) followed the iceberg theory.

to the North European Plain, including Drenthe. Earlier researchers had argued the same, but could not convince the supporters of the 'Drift theory' and the earlier periglacial 'Mud stream' theory.[365] The Dutch geologist F.J.P. van Calkar took Torell's side in 1881 and the Dutch geologist Jan Lorié [1852-1924] wrote in the *Nieuwe Drentsche Volksalmanak* (1887) that the boulders of the hunebeds demonstrated that the inland ice (*landijs*) theory was correct and that glaciers had transported them over land. He also described how periglacial* factors – particularly the cutting out of streams and the deposition of fine sands ('coversands'*) – governed the geomorphology* of Friesland and western Drenthe.

1861 and 1867: excavation and destruction of hunebed D49-Papeloze Kerk

A newspaper article from November 19, 1861 reported on what seems to be an expert report of an illegal excavation of hunebed D49-Papeloze Kerk by P. Keyzer. This and later documents show that the hunebed was heavily damaged:

> *'Recently, a hunebed named Papelooze Kerk was sold at Assen for removal. Excavation at the outset revealed a number of remarkable phenomena. A slightly elevated rectangular base, oriented E-W, measuring 7 m long and 4 m wide, is covered by a pavement consisting of regular laid cobbles; on this pavement, which lies on the natural soil, there is a layer of broken pieces of flint or stone, 30 cm thick, mixed with sand and a lot of smaller and larger sherds from urns or pots, which are light or dark yellow in colour and of which most are decorated with incised patterns (?) and foliage (beeld-, lof- of bloemwerk). Complete urns with ash or burnt bones, stone hammers or chisels (wedges) were not found, however. The hunebed is constructed with 22 unworked large boulders, each with an estimated volume of 50 cubic metres and weight of 4000 kilograms.*

---

365 Kahlke (1981, 15-22) summarises the complicated history of the different competing theories proposed since 1775 to explain the origin of erratics and glacial striae (*Gletscherkratzen*) on rocks in the North European Plain. The discussions in the 18th and 19th centuries in The Netherlands, which Kahlke ignored, played a negligible role in international discussions. L. Ali Cohen (1844, 369-80) cited Lyell's Drift theory to explain the origin of the boulders in Drenthe (in a somewhat fantastic way). Hermannus Hartogh Heijs van Zouteveen [1841-1891] only referred (1886) to Lyell's Drift theory, whereas Gratama (1884a; 1886, 187) mentioned, but did not choose between the theories of Lyell and Torell to explain the natural transport of the boulders to Drenthe. In 1892, the Dutch geographer Hendrik Blink [1852-1931] attributed (1892, 185-96) the inland glaciers theory to J. Lorié (1886), with no mention of Torell.

There were 'heavy boulders at the ends, 4 to the right and 5 to the left, 3 capstones (which had fallen down), forming a long rectangle, surrounded by 8 similar boulders, like watchmen at some distance'. By order of the King's Commissioner this work was stopped for the time being.'[366]

According to a report of the public prosecutor to the mayor of Sleen from February 7, 1862, 'the action consisted only of the removal of a bed of small stones, whereas the hunebed itself was not damaged.' The mayor added '… an existing layer of small stones [vlinten] removed as well as similar stones around the hunebed, which formed a sort of pavement on which the hunebed was raised; this caused a slight dislocation of the large boulders, but so little that the tomb is still almost in its original state. The owner offers it for sale for 240 guilders. … I have taken all possible action to prevent further damage.'[367]

The observation that there was a layer of broken flint and stone mixed with numerous potsherds on top of the floor pavement accords with those made by Van Giffen, myself and others in the 20th century. The thickness of the layer, however, is closer to 8-10 cm than to 30 cm. Because destruction of hunebeds in Drenthe was forbidden by law since 1734, the King's Commissioner and the mayor forbade further demolition of this tomb.

In 1867, further destruction was begun by a new owner. The mayor of Sleen stopped this, reported the damage to the King's Commisioner and suggested to instruct the state constable to see that no further damage was done. In 1871, the site was acquired by the State.[368] Apparently, the authorities saw the heavy boulders as the only important quality of the hunebeds, not their contents.

---

366 'Onlangs werd te Assen een hunebed, bekend onder de naam papelooze kerk, ter wegruiming verkocht. Bij aanvankelijke opgraving levert het menig opmerkelijk verschijnsel op. Op eene kleine hoogte bevindt zich een regthoekig grondvlak van het Oosten naar het Westen, ter lengte van 7 Ned. El en ter breedte van circa 4 el, regelmatig bevloerd met kleine keyen; op dezen vloer, die in den vasten bodem ligt ontwaart men eene laag geklopte flint of veldsteen, ter dikte van 3 palm, vermengd met zand en met eene menigte kleinere en grootere scherven van gebroken urnen of potten, licht- of donkergeel gekleurd en meest alle met ingesneden beeld-, lof-, of bloemwerk versierd. het hunebed bestaat uit 22 ongefatsoeneerde steenklompen, welker inhoud op 50 kub. Ellen of lasten, ter gewigt ieder van 4000 pond geschat wordt. Ingevolge aanschrijving van den commissaris des Konings is het werk voorloopig gestaakt.' (quotation from Provinciale Overijsselsche en Zwolsche Courant of January 12, 1863. This was an abbreviated version of reports in Nieuwe Rotterdamsche Courant, written on December 22, 1862, and Algemeen Handelsblad, December 27, 1862, all found by W. Arentzren, in June, 2010).

367 Document CdK 0040-301498 Nr 574, 07-02-1862. The documents dated to 1861-1862 in the Drenthe Archives about the demolition of this hunebed itemised by Van Giffen (1925, p. 196-7, nos. V33-35) refer to the same events.

368 Mrs Said Mooijman and W.A.B. van der Sanden have been kind enough to send me (June 28, 2010) the following documents; Articles in Provinciale Drentsche en Asser Courant of November 19 and 30, 1861); letter from King's Commissioner to mayor of Sleen (November 20, 1861, answer November 26, 1861), letter from King's Commisioner to Public Prosecutor (January 2, 1862, answer January 7, 1862) and undated letter from the mayor to King's Commissioner (1862).

1867-1886: Gratama's successful action to protect the hunebeds

About 1870, all Drenthe hunebeds – except one – passed into the ownership of the state or the province to prevent their demolition.[369] Thirty years after petitioning to the King, in 1841, Magnin's aims were realised for the hunebeds, almost exactly as he had advised.[370] A ditch was dug and wooden boundary posts placed around individual hunebeds and *grafkelders* (burial chambers', i.e. small hunebeds).[371] The person responsible was Lucas Oldenhuis Gratama [1815-1887], a Drenthe lawyer, politician, regional historian and amateur archaeologist.[372] He was not interested in sherds and defended the outmoded idea that the hunebeds, which recalled certain features of Christian churches, had been built during the time of the Vikings (1886, 56-71). In vain, he had tried to persuade the College of the Provincial States (representatives) of Drenthe, in 1867, to acquire the hunebeds for the Province. The following year he published an 'Open letter to the representatives of Drenthe about the care and maintenance of the hunnebedden' (Gratama 1868). Politicians, members of the Royal Academy of Sciences and Letters in Amsterdam and articles in several journals and periodicals showed serious interest in this matter and soon the Minister of Internal Affairs instructed the Governor of Drenthe to take action and gave him a budget.[373]

Unfortunately, the Governor and local mayors restored the hunebeds following Gratama's advice, without any supervision by attentive observers and recorders. Gratama's inspiration was a print of 'Avebury restored', a reconstruction on paper only,[374] which he mistakenly understood as showing that reconstruction of this huge prehistoric monument had actually taken place (Gratama 1886, 18-20). Moreover, he accepted Westendorp's theory (1815) that hunebeds had never had

---

369 According to the deeds of conveyance to the State and Province (Van Giffen 1925, 12-134), 12 of the 25 hunebeds owned by various collective ownerships (*Markegenooten*) were donated and the rest sold, and 6 of the 28 hunebeds owned by single or corporate private persons were donated and 22 sold. Hunebed G1-Noordlaren in the province of Groningen was bought from a private person by the State, in 1870 (Bakker 1983, 124). D6-Tynaarlo was the last hunebed that was acquired by the State or Province, in 1880 (Van Giffen 1925, 22). Presently, only D44-Westenes in Drenthe and U1-Lage Vuursche in Utrecht are privately owned.

370 The hundreds of barrows in Drenthe remained unprotected, however, like elsewhere in The Netherlands, and most would disappear with reclamations of heathlands or would be damaged by forestation in the following decades. Quite a number were excavated by Van Giffen and others before or even after destruction. Only in the second half of the 20th century were the remaining barrows legally protected.

371 As a consequence of Van Lier's study, the distinction between *grafkelders* (small hunebeds) and the larger hunebeds was made throughout the 19th century.

372 See his portrait photograph, from ca. 1875, in Van der Sanden (2007, 88).

373 Bakker 1979b, 1979c; Okken 1990.

374 '*General view of Abury restored*' in the English *Penny Magazine* of August, 1840 #, in which it is stated 'And thus has the genius of Dr. Stuckeley restored to the world the grand edifice we described'. The rather schematic drawing suggests a much smaller monument, which looks as if was recently restored. A later visit to the monument and a study of Stukeley's folio publication in Dryden's castle convinced Gratama of his error (Gratama 1884a, 40-1; 1886, 18-20).

a barrow and, consequently, thought that the remnants of hunebed barrows were wind-blown sand. At his instigation, remnants of barrows were dug away by labourers – without any scientific supervision.

Figure 46 shows the extreme case of D15-Loon where the barrow was removed, in March-April 1870, with the result that dislodged potsherds lay scattered around the tombs. Gratama wrote about this 'restoration' of D15-Loon by the King's Commissioner in Drenthe, Joan Lodewijk Gerhard Gregory [1808-1891, in office 1868-1875]:

> *'The interior was damaged and had been investigated earlier ... . An urn and sherds of pots and urns, some with crude decorations, and a juglet were found.'* (Gratama 1884a; 1886, 30, n. 3).

And:

> *'It is true that Mr. Gregory has stripped the sand from the hunnebed of Loon and other hunnebedden, but presumably sand will gradually settle there again.'* (Gratama 1886, 21).

Janssen's sketches of D15-Loon in 1847 (Figure 40) show that a barrow had covered the orthostats up to the base of the capstones; it was completely removed in 1870 (Figure 46).

Hunebeds D43-Emmen (a *langbett*) and D18-Rolde were restored by the mayor of Emmen and the Commissioner of Drenthe, but these works were at best very summarily documented, and these gentlemen did not supervise the work themselves on a daily basis. The stones from the nearby ruined hunebed D43a-Emmen were probably used for the restoration of *langbett* D43-Emmen.[375] The number of the other tombs from which quantities of the barrow sands were removed is considerable, as photographs made in 1874 show (see section '1867-1883').

A year before his death, Gratama published his studies of the hunebeds, which previously had appeared in *Nieuwe Drentsche Volksalmanak* 1883-1885 and in the *Provincale Drentsche en Asser Courant*,[376] in one volume with a useful, extensive bibliography (Gratama 1886). This book was reviewed by Serurier and A. de Mortillet in *L'Homme, Journal Illustré des Sciences Anthropologiques*, no. 18, September 25, 1886, p. 568 (Van Giffen 1925, 225, no. 101). In *Nieuwe Drentsche Volksalmanak* 1887 (p. 200-232), Gratama discussed the mayors' reports about the condition of the hunebeds and other antiquities in their municipality. Fifty years earlier he had written his first article about the hunebeds (Gratama 1838).

---

375 About *langbett* D43-Emmen and the possible use of stones from hunebed D43a for its 'restoration', see Bakker 1992, 15-22, figs. 12-4.

376 *Provincale Drentsche en Asser Courant* of September 12, 16, 20, 21 and 22, 1876; February 9, 1880; and January 14, 1885 (Van Giffen 1925, 223-4, nos. 85, 90, 96b)

Figure 46. Hunebed D15-Loon, in 1874, after removal of its barrow in 1870 (photograph by J. Goedeljee, Pleyte archives, National Museum of Antiquities at Leiden). See further Appendix 3.

1871-1879: Franks, Lukis & Dryden

In the summer of 1871, Augustus Wollaston Franks [1826-1897] came to Amsterdam for the auction of the collection of the botanist, palaeontologist and geologist Jacob Gijsbert Samuel van Breda [1788-1867].[377] Franks acquired 1900 fossils, plants and animals for the University of Cambridge and the British Museum of Natural History. He was director of the Christy Collection, a curator of the British Museum, and vice president of the Society of Antiquaries of London. In 1873, he would become its president for the second time. He was a collector of antiquities and one of the best known antiquaries of his time. During this trip, he also visited the hunebeds in Drenthe, the museums in Assen and Leiden, and also acquired a few archaeological objects at the auction.

---

377 Most of the contents of this section are covered, in more detail, in Bakker 1979c.

Franks reported to the Society of Antiquaries at London about the recent hunebed 'restorations', of which he strongly disapproved (Franks 1872). He collected sherds from the surface[378] and made the important observation that 'the whole style of the pottery agrees with what we know from Germany and Denmark as belonging to the Stone Age'. His remark 'I ventured, while at Assen, to call the attention of the members of the Commission of the museum to the value of fragments of pottery' seems to imply how little Gratama and others at Assen were aware of their value. Willem Pleyte, curator of the Leiden Museum, on the other hand, was aware and had collected sherds in 1870.[379] Franks and others, using the examples of Drenthe preservation measures and Danish monument protection laws (cf. Worsaae 1879),[380] argued for a bill that would protect prehistoric monuments in Britain. This bill ultimately became the Ancient Monument Act of Sir John Lubbock [1834-1913], in October, 1882.[381] Franks had asked Gratama for information about the Dutch preservation measures of hunebeds, and Gratama's translation into French of the brief summary of acquisitions and restorations made by L.J.G. Gegory, the King's Commissioner in Drenthe, was published in full in English (Franks 1873).

At the 1874 session of the Congrès International d'Anthropologie et d'Archéologie Préhistorique in Stockholm and the 1876 session of that in 'Buda-Pesth', Gratama spoke proudly about the protective measures and the restorations of the hunebeds. The protective measures were highly praised, but the restorations were unanimously disapproved of by the leading megalithic researchers, who maintained that one cannot restore without understanding the structure of such tombs. It must have been clear to the specialists that Gratama had no knowledge about stratigraphy and artefacts.

In 1878, the Reverend William Collings Lukis [1817-1892], Fellow of the Society of Antiquaries in London and rector of Wath near Ripon in Yorkshire, and Sir Henry Edward Leigh Dryden [1819-1899], who was fourth baronet of Canons Ashby, Byfield, in Northamptonshire, and Honorary Member of the Society of Antiquaries of Scotland, and who had already surveyed megaliths in the UK and Brittany, surveyed the Dutch hunebeds. Franks had initiated this survey on behalf of the Society of Antiquaries, and partly funded it. Unfortunately, by then,

---

378 Most of the sherds he brought home were given to him by W. Pleyte, however. His friend Hooft van Iddekinge also collected sherds from around the hunebeds and gave his well-administrated collection to the Assen museum (notes of W.J. de Wilde, from 1904-5).

379 Hooft van Iddekinge, member of the advisory board of the Assen Museum, was quite convinced of the importance of potsherds from the hunebeds, however. He collected sherds from around the hunebeds and gave his well-administrated collection to the Assen Museum (notes of W.J. de Wilde, from about 1904-5). Between 1905 and 1910, De Wilde collected sherds, which presumably still lay at the surface around most hunebeds (De Wilde 1910; pers. comm. W. Arentzen).

380 After 1807, 208 Danish ancient monuments – from dolmens to castle ruins – were legally protected. Another hundred were protected in and after 1873, when all ancient monuments were inventoried and described. But a general law for the protection of all ancient monuments was not made until 1937. Presently about 3000 dolmens and passage graves still exist in Denmark, which is probably 10% of the original number (Dehn et al. 2007, 273-4).

381 Thompson 1977, ch. VI; Evans 1956.

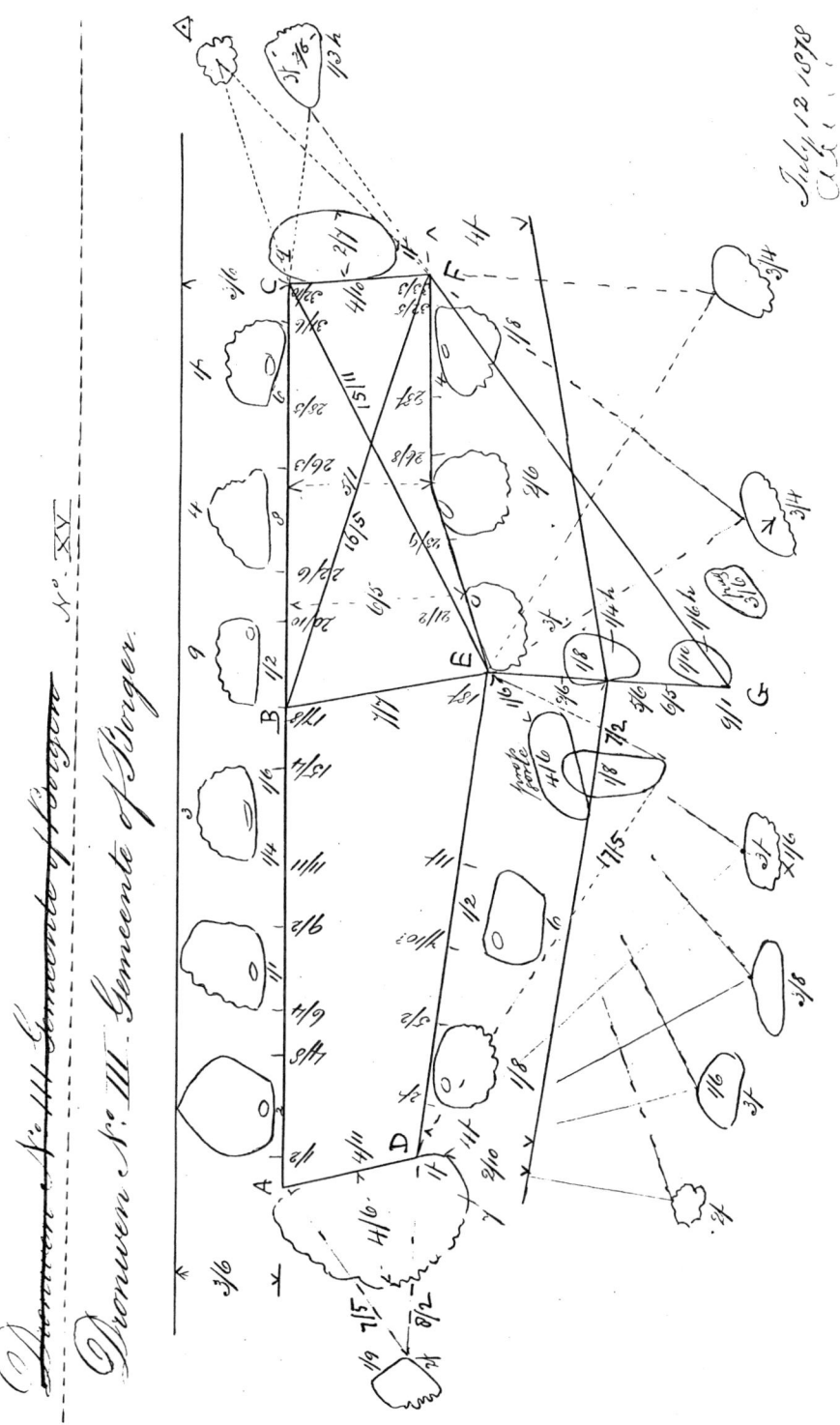

Figure 47. 'Sheet of measurements' of hunebed D26-Drouwenerveld by H. Dryden (photograph Society of Antiquaries, London). See further Appendix 3.

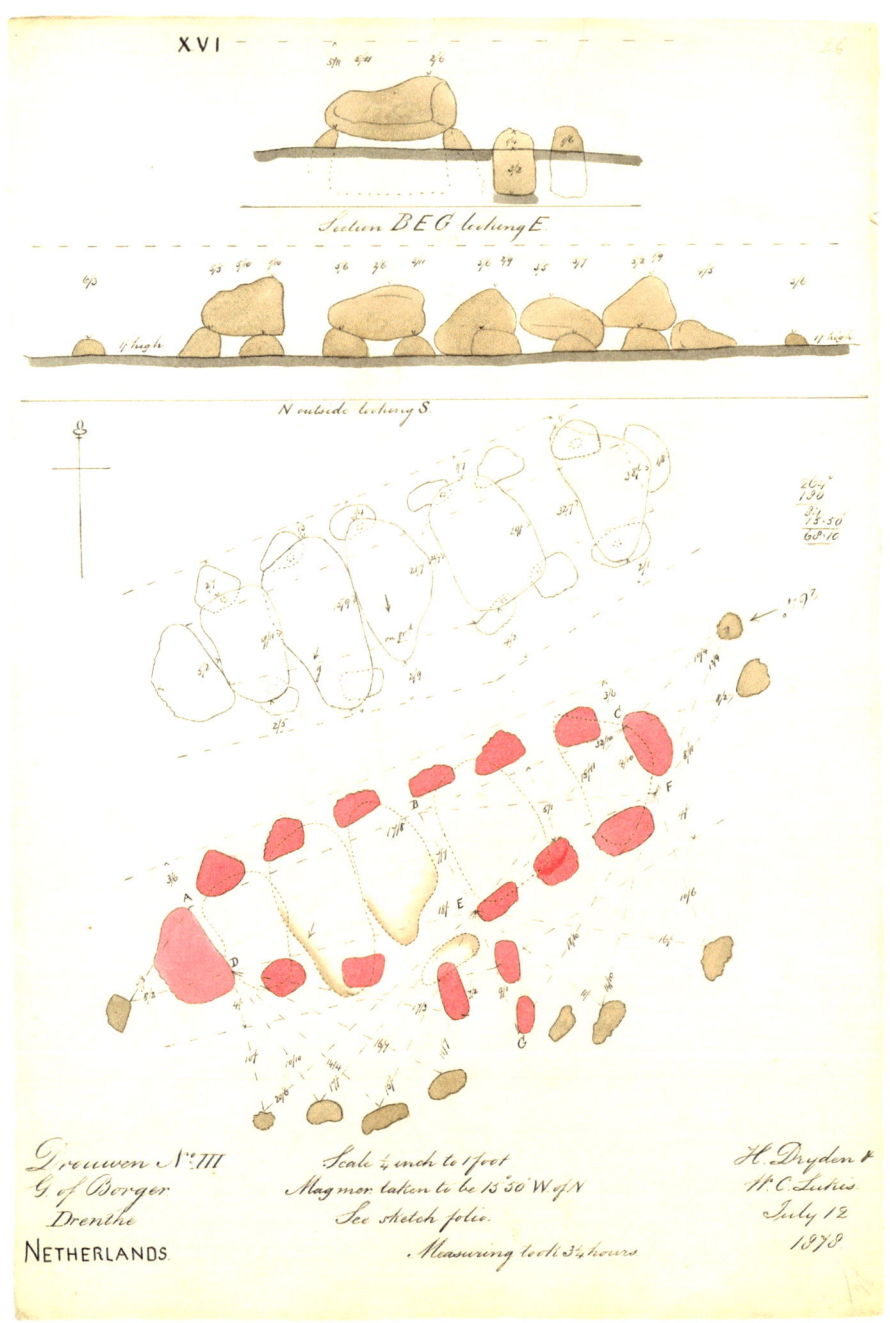

Figure 48. Plans and 'prospects' of D26-Drouwenerveld on July 12, 1878, by H. Dryden (photograph Society of Antiquaries, London).

Stunebed near Gieten. Drathe
Scale: 1/...
   W. C. Lukis. VSA. 8 July 1878

   View looking South.

Figure 49. Ink drawing, 36 x 23 cm, by W.C. Lukis of hunebed D14-Eexterhalte or Gieten, seen from the northeast, in 1878 (photograph Society of Antiquaries, London). See further Appendix 3.

the drastic restorations had already been done. Within three weeks, Dryden made painstakingly detailed ground plans and 'prospects' of 40 hunebeds, *viz.* three-quarters of those still extant (cf. Figures 47-48).[382] Dryden's plans were accompanied by 26 'sheets of measurements', which are kept by the Society of Antiquaries in Burlington House, London. Lukis described their form and topographical situation and drew views of these monuments (Figures 49 and 52) using a camera lucida (Figures 50-51). Although using a camera lucida required much practice, he preferred this light instrument to the cumbersome photographic equipment with its wet collodion plates, which was not always reliable and with which he had probably no experience.[383] He also dug several test pits. These were too small for studying the stratigraphy, but he sieved the excavated soil, a practice which would not become normal in Holland for another ninety years, in 1970.

Lukis illustrated a representative collection of the pottery and a few flint and stone tools from the hunebeds at full scale. He made beautiful full-scale watercolours of 27 TRB* pots in the Assen and Leiden museums and also of 105 decorated TRB* sherds, several of which he found himself. These were the first illustrations of TRB* sherds in The Netherlands.[384] Lukis was the first to recognise a ceramic disk, which he called a 'cover', and flint 'square-ended arrow points'[385]. The latter were transversal *petit tranchet* arrowheads, but he thought that the narrow base

---

382 Dryden and Lukis surveyed all Drenthe hunebeds except D1-4, D12, D32, D35, and D49-54, which are located to the west of the Hondsrug and the Ridge of Rolde.

383 Even the professional photographer Jan Goedeljee was not always successful when he photographed the hunebeds for Pleyte in 1874 (see the following section). Lukis's pencil drawing of hunebed D8-Anloo-N (pl. III) shows that he sat too close to the tomb, so that the size of the endstone in the foreground is exaggerated.

384 Lukis's manuscript from 1878 is kept by the Society of Antiquities of London; where I copied them in black-and-white, in 1976, cf. Bakker 1979c, p.15.

385 Lukis noted that at hunebed Bronneger III (D23-Bronneger), 'I found a square-ended arrow-point and fragments of urns close to the monument. W.C.L. 11. July 1878.'

A Description
OF THE
CAMERA LUCIDA.

By the means of this Instrument objects are represented on a sheet of Paper, so that an accurate Drawing may be made, even by those little accustomed to the Pencil.

In sketching from nature it is of the greatest use to the Artist; an indifferent draughtsman may make an accurate Drawing of the view before him.

Portraits may be corrrectly taken the size of life, or in any less proportion.

Paintings. Prints, Maps, Drawings of Machinery, Instruments, Furniture, &c. may be drawn in true perspective to any required scale.

Artists in various Trades will save much time by using this Instrument.

TO USE THE CAMERA LUCIDA.

Fix the Instrument to the table by the screw (or if it is the *Improved one,* it may be laid on the table, its weight being sufficient to balance it,) with the stem inclined. Place a sheet of Paper under the Prism, which must be turned, so that the face B may be exactly opposite the object to be drawn; by looking through the eye-hole downward on the Paper a picture of the object will be seen. The proper position of the eye-hole is of the first importance in the use of the Instrument; if the aperture is too far over the Prism, the Pencil will be indistinct, and if not far enough the object cannot be seen sufficiently clear: a little practice will make this perfectly easy. In first attempting to use this Instrument many persons lose sight of the Pencil, merely by the motion of the head in breathing, which they are not aware of. The longer the stem is drawn out the larger the object will appear, and the view less extended. If the object to be drawn is 2 feet from the Prism, and the Paper 1 foot, the copy will be half the size of the original; if the object is 1 foot from the Prism and the Paper 2 feet, the copy will be twice the size; and so in proportion for any intermediate distance.

This Instrument may be used with a Telescope or Microscope, (which must be an horizontal one) by placing the Prism close to the eye - glass: the magnified object may be drawn on a Paper beneath. Fig. 2 is a concave and convex glass for short or long sighted persons, which are sometimes framed to the Instrument: either of them may be used.

Figure 50. 'A Description of the CAMERA LUCIDA*', on a loose leaflet in the leather case of an early 19th-century English brass camera lucida. Author's collection.*

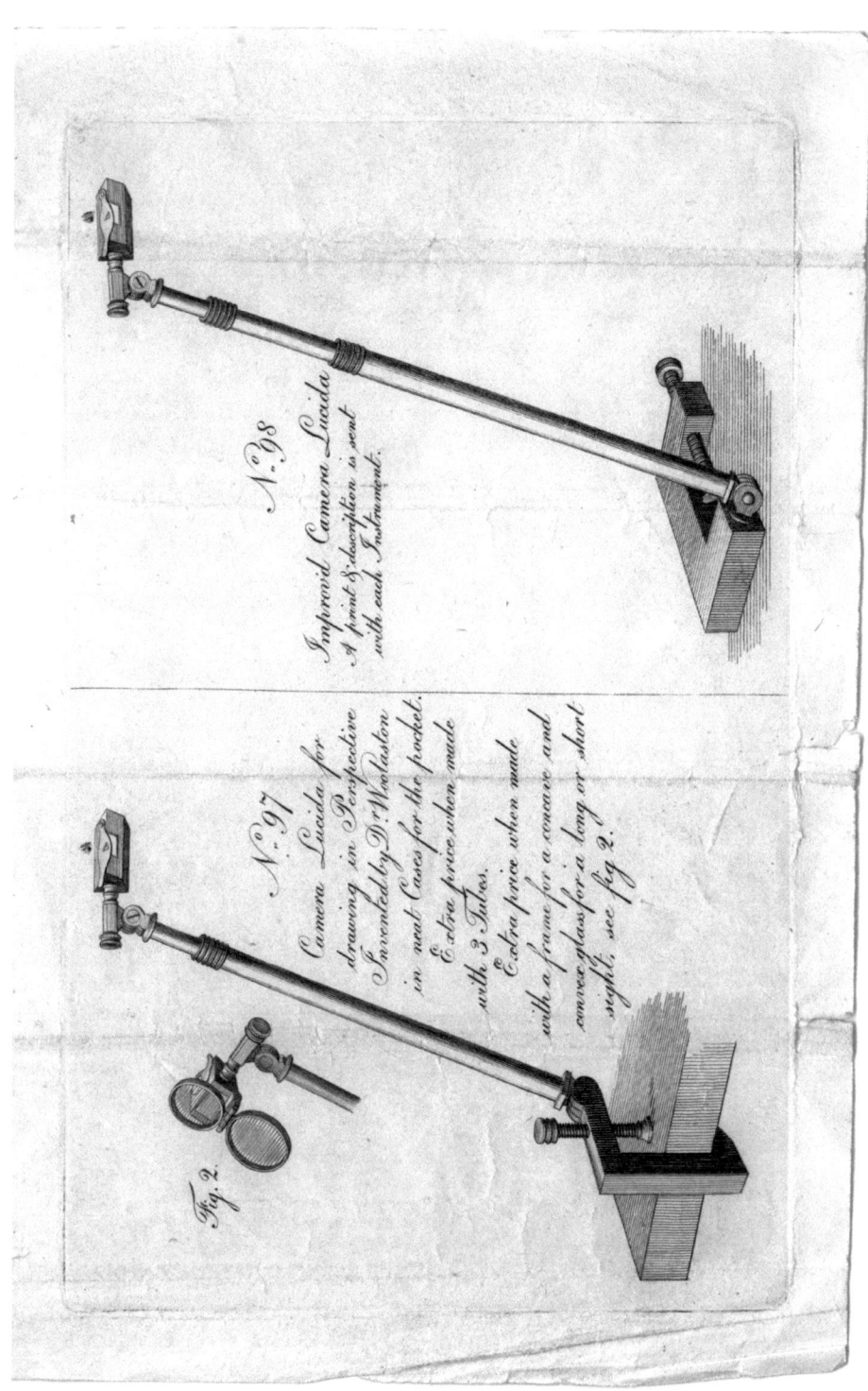

Nº.98

Improved Camera Lucida
A point & description is sent
with each Instrument.

Nº.97

Camera Lucida for
drawing in Perspective
Invented by Dr Wollaston
in neat Cases for the pocket.
Extra price when made
with 3 Tubes.
Extra price when made
with a frame for a concave and
convex glass for a long or short
sight. see fig 2.

Fig. 2.

Figure 51. The camera lucida can be used in a sitting or standing position, as early 19th-century and early 20th-century illustrations show. See further Appendix 3.

Figure 52. H. Dryden is surveying the Great Hunebed D27-Borger, July 13, 1878 (seen from the north). Pencil drawing by W.C. Lukis aided by a camera lucida (photograph Society of Antiquaries, London). See further Appendix 3.

was the tip.[386] Apart from 'bottles', i.e. collared flasks, he developed no further terms for the different 'urns' from the hunebeds.[387]

The results of this expedition were presented in a report to the Society of Antiquaries (Lukis 1879). In this excellent report Lukis expressed his doubts about the scientific value of the presentation of the hunebeds in Pleyte's *Nederlandsche Oudheden* ('Dutch Antiquities', 1877-1902) (see section '1867-1883'). Pleyte, who was publishing this book as a serial de luxe work – printed by E.J. Brill in Leiden – had probably shown him illustrations of hunebeds for the still unpublished parts of chapter I (1877-79) and the unpublished chapter II (1880-82) in the Leiden Museum, in 1878. No doubt because Pleyte was afraid that Lukis's disapproval would endanger the sale of his book, he defended it in the *Provincale Drentsche en Asser Courant*, the leading newspaper in Drenthe (February 13, 1880). In retrospect, Pleyte's defence is rather weak; he stressed that Lukis had not dealt with the publications printed before Janssen (1848) and that he did not know the chamberfill with its two floors. But whereas Pleyte's lithographs showing views of the hunebeds. made on the basis of photographs, are excellent, his plans are much inferior to Dryden's very accurate plans and 'prospects'.

---

386 Bakker 1979c. Lukis also drew a [Mesolithic] 'flint drill' and a stone axe fragment, both collected from a hunebed, and four later prehistoric pots and two bronze bracelets found elsewhere. He donated some of the sherds to the Assen Museum. The rest were sold together with his archaeological collection to the British Museum, in 1892, shortly before his death (Sebire n.d., 20). Lukis's Plate Ka, a watercolour showing 7 pieces of pottery from the western end of hunebed D27-Borger is reproduced (b/w) in Bakker 1979c, pl. VI.

387 In December 1976, when the currency rate guilders / pound was favourable, I photocopied the descriptions and the views of the Dutch hunebeds and drawings of artefacts from them made by Lukis, in Burlington House (cf. Bakker 1979c). I did not copy the plans and sheets of measures made by Dryden, which are very large, because a complete set is also kept in the Assen Museum. Nor did I photocopy Dryden's sheets of measurements. I did not study Lukis's original notes of Lukis in the Guernsey Museum. I do not remember if the pits dug by Lukis, which are indicated in the London set, are omitted in the Assen set, but this may be the case. I also studied the few artefacts collected by Franks and Lukis in the British Museum.
Van Giffen studied the Burlington House documents only after the publication of his *magnum opus* on the hunebeds (1925-1927). The second Dutchman who saw these documents before 1939, was Jan Butter [1881-1970], a geography teacher and amateur archaeologist, who also studied the artefacts that were found by Lukis, in the British Museum.

Dryden drew an extra set of his plans and sideviews for the Assen Museum of Antiquities at Gratama's request.[388] Unfortunately, costs prevented publication in both countries.[389] When A.E. van Giffen surveyed the hunebeds in 1918 and following years, he used the Assen set of Dryden's plans as an example for his own plans and copied Dryden's sideviews (atlas 1925-1927, pls. 117-8).

Lukis and Dryden had intended to publish a reduction of their plans, which were drawn to a scale of 1:48 (¼ inch to 1 foot). In 1925-1927, Van Giffen had his plans drawn to a scale of 1:50, which were fortunately not further reduced for publication (atlas). The size of Sprockhoff's three-volume atlas (1966, 1967, 1975) is almost the same size as Van Giffen's,[390] but his ground plans are on a scale of 1:100.

Van Giffen's diagram of hunebed orientations (1925, atlas-pl. 119 and p. 151-9) was obviously inspired by the one of Dryden in the Assen Museum (Figure 53). The same is true for a diagram made by De Wilde in the early 20th century, which remained unpublished and is now lost (see section '1904-1910').

With Franks's observations (1871-2), the surveys of hunebeds by Dryden and the expert drawings of TRB pottery by Lukis (1878-9), the Antiquarian Period of hunebed research came to an end in The Netherlands.[391] With all its defects, the systematic treatment of the Dutch hunebeds and the TRB* artefacts in Pleyte's monumental work on the 'Dutch antiquities' (1877-1902)[392] ushers in a new era in hunebed studies.

---

388 Four copies of Dryden's plans and sideviews are kept respectively in London (Society of Antiquaries, Burlington House), in Assen (Drents Museum), in Oxford (Dryden's bequest in the Ashmolean Museum, pers. comm. A. Sherratt) and in the Guernsey Museum (Lukis's bequest, pers. comm. H. Sebire, curator, 2006). Lukis's comments about and watercolours of hunebed pottery and flints as 'laid before the Society' together with Dryden's drawings made in 1878 (Lukis 1879) are in Burlington House. His original notes are in the Guernsey Museum [#] and the collected artefacts he brought home were bought by the British Museum shortly before Lukis's death. Gratama had offered to pay for one set of the hunebed plans and sideviews for the Assen Museum, but Dryden presented them as a gift.

389 Without a sponsor, complete publication is still hampered by costs. Particularly expensive are the full-scale reproductions of Lukis's ca. 40 watercolours of pottery, Plates A-H, Ia-c. Ka-b, L, N-R of TRB artefacts, and M and S-T of later objects, and camera lucida sketches of 16 hunebeds, which are in the archives of the Society of Antiquaries.

390 Van Giffen's atlas measures 51 x 33 cm and Sprockhoff's three atlases measure 48 x 32 cm.

391 Van Lier's book of 1760 was a prelude to this development. See section '1756-1760'.

392 See the following section '1867-1883'.

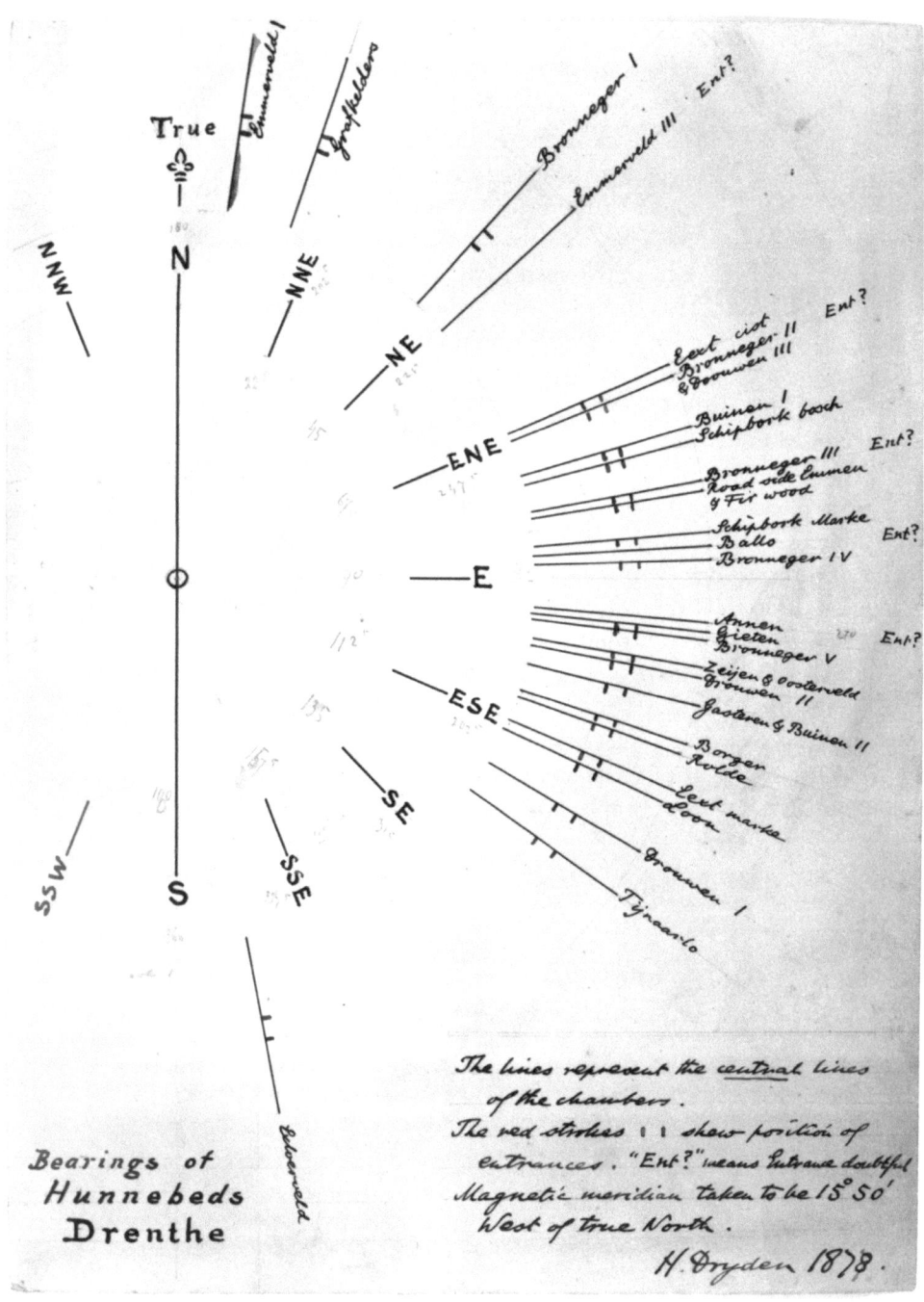

Figure 53. 'Bearings of Hunnebeds Drenthe' by H. Dryden, 1878 (Drents Museum, Assen, photograph by F. Gijbels, IPP). See further Appendix 3.

1867-1883: Pleyte, Leemans and Hooft van Iddekinge

The Drenthe archivist Magnin left his office in 1859. Janssen left the Leiden Museum at the end of 1868 and was succeeded as curator by Willem Pleyte [1836-1903], in 1869.[393] Pleyte, who had studied theology at the University of Utrecht, retrained himself in Egyptology when he found no appointment as Protestant minister. When he got a job at the Leiden Museum, his director Leemans, who also was an Egyptologist, made him curator for the Dutch Antiquities. Pleyte did not excavate any hunebeds himself. He discussed how hunebeds had been built in the first part (1877-9, 136-40) of *Nederlandsche Oudheden van de Vroegste Tijden tot op Karel de Groote* ('Dutch Antiquities from the Earliest Times until Charlemagne'), the de luxe serial publication describing and illustrating most archaeological remains in The Netherlands (1877-1902), which was scheduled to appear in two instalments per year.[394] The typochronological analysis of the artefacts is weak, many of the numerous lithographed colour illustrations on 198 folio-sized plates are inaccurate and reversed, and the local topography is incorrect at places.[395] Unfortunately, the serial character of the publication weakened Pleyte's style of writing: 'The unusual fragmented, illogical and inconsistent argumentation throughout this book impedes the reader from accepting the author's ordering of facts as well as his conclusions.'[396] Nevertheless, this catalogue of most artefacts and monuments known at the time remains most useful. Pleyte devoted his active years to this work, and such an enterprise has never been repeated in The Netherlands.

Although Pleyte (1877-9) quoted F. Wibel's more detailed version (1869) of Thomson's Three Age system at length, he hardly applied it to the Dutch artefacts in the rest of the book.

---

393 Having been led astray by the erroneous statement of Brongers & Wynia (2005, 29) that L.J.F. Janssen was director of the Coin Cabinet of Leiden University from 1863-1869, I asked colleagues at the Leiden Museum for information. Curator Mrs. A. Willemsen found in the Correspondence Archives that Janssen turned in his keys on December 28, 1868. Thus his appointment at the Leiden Museum ended December 31, 1868. On January 1, 1869, he probably became director of the Munt- en Penningkabinet ('Cabinet of Coins and Medals') of Leiden University (cf. *Jaarverslag* (Yearly Report) 1868 of the Leiden museum, 15) (pers. comm., March 18, 2010). Because C. Leemans, director of the Leiden Museum of Antiquities from 1839 to 1891, did not allow that Janssen combined his curatorship of that museum with the directorship of the Leiden Coin Cabinet, Janssen was obliged to leave the museum. W. Pleyte was appointed on January 11, 1869, as curator per February 1, 1869, by the Minister of Internal Affairs, who brushed aside Director Leemans's objections to a not so young Egyptologist (W. Arentzen, pers. comm., March 17, 2010).

394 Instalments covering antiquities in the provinces of Noord-Brabant and Limburg were never published; notes for them are bound in Pleyte's manuscript volumes (Leiden Museum).

395 See Van Giffen's corrections concerning hunebeds (1925, 89 n. 1; 93 n. 1-2; 97, n.2; 114, n. 1; 155-59, table).

396 De Wilde, unfinished manuscript 'De Hunebedden – Wat de schrijvers er van zeggen: W. Pleyte Nederlandsche Oudheden', p. 18: '*De ongewoon huppelende, nooit logisch en streng voortgaande argumentatie is overal in dit boek een ernstig beletsel om den schryver te vertrouwen, zoowel in zyne rangschikking der feiten als in de conclusies die hy trekt.*' (Arentzen 2010, 34).

In a way, Pleyte's work was the logical sequel to the inventories of Dutch sites where antiquities had been found, which was begun by Westendorp and, more or less simultaneously, by Reuvens and followed by Janssen. Reuvens's notes were published after his death as an inventory of sites with references to available information (Reuvens, Leemans & Janssen 1845). Janssen's extensive archaeological notes, which are in the Leiden University Library (MS. BPL 944), were published by G.M.C. Kramer-Clobus (1978). Ultimately, this practice of making inventories, which was continued by succeeding archaeologists, was the basis for the ARCHIS computer documentation of archaeological sites developed by the ROB / RACM / RCE in Amersfoort, which, unfortunately, still lacks illustrations of the archaeological objects concerned. The many illustrations of stray artefacts in Pleyte's work are therefore still valuable. Among the illustrations of TRB artefacts, polished axes of flint and other types of stone are most common. His illustrations of decorated TRB pottery are clear enough, although Lukis's unpublished drawings from 1878 are better.

Pleyte projected the localities near which antiquities had been found on a simplified version of Staring's 1:200,000 Geological Map of The Netherlands (1856-1867). This cartographic appendix was an important improvement since the small map by Engelberts (1790) and Reuvens et al. (1845) did not show the surface geology – or geomorphology.[397] A detailed soil map with the eleven hunebeds in the *gemeente* Borger and hunebed D30-Exloo, on a scale of 1:50,000, was also included separately.

Pleyte drew excellent lithographs of all hunebeds copied from photographs taken in 1874 by Jan Goedeljee [1824-1905]. This was perhaps the only occasion that this outstanding photographer, who was also bookbinder and undertaker, worked outside his hometown of Leiden. To bring his equipment to Drenthe and to photograph most hunebeds under Pleyte's supervision must have been quite an enterprise, but there are no detailed records of this trip. A small hooded carriage (*tentwagentje*), 'large enough to contain four persons,[398] a case with photographic liquids and equipment and the provisions' served as a dark room. It was moved as

---

397 Where the symbols for hunebeds etc. at one locality on the map were numerous, they were strung out and some of them appeared on the wrong soil type. J.H. Holwerda (1925) improved Pleyte's presentation by publishing three maps, on a scale of 1:600,000, with a simplified surface geology, using 5 soil types. On map I are plotted localities where the remains of 'the population of the Hunebeds' and 'the Beaker culture' occur; map II shows the localities of the 'Proto-Saxon, Gallo-Germanic and Germanic' remains; and on map III are plotted those of the Frisian-Batavian population, terps / *Wurten*, Roman sites and Frankish remains from the early Christian era. The locality names were indicated by short abbreviations in the colour that represented a culture or population, so that the sites were not printed on an incorrect type of soil.

398 Who these four persons were is not recorded. I suspect J. Goedeljee, W. Pleyte, J.E.H. Hooft van Iddekinge and, perhaps, W. Pleyte's brother P.B. Pleyte.
W. Arentzen found out that the *tentwagentje*, a closed carriage, is visible in the background, to the right, on Goedeljee's photograph of hunebeds D28-29, at Buinen (Leiden Museum). J. Zijlstra of the Rijtuigmuseum identified this hooded carriage as one of 'southern Dutch' type (letter to W. Arentzen, May 20, 2010). Pleyte 1877-1902: Drente, 1880-1882, pl. XXXV is a precise copy of the photograph, except that a horizon of his own invention was drawn above where the one on the photograph is.

closely as possible to each hunebed, but, even so, the walking distance was sometimes three minutes, which proved difficult, because the photographic 'glass plate
remained moist for only 7 minutes in the very high afternoon temperature on the
heath' (Pleyte 1877-1902: 1877-79, 139). Pleyte probably used reverse prints of
the photographs to draw the lithographs.[399] These excellent drawings clearly show
the whiteness of the boulders where the earth of the barrow had been taken away
by the 'restorations', around 1870; the trees often differ somewhat from the photograph (cf. Van der Sanden 2007, 103-7). Curiously, Pleyte drew the horizon ¾
cm above the real one in the picture of hunebed D15-Loon (Pleyte 1877-1902:
Drente, 1880-82, pl. LXIV). A similar thing happened with the lithograph of the
hunebeds D28 and D29-Buinen (Pleyte *ibid.*, pl. XXXV, see note 398), and probably much more. Irrelevant matters like the farm house behind hunebed D3-
Midlaren were omitted (Pleyte *ibid.*, pl. LIV).

Pleyte (*ibid.*, 1877-79, 136-40) thought that 'the most ancient Dutch and
builders of the hunebeds' occupied the region, perhaps, sometime after 3000 BC
and before 2000 BC. At the time, this was a relatively early date for Dutch and
northern European antiquities, although, as mentioned above, Willem Hofdijk
(1862) had dated the hunebeds to about 3000 BC (which is close to present-day
dates).

According to Pleyte (*ibid.*, Drente, 1880-82), the builders of the hunebeds
were Celts and related to the Tamehu, a light-skinned people who came from
Europe and built the dolmens in Egypt.[400] As an Egyptologist, Pleyte paid special
attention to these Tamehu and included two plates picturing them in his publication (Pleyte *ibid.*, Drente, pls. I-II). This idea about the Tamehu was already
fifteen years old at the time (W. Arentzen, pers. comm.). The Swiss archaeologist
Gustav Karl Freiherr von Bonstetten [1815-1892], alias Baron A. de Bonstetten,
had written in his *Essai sur les Dolmens* (1865, 49):

> *'Après avoir erré si longtemps de pays en pays, trouvèrent-ils enfin sur la terre
> d'Afrique la nouvelle partie q'ils chercheraint? L'histoire reste muette à cet égard,
> mais on croit retrouver en eux les ancêtres de la race blanche et tatouée des*

---

399 Under each plate is written 'W. Pleyte lith.' and 'P.J. Mulder impr.', and Hooft van Iddekinge
     (1877) stated that Pleyte drew the plates himself. Heavy retouches on the glass negatives of the
     hunebed pictures (by Pleyte) suggest, however, that they were actually drawn by others. As W.
     Arentzen concluded from these negatives (which are still kept in the Leiden Museum), most
     these pictures could not have directly been reproduced without heavy retouching.

400 In 1889, Pleyte specified that 'the Celts, which were related with the Tamehu' and had built the
     hunebeds, were not the Celts described by Caesar, but Celts who 'occupied the habitable sandy
     soils of our country, simultaneously with, or dominating, an older population, for which we have
     no other name, and which we call Celts as well, for brevity's sake' (Pleyte et al. 1889, 10-12, pers.
     comm. W. Arentzen). Pleyte thus became ensnared in his own words, probably because he had
     wanted to maintain, in his chapter Drente (1880-82), Westendorp's term 'Celts' for the hunebed
     builders, whose actual ethnic name was lost (the term 'primeval Celts' would have been much
     clearer). Perhaps it was also a reply to Stratingh's forty-year old idea (1849) that the builders of
     the hunebeds were a nameless preople. Pleyte may even have read Arend's *History* (1841ff.) in his
     youth (see section '1841 and 1849').

Tamhou (en égyptien, people du Nord) qui habitait sous les Ramsès le littoral de la Lybie.' [401]

Two years later the Leiden geologist and astronomer Elte Martens Beima [1801-1873], taking this account for a fact, wrote in *De Aarde vóór den Zondvloed* ('The Earth before the Deluge'; 1867, 547):

'No one knows from where these blond, blue-eyed people arrived; they inhabited ancient Numidia ... Désor saw there thousands of tombs and sacrificial places – named Dolmen and Menhir – which are identical to the tombs and monuments that are known as Celtic in Europe. Celto-Germanic tribes found their way to Europe via Spain and France.' [402]

In Pleyte's opinion, hunebed G1-Noordlaren should be excavated by gradually removing the chamberfill horizontally down to its base to locate the pots, potsherds, arrowheads, and stone implements. He also proposed that the soil at some distance from the stones of the chamber and the kerbstones be dug up (*omgespit*) to see if any artefacts were present (Pleyte *ibid.*, 1877-79). Fortunately, he did not act upon these proposals.

Pleyte had just been appointed as curator of the Dutch antiquities in the Leiden Museum when the hunebed 'restorations' were undertaken. This may explain why 'Leiden' took no action to stop them, even though Pleyte did not at all agree with them. Pleyte became clearly aware of the damage done when he made an inspection tours in 1870 and 1874 (Pleyte *ibid.*, 1880-82). Another factor was perhaps the persistent refusal of his director Leemans to go against the *laissez-faire* policy of the Minister of Interior Affairs towards the Province of Drenthe, which was only then gradually loosing its practical independence. Perhaps no one besides Pleyte was really aware of the damage done to the stratigraphy of barrow remains and chamberfills by the digging inherent to these 'restorations'.

Pleyte made his Drenthe tour of October, 1870,[403] together with Jan Ernst Henric Hooft van Iddekinge [1842-1881],[404] who's parental home Vennewoude at Paterswolde (just north of Drenthe) may have served as a *pied à terre*. P.B. Pleyte, W. Pleyte's brother, accompanied them.

Pleyte (1881) wrote a separate article about TRB* pottery collected near Hooghalen in Drenthe by the inn-keeper Kuiper, in *De Nederlandsche Spectator*. 'The question, where the builders of the hunebeds had lived, was now answered: they lived here. ... Curiously, no traces of them or of hunebeds were found on the

---

401   The Ramesside pharaohs reigned from about 1293 BC to 1070 BC.
402   Arentzen, pers. comm. Pierre Jean Édouard Désor [1801-1873] was a biologist and geologist, who visited the Sahara.
403   Pleyte, W. (1871), *Verslag van een bezoek der hunnebedden en de daarbij gevonden oudheden in den nazomer van het jaar 1870* ('Report of a visit to the hunebeds in the late summer of the year 1870', a manuscript of 21 p., Pleyte archives, Leiden Museum.
404   Pleyte (1877-1902) erroneously wrote that Hooft van Iddekinge was titled Jonkheer.

Veluwe'.[405] 'The pottery gleams when it is rubbed with a brush or a piece of cloth. Supposedly it was treated with wax. Its artistic design is by far superior to the pottery that was found in barrows.'[406] The TRB* pottery from Hooghalen, four complete funnel beakers (Pleyte 1877-1902, Drente, pl. LXXIV: 1-4), may have come from a flat grave cemetery, but there is no further documentation about the circumstances of their recovery.[407]

Conrad Leemans [1809-1893], director of the Leiden Museum between 1830 and 1891, who seems to have worked completely independently from his curators Janssen and Pleyte,[408] advised the Minister of Interior Affairs, in 1879,[409] after an inspection of the hunebeds, in 1877,[410] that:

'The floor of all extant hunebed chambers has been cleared; I am convinced that a deeper excavation would only render insignificant results; the same would be true for excavations of the soil around the tombs.'

---

405 The sandy Veluwe lies in the centre of the country, in the province of Gelderland. Holwerda (1909, 1911, 1912) found here TRB flat graves and a settlement in and next to the Hunneschans. And several other TRB sites were mapped there (Holwerda 1925). Pleyte (1881) overlooked the TRB artefacts and the possible hunebed U1 of Lage Vuursche, province of Utrecht (Pleyte 1902, pl. IV: 1, 2a-c, 5).

406 Viz. the plain Bronze-Iron Age pottery, which was secondarily interred in the upper part of barrows. Pleyte overlooked Corded Ware and Bell Beakers, especially the Veluwe type, which were buried underneath or lower in the barrows.

407 The above citations from Pleyte (1881) were loosely translated and abbreviated.

408 Leemans, who has an aggrieved expression on his best known photograph (Van der Sanden 2007, ill. p. 100), was disagreeable in his relations with his curators – first Janssen, then Pleyte. As a student-soldier, he had participated in the Ten Days Campaign of the Dutch army against the Belgian rebellion, in 1831, and was shot in his arm during the skirmishes at Boutersem, on August 11 (Jongstra 2010, 406). This made him a war hero. In 1839, the Dutch King finally consented to the Belgian independence from the United Kingdom of The Netherlands, to which the present Belgium had been assigned at the Congress of Vienna, in 1815. Cf. Otterspeer (1993) about Leemans.

409 Leemans sent the definitive report of this trip on October 24, 1879 to the Minister of Internal Affairs.
National Archives The Hague, Ministerie Binnenlandsche Zaken, afd. OKW 1848-1876, 2.04.08/1480 and 2.04.13/1481 (Van der Sanden 2007, 101-2 and pers. comm.).

410 Leemans was accompanied by Hooft van Iddekinge, in Drenthe in 1877. Leemans was chairman of the 'College van Rijksadviseurs voor de Monumenten van Gechiedenis en Kunst' (Board of State Advisers for the Monuments of History and Art', which existed from 1871-1877/8). Hooft van Iddekinge was its secretary and they visited the hunebeds in that capacity. Leemans numbered the hunebeds differently from Janssen (1848), but because his 1879 report remained unpublished, it had no effect on later studies. I leave here Leemans's quarrels with Pleyte and Hooft van Iddekinge about the hunebed trips and Hooft's hunebed plans (which Pleyte needed for his book) out of further consideration (see Bakker, in prep.).

Hooft van Iddekinge sketched plans of the hunebeds when he accompanied Leemans on his expedition through Drenthe in 1877.[411] Leemans measured their orientations with a compass. These sketches were tolerable, but they were clearly inferior to the exact plans drawn by H. Dryden in 1878. Pleyte, who did not have Dryden's drawings at his disposal, lithographed several of Hooft van Iddekinge's sketches for the 'Drente' chapter of his *Nederlandsche Oudheden* (Pleyte 1877-1902: 1880-82); these were not very precise and several were reproduced as mirror images.[412]

Hooft van Iddekinge (1877, 1879, 1880) reviewed successive issues of *Nederlandsche Oudheden* in *De Nederlandsche Spectator*, a much read periodical.[413] He wrote (1877) that archaeology had made less progress in Janssen's days than at present. Janssen had 'never presented much more than isolated facts ...The task of integrating these materials and building one edifice, seems to have been reserved for his successor, Dr. W. Pleyte.'

Leemans believed that all hunebeds were once covered by a barrow and that further excavation should await the discovery of new hunebeds in barrows. Actually, not any hunebed has been found in a barrow since 1809. It is fortunate, though, that Leemans's statement that all hunebed chambers had been cleared recently was patently wrong, for, given the deplorable excavation techniques in The Netherlands at the time, it was propitious that these erroneous pronouncements prevented the excavation of hunebeds for decades.

---

411 Leemans and Hooft van Iddekinge visited the hunebeds between May 28 and June 4, 1877, in 'a suitable cab and pair of horses and coachman' (*'een doelmatig ingericht rijtuigje met twee paarden en koetsier'*, Van der Sanden 2007, 101). Drawings made after Hooft van Iddekinge's sketches on brown oiled paper by the painter Jan B. Tetar van Elven [1805-1889], in 1877, are in the Pleyte archives, bound volumes 'Drenthe' i-ii Leiden Museum. See the illustration in Van Ginkel et al. 1999. p. 143 of the sketches of hunebeds D2-Westervelde, D1-Steenbergen, D3 and D4-Midlaren and G1-Noordlaren (but 'Pleyte' should be replaced by 'Hooft van Iddekinge' in the description). See also the illustration of Hooft van Iddekinge's sketches of D17 and D18-Rolde in Van der Sanden (2007, p. 103), who considered them 'very primitive'.

412 The plan of hunebed D15-Loon (Pleyte 1880-82, pl. LXIV, below left) is vertically mirrored and that of D41-Emmen (Pleyte 1880-82, pl. III:2) is upside down (the north arrow is reversed), for example. A long list of errors was compiled by De Wilde (1907), see Arentzen (2010). Pleyte wrote (1880, 12) about one of the hunebeds at Valthe, D36-D37: 'I made a photograph and Jonkheer Hooft van Iddekinge drew a plan.' This happened probably in 1874, but why he made the photograph himself is unclear. Did he mean 'I asked Goedeljee to make a photograph'?.

413 Hooft van Iddekinge did no further research on hunebeds. He published (1881) a book about 'Friesland and the Frisians in the Middle Ages. Contributions to the History, Jurisprudence, Numismatics and Geography of the Frisian Regions, in particular during the eleventh century'.

Finally it should be noted that Pleyte was an Egyptologist of international fame, who studied the important Egyptian collection of the Leiden Museum simultaneously with the Dutch antiquities.[414] When he studied a demotic magical papyrus in Leiden, for instance, he at once recognised the handwriting of its fellow in London.[415] The present-day Egyptologist H.D. Schneider once called Pleyte 'a genius'.[416]

Ca. 1868 and following years: photographs of hunebeds

Wet collodion glass negatives were invented by Scott Archer in 1851, but no photograph of a Dutch hunebed is known before the late 1860s. Janssen, Lukis and Dryden did not use photographs. In 1860, when the possibility of publishing Janssen's sketches of the hunebeds, from 1847, was discussed in the Dutch Institute of Letters and Sciences, professor Jan Ackersdijck [1790-1861] suggested to use photographs instead as examples for lithographic reproduction. This proposal was enthusiastically accepted by Janssen, but rejected by Leemans, because they would be less clear than drawings and, especially, because they would be much more expensive (Arentzen 2006, 211). Neither Janssen's sketches nor photographs were published at the time.

Van der Sanden's book about hunebeds D17 and D18 at Rolde (2007) contains a large selection of the great number of photographs of these hunebeds. Because the Rolde hunebeds were the best known and most portrayed hunebeds, this collection (which is not even complete) best shows how photography was used to document hunebeds.

The earliest known photograph, ca.11.5 x 9.5 cm, is of hunebed D18-Rolde and was bought by Pleyte in Assen, probably in H.P.A. van Gorcum's book shop, shortly after October 16, 1870.[417] The oak next to D18 has lost most, but not all of its leaves and low bushes are still in leaves, so the photograph was taken at the

---

414 W. Pleyte (1865) *Catalogue raisonné des types Égyptiens hiératiques de la fonderie de N. Tetterode à Amsterdam, dessinés par W. Pleyte.* Leiden: E.J. Brill (these fonts were still available in the 1970s); W. Pleyte (1866) *Études Égyptologiques I: Études sur un rouleau magique du musée de Leide.* Leiden; W. Pleyte & F. Rossi (1869-1876) *Le Papyrus de Turin.* Leiden: E.J. Brill; W. Pleyte (1879) *Études Égyptologiques III: L'Épistolographie Égyptienne.* Leiden: E.J. Brill; W. Pleyte & F. Rossi (1881-1882) *Chapitres supplémentaires du Livre des Morts.* Leiden: E.J. Brill; W. Pleyte & P.A.A. Boeser (1897), *Manuscrits coptes du Musée d'Antiquités des Pays-Bas à Leide.* Leiden: E.J. Brill. Separate studies on Dutch Archaeological subjects by Pleyte comprise Pleyte (1881) and Pleyte et al. (1889).

415 F.L. Griffith & H. Thompson (1904) *The demotic magical papyrus of London and Leiden* I, London (reprinted as *The Leyden Papyrus, an Egyptian Magical Book,* New York 1974). (W. Arentzen, pers. comm.).

416 See further Pleyte's long obituary (Boeser 1904).

417 Van der Sanden 2007, 90-4, ill. on p. 91, n. 10a: 10 on p. 206 (the photograph is in Pleyte's thick bound volume 'Drente'. Leiden Museum). W. Pleyte, *Verslag van een bezoek der hunnebedden en de daarbij gevonden oudheden, in den nazomer van het Jaar 1870* ('Report of a visit to the hunnebeds and the antiquities found near them, in the late summer of the year 1870'), manuscript report, finished March 9, 1871, in the Leiden Museum, in the mentioned volume 'Drente' in the Pleyte archives: 'Later on we bought a photograph of the best preserved [Rolde hunebed] in Assen.' (p. 6).

end of October, in November, or, perhaps, early December.[418] An almost identical photograph was reproduced as a print with the erroneous title 'Dolmen at Ballo' by James Fergusson in his *Rude Stone Monuments* (1872, 321), which went to the printer on December 1, 1871. This photograph was made just before or just after the one in Van der Sanden, because the two young men used to indicate the size of the tomb, have different positions on each photograph. Because it seems improbable that these photographs were taken immediately before Pleyte bought his, they must have been made in the autumn of 1869 or preceding years. The photographer was probably Friedrich Justus von Kolkow [1893-1914], who came from Danzig to Groningen in 1863, where he worked as a photographer.[419]

Jacob Dirks [1811-1892] showed one or more photographs of hunebeds on the 5th session of the Congrès International d'Anthropologie et de Préhistoire in Bologna in 1871.[420] Probably they were Von Kolkow's photographs.

Another photograph of D18-Rolde was made by Von Kolkow, in 1873.[421] As Van der Sanden noted (p. 93), the photograph was made in the spring of 1873, after a board with the inscription 'ROLDE' on a red and white blocked pole had been erected next to the hunebed. Von Kolkow made pairs of stereo photographs, in 1873, of hunebeds D6-Tynaarlo, D3-D4-Midlaren, D17 and/or D18 at Rolde, D43(?)-Emmen and D53-Havelte (Van der Sanden 2007, ill. p. 92-3) and showed them at the International Exhibition in Vienna in 1873, together with photographs of archaeological objects from Assen; he won a medal (Van der Sanden 2007, 93, 206 n. 12). The photographs of D18-Rolde show this tomb in the summer, before it was restored by L.J.G. Gregory between September and December, 1873.[422]

---

418 That the oaks were defoliated, in April-May, by caterpillars of the European oak leaf roller (*Tortrix viridiana*) or winter moth (*Operophtera brumata*) is unlikely.

419 About Von Kolkow, see Rooseboom (2008), about early photography in Drenthe, Goslinga (2008).

420 The Frisian antiquary Dirks, who was also active in Groningen, Drenthe and Overijssel, spoke in Bologna for fifteen minutes about the Drenthe hunebeds, a *terramare*-like formation at Paterswolde, Groningen, and the *terpen* of Friesland and Groningen. Gratama (1886) stated that Dirks showed one or more photographs of hunebeds. Dirks (1873, 96) reported that the lectures in Bologna were subdivided according to 'the well known Stone, Bronze and Iron Ages'. The Frisian antiquaries used the Three Age system much earlier than the archaeologists of the Leiden Museum.

421 Van der Sanden 2007, ill. p. 92 (above), 93, n. 10-1, 11 on p. 206. This photograph was also bought by W.C. Lukis, in 1878, in Assen (archives of the Society of Antiquaries of London). It measures 31.5 x 21.5 cm; the reproduction (or the original) in Van der Sanden is trimmed to the right and left and below.

422 Van der Sanden 2007, 94-7.

Pleyte, who was an amateur photographer himself,[423] introduced photography to Dutch archaeology, in 1874, when he had all hunebeds and many artefacts photographed for his 'Dutch Antiquities' (*Nederlandsche Oudheden*, 1877-1902). His successor Holwerda, in Leiden, and Van Giffen, in Groningen, used photography as an important tool for documentation.

As Pleyte described (see the preceding section), the Leiden photographer Jan Goedeljee used the wet plate collodion process in the hot summer of 1874, when he photographed most hunebeds. The wet plate method, which replaced the much more expensive daguerreotype, was invented by Frederick Scott Archer, in 1851, and it was generally used during the following 30 to 40 years – probably also for the two mentioned earliest photographs of D18-Rolde. This process allowed the photographer to make an unlimited number of prints from a single glass negative, but a major disadvantage was that the entire process, from coating to developing, had to be done before the plate dried. This gave the photographer about 10 minutes, sometimes less, to complete everything. The method required numerous chemicals and liquids, all mixed in a portable dark room if the pictures were taken outside. The camera was as large as a shoebox and a heavy tripod was indispensable.[424] Goedeljee used a *tentwagentje*, a hooded carriage, which was 'large enough to contain four persons, a case with photographic liquids and equipment and the provisions' and also served as a dark room. It was moved as closely as possible to each hunebed, but even so, the walking distance was sometimes three minutes, which proved difficult, because the photographic 'glass plate remained wet for only 7 minutes in the very high afternoon temperature on the heath' (Pleyte 1877-1902: 1877-79, 139). The prints and the negatives of these photographs in the Leiden Museum show as it were, how 'the technical possibilities of that time were stretched to their limits' (pers. comm. W. Arentzen, 2010). Most photographs have scratches caused by an ill-functioning transport of the plates.[425]

One should realise, however, that other photographers may also have taken the aforementioned photographs. The Groningen photographer Johannes Gerhardus Kramer [1845-1903] photographed townscapes in Groningen and views in surrounding villages, and he visited Drenthe several times around 1870 and following years. The uppermost photograph on p. 130 and described on p. 127 in Van

---

423 Pleyte signed a letter to the mayor of Assendelft, on October 9, 1879, 'W. Pleyte Mzn, amateurphotograaf, Diefsteeg No. 1 te Leiden' (Beeldbank Leiderdorp, pers. comm. W. Arentzen). He 'took a photograph [of a hunebed at Valthe, in 1874], while J. Hooft van Iddekinge sketched a plan' (Pleyte 1880-82, p. 25). Or did J. Goedeljee actually make this photograph at Pleyte's request?

424 The preceding is mainly based on the article 'The Wet Collodion Process' on Youtube on the internet, by an anonymous author.

425 In 1874, Von Kolkow proposed to the 'Board of State Advisors for the monuments of History and Art' (*College van Rijksadviseurs voor de Monumenten van Geschiedenis en Kuns*t, viz. chairman Leemans and secretary Hooft van Iddekinge) that he photograph all hunebeds, but this was not accepted (Van der Sanden 2007, 206 n. 11). Was he too expensive, was Goedeljee preferred by Pleyte, or had Goedeljee already agreed to the undertaking? And did Leemans, Pleyte and Hooft van Iddekinge freely discuss this offer among each other? In 1874, Leemans had not yet seen the hunebeds himself.

der Sanden (2007) was actually taken by Kramer. His 11 x 6 cm cabinet photograph of D17-Rolde, pasted on cardboard with a hand written date *Aug. 1887* on the back, is signed *J. G. Kramer* GRONINGEN on the front. A sticker on the back indicates that it was sold by the Van Gorcum en Comp. book shop in Assen.[426] This photograph was taken just before or after Kramer's cabinet photograph, because they are identical except for the position of the boy on top of the capstone. The lower photograph (ibid.), was probably made on the same day by Kramer, because the view is similar and the same boy is in the picture. This photograph was published about 1900 as a postcard by Van Gorcum en Comp. in Assen.[427]

A unique album *Photographieën van Assen* was presented, on September 7, 1895, to the 15-year-old Queen Wilhelmina [1880-1962] and her mother, Queen-regent Emma of Waldeck and Pyrmont, Princess of Orange and Nassau [1858-1934], when they visited Drenthe; it is now in the *Koninklijk Huisarchief* in The Hague. It contains photographs of the hunebeds D3-Midlaren, D4-Midlaren and D6-Tynaarlo, in addition to Kramer's photographs of D17 and D18 at Rolde (Van der Sanden 2007, 127, ills. on p. 130-1).[428] It is not known if these were also taken by Kramer.

In 1896, the tax collector and amateur archaeologist Geert Jannes Landweer [1859-1924] presented his photograph of hunebed D45-Emmerdennen, which was taken in 1895, to the Assen Museum. Two years earlier, on October 1893, the well-known photograph of Harm Tiesing [1853-1936], small farmer and writer about regional history, who was leaning against the large Borger hunebed, D27, was taken.

Dry plate negatives were invented in 1871 by Richard L. Maddox. They were industrially made, in 1878, by Wratton & Wainwright, in London, and the Liverpool Dry Plate and Photographic Company.

De Wilde, who is discussed in the following section, used dry negative photography for his hunebed documentation, in 1904-6. He used two box-like cameras, one of which was loaded from packs with 10 or 15 glass plates that were 9 x 12 cm, the other with that number of 13 x 18 cm plates. They were probably orthochromatic plates, viz. insensitive to red and deep orange light, so that they could be inserted in the camera in a dark room with red light. His first series, made in 1904, went amiss in the dark room, and the next year he made a new series.[429] In August, 1906, he photographed Neolithic objects in the Museum and, again, hunebeds – a relatively high number of glass plates failed again in the process.

---

426 On October 1, 1872, the book-shop H.P.A. van Gorcum and the publishing house Van Gorcum were merged to form 'Van Gorcum en Comp.'.

427 See M. Goslinga, Een Kabinetfoto van J.G. Kramer, *Waardeel* 2009 (4), p. 16.

428 Van der Sanden noted that the photograph of hunebed D17-Rolde was taken earlier, as is shown by the presence of an oak tree that had disappeared by 1891. As mentioned above, Kramer took it before August, 1887.

429 Arentzen, pers. comm. 2010

When Van Giffen photographed the hunebeds himself in 1918, he used a large mahogany-framed camera, a heavy wooden tripod, and a black cloth over his head. Almost all of these excellent photographs were printed in his atlas (1925-1927).[430] Holwerda or his technician would have used similar equipment, in 1912-14. As W. Arentzen remarked, photographic techniques were probably much improved since De Wilde's time.

After the introduction of roll film cameras, around 1914, and tourism was becoming increasingly popular, numerous photographs of the hunebeds were taken. Since the tombs were easy to photograph and unusual objects, they gradually became symbols of Drenthe throughout The Netherlands; the Drentians themselves had been much earlier convinced of their value by Picardt (1660).[431] To celebrate its 25th anniversary, the Dutch touring association ANWB held a competition for photographers, and an ample selection of the photographs that were sent in was reproduced in *Ons eigen land* (1908, 'Our Own Country'), consisting of five volumes. Photographs of hunebeds D6-Tynaarlo, D17-Rolde and D27-Borger appeared in volume 3, opp. p. 45 and 47.

Beginning about 1900, picture postcards of hunebeds were sold to visitors by the thousands (Ten Anscher 1988).[432] Several are quite useful, because they show the situation before Van Giffen's drastic restorations, which took place mainly after 1945.[433]

1885: a wall painting of hunebed building, in Assen

When the new *Provinciehuis* (Province House) in Assen, Drenthe, was opened, in 1885, one wall of its *Statenzaal* (council hall of the provincial representatives) was decorated with five monumental wall paintings of the most important episodes

---

430 A few photographs in a pre-print of the book, which is still kept in the Groningen Institute, were omitted in the definitive publication.

431 A geography and history textbook for the primary schools in Drenthe (Oostkamp 1822) briefly mentioned the Celtic Fields* (*legerplaatsen*), tumuli and the 'since long renowned' hunebeds [following Picardt 1660 and Van Lier et al. 1792]. The hunebeds were discussed in ca. 270 words, with reference to Van Lier (1760) and Westendorp (1815).

432 Ten Anscher (1988) described some of the collections of hunebed photographs on postcards, but completeness was impossible. He assumed that the names of the localities printed on the postcards were correct, but several of the pictured hunebeds have an incorrect locality name, or one which does not conform to those used in Appendix 1.

433 From 1918 on, Van Giffen repositioned the sidestones and capstones of the hunebeds he investigated to enable the excavation of the chamber fills. In 1912-3, Holwerda did the same. After that, touristic interference made the repositioning of such stones often necessary. Between ca. 1945 and 1973, Van Giffen systematically restored all Dutch hunebeds (including the kerbstones). See further M. Goslinga, Portret bij 't hunebed. Mensen bij hunebedden op ansichten, circa 1900-2000, *Waardeel* 2007 (2), 24-32. #

het · bouwen · van · eene · grafstede ·
door · de · oudste · bewoners · van ·
Drenthe ·

Figure 54. 'The building of a burial monument by the earliest inhabitants of Drenthe', wall painting by Georg Sturm (1885) in the Council-hall of the Provincial Gouvernement of Drenthe in Assen (photograph by Vincent van Vilsteren, Drents Museum). See further Appendix 3.

from the history of Drenthe.[434] They were designed by Georg Sturm [1855-1923] and painted on the wall by the German painter F. Florack and his brother. Sturm was born and active in Vienna, until he came to The Netherlands, in 1882, to design historical wall paintings for the Amsterdam *Rijksmuseum*, and stayed. He also designed this type of wall painting for the *Statenzaal* in the new *Provinciehuis* in Zwolle for the province of Overijssel (1898). Presumably, Lucas Oldenhuis Gratama [1815-1887] was the main adviser about the choice of the five episodes to be depicted. Probably he also advised Sturm about how to represent 'The building of a burial monument by Drenthe's earliest inhabitants' (Figure 54). He and the representatives were well aware of Picardt's assertion (1660) that the hunebeds were among Drenthe's most valuable properties.[435]

Hunebed builders had been depicted, in 1859, in a drawing by Rochussen (see section '1856-1862') showing them cutting a tree. The first to depict them, of course, was Picardt (see section '1660' and Figures 6-8). Sturm did not improve on these former representations. As mentioned before, Picardt's clothes of animal skins were inspired by those of medieval Wildmen and it would be a long time before Isings gave the builders simplified, woven Bronze Age clothes in 1959 (Figure 3).

In the Assen painting, the handling of a boulder using cords, a lever and a roller by the four men in the foreground appears rather clumsy. Picardt's (1660) hunebeds are better rendered than Sturm's. The latter's hunebed is standing free without an enclosing barrow or dry walling stones and its entrance in an unusual place – or was the heavy stone in the foreground meant to fill the gap between the orthostats? The architecture of this tomb is enigmatic and shows that neither Sturm nor Gratama had a clear idea of it. They should have consulted Lukis, Dryden, Hooft van Iddekinge, or Pleyte!

An accurate uncoloured lithographic reproduction of Sturm's painting of Drenthe's hunebed building inhabitants appeared in *De Nieuwe Drentsche Volksalmanak* of 1885 as an illustration for part II of Gratama's study 'The Hunnebeds in Drenthe' (1885).[436] When Carel Vosmaer [1826-1888], the editor of *De Nederlandsche Spectator*, discussed this edition of the *Volksalmanak* in his weekly, he remarked (1885, p. 111) that this illustration showed that Gratama disagreed with the former King of Sweden 'about the manner in which these huge stone masses were placed on top of each other'.

---

434 For 'the building of a burial monument by Drenthe's earliest inhabitants' (*het bouwen van eene grafstede door de oudste bewoners van Drenthe*), see Figure 54. The four other pictures are titled 'The preaching of the Christian faith by Willehad', 'The conquest of Drenthe by Charlemagne', 'The Gift of Drenthe to the Bishop of Utrecht', and 'The Province Aldermen devise the *Landrecht* [the first Drenthian code of law]. After the provincial representatives of Drenthe left the *Provinciehuis*, in 1973, the former *Statenzaal* became part of the Assen Museum.

435 See section '1660'.

436 The lithograph is signed 'G. Sturm inv.' and 'Lith. Gebr. Braakensiek. Amst.'. In it, the tattoos of the men are much clearer rendered than in the wall painting (Figure 54).

Actually, Vosmaer should have attributed the implied theory to King Frederik VII of Denmark (1857), not the former King of Sweden, and he could also have mentioned Janssen (1853a) or even Bödiker (1828), who had similar theories.[437] All three had argued that an earthen barrow around the standing stones of a hunebed chamber reached to their tops; the capstones could thus be moved up the barrow on rollers into position. In Sturm's painting, such a barrow was absent and so were alternative devices, such as scaffolding or a wooden ramp.

When Gratama reprinted his (1884-85) study in a book (1886), he used the lithograph as frontispiece and reacted to Vosmaer's critique on p. 190-192, mainly by quoting an enthusiastic description of the picture in the *Handelsblad*. In no less than 187 words, this newspaper described what is shown in the picture, probably because it had no illustrations at the time. 'The race of giants, so powerfully built, that created such giant's graves[438] and expressed their veneration in such a majestic manner for the dead and the King of Terrors,[439] who was maybe the only one they worshipped. ... We were actually transported back to the Stone Age or, as Prof. ECKER puts it, the Pre-Metal Age.'[440]

Vosmaer reviewed this book in *De Nederlandsche Spectator* (1886, p. 109-10) and stated that Gratama 'did not fully agree' with the contents of the painting.[441]

1904-1910: De Wilde

Willem Johannes de Wilde [1860-1936] was a chief assistant of physiology at Utrecht University until he resigned, in 1902. He spent part of the summers of 1904, 1905 and 1906 as a private archaeologist in Drenthe. His main concern was the outer appearance of the hunebeds. He excerpted information about them from all the relevant publications he could find, copied Dryden's hunebed plans from

---

437 See section 'How was a hunebed constructed?' Bödiker's 1828 study may have been unknown in The Netherlands.

438 'Race of giants' and 'giant's graves' are used here metaphorically; the hunebed builders are not depicted any larger than the individuals in the other wall pictures.

439 'King of Terrors' means death in person (Job 18: 14).

440 Where the anonymous journalist of *Handelsblad* picked up Ecker's 'Pre-Metal age' is unknown. Alexander Ecker [1816-1887] was one of the founders of German physical anthropology (craniology). He was a professor in Physiology and Anatomy at the universities of Basel, Switzerland, and Freiburg in Breisgau, Germany. Together with Ludwig Lindenschmit [1809-1893] he edited the volumes of the periodical *Archiv für Anthropologie* (1886-1942) and wrote (1863-1865) *Crania Germaniae meridionalis occidentalis*, mainly about skulls from early medieval cemeteries (Gummel 1938, 412-3). None of the lengthy quotations from his editorial considerations in Gummel (1938) mentions 'a Pre-Metal Age', but prehistoric chronology and the Three Age system were a common topic of discussion in German archaeological circles at the time. Ecker does not occur in bibliographies about Dutch hunebeds and megalithic tombs elsewhere in Europe (e.g. Van Giffen 1925: 212-29; 1927: 510-49).

441 This is not evident to me from Gratama's text (1886). Apparently Gratama did not understand Vosmaer's words, because he had not studied Frederik VII's publication (1857 or 1863) himself.

the set kept in the Assen Museum[442] and checked their accuracy on the spot. He drew plans of the hunebeds that were missing from the set Dryden made and took several photographs of all of them. He gave the hunebeds new locality names, numbered them in alphabetic order and filled out a long questionnaire about architectural details and the locality of each tomb. This documentation was bound in nine notepad-size volumes, of which only one is still preserved; it includes hunebeds '28. Gasteren-N' [D10-Gasteren], '29. Gieten-ZW' [D14-Eexterhalte], '30. Loon-N' [D15-Loon], '31. Midlaren-WI' [D3-Midlaren] and '32. Midlaren-WII' [D4-Midlaren] along with bleached photographs and sketches of the shapes of the orthostats.[443] Dryden's compass rose of hunebed orientations in the Assen set inspired De Wilde to make a new one, which was never published and is now lost.[444]

De Wilde knew the Dutch, and several German, Danish, and Swedish archaeological publications, stressed the importance of modern excavations and argued that, following the Danish example, an Inspector of the Hunebeds should be appointed. Holwerda would begin modern excavations in 1912-13 and Van Giffen would continue this and would begin acting as a *de facto* inspector in 1918 (Bakker 2004, 144-7; Van der Sanden 2007, 137).

As mentioned above, De Wilde complained in 1905:

> 'our Hunebeds are a completely neglected part of our archaeology; so that, in fact, we do not even know the simplest things about them. It is more than high time to finally put the hands, or rather the minds into action.'[445]

In a publication of 1906, entitled 'A legendary omnipresence', he pointed out that King Louis Napoleon on horseback had posed on the large and flat capstone of hunebed D45-Emmerdennen, in 1809, and not on capstones of various other hunebeds, as was later claimed.[446]

---

442 J.A.R. Kymmell, the curator of the Assen Museum of Antiquities allowed him to borrow and copy these at home in Utrecht. De Wilde's pen-and-watercolour copies of Dryden's drawings are very similar to the originals, but are on notepad-size paper (ca. in quarto). (Bakker 2004, 144-7; Arentzen 2010). On Sundays in August, 1906, De Wilde studied the Neolithic artefacts in the Assen Museum. He analysed and sketched several details of TRB decoration, stone axes, battle-axes and flints. Then he also photographed hunebeds, but several glass negatives failed.

443 Van der Sanden illustrates (2007, 137), some of these notes by De Wilde.

444 Among his papers is the typed draft of [the well-written introduction to] a study about the orientation of the hunebeds.

445 Letter to the curator of the Drenthe Museum of Antiquities in Assen, December 10, 1905.

446 Van Giffen (1925, 226) omitted this article by De Wilde (1906) from his bibliography concerning hunebeds, probably because he thought it irrelevant, but he briefly mentioned the event on p. 166n.

De heide met Hunebed bij Tinaarloo.

Figure 55. View of hunebed D6-Tynaarlo. School picture from 1901 by Bernard Bueninck [1864-1933]. See further Appendix 3.

One year later, he wrote a scornful critique of Pleyte's *Nederlandsche Oudheden* (1877-1902), which J.H. Holwerda (1906) had called 'a standard work' (De Wilde 1907). He emphasised Pleyte's mirrored illustrations of hunebed plans and arte-facts and other errors. According to De Wilde, Holwerda admitted that his praise had been exaggerated.[447]

In an unfinished manuscript, De Wilde wrote in 1907:

'I myself have seen traces, and certainly recent ones, of disturbances in the soil in virtually all hunebeds. And once one knows that the 'culture layer' in the hunebed soil, that is, the layer in which the burial remains are found, lies at most a half meter under the surface, but more usually right at the surface, it is easy to imagine that even a simple pocket knife in the hands of an unqualified person can create an archaeological disaster. Do not suppose that I express this too strongly, because a good archaeologist must be aware that also the smallest potsherd can be of signifi-

---

447 According to De Wilde's letter of March 3, 1907 to J.A.R. Kymmell, curator of the Assen Museum.

*cance for his science and may even have decisive value for systematics and knowl-
edge of prehistoric phenomena in our country. But a site that is disturbed one time
by an incompetent person is lost and has become almost completely worthless.'*[448]

Hardly any of the sherds from such unauthorized grubbing reached the museums, most were thrown away, I might add.

As W. Arentzen (2010, 88) noted, De Wilde (1908) was the first who used the history of the Dutch archaeology to explain how the thinking about this discipline had developed.

In a lecture given in Assen, in January, 1909, De Wilde discussed the differences between the southwestern European megalithic tombs and the Dutch hunebeds, which closely resembled the megalithic tombs in German Hanover (now Lower Saxony). Jan Gualtherus Christian Joosting [1846-1944], *rijksarchivaris* (state archivist) in Drenthe, related the contents of De Wilde's lecture at length to the Historical Society in Groningen on Saturday, January 23, 1909, at the house of Jonkheer Johan Adriaan Feith [1858-1913], *rijksarchivaris* for Groningen:[449]

'*The hunebeds are constructed, in his opinion, like a child's game of dominoes:
first two standing stones with a capstone, followed by a small chamber with one
open side, then a closed chamber, ultimately making one large room by elongation
and widening.*[450] *The first forms are found in Africa and England, the following
in France, Hanover and our country. Large elongated chambers occur in France,
widened chambers in our country and Hanover. De Wilde concludes from this
that the development did not go from Northern Africa, to Spain, France, The
Netherlands; thus our hunebeds are not Celtic but Germanic (Nordic or Saxon).*'

---

448 'Ik zelf heb by zoogoed als alle Hunebedden sporen, en wel zeer recente sporen van omwroeting van den bodem gezien. En wanneer men nu weet dat de "kultuurlaag" in den Hunebedbodem, d.w.z. de laag waarin de begraafresten gevonden worden, hoogstens een halve meter diep onder de vrije oppervlakte ligt en meestal zelfs al begint onmiddellyk aan de oppervlakte, dan is het gemakkelyk in te zien dat zelfs een eenvoudig zakmes al in den vuist van een onbevoegde een archaeologische ramp kan veroorzaken. Men meene niet dat ik my hier te sterk uitdruk, want een goed archaeoloog moet het besef hebben dat ook de kleinste potscherf van belang is voor zyn wetenschap en zelfs mogelyk van beslissende waarde kan worden voor nadere systematiek en kennis der oudheidkundige verschynselen in ons land. Maar wat eenmaal door een onbevoegde is ontgraven is verloren en zoogoed als geheel waardeloos geworden.' De Wilde 1907, unfinished manuscript *De richting der megalithische graven in Nederland*, p. 4; Arentzen 2010, 43.

449 Letter from W. Arentzen, 8.9.2009. Carl Wilhelm Vollgraff [1876-1967], professor in Greek Language and Literature at Groningen University and Jacob Adolf Worp [1851-1917], man of letters, historian and teacher at the Groningen gymnasium, were also present. Michael Schoengen [1866-1937], external lecturer in palaeography at Groningen University, who became *rijksarchivaris* of Overijssel in 1909, was absent. Feith spoke about the round churches of Bornholm. Cf. Van Berkel (2009) about the Groningen *Historisch Genootschap* ('Historical Society').

450 This description of hunebed architecture is as confused in the Dutch original version as in translation, probably because Joosting or the writer of the minutes had no clear image of hunebed architecture. Obviously no actual dominos were used to explain the principles of hunebed construction in the Groningen lecture! In my opinion, De Wilde may have described a hunebed as a row of elements, each consisting of two sidestones covered by a capstone, closed by an endstone at both ends. No reference is made to an entrance in the middle of one long side in the description; 'widening' may or may not have referred to the widening of the chamber in the middle.

'Most important was De Wilde's theory about the height of the hunebeds above A.P.[451] The orientation of the hunebeds provides no clue, because they point in all directions,[452] which argues against a religious reason for their location. It appears that all hunebeds are located on diluvium [glacial deposits], just beyond the bounds of the alluvial deposits, and almost all at the same elevation. Since alluvium is deposited in shallow water, the hunebeds were placed near the beach of an ancient sea. Their orientation was determined by that of the beach. If one assumes with De Wilde that Drenthe did not become inhabited until just before this sea changed into peat bogs, one should date the hunebeds some thousands of years before Christ. To which may be added that surrounding peoples, if need be Vikings, may have brought their dead to the coast of Drenthe for burial in order to overcome the well-known fear of the deceased, by transporting them overseas.[453] Geological research has to confirm De Wilde's hypothesis further, but undoubtedly it is important, because it could generate hypotheses to explain the hunebeds.'

In the same year, De Wilde (1909a, 122-3) stated that Drenthe first was inhabited around 3000 BC by the pastoral descendants of the Danish Kjökkenmöddinger people, who built the hunebeds and who gradually migrated through Schleswig-Holstein, Oldenburg etc. He promised to explain the reasons for this assumption in a later study, but never did.

Also in 1909, De Wilde (1909b) pointed out that archaeological excavations under and around the Stone of Lage Vuursche (the possible hunebed U1) would have interesting results; he stated that he was available to supervise such excavations.

It irritated him that Jan Hendrik Gallée [1847-1908] made in a study about 'Traces of Indo-Germanic ritual in Germanic funeral ceremonies' (1900-1901, 134-5) no less than ten mistakes in a short discussion of the hunebeds, as he explained in six closely written pages among his notes.[454]

In a lecture in Amsterdam, in 1910, De Wilde (1910b, 12-13) said:

'[The hunebeds D53 and D54 at Havelte-Darp] are not identical in orientation, but their axes are parallel to the slope of the hill. It is known, moreover, that the [water of the] Steenwijker Aa [book] reached the foot of the hill [Havelterberg], but it was shallow and stagnant and not flowing as a stream.'

De Wilde's theory used Lorié's (1887) description of geomorphology the periglacial landscape extensively, and connected its development to the hunebed period. Although he knew that the moraines from the Ice Age in Drenthe were 'very

---

451 A.P. means Amsterdam Ordnance Datum, more or less equivalent to the mean sea level (today it is N.A.P.).
452 This is exaggerated, see Part A.
453 This may have been Joosting's own comment, in my opinion (the Dutch sentence is somewhat longer).
454 Unfinished manuscript *Nederlandsch Keltisme* (1913), cf. Arentzen 2010, 73-6.

old' (*overoud*),[455] he apparently overlooked or disagreed that Lorié's periglacial sandy landforms dated from the Diluvium / Pleistocene and were much older than the hunebeds. As the text of his Assen lecture, cited above, shows, De Wilde seems to have thought that most peat bogs in Drenthe were open water at the time when the hunebeds were in use. A few indications in his available notes seem to confirm this, but there is no evidence that he questioned why stone axes and bronzes occurred in the peat and were not found on their sandy subsoil.

In 1910, De Wilde (1910a) wrote a long, informative article about the outer appearance of the hunebeds in the popular *De Kampioen*, publication of the ANWB touring club, in which his considerable knowledge of the monuments is evident. He used reductions of Dryden's hunebed plans and added his own plans of hunebeds D53-Havelte and D13-Eext,[456] and also discussed the split boulders in the walls of the churches of Odoorn and Emmen.

De Wilde was the only Dutchman of his generation who studied the architecture of each of the 53 hunebeds, and he did this extremely carefully.[457] Although he described and sketched the pottery and stone artefacts from the hunebeds that were in the Assen Museum scrupulously – with clear comprehension of stab-and-drag decoration techniques –,[458] he did not concern himself with what now would be called the 'cultural background' or even the 'culture' of the hunebed builders, because he, like most archaeologists of his time, was not aware of the 19th-century concept of 'an archaeological culture', which Kossinna would elaborate between 1909 and 1921, and which was refined by Jażdżewski for the TRB culture, in 1932 and 1936, and by Childe for archaeological cultures in general, in 1950 (see the following section).

---

455 In De Wilde's quire *Uittreksels*, p. 3. 'Pod. 10'. He also excerpted a study by the geologist F.J.P. van Calkar (1885) about the Diluvium [Pleistocene] near Nieuw-Amsterdam in Drenthe (in the same quire).
 H. Meijer's chapter 'In het land van de Hunnebedden' (In the country of the hunebeds) in the book *Ons eigen land* ('Our own Country', 1908, vol. 3, p. 37-9) shows that Torrell's theory (1875) about how Scandinavian glaciers had brought the 'immense granite boulders' of the hunebeds to Drenthe was general knowledge at the time. 'The contents of the hunebeds prove that the people who used them burned their dead and collected the ash in crude urns made of loam, and that they used primitive stone tools.' (*ibid.*).

456 Dryden's plan of D13 had been sent as a specimen to the Leiden Museum, where it is kept in the Pleyte archives.

457 See further the study about De Wilde's life and hunebed research by W. Arentzen 2010. I am much indebted to Wout Arentzen for allowing me to use several new data from this study.

458 Quire *Eigen beschrijving. I. Voorwerpen in en onder de hunebedden gevonden* ('Own description. I. Objects found in and under the hunebeds'), 1906. De Wilde drew a trapezoidal arrowhead in it, which was 'found by W.C. Lukis, hunebed Emmerveld n° 3, 1878' [D38] with the blunt base (a) at the top and the cutting edge (b) at the bottom, like Lukis had done in his unpublished drawings. De Wilde commented that [the top of] (a) was 'apparently broken off' and that (b) was 'very sharp'. Neither Lukis, nor De Wilde was aware that the 'very sharp' edge (b) was the actual cutting edge (cf. section '1871-1879'). Apparently, Lukis's interpretation was perpetuated in the Assen Museum.
 De Wilde's notes on [Neolithic] artefacts were followed by a description without drawings of the bronze artefacts in the Assen Museum. There are no notes left about similar studies in the Leiden Museum.

In 1913, De Wilde drew the outlines of a large study 'Nederlandsch Keltisme' (Dutch Celtism) in sections marked § 1-21.[459] In the draft, De Wilde stated in § 13 that the succession of prehistoric periods in Denmark was:

1. Maglemose
2. earliest Kjökkenmöddinger period
3. latest Kjökkenmöddinger period
4. earliest Megalithic period
5. middle Megalithic period
6. latest Megalithic period (with indications of a transition to a Copper Age and Bronze Age).

Only stages (5) and (6) were represented in The Netherlands, and they could have been somewhat later in absolute years than they were in Denmark. In § 20 he dated the *Hunebeddentyd* (Hunebed Period) to 3000-1000 BC.[460]

Joosting's report of De Wilde's Assen lecture, cited above, shows how hunebed research – restricted to the outer appearance as it was – stagnated almost completely before systematic excavations of whole hunebeds started. De Wilde was only too well aware of this, but when J.H. Holwerda and A.E van Giffen began their hunebed excavations, in 1912 and 1918, respectively, he stopped his archaeological activities.[461]

1886-1911: undocumented 'exploration' of hunebeds goes on

No other research of hunebeds worth mentioning took place till 1912. Unsystematic digging in the chamberfills by robbers went on, however, until the early 1980s,[462] and hardly anything recovered reached the museums.

As early as 1848, Petrus Speckman van der Scheer [1820-1858], book-seller, printer, and publisher at Winschoten, who had an interest in archaeological and historical subjects, wrote:

---

459 Arentzen 2010, 73-6.
460 A reference to Holwerda (1907) provides a *terminus post quem* for this typescript.
461 Between 1914 and his death in 1936, De Wilde did not publish at all, for unknown reasons. Strikingly, he did not take part in the excursion to Holwerda's excavation of hunebeds D19 and D20-Drouwen, in 1912, by the Nederlandsche Anthropologische Vereeniging ('Dutch Anthropological Society'), the excavation's sponsor. Although many persons in the group photograph taken that day (reproduction in Van Ginkel et al. 1999, 33) cannot be identified anymore, De Wilde appears to have been absent. The sturdy man with straw hat in the middle background almost certainly was Prince Hendrik of Mecklenburg-Schwerin, consort of Queen Wilhelmina, and not De Wilde.
462 In 1983-85, a pavement of perforated concrete blocks (the kind used for parking lots) was laid about 15 cm below the surface of all chamberfills of the Dutch hunebeds that had not yet been systematically excavated (Bakker 1992, 7, fig. 3; Van Ginkel et al. 1999, ill. p. 154).

'There is no denying that many if not all hunebeds have been completely or partly dug previously. Diverse persons confirmed this to us personally; but what was found have remained secret.' [463]

In 1872, the visiting English archaeologist Augustus Wollaston Franks noted:

'Nearly all the Hunebedden having been explored by treasure seekers and others, there is little hope of obtaining from them complete urns, and although many urns are preserved in the museum at Assen, there are scarcely any that are known for certain to have been found in the Hunebedden; they were mostly collected years ago by persons who were content to attach to them the names of the villages near which they were found, without [providing] *any further particulars.'* (Franks 1872, 5).

And, in 1873-74 and 1877, the amateur archaeologist Douwe Lubach [1815-1902] wrote:

'It is my opinion that all hunebeds have been explored' (Lubach 1873-74; 1877, 166). [464]

As we have seen, several hunebeds were dug into by gentlemen in the 18th century. This digging went on in the 19th and 20th centuries. Hunebed D10-Gasteren 'was excavated in May 1854, a stone chisel, a few urns, a small pot etc. were found.' [465] 'The hunebed at Vries' [D5-Zeijen] was bought by the Province, in 1856-1857, through the mediation of the King's Commissioner and the Archivist Magnin; this purchase ensued after the mayor of Vries, in 1856, stopped a stone seeker from collecting further floor stones etc. of the tomb, after reporting that 'a chisel was excavated from it and presumably more can be found in it'. [466] In April, 1878, J.H. Textor, master of the Vries-Zuidlaren railway station, excavated two large fragments of collared flasks from the chamber of hunebed D6-Tynaarlo and turned them over to W.C. Lukis, who gave them, together with two small sherds that he recovered himself, to the Assen Museum. [467] In 1904-5, De Wilde found traces of recent digging in nearly all hunebeds. Van Giffen (1927) mentions other – documented! – diggings in the hunebeds throughout the 19th and early 20th centuries.

---

463 P.S. van der Scheer, *Kronyk van het Historisch Gezelschap te Utrecht* 1848, 190 (cf. Arentzen 2006, 140).

464 D. Lubach was State Inspector of Health Care in Overijssel and Drenthe (Gratama 1884a, 30).

465 Arentzen (2006, 119), citing Janssen, who quoted the *Leidsche Courant* of May 7, 1854 and the *Haarlemsche Courant*

466 Arentzen (2006, 120) citing Janssen, who quoted from *Haarlemsch Dagblad* [*Haarlemsche Courant?*] of December 24, 26, 27 or 28, 1856. The deed of acquisition of D5-Zeijen, in July, 1857, for 68.00 guilders, indicates that actually D5 was concerned (and not D6-Tynaarlo in the same municipality, which was not bought by the State until 1880; cf. Van Giffen 1925, 21, 23).

467 See Lukis's manuscript plates B: 1-4. His other plates show many other pieces of pottery and axes from several hunebeds in Dutch and his own collections.

Fortunately the statements by Van der Scheer, Franks and Lubach were not completely true, at least not the implication that nearly all hunebed chamber fills had been dug up and cleared. From 1912 onwards, systematic and complete excavations, although too hastily executed, of Dutch hunebed chambers and sites of destroyed tombs began to be undertaken and published by Holwerda (1913a; 1913b; 1914) and Van Giffen (1919; 1924; 1925-1927; 1927; 1943a, 1943b). The full variety of pottery forms and styles of the TRB culture emerged from the astoundingly numerous sherds and pots recovered from the hunebed chambers (Frontispiece), which had previously been only partly represented by the drawings of Pleyte.[468]

Regional Groups and the concept of a 'TRB culture'

James Fergusson [1808-1886] dated the Drenthe hunebeds to a period ranging possibly 'from the Christian era down to the time when the people of this country were converted to Christianity, whenever that may have been' (1872, 322), more or less similar to Gratama's idea. Nevertheless, a Stone Age date for the Funnel Beaker* or TRB Culture*, its types of pottery and megalithic tombs, its distribution and regional sub-groupings was gradually perceived during the 19th century. The first to do so were archaeologists who studied related monuments and artefacts outside their own local regions and had a wide geographic overview.

As early as 1815, Nicolaus Westendorp, who had surveyed the megaliths and their contents in NW Germany on a special trip in the early summer of 1813 (Bakker 2004, 130-1), argued that the hunebeds in northwestern Germany were made by the same people as those in Drenthe:

> 'Whoever has seen the orientation and the general outer aspect of the latter [hunebeds], would not be convinced? Everywhere the same urns, weapons, outer appearance, architecture, building-material and orientation! Could these similarities be a coincidence? Aren't they proof of identical customs of a people, an identical religious faith and superstitious worship, an identical way of interment, based on the same ideas and institutions? How could this proposition be better supported than by this similarity in aspects where the people do not allow any arbitrariness?' (Westendorp 1815, 285-6).

He was also aware of the similarities between the Dutch hunebeds and those of North Germany, Denmark and Sweden, which he knew from the literature. He did not focus further on the group of Dutch-northwestern German hunebeds, because he wanted to stress the uniformity of one single, very early Celtic people, who had built all megalithic tombs in a broad zone along the North Atlantic coasts, from southern Sweden to Spain and from Ireland to the Oder (Figure 36).

468　The excellent watercolours of pottery from Drenthe hunebeds by W.C. Lukis, from 1878, in the files of The Society of Antiquaries of London, were (and are) little known.

Augustus Wollaston Franks [1826-1897] noted (1872) the similarities existing between tombs and artefacts of what are now called TRB West and North Groups:

> 'In several of the Hunebedden I discovered fragments of pottery ... and I saw in Leyden a similar collection, as well as a flint arrowhead, obtained in the various Hunebedden by Mr. Pleyte and Mr. Hooft van Iddekinge, some of which they were good enough to give me. These fragments are of considerable value. I ventured, while at Assen, to call the attention of the members of the Commission to the value of fragments of pottery, which with due search might probably be found in most of the Hunebedden.[469] These fragments enable us to judge the character of the pottery found in these sepulchres and I beg to exhibit drawings of some of the urns from Assen, of which several, from the similarity to the fragments, must have been found in the Hunebedden.[470] The whole style of the pottery agrees with what we know from Germany and Denmark as belonging to the stone age, and stone implements seem unquestionably to have been found in these structures...'[471]

Eighteen years later, the TRB West Group* was identified (1890) in so many words by the German archaeologist Otto Tischler [1843-1891], from Königsberg (East Prussia):

> 'Within the whole area of the megalithic graves, different local territories can be defined, every one of which displays an inventory of completely uniformly styled pottery. Such a territory comprises, for example, Hanover, Oldenburg, northern Westphalia and the eastern Netherlands'.

In the early 20th century, the German archaeologist Gustaf Kossinna [1858-1931] discerned the geographical extension of what he recognised as one TRB *culture* (*Trichterbecherkultur*) and four regional groups on basis of pottery types: the Northern, Western, Eastern and Southern TRB Groups (Kossinna 1909-10; 1921, 143-51, fig. 9; Midgley 1992, 32-3). Two generations later, the Polish archaeologist Konrad Jażdżewski (1932; 1936, 227-30) provided a fuller description of the TRB culture and its regional groups, and divided the Eastern group further into Eastern and Southeastern components. This regional division of the TRB culture is used to this day, although the boundaries between adjacent groups are not sharp (see Figure 1, cf. Midgley 1992, 32-3).

The 19th-century concept of a prehistoric 'culture' (cf. Meinander 1981), which Kossinna elaborated, was clearly defined (1950, 2) by Vere Gordon Childe [1892-1957]:

> 'A culture is defined as an assemblage of artifacts that recur repeatedly associated together in dwellings of the same kind and with burials by the same rite. The

---

469 This remark makes quite clear how little aware Gratama and other Drenthians were of the importance of sherds.

470 It is not always clear in the Assen Museum administration where its TRB pottery was found before 1916, when Van Giffen began to reorganise the archaeological department.

471 Where Franks's sherds and drawings are kept is unknown to me.

arbitrary peculiarities of implements, weapons, ornaments, houses, burial rites and ritual objects are assumed to be the concrete expressions of the common social traditions that bind together a people'.

In 1968, David Clarke [1937-1976] redefined it:

'An archaeological culture is a polythetic set of specific and comprehensive artifact types which consistently recur together in assemblages within a limited geographical area.' (Clarke 1968, 285).

Although it was *bon ton* to argue against this concept in the 1970-90s in the University of Amsterdam Institute for Prae- and Protohistory, where I was teaching, and although it does not always apply well to Metal Age and later archaeology, I have never doubted that 'the TRB culture' represents a prehistoric reality. As Kossinna observed, it has sharp, distinct boundaries, despite a few outlying artefacts that were exchanged with members of surrounding cultures (see Bakker 2001a).

Epilogue

Andrew Sherratt [1946-2006] posed (1996) a dialectic between 'Enlightenment' and 'Romanticism' as modes of thought in European post-medieval cultural and intellectual history and applied it to the history of archaeological thought (Figure 56). These two modes reflect an alternation of 'action' and 'reaction', but rarely does the one become completely silenced by the other. In an attempt to reconcile both modes of thought in archaeology, Sherratt noted that both research traditions could be united within the work of the same author.[472] Undeniably, there had been also a geographic or cultural bipolarity between the developments in Germany and France. His scheme (Figure 56) detailed the new elements in both modes of thought.[473] Timothy Darvill (2006, Table A) placed an 'Age of myth and legend' before the 'Reformation' as the earliest, medieval and 16th century stage of the 'Romantic' mode in this scheme, when he subdivided the research history of Stonehenge accordingly.[474]

At first sight it would seem rather easy to discern the same alternation within the megalithic research in Drenthe. The medieval word *hunebed* reflects the 'Age of myth and legend'; Schonhovius (1547) worked in the 'Humanist Renaissance tradition'; the Calvinist Picardt (1660), with his Nordic giants, and the Calvinist jurist and historian Van Leeuwen (1685), who adhered to this theory, may be classed under 'Reformation'. Smids (1694), J. Hofstede (1706), Van Lier and Vosmaer (1760), P. Camper (1768-1781), J. and P. Hofstede (1809) represented

---

472 Sherratt added a note 'This is not to imply that individuals mechanically obey the dictates of the *Zeitgeist*; only that each of these opposing structures is more attractive than others. Individuals may try to create their image in the likeness of one or the other, often rhetorically exaggerating the difference – Van Giffen and Holwerda, perhaps?' (Sherratt 1996, n. 2).

473 Piggott (1950) described in great detail how the various scientific approaches of the 18th century influenced William Stukeley, but nowhere did he formulate the opposition of rationalist and romantic approaches as pronouncedly as Trigger (2006, 537) might seem to imply. In this respect, Piggott's 1950 formulation was not a direct predecessor of Sherratt's 1996 model (which is not discussed by Trigger).

474 Piggott's subdivision (1976, back cover) of the history of antiquarian and archaeological thought about and research in the United Kingdom until the 1830s cannot be applied to the history of the study of the Dutch hunebeds, as described here. He identified four successive stages between the Elizabethan and the Victorian ages in British archaeology: (1) The 'great 17th century period, associated with the spirit of description, identification, and classification of field-monuments and artifacts'. (2) The 'decline in antiquarian scholarship in the period after 1720, typical of the fall of standards of medieval studies, generally, in the 18th century.' (3) The 'replacement of the older scientific rigour by a romantic approach to the past, with its "soft primitivism" of Noble Savage and of Golden Age, and its cult of the Picturesque.' (4) A 'return to a more analytic methodology with the emergence, in the 1830's, of the country archaeological societies, themselves much influenced by the Tractarianism movement and the revival of interest in church architecture.' Please note that Piggott situated a 'romantic approach' in his third period, i.e. subsequent to Darvill's period of Romanticism and *Volksgeist*, between 1720 and 1800 (2006, Table A). Darvill adhered to Piggott's idea of a fundamental change occurring about 1720, although it has been argued that Piggott's recognition (1950) of a striking contrast between an early, matter-of-fact Stukeley and his 'intellectual decline and fall after about 1720-30´ cannot be upheld (cf. Piggott 1976, 49-50).

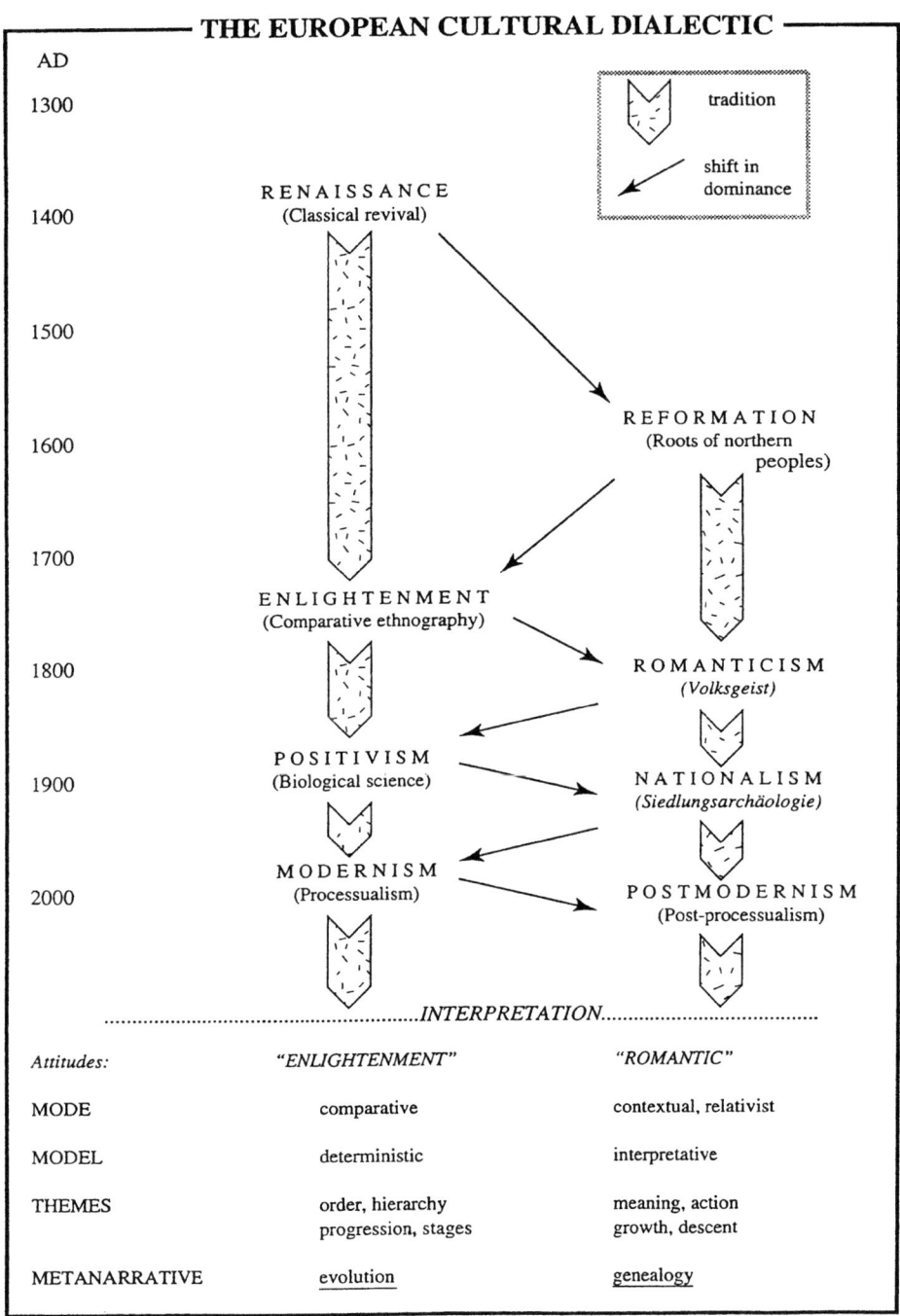

Figure 56. 'The European cultural dialectic' (A. Sherratt 1996, fig. 1). The title reads: 'The alternation of attitudes in European cultural and intellectual history: the succession of movements which have given rise to and influenced archaeology, conceived as a dialectic between ideologies of stability and revolt. These movements reflect both temporal fluctuations in economic prosperity and geographical oppositions (especially North / South, though most recently between Europe and the USA).'

the 'Enlightenment' mode, although most of them actually represented a physio-theological version of it, which regarded Nature as displaying God's works, and was prevalent in The Netherlands at the time.[475] On the other hand, A.G. Camper (1808), Westendorp (1815, 1822), Janssen (1847-1869), Gratama (1867-1886) and Pleyte (1877-1882) represented the 'Romantic' mode, whereas their visiting English colleagues Franks (1872), Lukis (1879) and Dryden, and the Dutchman De Wilde (1904-1910) represented the enlightened-positivist attitude.

On a closer look, it is only too evident that adherents to a new mode retained essential elements of the old mode, as Sherratt correctly argued. Schonhovius worked in the humanist tradition of the Renaissance, but still accepted the Devil's Cunt myth and the giants (in the guise of 'Herculeses'), which derived from the 'Age of myth and legend'. Picardt (1660) thought that the devil formerly had been active near hunebeds. Van Leeuwen (1685) still believed in the former existence of giants and their role as builders of hunebeds. Smids (1694), in examining the human bones taken during the first excavation of a Dutch hunebed, saw that they were of normally sized people; but a quarter century later, he reverted to the theory that giants built the hunebeds (1711). J. Hofstede (1706) wrote a brief, straightforward excavation report, but used ideas of the Italian Renaissance author Alessandri for his theory that some of the pottery had contained provisions for the interred. Van Lier (1760) discussed hunebed D13 and its contents at length in five essays in a book, for which he used archaeological and ethnographic studies, as well as classical sources about the age and the civilisation of the builders. This was also done by the 'romantic' researcher Westendorp, who paid close attention to the stages of development of the hunebed builders – typical for the Enlightenment – and consulted the classical and ethnographic sources as well. Adriaan Camper was a typical enlightenment empirical scientist,[476] like his father Petrus Camper, Van Lier and Vosmaer, but he took a 'romantic' interest in the ethnic identification of the hunebed builders (1808).

According to the Dutch-German education system, one would perhaps be inclined to divide the attitudes towards Dutch hunebeds between the languages and history (*alpha*) and the natural sciences (*beta*) research traditions, with sociology (*gamma*) as a more recent development. This division is roughly comparable to

---

475 As exemplified by *Kathechismus der natuur* ('Nature's Cathechism') by the Mennonite clergyman J.F. MARTINET: Amsterdam, J. Allart, 1777-1779, 4 volumes in 8 tomes, an extremely popular, richly illustrated encyclopaedic introduction to Creation aimed at reconciling science with the Revelation. It was reprinted a number of times and translated into several languages. It does not mention hunebeds.

476 Adriaan Camper had been privately educated in mathematics, physics, natural history and classical and modern languages in his parental home, after which he studied medicine and natural history in Groningen and Leiden. Den Tex (2004) has called him 'a remarkably modern geologist' for his conclusion that a basalt terrace, containing granite but also boulders from the Volane valley bottom, demonstrated that the basalt had flowed over a boulder bed, 'a purely inductive hypothesis explaining a geological scene'.

Sherratt's, but the Renaissance study of Roman and Greek sources would then be placed under the 'Romantic' mode, and the beauty of the antiphony in Andrew's scheme would be disturbed.[477]

The concept of *Volksgeist* ('national character'),[478] so typical of German history and archaeology in the 19th century (Figure 56),[479] was almost absent from contemporary Dutch archaeology (Eickhoff 2007).[480] Nationalism, which arose in such an extreme form in Germany around 1900 (Figure 56), with Gustaf Kossinna in the forefront, was never an important factor in Dutch hunebed or other archaeological studies.[481] In 1760, Vosmaer opposed Van Lier's supposition (1760) that the hunebed builders were the (ancient Germanic) ancestors of the Dutch, because their tombs occurred only in a small corner of the country. Westendorp (1815; 1822) argued that the hunebed builders were ancient Celts, in the first History of our Fatherland. And although Janssen denoted them again as the most ancient, Germanic ancestors of the Dutch, between 1848 and 1856, this gave no rise to a general national pride in the prehistoric past that was in any way comparable to that of 19th and early 20th century Germany and Denmark. Between 1795 and 1815, a Dutch nation state was forged from the former United Provinces. It had renounced its expansionist aims in Europe[482] and the source of its national pride was its artists and the deeds and wealth of the 15th to the 17th centuries. The poorly known prehistoric past was left out of consideration. According to the Dutch historian E.H. Kossmann (2007, 148):

---

477 Moreover, it is not completely true that Humanism brought 'modern, rational' approaches to late medieval historiography in western Europe, between 1450 and 1550 (which has often been maintained). It added data from classical sources such as Tacitus, but usually retained the old myths and added new ones about the origin of tribes, and towns and noble families. Moreover, humanistic historiography had distinct local patriotic traits, of which the 'Batavian myth', which located the Insula Batavorum and the Batavians of Tacitus in Holland and Utrecht, rather than in the Betuwe in Gelderland, is an example (Ebels-Hoving 1987, 234ff.; Tilmans 1987).

478 For the concept of *Volksgeist* (*Volksseele, Nationalgeist, Volkscharacter*), suggested by Herder and coined by Hegel in 1801, its earlier forms in the 17th and 18th century, and its 19th-century impact in Germany, on Slavic authors, and in America, see N. Rothenstreich in *The Dictionary of the History of Ideas*, 2003, Charlottesville, Electronic Text Center # (internet), p. 490-6. 'It is a term connoting the productive principle of a spiritual or psychic character operating in different national entities and manifesting itself in various creations like language, folklore, mores, and legal order' (p. 490-1). There were no written sources on the character of the hunebed builders, of course, in contrast to Tacitus's observations of the Germani. The Germanic people played an essential role in the historiography of the Batavians in The Netherlands between 1500 and 1800 (Langereis 2004).

479 Darvill (2006, Table A) located 'Romanticism / 'Volksgeist', rather anachronistically, between 1720 and 1800.

480 Eickhoff (2007) describes how late 19th-century German classical philologists and archaeologists looked down upon Reuvens and Leemans for this reason. Neither Janssen nor Pleyte theorised about the ancient *Volksgeist* in prehistory. It could be argued that level-headedness and common sense – often rather banal – are a constant factor in Dutch 19th- and 20th-century archaeology.

481 Bakker 1990a, 30-31 discussed Dutch nationalism in school education, school pictures and the popular romanticised histories of W.J. Hofdijk.

482 Especially after the secession of Belgium in 1830-39, the (northern) Netherlands consolidated their local colonies in Indonesia by incorporating the areas between them to form the colony of the Dutch East Indies, the present Republic of Indonesia.

'After a hesitant rise in the eighteenth century, [Dutch] *nationalism changed during the course of the nineteenth century into a quiet pride of former, not repeated achievements, which created self-esteem but no dynamic perspective for the future. History was presented in a national perspective, also in The Netherlands; but no one believed that the ancient greatness would revive.'*

A good example of this calm, retrospective national pride without expansive tendencies are the popular, carefully composed and dramatised scenes from prehistory and history that were written by Willem Jacobsz Hofdijk [1816-1888]. They carry titles such as *The Dutch Nation Sketched in the Various Epochs of its Progress* (1856a), *Historical Landscapes* (1856b) and *Our Ancestors, Sketched in Daily Life* (1859-1865). They begin with a scene from the daily life of the hunebed builders, which was based mainly on Janssen's studies, but also on various articles by Haasloop Werner and others.[483]

Thanks to Hofdijk (1856b), the hunebed builders entered popular historical and school books as the most ancient and only described prehistoric people of The Netherlands, apart from the Batavians. In recently prescribed teachings on Dutch history in schools (2006-7, see Hellinga 2007), the first chapter is about the hunebeds. The second chapter deals with the Romans and the Batavians are absent (Hellinga 2007).

In some ways, the approach taken by hunebed researchers reflects their education. Schonhovius, Picardt, J. Hofstede (1706), Engelberts, Westendorp, Janssen and Pleyte were educated in theology as priests or pastors. Van Leeuwen, Van Lier, J. and P. Hofstede (1809) and Gratama studied law and classical languages. Picardt, Smids, P. and A.G. Camper studied medicine; the Campers specialised in anatomy and palaeontology. Vosmaer was a self taught collector and zoologist. Titia Brongersma was one of the rare poetesses of her time; Smids was a poet, playwright and historian. In 1785, both were Roman Catholics in Groningen. Smids moved later to Amsterdam and converted to the Dutch Calvinistic Church (before 1711). De Wilde, however, had studied medicine.

---

483 See Bakker 1990a about Hofdijk's works on prehistory.

Latin, French and German were read by the educated; English publications were often studied in French translation. In 1870-80, the visiting British hunebed researchers corresponded in French with the Dutch archaeologists in Leiden and Assen.[484]

A main obstacle for applying Sherratt's scheme (Figure 56) to the history of Dutch hunebed research, as Darvill (2006) did to that of Stonehenge, is, however, that clear exponents of both attitudes occur in the Stonehenge studies, whereas the Dutch sample of hunebed studies is rather meagre and several authors displayed no distinct approach or theory.

Several 'enlightenment' authors in Holland and Britain hardly theorised, which seems very 'reasonable'. If we knew Stukeley only through his excellent drawings and descriptions (Piggott 1950; 1983[2]), he would figure as one of the most 'reasonable' researchers of his enlightened age, but his vague, romantic, deist and masonic digressions reveal a theoretical disposition belonging to the 'Romantic' mode. Apart from Picardt, several Dutch authors seem more often followers than innovators of theories about megaliths. Hunebeds were not a central issue in Dutch intellectual discourse,[485] and Drenthian amateur researchers often lagged behind in their knowledge of international theory. Gratama (1886) is an example of this backwardness, but his comparison of hunebeds to Christian churches reaches back to Petrus Camper (1780).

However, Van Lier's book on D13 and a few other Drenthe hunebeds (1760), Westendorp's work on west European megalithic tombs (1815, 1822), the legal protection of Drenthe hunebeds in 1734, and their acquisition by state and province in 1868-80 were most uncommon at the time. Van Lier was the first to discern a Stone Age* preceding a Metal Age* in The Netherlands.

A final word can be said about the intriguing development of what now can be considered 'incorrect theories'. All were incorporated in closely reasoned logical systems. Picardt's giants (1660) and the cremation urns in his book and in the excavation reports, between 1685[486] and the early 20th century, appear to have

---

484 The following six museums that were open to the educated public paid attention to the hunebeds or had objects from them in their collections: (a) the Prince's collection in the Hague (1758-1795), (b) the Hofstede collection in the Royal Museum in Amsterdam (1809-1825), after which it was transferred to the Leiden Museum; (c) the National Museum of Antiquities in Leiden, from 1818 onwards [it was officially called 'Archaeological Cabinet of Leiden University' till the second half of the 19th century (Hoijtink 2003), but Leemans and Janssen called it 'the Dutch Museum of Antiquities' in their publications (e.g. Reuvens, Leemans & Janssen 1845), although they were obliged to use the old name in their letters to the Minister of Interior Affairs and the King]; (d) the private museum of W.J.H. baron van Westreenen van Tiellandt in the Hague (now the Museum Meermanno-Westreenianum in the Hague), since the early 19th century; (e) the Provincial Museum of Antiquities from Drenthe in Assen, since 1854; (f) the section Germanic Antiquities of the Museum for Natural History of Groningen University had nothing regarding the hunebeds until a model of D6-Tynaarlo was made, in 1843 (see section '1840-1869').

485 Cf. Westendorp (1815, Introduction): 'Formerly our most distinguished scholars usually studied Roman antiquities and our [hunebeds] were generally looked upon with contempt.'

486 Actually, Picardt (1660, 33) speculated already that the giants were cremated and that their remains were 'carefully collected in earthenware pots or jugs'. These were buried and a hunebed was built over them.

been 'common knowledge', which fitted with current models of thought and were congruent with the written sources.[487] Smids (1711) still stuck to Picardt's giants theory, although the bones from the Borger hunebed and discussion with another medical doctor should have suggested otherwise.

Other 'incorrect theories' originated contrary to better judgement, as it were. Westendorp, writing from 1812 to 1822, chose to identify *one* historically known people, the Celts, as builders of the 'hunebeds' found from Cape St Vincent and Lyon to Ireland, Stockholm and Berlin, and rejected the possibility that the builders may have been more than one people, as was suggested in the prize question of 1808-1814. He did not question why the Celts had not constructed any megaliths in central and southeastern Europe and Asia Minor, where they had also lived. But given the scarce evidence at the time, he created a magnificent conception, albeit with few empirical underpinnings, that allowed him to portray the Stone Age life of 'the first inhabitants of our Fatherland'.

Another example is Janssen's estimate of the age of the 'fireplaces' with 'stone tools' near Hilversum, fabricated by the shrewd agricultural labourer Westbroek, in 1853, which he changed from the Stone Age to ultimately the Roman Period, arguing that this had been a culturally backward and isolated spot, where stone tools were still used. At first Janssen dated a sandstone block with a carved mould, which was part of the wall of one of the supposedly Stone Age 'fireplaces', to the 15th and 16th centuries AD[488] (which is correct), but soon changed this to the Roman Period to make it congruent with his (incorrect) observation (1848) that hunebed D44a-Zaalhof dated from the Roman period. He thus argued, in 1856, that the Stone Age of the hunebeds lasted till the Roman Period and that a genuine Bronze Age was absent in The Netherlands.

In preparation for an 'archaeological system' for The Netherlands and the exposition of the Leiden Museum (1907), J.H. Holwerda made a museum tour through southwestern Germany and The Netherlands. En route, in August and September, 1904, he apparently read Janssen's *magnum opus* on the – fraudulent – Hilversum antiquities (*Hilversumsche Oudheden*, 1856), and worked out his own vision on Dutch archaeology. His short *aide-mémoire* notes about Janssen's 1856 book read:

> *'Janssen Hilversumsche Oudheden. First the fireplaces with the strange small stones. I think there is positive evidence that they are from a very late period. A few things make me even doubt their authenticity. Further advice about this find and*

---

487 Although W.K. Grimm, in his review (1824, 693) of Westendorp's 1822 book, had asked for reliable evidence that the 'urns' in hunebeds did actually contain human cremations.
488 Arentzen 2007.

comparison with all sorts [of things is required], but will yield nothing. It remains a strange story. Further all sorts of quotations that I could well use ... ' [489]

But at this fork in the road he chose the wrong course, put his doubts aside and made the Hilversum artefacts one of the main pillars of his argument that The Netherlands had never known a Bronze Age and that the Stone Age lasted until the Roman Period – in agreement with Janssen and Van Lier.

Pleyte, also in Leiden, rejected Janssen's dating of the last hunebeds to the Roman Period, however. His own dating of the of the hunebeds, supposedly built by relatives of the Tamehu, who were known from Egyptian sources, to 'perhaps' between 3000 and 2000 BC (Pleyte 1877-1902: Friesland etc, 1877-79, 136-40, Drente, 1880-82, pls. 1-2) was as new for Dutch archaeology as Picardt's dating of the hunebeds to before 1660 BC (Picardt 1660, 131). But even more remarkable is Hofdijk's dating of the hunebeds to around 3000 BC in 1862. [490]

Janssen's erroneous late date for the last hunebeds regained validity – with J.H. Holwerda in Leiden only! – from 1908 until 1938-1945. Future generations will perhaps note how our present generation turns a blind eye to other 'obvious' realities.

On the other hand, Van Lier, who initially was not an antiquarian and did not have an extensive library at his disposal, did have an open mind and an enlightened inquisitive approach. He arrived at quite modern conclusions in many respects, and his precise research report remains valid till this day. The same is true for the research reports of Johannes Hofstede (1809) and Lukis and Dryden (1878-9). Lukis's fine watercolours of Drenthe hunebed pottery foreshadowed the ceramic studies of the 20th century (although no Dutch archaeologist saw them before the 1920s and 1930s). [491] And Dryden's 1878 hunebed plans helped to shape those of Van Giffen's atlas (1925), in which the sideviews of the hunebeds were copied from Dryden's drawings in Assen (atlas-pls. 117-8). Dryden's compass card of hunebed orientations inspired De Wilde and Van Giffen to make their own (Van Giffen 1925, atlas-pl. 119; Bakker 1979c, pl. va-b). [492]

I will end by citing from Timothy Darvill's reaction to the preceding study. [493] He concluded:

---

489 Theo Toebosch gave me a photocopy of Holwerda's note (1904):

> '*Janssen Hilversumsche Oudheden. In de eerste plaats over de haardsteden met het rare kleine steenen goed. Er zijn dunkt mij positieve bewijzen dat ze uit zeer late tijd zijn. Enkele dingen doen me zelfs aan de echtheid twijfelen. Verder hulp over deze vondst en vergelijking met allerlei, wat niets geeft. Het blijft een vreemde geschiedenis. Dan allerlei citaten waar ik wel wat aan heb ..'*

A longer quotation is in Bakker 2004, 162.

490 See section '1856-1862: Hofdijk'; cf. Figure 2 and section 'A1'.

491 When J. Butter and A.E. van Giffen saw them in London.

492 De Wilde's scheme is lost. González-Garcia and Costa-Ferrer (2007) measured the Dutch and German hunebed orientations once more, and drew precise compass cards, but developed no new insights.

493 E-mail of 18.2.2009.

'What it also shows, of course, is that there is work to be done on the timing and relationships of the various academic traditions applied in a field of archaeology across Europe. In my mind's eye is one of Louwe Kooijmans' wonderful culture-diagrams but with the history of our discipline mapped out (maybe he has already done it?).'

This is not the case, and such synoptic tables of the history of megalithic or any other archaeological research across Europe seem promising goals for further study – by a younger generation.

Acknowledgements

I am very much indebted to Wout Arentzen, a scrupulous reader of texts and sources of 19th-century and early 20th-century archaeologists (Arentzen 2005; 2006; 2007; 2009a; 2010), for unceasing tips, additions, corrections, stimulating discussions and for providing me with photographs for Figures 30, 31, 37, 38 and 42.[494] I also thank Wijnand van der Sanden, Provincial Archaeologist of Drenthe. He studied the complete documentation on the Rolde hunebeds (Van der Sanden 2007), aided by Henk Luning, who examined the Assen archives, and gave me the photographs for Figures 32 and 45 and furnished several data. I thank Karl-Göran Sjögren, Malmö, for his information about early Scandinavian megalith research, and Cyrille Chaigneau, Vannnes, for that in France. Camilla Haarby Hansen kindly provided information about the number of Early Neolithic flat graves in Denmark. Christian Adamsen, editor of the famous Danish periodical *Skalk*, at Højbjerg, kindly provided transcripts of the documents cited in Appendix 2B. As always, Jan Nanning Lanting with his extensive factual knowledge and Anna Lucia Brindley, both of the Groningen Institute for Archaeology of the State University at Groningen, kindly provided all detailed information I asked for. The National Museum of Antiquities at Leiden (called 'Leiden Museum' in the text) furnished the Frontispiece and Figure 37 and allowed Fred Gijbels, renowned photographer of our former Institute voor Pre- en Protohistorie of Amsterdam University, to copy Figure 46 in the 1970s.

My late Groningen colleague Albert Etto Lanting [1945-2004] was a much appreciated discussion partner and helpful for sorting out details and pointing out mistakes in my former work. He commented on the typology of the Diever battle-axe, in the British Museum, on basis of my drawing.

My late Amsterdam colleague Ben L. van Beek [1938-2005] bought Maaskamp's aquatint (ca.1812) of hunebed D41, after its discovery in 1809, in an antiquarian bookshop and presented it to me in 1973. The publication from which it was taken was identified by Amsterdam antiquarian booksellers.

For personal comments I am indebted to professor Tjalling Waterbolk, Haren (for his explanation of a passage in Picardt 1666, 23); to professor Stefan Radt, Onnen (for his comments on a passage in Strabo); to Dr. J. van Campen, Amsterdam and J.P. Puype, both of the Army Museum, Delft, and to J. van Heel of the Museum Meermanno-Westreenianum in The Hague (about the sword of Claudius Civilis); to Evert Kramer, Fries Museum / Tresoar, Leeuwarden (about the Quaestius collection); to Yannick Henk, RAAP-West[495], Leiden (about the TRB canoe from Dijkgatsweide); to professor Nico Roymans, Amsterdam (for

---

494 Arentzen's 2010 book and the present work were simultaneously written and discussed, with notable mutual influences.

495 RAAP = Regional Archeologisch Archiverings Project.

drawing my attention to the 1986 study by Claudia Liebers); to Marc Spanjer (September 23, 2003) and Dr. Heather Sebire (2009), former curator of the Guernsey Museum (about the plans of Drenthe hunebeds in the W.C. Lukis bequest in that museum); to Dr. H. Nijkeuter (about hunebed poems); to Theo Toebosch (about Holwerda's notes); to Dr. Leo Verhart, Luc W.S.W. Amkreutz and Annemarieke Willemsen (for information from the Leiden Museum and for permission to reproduce the Frontispiece and Figures 30, 31, 37 and 46); to my Amsterdam colleagues professor Anthonie Heidinga (about Dutch Romantic literature and critically reading a previous version of the text) and professor Willy Groenman-van Waateringe (for reading an earlier text version); to Mrs Florence J.J.M. Pieters, formerly Artis Library, Amsterdam (about Van Lier and Vosmaer). Further I am indebted to Mr. Vincent van Vilsteren, of the Drents Museum, in Assen [called 'Assen Museum' in the text] (for Figure 54); to the Drents Museum for permission to reproduce Figures 13, 32a-b, 40-41, 45, 53-54; to Dr. J. Bervoets (about Ver Huell); to professor Wim Gerritsen, Utrecht (details about the words *hun* and *hunebed*); to the Society of Antiquaries of London (for Figures 47-49 and 52); to J.B. Meijer (for information about hunebed D5-Zeijen); and to Dr. A.D. Verlinde (about TRB finds in Overijssel). But many more have helped me with the preparation of this study (2006-2010) and previous work on which it is based. I thank them all very much indeed.

Dr. Egge Knol, curator of the archaeological collection of the Groninger Museum, helped me with several data and arranged the photographs for Figures 14 and 39 to be taken by Marten de Leeuw. Uniepers Abcoude kindly provided Figures 2, 9, 15, 44, 52 (from Van Ginkel et al. 1999, ills. p. 40, 128, 121, 144, 142, 146) for reproduction. Sidestone Press provided Figures 5-8. The Onderwijsmuseum in The Hague kindly provided Figure 55. Amsterdam University Library provided the photographs for Figures 4, 10, 20-28 and 43. Permission for reproduction was allowed by all concerned.

Finally, I am extremely grateful to Susan Holstrom, Amsterdam, for considerably clarifying and improving the English and the composition of my text, and to my friend and colleague professor Dr. W. Haio Zimmermann, Wilhelmshaven-Bockhorn, Germany, and his wife Gundel for the translation / re-writing of the German texts (Appendix 2A and 2B), and sending me Christian Adamsen's transcripts for Appendix 2B. I am also much indebted to Karsten Wentink and Corné van Woerdekom for the pleasant and expert way they prepared this book for publication by Sidestone Press.

A reflection of the Dutch novelist Maarten 't Hart applies very well to the writing of this book, between 2006 and 2010:

> *'But when writing, you are never ready. You are never completely satisfied with a written text and keep changing, improving, even in the galley proofs. [...] The liberating feeling: finito! never comes about. When something is laid aside for a rest, I am unremittingly walking about, wishing to take it out, read it again and correct it, almost all the time.'* [496]

Baarn, 2006-2010

About the author

Dr. Jan Albert Bakker (1935), is a former senior lecturer (*universitair hoofddocent*) in Prehistoric Archaeology of Northwestern Europe at the University of Amsterdam, at the former Institute for Prae- and Protohistory (IPP), which is now part of the Amsterdam Archaeological Centre (AAC).

Bothalaan 1
NL-3743 CS Baarn
The Netherlands

bakker06@planet.nl

---

[496] *'Maar als men schrijft komt men nooit klaar. Nooit is men geheel tevreden over een geschreven tekst. Men blijft er maar aan veranderen, sleutelen, tot in de drukproef toe. [...] Nooit ontstaat het bevrijdende gevoel: finito! Terwijl iets rijpt in een lade, loop ik rusteloos rond, wil ik het er telkens uithalen om het te herlezen en te verbeteren, en dat gebeurt dan ook voortdurend.'* Maarten 't Hart, *Het roer kan nog zesmaal om*, Amsterdam [1984[1]] 2000[8], 152 (the translation is mine).

Appendix 1

List of the Dutch hunebeds

This list is an improved version of my previous list of extant and former hunebeds (Bakker 1992, 209-211). The list by Van Ginkel et al. (1999, 161-99), which was based on the one by Klok (1979) and the Hunebed Committee (1980s), uses longer topographical names for these tombs. Ultimately, of course, all these lists are based on Van Giffen's *fundamental* inventory of extant hunebeds (1925, 9-138) and his inventory of hunebeds by province, *gemeente* (municipality) and village, including former, no longer existing hunebeds that were mentioned in the literature (1925, 160-91). Van Ginkel et al. 1999 (*ibid.*) took account of the new subdivision of Drenthe by municipality of the preceding year and presented location maps and photographs of the extant hunebeds and brief research histories of extant and former hunebeds.

Colour pictures of all extant Dutch hunebeds can be found on the website of J.B. [Hans] Meijer, www.hunebedden.nl / Dolmens in The Netherlands; Picture gallery.

Google Earth uses Van Giffen's hunebed codes (G1, D1-D54) and the hunebeds are clearly visible on air photographs if not obscured by the shadows of trees. Side views from ground level, short descriptions and sometimes an old picture are also provided.

With Google the Dutch word *hunebed* has 9,760 hits, which is more than double 4,480 hits for *grafheuvel* (earthen tumulus, barrow) – although barrows are much more numerous in The Netherlands. *Hunebedbouwers* (hunebed builders) has ca.1620 hits, including *Leylijnen & Wichelroede* (ley lines and divining-rod), *aardstralen* (earth-rays), and stories in Drenthe dialect by Harmjan van Steenwijk and Jan Veenstra (February 2, 2010).[497] This relative popularity of the hunebeds is due to the fact that they are the first subject covered in history lessons in primary schools. And they are the oldest archaeological sites that can be visited in The Netherlands (together with Neolithic flint mines east of Maastricht), located in

---

497 Between February 3 and March 17, 2010, other terms had the following number of hits: *hunnebed* (1,380), megalith (54,900), *Grosssteingrab* (2,520), *Hünengrab* (6,680), dolmen (354,000), passage grave (1160,000), *Ganggrab* (1,080), *ganggraf* (1,240), Funnelbeaker (1,040), *Trechterbekercultuur* (695), *Trichterbecherkultur* (1,480), TRB culture (18,000 / 15.900), Johan Picardt (325, including a club of Leiden students in archaeology). These numbers were approximative and there were many duplicates among the hits.

one of the most popular regions for tourists in this overpopulated country. And their construction using large boulders is impressive visually, inviting intriguing questions and kindling the imagination…

Figure 57 is a general map of the hunebeds in the provinces of Drenthe, Groningen, Fryslân / Friesland and Overijssel. The Stone of Lage Vuursche (U1), possibly a remnant of a hunebed, is in the municipality of Baarn, in the province of Utrecht, 12 km northeast of the town of Utrecht (centre), in the middle of The Netherlands.

According to this list, there are **53 extant hunebeds** at their original sites. Hunebed G5-Heveskesklooster was reconstructed from the original stones in the Aquarion Museum in Delfzijl. The sites of **24 demolished megalithic tombs** were verified by excavations: 20 passage graves, 1 dolmen (G5), 1 passage grave of cist (D13c), and 2 cists (D31a and F1). Their numbers are marked by **. The **possible sites of 3 other demolished hunebeds** have not yet verified by excavations (marked by **). The extant Stone of Lage Vuursche (***U1) is included in the list, even though it is not certain that it represents a former hunebed. In the provinces of Utrecht, Gelderland and Overijssel, as well as in Friesland-Drenthe-Groningen other hunebeds may have disappeared before they were recorded, because *Hünengräber* occur in neighbouring Germany as far south as the Rivers Lippe and Emscher, directly north of the Ruhr.

Originally there may have been about one hundred hunebeds in The Netherlands. Picardt's guess (1660, 131) that half the original number of hunebeds had disappeared would even suggest an original number of about 125, if we were to take him literally and assume that he knew all hunebeds that were extant then and not covered by a barrow (such as D13-Eext and D41-Emmen) – *quod non*.[498]

'N', 'NO', 'O', 'ZO', 'Z', 'ZW', 'W', 'NW' in hunebed names indicate the cardinal and intercardinal directions N, NE, E, SE, S, SW, W, and NW in Dutch.

References to the publications of recent research of each tomb and its contents have been added, and are included in the 'References'. The statements 'Dryden and Lukis 1878, pl. X' refer to the plans and sideviews of 40 hunebeds made by H. Dryden and the short descriptions and sideviews of these, which were made by W.C. Lukis, in 1878 (see section '1871-1879').[499] Lukis's drawings, on 22 plates,[500] of pottery and other artefacts in Dutch collections or in the one of his own are separately mentioned. L.J.F. Janssen's two sets of drawings of most hunebeds, made in 1846 and 1847 (which are in the Assen and Leiden Museums), are usually not referred to, nor are most of my previous publications.

---

498 Before Van Giffen's thorough inventory of the available sources (1925, 168-88), De Wilde (1910, 243) thought that 12-14 demolished hunebeds could be located and that originally there had been more than 100, perhaps even up 200 or 300 hunebeds in the provinces Drenthe, Groningen and Friesland (Van Giffen 1925, 186).

499 Lukis's descriptions are arranged in the order of Dryden's plans I-XL.

500 These plates of Lukis were named by him Plates A-T, but pl. I was triple (Ia-c) and pl. K was double (Ka-b).

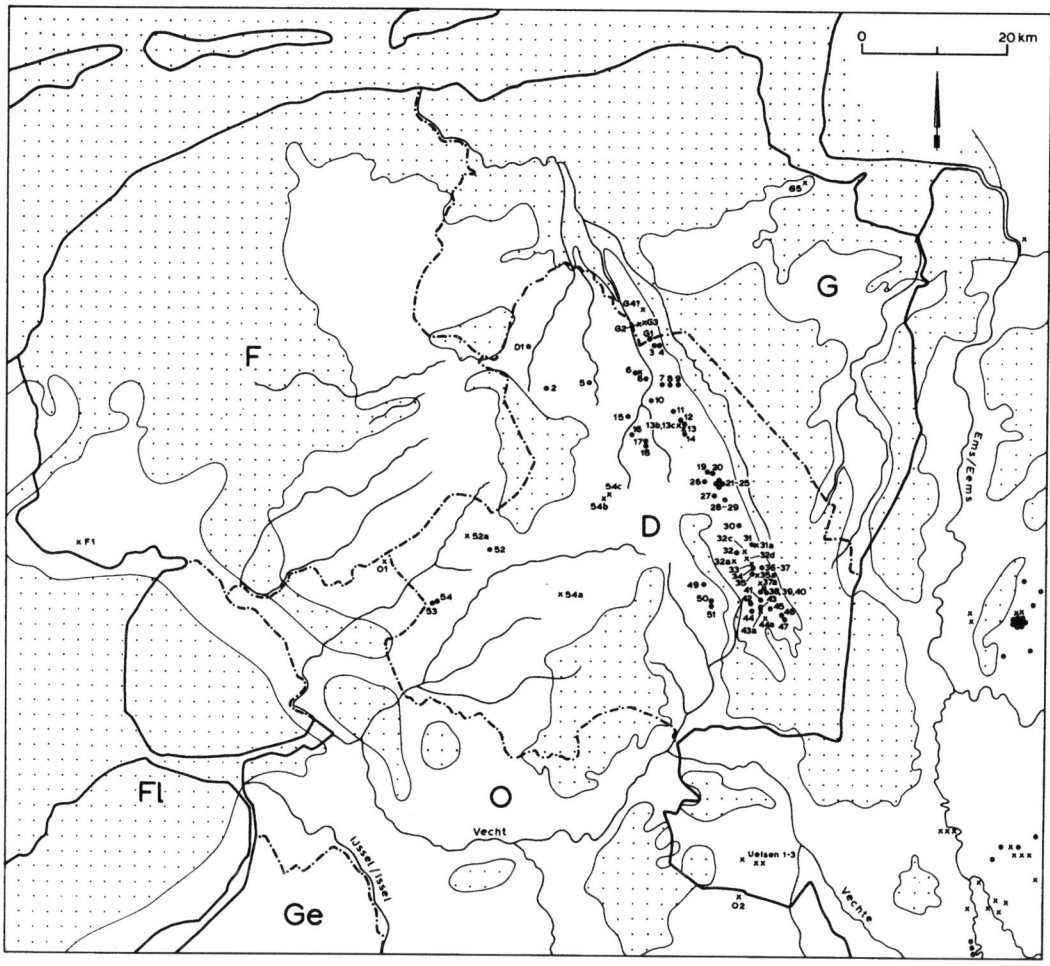

Figure 57. Distribution of the Dutch hunebeds in the provinces of Groningen (G: G1, *G2-*G5), Drenthe (D: D1-54 including demolished tombs), Fryslân / Friesland (F: cist *F1), Overijssel (O: *O1-*O2) and German borderland. Extant hunebeds are indicated by a dot (•), demolished tombs by a cross (x) (Bakker 1992, fig. 1).

In my books about the TRB West Group and the Dutch hunebeds (Bakker 1979a; 1992) the interior lengths of the hunebed chambers are statistically compiled, and what is known about the eldest Brindley horizons found in each is reported. The oldest MNA TRB pottery (horizon 1 of Brindley 1986b = phase A of Bakker 1979a) is found only in short hunebeds, which have 2-5 yokes or pairs of sidestones (**PS**). The less clear-cut relations between the interior chamber lengths of the larger Dutch hunebeds and Brindley's horizons 2-7 or phases Bakker B-G is also discussed in Bakker 1992, 62; cf. Bakker 1979a, 148-58. Stylistic TRB pottery 'horizons' mentioned below are those of Brindley 1986b, 'phases' those of Bakker 1979a. 'Phases' of EGK and Bell Beaker pottery, which are subsequent to the TRB period, are those of Drenth & Lanting 1991.

The **PS** (number or pairs of sidestones) and **CL** (interior chamber length at surface level) are given below for each hunebed, as well as their floor length (**FL**), if available (from Bakker 1978a, 150-151; 1992). The presence of a kerb is also mentioned. The measures in parentheses for **CL** and **FL** are estimated.

The Dutch **provincies**, provinces, are subdivided into **gemeenten**. The Dutch and Frisian term *gemeente* is usually translated by 'municipality' in English, although a gemeente often comprises the area of a number of villages without a town (Lat. *municipium*), as 'municipality' would suggest (cf. German *Gemeinde*, Polish *gmina*).

Provincie Fryslân / **Province of Friesland**[501]

Not a hunebed but a cist: **F1-Riis*, gemeente Gaasterlân-Sleat (formerly called hunebed '*F1-Rijs*, gemeente Gaasterland'). 5 PS, CL (ca.3.8 m), FL about 4.3 m, interior chamber width 0.8 m. Discovered in 1849 during forestation and immediately almost completely demolished. Its site was excavated in 1849 by L.J.F. Janssen (1850; 1853) and in 1922 by A.E. van Giffen (Van Giffen 1924; Van Giffen 1927, 66), who, in 1958, marked the place of the orthostats by concrete slabs ('*plomben*') at the surface (photograph: Van Ginkel et al. 1999, 115). Later investigation of sources and the site by J.N. Lanting, in 1996, led to the conclusion that the structure was a stone cist, not a hunebed, which was evidenced by the small dimensions of the tomb and the fact that it was constructed below surface. According to Lanting (per. comm.. 2010) this tomb lay below the old ground surface, but according to Kossian (2005, no. 333A), it was enclosed in a low barrow (*im flachen Primärhügel*). The tomb contained the sherds of 15-25 pots from Brindley 1 and 2 only. Also found were one 15 cm long, 'rectangular' flint axe, polished on its long sides, cf. Type Lindø, and 3 short, 6.7-15.0 cm long, 'rectangular' flint axes, polished on all sides except the butt (Van Giffen 1927, atlas-pl. 152). Since 18 pots is the maximum known from earth graves of the West Group (Hooghalen 5 and Mesum: Bakker 1970), the relatively large number of pots and axes may show that the cist was used, like a hunebed, for successive interments at the beginning of the MNA period. Its locality is notably distant from the Drenthe Plateau and the other sandy soils of The Netherlands, where the other examples of such early pottery have been found (cf. the map fig. 37 in Bakker 1979a; three similarly early sites have subsequently been found on the western Drenthe Plateau).

> (Janssen 1850; Janssen 1853; Van Giffen 1924; Van Giffen 1927, 66, 323-37, atlas-pls. 150-2; Boeles 1951; Bakker 1992, 144, 174; Lanting 1997; Van Ginkel et al. 1999, 193).

---

501 The Frisian locality name is first given in the Frisian language, followed by the Dutch name.

Province of Groningen

G1-Noordlaren, gemeente Haren. 5 PS, CL (ca. 7.1 m), FL 7.6 m. Its plan is shown in Figure 58. First mentioned by M. Bolhuis in 1694. Drawn by Petrus Camper in 1768 (Figure 24). Completely excavated by Van Giffen, Bakker and students of Amsterdam University in 1957. Architecture, inventory and research history are given in Bakker (1983). TRB pottery dates from my phases B-D2 and F-G, viz. Brindley 2-4 and 6-7.

(Bakker 1983; Brindley & Lanting 1992; Van Ginkel et al. 1999, 164).

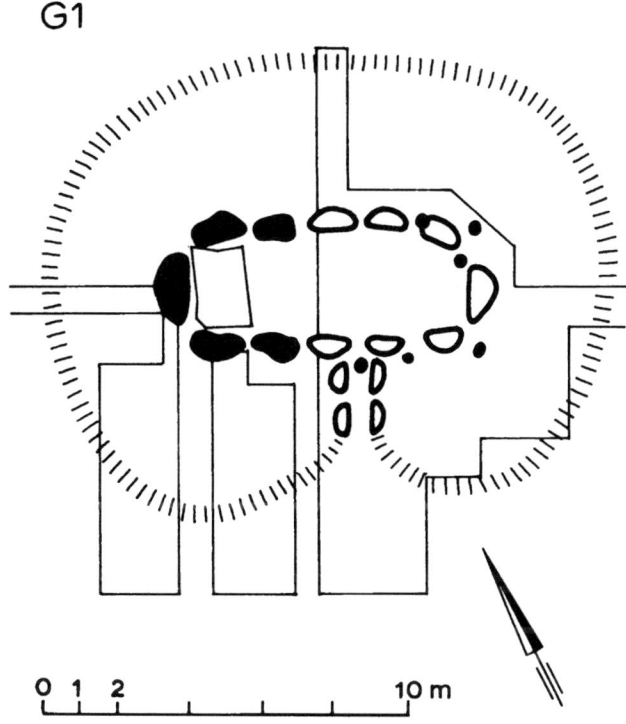

G1

0 1 2   10 m

Figure 58. Plan of hunebed G1-Noordlaren (Bakker 1983). Remnant stones are in black, location of missing stones are outlined. Dots indicate postholes. The extent of the excavated area and of the foot of the hunebed barrow are also shown (Bakker 1992, fig. 17).

*G2-Glimmen-N, gemeente Haren. 7 PS,[502] CL (ca.11.5 m), FL about 12.0 m. Site discovered by J.E. Musch in 1972, excavated by J.N. Lanting in 1969 and 1970 (Lanting 1975). Inventory analysed by Brindley (1986a).

(Lanting 1975; Brindley 1986a; Van Ginkel et al. 1999, 193).

---

502 Bakker (1979a, 150) incorrectly reported 6 PS.

G3-Glimmen-Z, gemeente Haren. 2 PS, CL (ca.2.7 m), FL about 3.2 m. Site discovered by J.E. Musch in 1972, excavated by J.N. Lanting in 1971 (Lanting 1975). The inventory was published by Brindley (1983). I discussed a dolmen flask from G3 and the age of G3 in Bakker (1994), which was contested by J.N. Lanting (pers. comm.). For a synopsis of these discussions, see Bakker (2004, 178-179).

(Lanting 1975; Brindley 1983; Van Ginkel et al. 1999, 193).

**G4-Onnen*, gemeente Haren. Site discovered by J.E. Musch in 1961, not excavated.

(Bakker 1983; Bakker 1988, 65-66; Van Ginkel et al. 1999, 194).

**G5-Heveskesklooster*, gemeente Delfzijl. 3 PS, CL about 2.5 m, FL 2.7 m. The plan is shown in Figure 59. Discovered in 1982 under a medieval *terp* by J.W. Boersma and excavated by J.N. Lanting in 1983. It is a 'rectangular dolmen'. Unsuspected by the archaeologists, this dolmen was partly dismantled during the Corded Ware or Beaker period, about 2000 cal BC, before it was overgrown by peat. There was no sizable earthen barrow present. This tomb has been rebuilt in the Aquarion Museum in Delfzijl (Van Ginkel & Verhart 2009, ill. 27.22; Wikipedia: 'Hunebed'). An excavation report about stratigraphy and artefacts has not yet appeared.

(Bakker 1992, 108-109: n. 13; Bakker 1994; Van Ginkel et al. 1999, 194; Van Ginkel & Verhart 2009, fig. 4.12 is *not* G5, but a cist next to it – which is exhibited in the Hunebed Centre at Borger).

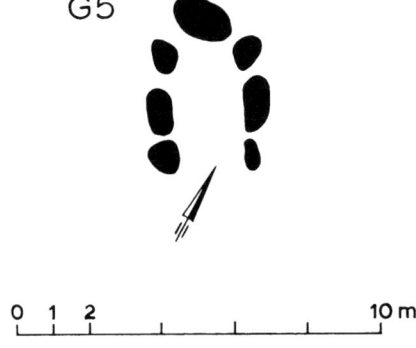

Figure 59. Plan of dolmen G5-Heveskesklooster (Bakker 1992, fig. 5).

Province of Drenthe[503]

D1-Steenbergen, gemeente Noordenveld. 6 PS, CL about 10.3 m. Not systematically excavated. Restored in 1953, 1954, about 1965, 1993 and 1997.[504]

(Van Giffen 1925, 12-4; Klok 1979, 86-89; Van Ginkel et al. 1999, 164).

D2-Westervelde, gemeente Noordenveld. 4 PS, CL about 6.0 m. Not systematically excavated. First mentioned in 1869. Restored in 1928, 1952 and 1965.

(Van Giffen 1925, 14-6; Van Ginkel et al. 1999, 165).

D3-Midlaren-W, gemeente Tynaarlo.[505] 6 PS, CL 9.1 m, was first drawn by Cornelis Pronk on July 30, 1754 (Figure 14). It was also drawn by Petrus Camper about 1768-1769 (Figure 25) and by Antoine-Ignace Melling in 1812 (Boschma & Perot 1991, 132-3). Not systematically excavated. Pleyte (1877-1902: Drente, 1880-82) recorded that a piece of tuff had been found in or at the Midlaren hunebeds. It is worth to retain this, because all samples of stone without traces of use have been discarded in the Leiden Museum. Tuff (tephrite) was imported from the Eiffel area since about 700 BC and used for querns or medieval buildings.

(Pleyte 1877-1902; Van Giffen 1925, 16-9; Van Ginkel et al. 1999, 166).

D4-Midlaren-O, gemeente Tynaarlo. 7 PS, CL 12.6 m. Drawn by Petrus Camper about 1768-1769 (Figure 26) and by Antoine-Ignace Melling in 1812 (Boschma and Perot 1991, 132-3). Not systematically excavated. Pleyte (1877-1902: Drenthe, 1880-82) recorded that a piece of tuff had been found in or at the Midlaren hunebeds. It is worth to retain this, because all samples of stone without traces of use have been discarded in the Leiden Museum. Tuff (tephrite) was imported from the Eiffel area since about 700 BC and used for querns or medieval buildings.

(Pleyte 1877-1902; Van Giffen 1925, 19-21; Van Ginkel et al.1999, 166).

D5-Zeijen, gemeente Tynaarlo. 4 PS, CL 6.1 m. 'Originally only the capstones appear to have been visible' (Janssen 1848, Table). Through the intercession of L.O. Gratama this hunebed was bought, in 1857, for 40 guilders, by the Province of Drenthe from a stone seeker, who was about to demolish it (despite the legal protection of hunebeds in that province). W.C. Lukis found three sherds in 1878

---

503 The 29-34 *gemeenten* (municipalities) of Drenthe from 1813-84 were reduced to 12 *gemeenten* in 1998 (Gerding et al. 2003, 335-6 with map). Simultaneously the orthography of the locality names was fixed, which is followed by Gerding et al. 2003.

504 D1-Steenbergen and D5-Zeijen were first visited by N. Westendorp in 1814 (Westendorp 1815, 277) and not in 1811 or 1812 (Van Ginkel et al. 164, 166). See Arentzen (2009) and Bakker (in prep).

505 Tynaarlo was formerly often spelled 'Tinaarlo' or 'Tinaarloo'.

(plate A: 1-3). Not systematically excavated. This hunebed deserves further attention, because it lies in a depression in the surrounding (now flat) surface, instead of on it. This was already the case in 1878.[506]

(Dryden & Lukis 1878, plan I; Van Giffen 1925, 21-23; Van Giffen 1927, 44-52; Van Ginkel et al. 1999, 166).

D6-Tynaarlo-W, gemeente Tynaarlo. 3 PS, CL about 3.9 m. Was for a long time the only intact hunebed. It was illustrated a number of times, including by Engelberts in 1790 (Figure 28), Westendorp in 1815 and 1822 (Figure 35), Jan van Ravenswaay in 1845-9; Alexander Ver Huell in 1859 (Figure 44) and on a school picture by Bernard Bueninck in 1901 (Figure 55). Scale models were made in 1843 (Figure 39, see section '1840-1868'). W.C. Lukis drew 2 sherds found on its floor by himself and 2 fragmentary, undecorated collared flasks that were excavated by the Station Master. J.H. Textor and given to him (1878, pl. B: 1-4). Not systematically excavated, but see section '1871-1879'.

(Dryden & Lukis 1878, plan II; Van Giffen 1925, 23-5; Van Ginkel et al. 1999, 167).

*D6a-Tynaarlo-O, gemeente Tynaarlo, formerly called D6e-f-Tinaarlo and considered by Van Giffen as two demolished hunebeds. D6a had 4 PS, CL (4.2 m), FL 4.8 m. The plan is shown in Figure 60. Investigated by Van Giffen in 1928.

Van Giffen (1944a) thought that he found the remnants of two hunebeds and named them D6e and D6f. In 2002, J.N. Lanting argued that there was only one demolished hunebed and that the supposed second hunebed site was a deposit of debris from the first hunebed. Because the alleged demolished hunebeds D6a-d and D6f at Tynaarlo (as listed by Van Giffen 1925, 170-2, table opp. p. 156) probably never existed, he renamed the D6e tomb 'D6a' (Brindley, Lanting & Neves Espinha 2002). In 1928, Van Giffen found the ten extraction holes of the orthostats of this former hunebed and 3 pairs of postholes, with discolorations of horizontal beams (?) between them.

(Van Giffen !925, 170-2, table opp. p. 156; 1944a; Bakker 1992, 144, 194; Van Ginkel et al. 1999, 194; Brindley, Lanting & Neves Espinha 2002; Kossian 2005, 475, pl. 207).

---

506 Since 1998, the orthography is *Zeijen* instead of *Zeyen*, which was generally used in the archaeological literature. See note 503.

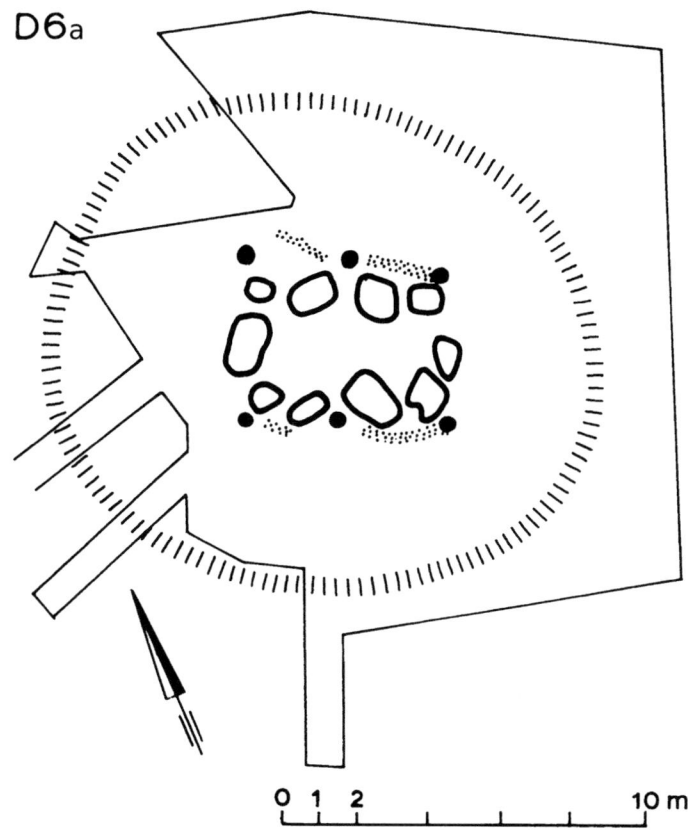

D6a

0 1 2   10 m

Figure 60. Plan of demolished hunebed D6a-Tynaarlo, formerly called D6e-Tynaarlo (Van Giffen 1944a) Extraction holes of orthostats, postholes, traces of horizontal beams (?), barrow foot and excavated area are shown (Bakker 1992, fig. 17).

D7-Schipborg, gemeente Aa en Hunze. 4 PS, CL 7.2 m. Lukis wrote in 1878 'Much pottery and fragments of human bones are scattered over the surface near the monument. I found a considerable quantity in the entrance passage, many fragments being richly decorated. The greater portion of the fragments I placed in the Assen Museum, but a few specimens are now exhibited [to the audience of his lecture to the Society of Antiquaries].' See his drawings on pl. C: 1-11. Not systematically excavated.

   (Dryden & Lukis 1878, plan VI; Van Giffen 1925, 25-7; Van Ginkel et al. 1999, 167)

D8-Anloo-N (Kniphorstbos), gemeente Aa en Hunze. 4 PS, CL 5.7 m. Drawn by Petrus Camper in 1768 (Figure 23). Not systematically excavated.

   (Dryden & Lukis 1878, plan V; Van Giffen 1925, 27-30; Van Ginkel et al. 1999, 168).

**D8a-Anloo-Z1*, gemeente Aa en Hunze. Discovered by S.W. Jager in 1992, not systematically excavated.

(Jager 1994; Van Ginkel et al. 1999, 194).

**D8b-Anloo-Z2*, gemeente Aa en Hunze. Discovered by S.W. Jager in 1992, not systematically excavated.

(Jager 1994; Van Ginkel et al. 1999, 1994-5).

D9-Annen,[507] gemeente Aa en Hunze. Drawn by Petrus Camper in 1769 (Figure 20). First mentioned by L. Smids (1711). Investigated by H. Dryden and W.C. Lukis in 1878 (plan IV). Excavated by Van Giffen in 1952.

(Dryden & Lukis 1878, plan IV; Van Giffen 1925, 30-1; Bakker 1979, 16; De Groot 1988; Brindley & Lanting 1992, 138-9; Van Ginkel et al. 1999, 168).

D10-Gasteren, gemeente Aa en Hunze. 4 PS, CL 5.0 m. Investigated by H. Dryden and W.C. Lukis in 1878 (plan III, plate I(2)). Not systematically excavated.

(Dryden & Lukis 1878, plan III; Van Giffen 1925, 32-3; Van Ginkel et al. 1999, 169).

D11-Anloo-Z (Evertsbos),[508] gemeente Aa en Hunze. 5 PS, CL 7.6 m. Investigated by H. Dryden and W.C. Lukis in 1878 (plan VII, plate IVa-b, artefacts in British Museum). Not systematically excavated.

(Dryden & Lukis 1878, plan VII; Van Giffen 1925, 33-5; Van Ginkel et al. 1999, 169).

D12-Eext Es, gemeente Aa en Hunze. First mentioned by Van Lier (1760), excavated and restored by Van Giffen in 1952.

(Van Giffen 1925, 35-7; Van Ginkel et al. 1999, 170).

D13-Eexter grafkelder,[509] gemeente Aa en Hunze. 3 PS, CL 3.2 m. Discovered about 1735 under a barrow and investigated by J. van Lier in 1756, who wrote the first monograph of a hunebed (Van Lier 1760, see '1756-1760' and Figures 18-19). Drawn by Cornelis van Noorde in 1756 (Figure 15) and by Petrus Camper in 1768 (Figure 20). According to W.J. de Wilde's notes, in 1904, the steps, floor and barrow were repeatedly damaged by visitors and erosion and duly repaired.

---

507 D9 was called D9-Noordlo by Van Giffen (1925), but the hamlet Noordlo has now become part of Annen.
508 The Evertsbos ('Evert's Woods') was planted in the early 20th century. Today it is part of the woods on the Terborgh Estate.
509 *Grafkelder*, literally means 'burial vault', but this small hunebed with a stepped entrance had a flat ceiling of capstones and stones instead of an arched roof. I translate it therefore as 'burial chamber'.

Van Giffen's photograph of 1908 (Van Giffen 1927, text fig, 2, cf. p. 15, n. 3) shows the bare landscape and the deterioration of the monument. A photograph published in 1913 shows that large parts of the barrow were freshly dug away (see Bakker 1990a, fig. 5).

Later excavations were undertaken by by Van Giffen, in 1927, and J.N. Lanting, in 1984. According to Lanting (pers. comm., 1992), the top of the barrow, which once also covered the capstones, dates from the Bell Beaker period. This hunebed is unique for its three steps and the relatively thin orthostats and capstones, constructed with almost no gaps or dry walling stones between them. The repeatedly restored floor of the monument lies now much higher than the land surface around the barrow foot because the surrounding sandy soils have been dug and levelled. D13 was originally placed on top of a narrow coversand ridge,[510] which was dug away by the villagers.

> (Dryden & Lukis 1878, plan VIII; Van Giffen 1925, 37-40; Van Giffen 1927, 12-25; Van Giffen 1943a; Lanting 1978; Klok 1979, 91-6; Van Ginkel et al. 1999, 170).

D13a-Eext,[511] gemeente Aa en Hunze. PS, CL. Discovered and destroyed by H. Brinks in his farmyard, in 1923. Because the salvaged sherds belong to *several* ceramic horizons, D13a was probably a small hunebed (and not a stone cist, as suggested by Van Ginkel et al. 1999, 195).

> (Van Giffen 1927, 275-81; Van Giffen 1944b; Jager 1994; Van Ginkel et al. 1999, 195; Kossian 2005, 462-3).

D13b-Eext, gemeente Aa en Hunze. PS, CL Excavated by Van Giffen in 1927. A small hunebed or a stone cist.

> (Van Giffen 1944c; Lanting 1997, 49; Van Ginkel et al. 1999, 195).

D13c-Eext, gemeente Aa en Hunze. PS, CL Excavated by Van Giffen in 1927. The extraction holes of 9 orthostats and the few TRB and Bell Beaker sherds from the site indicate that this was a small hunebed or a stone cist.

> (Van Giffen 1944c; Lanting 1997, 49; Van Ginkel et al. 1999, 195).

---

510 The narrow and hair-straight periglacial coversand ridges, that were less than 10 m high and less than 20 m wide, were a much sought locations for hunebeds and barrows in the often completely flat coversand regions of The Netherlands and northwestern Germany, because the monuments were then visible from some distance. They are called *haar* ('hair') and if they stuck out in peat bogs *tange* in Dutch locality names (cf. English 'tang').

511 Van Ginkel et al. 1999 called this tomb 'D13a-Eexterhalte', but to avoid confusion with hunebed D14-Eexterhalte, I call it 'D13a-Eext'.

D14-Eexterhalte,[512] gemeente Aa en Hunze. 9 PS, CL 15.9 m, FL 15.8 m? Kerb. First mentioned by Van Lier (1756). Drawn by Cornelis van Noorde in 1756 (Sliggers 1982, 33), by Petrus Camper in 1769 and by W.C. Lukis in 1878 (Figures 21-22, 49). Excavated by Van Giffen in 1927. A.L. Brindley (pers. comm., 2009) is preparing a publication of the artefacts.

(Dryden & Lukis 1878, plan IX; Van Giffen 1925, 40-3; Bakker 1990a, 35-7; Bakker 1992, 58-9, 144; Van Ginkel et al. 1999, 171).

D15-Loon, gemeente Assen. 5 PS, CL 8.0 m. Kerb. The plan is shown in Figure 61. Excavated by J. Hofstede in 1809 and L.J.G. Gregory in 1870. Originally its barrow reached up to the base of the capstones (Figure 40), but in 1870 the entire barrow was removed during 'restoration' (Figure 46). W.C. Lukis illustrated much pottery and a microlithic borer from this tomb (pls. D:1,[513] Ia: 1-12, Ib: 1-11, Ic:1. He wrote 'Until recently the mound was three feet six inches higher than it is now, the former surface being marked upon the capstones and supports. I found a large quantity of potsherds within and without the monument. They were very likely thrown out by the first demolishers. On the north side between the cham-

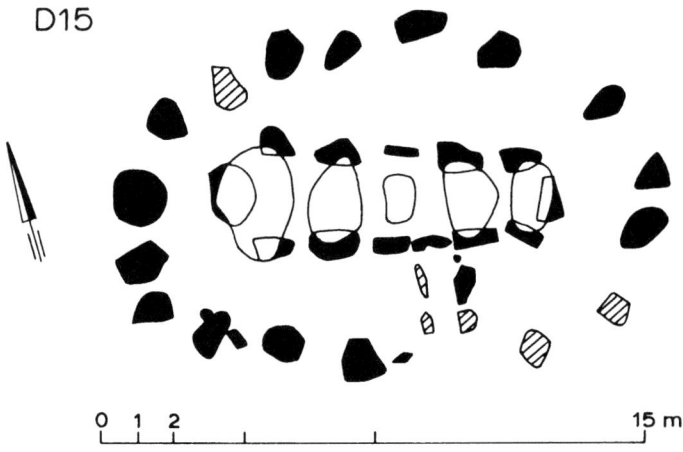

Figure 61. Plan of hunebed D15-Loon, the shortest chamber with a kerb (Bakker 1992, fig. 7).

512 Eexterhalte was the station of a tramway through Drenthe (ca.1900-1940), on the old road between Rolde and Gieten. In the older literature this hunebed was often called the hunebed of Gieten.
513 This large fragment of a richly decorated tureen, Leiden Museum C.139, was assigned by Pleyte (Drente,1880-82, pl. XI: 1) to Emmen.

ber and the enclosing line of stones I found a delicately formed flint drill which. together with the pottery I gave to the Museum of Assen. Dr Pleyte of Leiden has many fragments of vessels which he found here. [etc.]'

Not systematically excavated.

(Dryden & Lukis 1878, plan X; Van Giffen 1925, 43-6; Van Giffen 1927, 25-42, 58-64; Van Ginkel et al.1999, 171 with reference to illegal finds in the entrance).

D16-Balloo, gemeente Aa en Hunze. 9 PS, CL 13.8 m. Not systematically excavated, restored in 1952 and 1954.

(Dryden & Lukis 1878, plan XIII; Van Giffen 1925, 47-9; Bakker 1992, 31-32; Van Ginkel et al. 1999, 172).

D17-Rolde-N, gemeente Aa en Hunze. 8 PS, CL 12.0 m. Not systematically excavated. See section '1706'. Drawn by L.J.F. Janssen in 1847 (Figure 41).

(Dryden & Lukis 1878, plan XII; Van Giffen 1925, 49-53; Van Giffen 1927, 9-12; Van Ginkel et al. 1999, 172; Van der Sanden (2007) compiled all available documentation produced since 1642).

D18-Rolde-Z, gemeente Aa en Hunze. 7 PS, CL 10.5 m. See Figure 45 for the situation before its restoration in 1873. Not systematically excavated. Van der Sanden (2007) published a great number of illustrations. *Ons eigen land*, 1908, opposite p. 45 has a photograph from the north.

(Dryden & Lukis 1878, plan XI; Van Giffen 1925, 53-6; Van Ginkel et al.1999, 173; Van der Sanden (2007) compiled all available documentation produced since 1642).

D19-Drouwen-W, gemeente Borger-Odoorn.(Van Giffen 1925, 56-60). 9 PS, CL 13.9 m. The plan is shown in Figure 62. Excavated by J.H. Holwerda in 1912 (Holwerda 1913a, b). Restored in 1962 and 1998. More than 400 pots were identified. Two strips of copper (Schlicht 1968) were not spectrally analysed. The

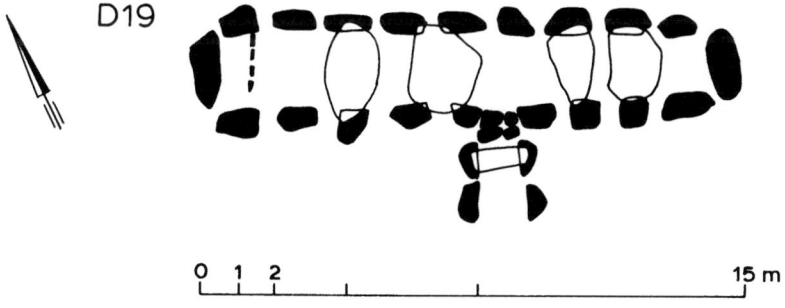

Figure 62. Plan of hunebed D19-Drouwen (Bakker 1992, fig. 7).

Frontispiece shows some of the pottery, beads and 12 axes from the chamber. Lukis excavated much pottery (sherds of 'at least 25 urns'), 3 transversal arrowheads and a chip of flint from a pit of 30 x 45 cm in the west end of the chamber (pls. Ka: 1-7, Kb:1-10).

> (Dryden & Lukis 1878, plan XIV; Van Giffen 1925, 56-60; Van Giffen 1927, 81-96; Van Ginkel et al. 1999, 173; Van Ginkel & Verhart 2009, fig. 4.14. See Figure 62 and the Frontispiece.

D20-Drouwen-O, gemeente Borger-Odoorn. 7 PS,[514] CL 10.0 m. The orthostats of the kerb were pulled down in prehistory. Excavated by J.H. Holwerda in 1912 (Holwerda 1913a, b) and by A.E. van Giffen in the 1960s, who found the pulled down kerbstones. Two ritual deposits were found outside the kerb by Van Giffen and J.E. Musch.

> (Dryden & Lukis 1878, plan XV; Van Giffen 1925, 60-3; Van Giffen 1927, 81-3, 96-100; Van Giffen & Glasbergen 1964, but see Bakker 1979a, 116-118, fig. 61, P-Q; Klok 1979, 99-102; Van Ginkel et al. 1999, 174; Kossian 2005, 461-2).

D21-Bronneger-W, gemeente Borger-Odoorn. 4 PS, CL 6.1 m, FL 6.5 m. Investigated by H. Dryden and W.C. Lukis in 1878 (plan XVI). Lukis, in searching for the floor, 'found a few fragments of urns' (1878, pl. L:1-6). Excavated by Van Giffen in 1918 (Van Giffen 1927, 231-71. According to a re-analysis of the then published inventory (Bakker 1992, 48-9; cf. 144), the tomb contained TRB pottery of Brindley 1-5, a zigzag beaker, 2 pot beakers and other EGK and Bell Beaker ware. Knöll's idea (1959, cf. pls. 43-44) that the stratigraphy of this chamber provided a basis for ordering the pottery typochronologically, was not tenable.

> (Dryden & Lukis 1878, plan XVI; Van Giffen 1925, 63-5; Van Giffen 1927, 231-71; A.E. Lanting 1983; Bakker 1992, 48-9, 144; Van Ginkel et al. 1999, 174; Kossian 2005, 458).

D22-Bronneger-O, gemeente Borger-Odoorn. 2 PS, CL (ca.3.3 m), FL 3.7 m. Investigated by H. Dryden and W.C. Lukis in 1878 (plan XVIII). Excavated by Van Giffen in 1918, restored in 1960.

> (Dryden & Lukis 1878, plan XVIII; Van Giffen 1925, 66-7; Van Giffen 1927, 231-71; Van Ginkel et al. 1999, 171).

D23-Bronneger-N, gemeente Borger-Odoorn. 4 PS, CL about 6.0 m. Not systematically excavated. Lukis & Dryden collected a few pottery fragments in 1878 (Bakker 1979, 16). One pot is discussed by Bakker (1980) and Drenth & A.E. Lanting (1990).

---

514 Bakker (1979a, 150) reported erroneously that D20-Drouwen-O had 6 PS.

(Dryden & Lukis 1878, plan XIX; Van Giffen 1925, 67-9; Van Ginkel et al. 1999, 176)

D24-Bronneger-ZW, gemeente Borger-Odoorn. 4 PS, CL 5.6 m. Not systematically excavated.

(Dryden & Lukis 1878, plan XX; Van Giffen 1925, 69-71; Van Ginkel et al. 1999, 177)

D25-Bronneger-ZO, gemeente Borger-Odoorn. 4 PS, CL 5.8 m. Investigated by H. Dryden and W.C. Lukis in 1878 (a few artefacts are in the British Museum). Not systematically excavated.

(Dryden & Lukis 1878, plan XXI; Van Giffen 1925, 71-3; Van Ginkel et al. 1999, 177).

D26-Drouwenerveld, gemeente Borger-Odoorn. 6 PS, CL 9.9 m, kerb. First mentioned in 1812 by N. Westendorp. Investigated by H. Dryden and W.C. Lukis in 1878 (a few sherds are in the British Museum; see Figure 48). Completely excavated by W. Glasbergen, A.E. van Giffen, J.A. Bakker and students in 1968 and 1970. A selection of the restored pottery and flint artefacts is shown in the Hunebed Centre at Borger. The other artefacts are in the Archaeological Depot at Nuis (Gr.). A final research report is in preparation (Bakker in prep.). 157 TRB pots have been assigned to late Brindley 2 or early-3 through early-5. Two EGK amphorae and two battle axes are from phases 1-2 to early 4. Finally a Harpstedt type Iron Age pot was found in the chamber.

(Dryden & Lukis 1878, plan XVI; Van Giffen 1925, 73-5; Bakker 1992, 49-51, figs. 19-20; Van Ginkel et al. 1999, 178; Kossian 2005, 462; Bakker in prep.).

D27-Borger, gemeente Borger-Odoorn. 9 PS, CL 20.0 m. Kerb. Longest hunebed of The Netherlands. Titia Brongersma led diggings in its chamber in 1685, the first known hunebed excavation in The Netherlands (see section '1685', and Figure 9). Surveyed by H. Dryden and W.C. Lukis in 1878 (a few artefacts are in the British Museum; see Figure 52). Lukis noted, 'The recent lowering of the mound is indicated by a line of demarcation on the supports two feet above the present-day ground level.' He illustrated eight small 'Fragments of Urns found in the great Hunebed of Borger, Drenthe, by W.C. Lukis.' (pl. H: 1-8). Fig. H: 8 is a handle of a Brindley 7 pot, H: 4 and H: 6 represent a bowl or amphora from Brindley 5, the others cannot be further identified than 'from Brindley 2-4'. The tomb was not systematically excavated. Restored by Van Giffen in 1937. The eastern half of the capstones, which had slipped from the orthostats, were left as they were to show how the tomb had looked for so long. But later on, Van Giffen also repositioned these capstones. A few recently found sherds are illustrated in Koops (2009).

A note from 1835 records that [extraction holes of a former kerb] were visible as depressions around the tomb. A single orthostat southeast of the entrance is not shown on Van Giffen's 1925-7 atlas-pl. 58. Perhaps this orthostat was found here by Van Giffen, as the last remnant of a kerb. There are no records about the former position of this stone, but Van Giffen told me that he was unable to find any traces of a kerb because the ground had been deeply disturbed. In the 19th century, D27, the longest hunebed of Drenthe, was the pride of the village of Borger, and flower beds were planted in the front, for which the ground was dug deeply. The flower beds are shown on a photograph in *Ons eigen land*, 1908, vol. 3, opp. to p. 47.

> (Dryden & Lukis 1878, plan XXIV; Van Giffen 1925, 75-9; Van Giffen 1927, 3-9; Bakker 1984; 1992; Van Ginkel et al. 1999, 178; Koops 2009; Van Ginkel & Verhart 2009, fig. 4.15, from NE).

D28-Buinen-N, gemeente Borger-Odoorn. 4 PS, CL 5.8 m, FL 5.9 m. Excavated by A.E. Van Giffen in 1927 and by J.N. Lanting in 1985. The TRB pottery belongs to Brindley 3-5. Single Grave and Bell Beaker pottery was also found. Two identical cocoon-shaped spiral beads of unique form were made of copper. The spectral analysis of both is unsatisfactory, because each had different results, neither of which fit into the known spectra (Butler & Van der Waals 1967, 76; Bakker 1979a, 129-131).

> (Dryden & Lukis 1878, plan XXIII, pl. XI; Van Giffen 1925, 79-81; Van Giffen 1943b; Brindley & Lanting 1992; Bakker 1992, 49; Van Ginkel et al. 1999, 179).

D29-Buinen-Z, gemeente Borger-Odoorn. 4 PS, CL 6.3 m. W.C. Lukis found 5 sherds in 1878 (pl. A: 4-7). Not systematically excavated.

> (Dryden & Lukis 1878, plan XXI. Van Giffen 1925, 81-3; Van Ginkel et al. 1999, 179).

D30-Exloo-N (Exlooërbos), gemeente Borger-Odoorn. 4 PS, CL 5.9 m, FL 6.3 m. The plan is shown in Figure 63. Not systematically excavated.

> (Dryden & Lukis 1878, plan XXV; Van Giffen 1925, 83-4; Van Giffen 1927, 207-30; Klok 1979, 105-110; Brindley & Lanting 1992, 123-7; Van Ginkel et al. 1999, 180; Kossian 2005, 466-7, pl. 201).

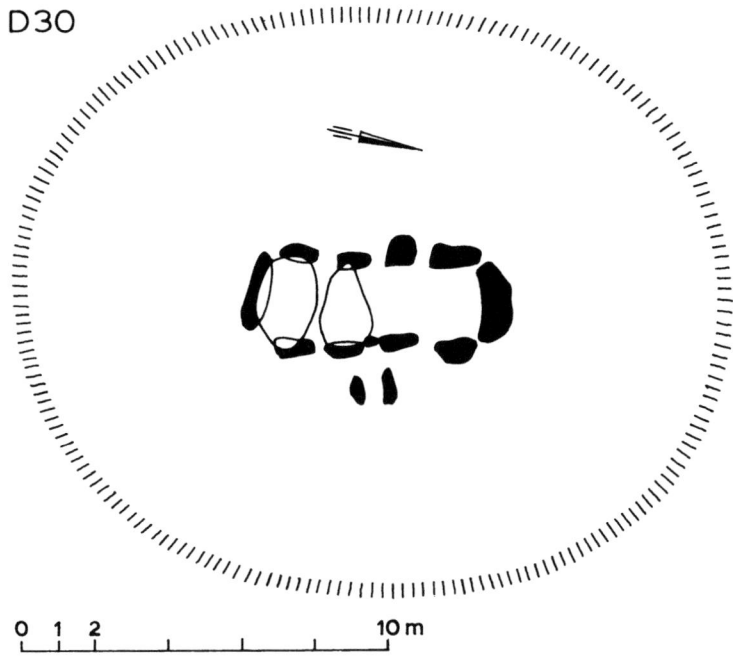

Figure 63. Plan of hunebed D30-Exloo (Bakker 1992, fig. 5).

D31-Exloo-Z (Hunzebos), gemeente Borger-Odoorn. First mentioned in 1818. Investigated by H. Dryden and W.C. Lukis in 1878 (plan XXVI). Completely ruined in 1918 (Van Giffen 1925, atlas pl. 66). Restored by Van Giffen in 1952 with 4 PS and a CL of 5.6 m (unpublished plans are in GIA archives). Van Giffen found the extraction holes of one pair of entrance stones in 1965.

(Dryden & Lukis 1878, plan XXVI; Van Giffen 1925, 185-7; Van Ginkel et al. 1999, 180).

Not a hunebed but a cist: *D31a-Exloo* (Zuiderveld), gemeente Borger-Odoorn. This tomb was first described and studied in 1843. It was excavated by L.J.F. Janssen in 1846, who found a human cremation compressed in the form of a ball [had it been wrapped in a piece of cloth? – B.]. In 1846 or 1847 he drew this tomb (three large boulders in a depression). He reconstructed it with one capstone resting on three orthostats and the fourth missing (Janssen 1848, 'Exlo 3' in Table; the capstone should also have been stippled). Between 1848 and 1855 or 1875, its last stones were taken away. Van Giffen wrote on Janssen's 1848 hunebed table (BAI library) that the site of D31a was completely unknown locally in 1918 (cf. Van Giffen 1925, 180). J.E. Musch rediscovered the site in 1968. J.N. Lanting excavated it in 1993. Three orthostats and a chamber floor were found in a round pit (ca.4m in diameter), conforming to Janssen's schematic plan. According to Lanting (1994) this was not a dolmen, but a cist below surface. It contained 'the earliest TRB pottery of The Netherlands'.[515]

> (Janssen 1848, 17; drawing by L.J.F. Janssen from 1847 or 1846 in Drents Museum Assen; Van Giffen 1927, 54-6; Lanting 1994; Lanting 1997, 49; Van Ginkel et al. 1999, 195).

D32-Odoorn, gemeente Borger-Odoorn. 5 PS, CL 6.3 m. First mentioned in 1818. Not studied by Dryden and Lukis in 1878. Not systematically excavated. Restored in 1953, 1958 and 1995. A flat grave was found next to the tomb.

> (Van Giffen 1925, 87-9; Van Ginkel et al. 1999, 191; Kossian 2005, 471-2, pl. 2004).

*D32a-Odoorn-Westeres, gemeente Borger-Odoorn. 8 PS, CL (ca.11.5 m), FL about 12.0 m. In 1818 three large boulders remained, but they were removed between 1854 and 1869. J.N. Lanting excavated the site in 1983 and found the foundation and the extraction holes of orthostats, and the stone floor with the cited dimensions. Sherds of 165 pots are from Brindley 3-5.

> (Taayke 1985, 127-38; Brindley & Lanting 1992, 138; Van Ginkel et al. 1999, 196).

[**D32b-Odoorn*, as recorded by Van Giffen (1925), is **non existent**. Nothing could be found at its supposed site. Moreover, J.E. Musch fitted one piece of a flint axe 'from D32b' to another found in D32d (Taayke 1985).]

*D32c-Odoorn-Noorderveld, gemeente Borger-Odoorn. 4 PS, CL (ca.4.5 m), FL (ca.5.0 m). By 1929, this tomb had been robbed of its huge stones and only a low barrow remained. In 1984, only a gravelly patch in a ploughed field remained. J.N. Lanting excavated this site and found extraction and foundation holes of a chamber measuring 5 x 1.8-2.0 m.

> (Taayke 1985, 138-40; Van Ginkel et al. 1999, 196)

*D32d-Odoorn-Noorderveld, gemeente Borger-Odoorn. 3 PS, CL (ca.5.0 m), FL about 5.5 m. This damaged hunebed was not noted until 1943. J.E. Musch found its site again in the 1960s. The site was excavated by J.N. Lanting, in 1984, who found the pits of 3 PS and two endstones, but no floor pavement. Sherds of ca.150 pots were collected, which were assigned to Brindley 2-5 and 7. A small

---

515 Kossian 2005 (p. 23, n. 122) erroneously understood that Lanting (1997) had interpreted this tomb as 'the only dolmen that is known, until now, from The Netherlands'. I consider G5-Heveskesklooster as a dolmen, see above.

ceramic lid is unique for the TRB West Group. Fragments of Gouda tobacco pipes suggest that the tomb was demolished in the early 19th century.

(Taayke 1985, 140-2; Kamlag 1988; Van Ginkel et al. 1999, 196).

*D33-Valthe-Valtherveld, gemeente Borger-Odoorn. The site of D33 lies about 150 m to the north of D34. FL 7-7.5 m. In 1918, only nine loose large boulders remained (Van Giffen 1925, 89-91). After putting aside the *eleven* loose large boulders in December, 1954, A.E. van Giffen excavated the perimeter of a 7-7.5 m long stone pavement, the interior of which was completely destroyed. On March 23, 1956, the *Genie* (military corps of engineers) transported the large boulders from the site of hunebed D33 to D49-Papeloze Kerk for use in its reconstruction. Thus hunebed D33 was 'abolished' (*opgeheven*), as Van Giffen put it.

(Dryden & Lukis 1878, plan XXIX; Van Giffen 1925, 89-91; Van Giffen 1961, 1969; Bakker 1979a, 174; Van Ginkel et al. 1999, 196).

D34-Valthe-W, gemeente Borger-Odoorn. 5 PS, CL 7.1 m. First mentioned in 1818. Demolished in 1869. Investigated by H. Dryden and W.C. Lukis in 1878 (plan XXX). In 1952, Van Giffen found that the floor and the grave goods had completely disappeared.

(Dryden & Lukis 1878, plan XXX; Van Giffen 1925, 91-3; Van Ginkel et al. 1999, 181).

D35-Valthe-ZW (Valtherbos), gemeente Borger-Odoorn. 5 PS, CL 6.9 m. First mentioned by N. Westendorp in 1815. Not studied by Dryden and Lukis in 1878. Not systematically excavated. Restored in 1952.

(Van Giffen 1925, 93-5; Van Ginkel et al. 1999, 182).

*D35a-Valthe-Valtherspaan, gemeente Borger-Odoorn. 5 PS, FL 7.1 m. Described by C.J.C. Reuvens (1833) and L.J.F. Janssen (1847), who found an exterior? chamber length of 12 m. Demolished in the 1870s. Van Giffen could not recognise the plan of the tomb when he excavated the site in 1920 (Van Giffen 1927, 271-75). Van Ginkel et al. (1999, 197) point out that actually two different hunebeds may be concerned.

D36-Valthe-O2-Oosteres, gemeente Borger-Odoorn. Lies few meters north of D37. 5 PS, CL 7.9 m. Not systematically excavated.

(Dryden & Lukis 1878, plan XXVII; Van Giffen 1925, 95-7; Van Ginkel et al. 1999, 182).

D37-Valthe-O1-Oosteres, gemeente Borger-Odoorn. 6 PS, CL 9.6 m. Lies few metres south of D36. Not systematically excavated.

(Dryden & Lukis 1878, plan XXVIII; Van Giffen 1925, 97-9; Van Ginkel et al. 1999, 183).

D37a-Weerdinge, gemeente Emmen. ? PS, CL (ca.5.0 m), FL (ca.5.5 m). Excavated by J. Kouwens de Sille in 1837, A.E. van Giffen in 1925 and J.N. Lanting in 1993.

(Van Giffen 1927, 52-4, 185-310; Lanting 1997, 40; Van Ginkel et al. 1999, 197; Kossian 2005, 477, pl. 210).

D38-Emmerveld-N, gemeente Emmen. Forms a trio with D39 and D40. 5 PS, CL 6.6 m. First mentioned on the Hottinger map (1788-1792). Not systematically excavated. Restored in 1960.

(Dryden & Lukis 1878, plan XXXII; Van Giffen 1925, 99-101; Van Ginkel et al. 1999, 183).

D39-Emmerveld-ZW, gemeente Emmen. 3 PS, CL 3.2 m. First mentioned on the Hottinger map (1788-1792). Excavated by A.E. van Giffen in 1925 and J.N. Lanting in 1984. Restored in 1960. Forms a trio with D38 and D40.

(Dryden & Lukis 1878, plan XXXIII; Van Giffen 1925, 101-2; Van Ginkel et al. 1999, 184).

**D39a-Emmenerveld-ZW*, gemeente Emmen. Directly northeast of D39, S.W. Jager discovered a depression with stone gravel (5-5.5 x 2-2.5 m) in a slight rise with many stones. A cist?

(Jager 1996; Van Ginkel et al. 1999, 197).

D40-Emmerveld-ZO, gemeente Emmen. Forms a trio with D38 and D39. 2 PS, CL 3.4 m, FL (ca.4.0 m). The plan is shown in Figure 64. First mentioned on the Hottinger map (1788-1792). Excavated by A.E. van Giffen in 1918 and 1921, and by J.N. Lanting in 1987. Restored in 1960.

(Dryden & Lukis 1878, plan XXXIV; Van Giffen 1925, 102-4; Van Giffen 1927, 165-207; Klok 1979, 110-1; Brindley & Lanting 1992, 102-22; Van Ginkel et al. 1999, 184; Kossian 2005, 463-4, pl. 198).

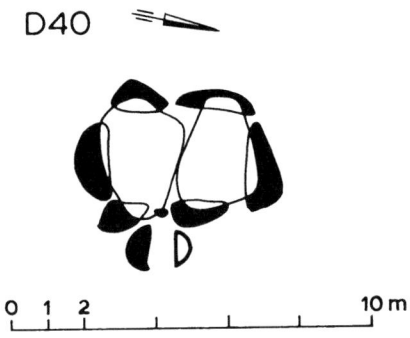

Figure 64. Plan of hunebed D40-Emmerveld (Bakker 1992, fig. 5).

D41-Emmen-N, gemeente Emmen. 4 PS, CL 4.5 m. Discovered in 1809 in a barrow and documented by J. Hofstede (see section '1809' and Figures 30-31 and 34). A.E. van Giffen and P. Kjaerum [1926-2010] found the sill stone of an entrance in 1960.

> (Dryden & Lukis 1878, plan XXXIX; Van Giffen 1925, 104-106; Van Giffen 1962, 112-3; Van Ginkel et al. 1999, 185).

D42-Westenes-N (op de Stienkamp), gemeente Emmen. 10 PS, CL 15.8 m. Depicted on the Hottinger maps (1788-1792). The chamber was not systematically excavated. A.E. van Giffen found the extraction holes of *three* pairs of entrance sidestones in 1965 (which is unique for The Netherlands). A Middle Bronze Age leaf-shaped and double-edged bronze razor from 1400-1200 BC was found in the spoil heaps of these excavations.

> (Dryden & Lukis 1878, plan XXXVI; Van Giffen 1925, 106-8; Bakker 1992, 59; Van Ginkel et al. 1999, 186)

D43-Emmen-Schimmeres, gemeente Emmen. *Langbett* with two hunebeds within its 40.3 m long and 6.8 m wide kerb: D43N (3 PS, CL 3.4m) and D43Z (5 PS, CL 6.5 m). The kerb is unique for its two rounded ends. This largest megalithic monument of The Netherlands was inexpertly restored in 1869. It was excavated by J.H. Holwerda in 1913 and by A.E. van Giffen in 1960. Figure 65 shows the plans drawn by both last named and Figure 66 the situation in 1968.

> (Dryden & Lukis 1878, plan XL; Van Giffen 1925, 108-12; Van Giffen 1927, 100-24; Van Giffen 1962; Bakker 1992, 15-21, figs. 12-4; Van Ginkel et al. 1999, 186; Kossian 2005, 464-5, pl. 199).

*D43a-Emmen, gemeente Emmen. 3 PS, CL about 3.8 m. Located south of nearby D43. First mentioned in 1819. L.J.F. Janssen drew it in 1847. Demolished in 1869-71; possibly some of its boulders were used to restore D43 in 1869. J.E. Musch discovered its site in 1968 and J.N. Lanting excavated it in 1984. 5500 sherds enabled reconstruction of 114 pots. At least 89 belonged to the TRB culture (Brindley 1-5).

> (Bakker 1992, 16; Molema 1987; Brindley & Lanting 1992, 138-9; Van Ginkel et al. 1999, 197).

D44-Westenes, gemeente Emmen. First mentioned by Janssen (1848, table), who thought that it originally was a hunebed with 6 PS, of which 8 sidestones, two endstones and 4 capstones were still present. Then and now it lay in a farmyard and is still the only privately owned Dutch hunebed. For some time its remnants were part of a pigsty. In 1918, only six large boulders remained: 3 orthostats and one capstone *in situ*, one capstone with a row of wedge holes and one loose sidestone (Van Giffen 1925, atlas-pl. 93). A.E. van Giffen excavated the site and

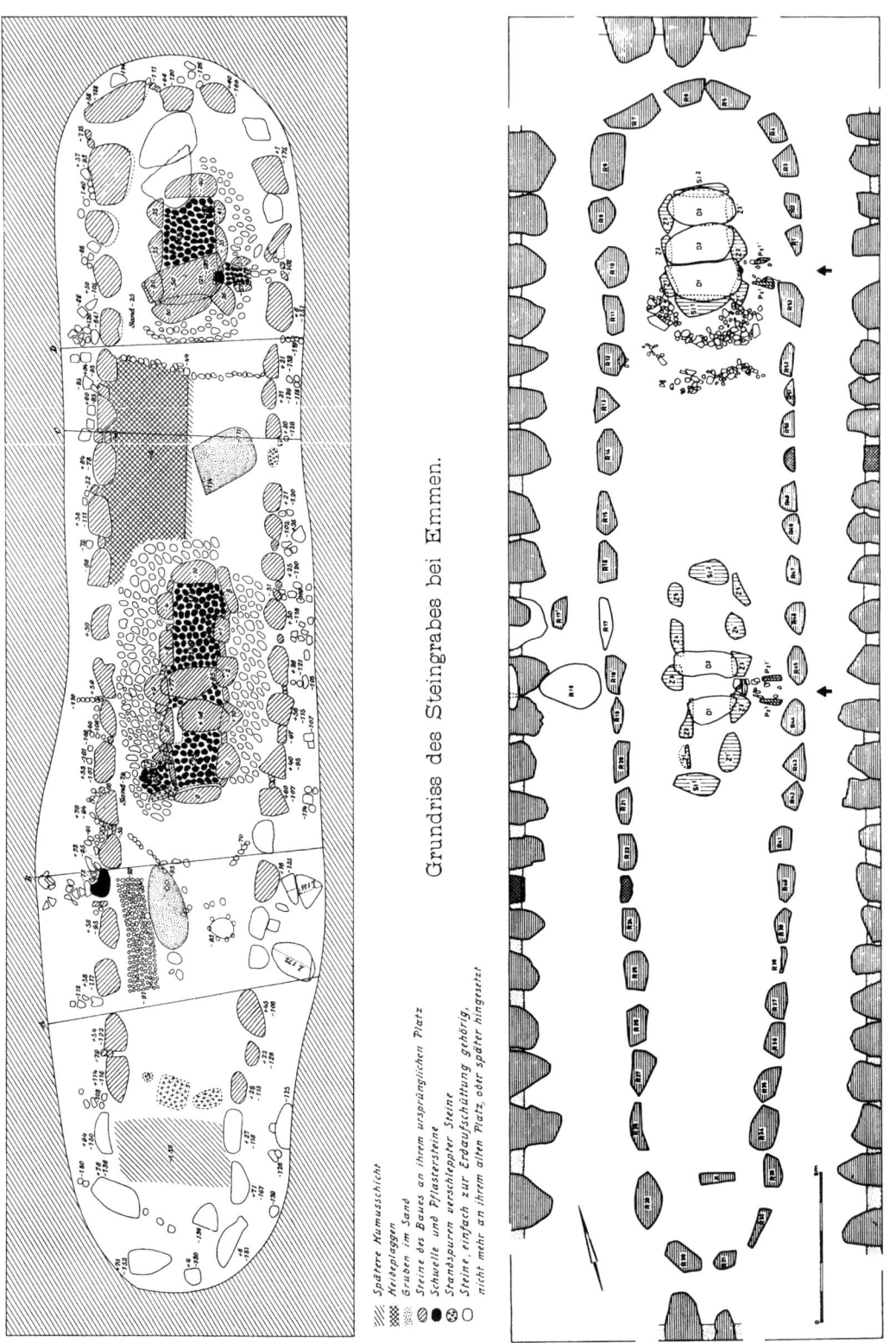

Grundriss des Steingrabes bei Emmen.

Figure 65. Langbett D43-Emmen-Schimmeres. Excavation plan by J.H. Holwerda (1914) and plans and sideviews by A.E. van Giffen (1962) (Bakker 1992, figs. 12-13).

Figure 66. Langbett D43-Emmen-Schimmeres from the southwest, in April, 1968, after Van Giffen's restorations of 1960 (photograph IPP-1968-736-31A by Fred Gijbels, from the trunk of an uprooted oak tree). See further Appendix 3.

restored the ruin a bit in 1961, but was not able to find the extraction holes etc. because the soil was too deeply disturbed.

(Dryden & Lukis 1878, plan XXXV; Janssen 1848, table; Van Giffen 1925, 112-4; Van Ginkel et al. 1999, 187).

D44a-Zaalhof, gemeente Emmen. FL 5.5 m. C.J.C. Reuvens drew the two remaining orthostats, one of which had a row of wedge holes (Brongers 1973), which were first mentioned by J. Picardt (1660, 80: 'some marked large boulders' (*eenige groote gemerckte Keselingen*); one stone was 'marked' by cleavage holes). Excavated by L.J.F. Janssen in 1846 (Janssen 1848). See sections '1660' and '1840-1860'). The site was destroyed by house construction in the early 20th century.

(Van Giffen 1927, 56-8; Bakker 1988, 64-5; Van Ginkel et al. 1999, 198)

D45-Emmerdennen, gemeente Emmen. 9 PS, CL 15.4 m and a kerb. The plan is shown in Figure 67. Occurs on the Hottinger maps (1788-1792). Inexpertly restored in 1870, investigated by H. Dryden and W.C. Lukis in 1878, and heavily damaged about 1885. When Van Giffen excavated and restored it, in 1957, the hunebed floor had vanished completely. In 1968, he added *plombes* (slabs of concrete and broken erratics on the ground surface) to indicate where the missing kerbstones had been. See my discussion of the position of the kerbstones and former restorations (Bakker 1992, 112-3, fig. 7, based on Van Giffen's 1957 field drawings and my own observations in 1968: see Figure 67).

A row of wedge holes is in capstone D4. The largest capstone, D6, had been large enough to widen the chamber in the form of a recess. In 1809, King Louis Napoleon of Holland, on horse-back, posed on this capstone, which has a flat surface.[516] Three other capstones [D7-D9] are missing.

(Dryden & Lukis 1878, plan XXXI; Van Giffen 1925, 114-7; Bakker 1992, 112-3, n. 30; Van Ginkel et al. 1999, 187).

---

516 This story was later told of a number of Drenthe hunebeds and also of Stone U1-Lage Vuursche. But as De Wilde (1906) noted in an article named 'A legendary omnipresence', this happened only here.

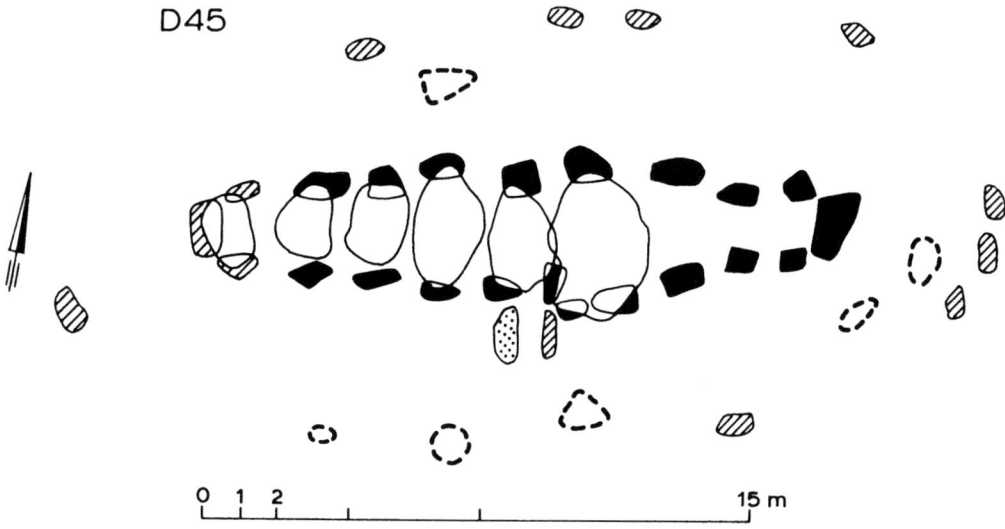

D45

0 1 2   15 m

Figure 67. Plan of hunebed D45-Emmerdennen (Bakker 1992, fig. 7). See further Appendix 3.

D46-Angelslo-N (Folkinger Slag), gemeente Emmen. 5 PS, CL 7.4 m. Occurs on the Hottinger map (1788-1792). D46 or D47 was excavated by J. Hofstede in 1809. Not systematically excavated. One capstone has a row of wedge holes. Restored in 1960 and 1997. It lies now in a small grove in the built-up area of the town of Emmen.

(Dryden & Lukis 1878, plan XXXVII; Van Giffen 1925, 117-9; Van Giffen 1927, 43-4; Klok 1979, 116-20; Van Ginkel et al. 1999, 188).

D47-Angelslo-Z (Haselackers), gemeente Emmen. 5 PS, CL 6.1 m. D46 was excavated by J. Hofstede in 1809. Mentioned in 1819, by L. Willinge. Restored and excavated in 1960 and 1997. Capstone D5 is a large boulder from elsewhere which was added in 1960.[517]

(Dryden & Lukis 1878, plan XXXVIII; Van Giffen 1925, 119-21; Van Giffen 1927, 43-4; Klok 1979, 116-20; Van Ginkel et al. 1999, 188).

[*D48-'Stone of Noordbarge'* is a large erratic boulder, **not a hunebed**]. Janssen (1848, table) drew a schematic plan of a 3 PS (*in situ*) hunebed, but remarked that 'only 5 large boulders remain'. Van Giffen (1925, 121-2, atlas-pl. 102) identified it as a single erratic boulder (4.15 x 3.40 m), not a hunebed. On September 2, 1967, he noted that there were 7 bore-holes for blasting with gun powder in the boulder, and that one corner of the boulder had broken off from the borehole (Van Giffen's notes about hunebeds in RCE, Amersfoort).

---

517 Van Ginkel et al. 1999, 188 wrote that two boulders from elsewhere were added as capstones, but their photo shows only the two capstones of 1918 and the one from 1960.

D49-Papeloze Kerk ('Popeless Church'; possible explanations of this name are given on p. 34) at Schoonoord, gemeente Coevorden. 6 PS, CL 10.2 m. Kerb. First mentioned in 1812. Heavily damaged about 1861 and 1867 by stone seekers, see section '1861 and 1867' and Van Giffen 1925, atlas-pl. 104. Not studied by H. Dryden and W.C. Lukis in 1878. Excavated in 1938 and 1958 by A.E. van Giffen, who reconstructed it as a demonstration model of a Dutch hunebed. All stones were restored, partly with large boulders from elsewhere (eleven stones were from hunebed *D33-Valthe-Valtherveld*). Half of the tomb was covered with earth and the chamber reconstructed with dry walling stones. The other half of the tomb was restored as a hunebed 'skeleton'. Copies of TRB pottery were put in the reconstructed chamber half; these were stolen within weeks and sold to the Harderwijk Museum and collectors as genuine artefacts.

(Van Giffen 1925, 122-4; Van Giffen 1961; Van Giffen 1969; Klok 1979, 120-3; Bakker 1992, 8; Van Ginkel et al. 1999, 189).

D50-Noordsleen-N, gemeente Coevorden. Lies southwest of D51. 8 PS, CL 15.6 m. Kerb. First mentioned on the Hottinger map (1788-1792). Not studied by H. Dryden and W.C. Lukis in 1878. The chamber was not systematically excavated. Restored by A.E. van Giffen in 1962, later once more, in 1998. Now one of the most magnificent hunebeds.

(Van Giffen 1925, 124-7; Van Ginkel et al. 1999, 190).

D51-Noordsleen-Z, gemeente Coevorden. Lies northeast of D51. 7 PS, CL 11.2 m. First mentioned on the Hottinger map (1788-1792). Not studied by H. Dryden and W.C. Lukis in 1878. The chamber was not systematically excavated. Restored by A.E. van Giffen in 1962, who found that the chamberfill was 'deeply disturbed'.

(Van Giffen 1925, 127-9; Van Ginkel et al. 1999, 190).

D52-Diever, gemeente Westerveld. 7 PS, CL (ca.12.4),[518] FL (ca.12.6). First mentioned in 1818. Not studied by H. Dryden and W.C. Lukis in 1878. The chamber was not systematically excavated. Restored by A.E. van Giffen in 1953, and in 1995.

(Van Giffen 1925, 129-31; Van Giffen 1925, atlas-pl. 108; Klok 1979, 123-6; Van Ginkel et al. 1999, 191).

*D52a-Wapse-Diever-Pottiesbarchien, gemeente Westerveld. 8 PS, FL 15.3 m. In 1734, all hunebeds in Drenthe were legally protected (see section '1730-1734'), but early in 1753 an exception was granted for the demolition of D52a, which was partly covered by drift sand. Ostensibly this was 'because the beauty of the view

---

518 Bakker (1978a, 150) reported that D52-Diever had a CL of 12.7 m.

was not harmed', but probably it was because arrangements for this demolition had been made before the new law was made. In the early 20th century, what was left of the barrow on the Berkenheuvel estate was called *Pottiesbarchien* ('pottery hillock'), because sherds could easily be collected here. In 1929, A.E. van Giffen excavated the site and left many sherds and flints in the spoil heaps (as usual). In 1988, J.N. Lanting excavated the site once more, including the seven spoil heaps, and recovered ca.15,800 sherds, which have yet to be sorted. He also restored the hunebed barrow.

(Van Ginkel et al. 1999, 198).

D53-Havelte-W, gemeente Westerveld. 10 PS, CL 17.0 m, FL 17.3 m. Kerb. Three instead of one endstones are at each end. This hunebed was first mentioned by A. Schoemaker in 1732 and drawn by Cornelis Pronk on July 1, 1732 (Gevers & Mensema 1985, fig. 34) and by Abraham de Haen on September 16, 1737 (Figure 13). Not studied by H. Dryden and W.C. Lukis in 1878. Completely excavated by A.E. van Giffen in 1918. The TRB pottery dates from Brindley 3-7. The initial estimate that the tomb contained about 600 pots is too high, according to J.N. Lanting (pers. comm.). At the end of World War II, the German occupiers demanded that A.E. van Giffen remove the tomb completely to make way for an air strip. Early 1945, he buried the boulders in a 6 m deep pit with the help of a dragline. The hunebed floor remained in place. The boulders were lifted again in 1947 and the tomb was reconstructed in 1949 by Van Giffen. It was restored in 1991.

(Van Giffen 1925, 131-33; Van Giffen 1927, 124-64; Van Giffen 1951, 102-4; Klok 1979, 126-31; Brindley & Lanting 1992, 138-9; Van Ginkel et al. 1999, 191).

D54-Havelte-O, gemeente Westerveld. 7 PS, CL 10.7 m. First mentioned by A. Schoemaker in 1732 and drawn by Cornelis Pronk on July 1, 1732 (Gevers & Mensema 1985, fig. 35). Not studied by H. Dryden and W.C. Lukis in 1878. Not systematically excavated. Restored in 1955, 1966 and 1995.

(Van Giffen 1925, 134-6; Bakker 1990a, 37-40; Van Ginkel et al. 1999, 192).

*D54a-Spier, gemeente Midden-Drenthe. 5 PS, FL about 8.0 m. W. Beyerinck discovered this demolished hunebed in a barrow in 1923 and excavated it in 1921 and 1923. The site was excavated by A.E. van Giffen in 1949. More than 4200 TRB sherds were collected (attributed to Brindley 2-7; clay discs, of which 18

fragments were recovered, are unique to this Dutch hunebed). Outside the tomb, 5 secondary burial and/or other ritual deposits were found near the supposed entrance in or below the hunebed barrow.

(Van Giffen 1927, 281-5; Meeüsen 1983; Van Ginkel et al. 1999, 198; Kossian 2005, 474, pl. 209).

D54b-Hooghalen, gemeente Midden-Drenthe. 5 PS, CL (ca.5.6 m), FL about 6.1 m. Discovered during forestation in 1946. Most stones were gone. Excavated by A.E. van Giffen in 1947. Unfortunately the artefacts collected from the chamber-fill were mixed up with those from D54c.

(Bouma 1985; Brindley & Lanting 1992, 138-9; Van Ginkel et al. 1999, 199).

D54c-Hooghalen, gemeente Midden-Drenthe. 2 PS, CL (ca.3.2 m), FL about 3.7 m. Found and excavated as D54b. The collected artefacts were mixed up with those from D54b.

(Bouma 1985; Brindley & Lanting 1992, 138-9; Van Ginkel et al. 1999, 199).

Province of Overijssel

O1-De Eese,[519] gemeente Steenwijk. Drawn by Petrus Camper in 1781 (Figure 27). Most boulders were carried off, probably in the 1840s. The site was excavated by A.E. van Giffen in 1918, who reported (1927, 319) a chamber length of 6.5-7.0 m (Van Giffen 1927, atlas-pls. 148-149). J.N. Lanting, however, after excavating the site once more in 1985, reported 6, perhaps even 7 PS, a CL of 14-15 m, and possibly a kerb. Parts of the barrow are still present. The pottery has not been systematically analysed, but comprises at least Brindley 3-5.

(Van Giffen 1927; 311-22; Brindley & Lanting 1992, 97-108; Van Ginkel et al. 1999, 199).

O2-Mander (Manderstreu), gemeente Tubbergen. Probably 6 PS and exterior CL of 13 m. Discovered shortly before 1957 and excavated by C.C.W.J. Hijszeler in 1957. Re-excavated by A.D. Verlinde in 1995. The TRB pottery from the chamber comprises Brindley 3-5, but two probably ritual pits in front of the former entrance of the tomb, which date from Brindley 2, indicate that the hunebed was built during that horizon. Sherds of at least 300 decorated pots in the former chamber fill were found. An adjacent TRB flat grave cemetery comprised at least 8 TRB flat graves (late Brindley 4 to early 5).

---

519 Van Giffen (1927, 311ff.) spelled the location 'De Eeze', but Van Ginkel et al. (1999, 199), spell it 'De Eese', conforming with most maps made since 1812 and with the Dutch *Topographische Kaart* (Topographical Map) since 1850. Hunebed O1-De Eese is not indicated on the maps made by the French 'Corps Impérial des Ingénieurs Geographes' between 1811 and 1813 (Versfelt & Schroor 2001, blade 11), which indicated several hunebeds, but not all. O1-De Eese is also absent from the *Topographische Kaart van het Koningrijk der Nederlanden* 1:50,000 (1850).

(Ufkes 1992; Van Ginkel et al. 1999, 199; Lanting & Brindley 2004; Van Beek 2009).

Province of Utrecht

***U1-Lage Vuursche, gemeente Baarn. The Stone of Lage Vuursche, a large boulder resting on three orthostats, was first drawn ca.1781. There are no indications that this is a 17th-century 'folly'; rather, it may be the remains of a hunebed. If one of the orthostats under the capstone really measured 2.23 x 1.6 x 1.16 m (Scheltema 1833) and if 2.23 is a misprint for 1.23, there is a fair chance that these boulders are remnants of a hunebed. On the other hand, the top of the 'capstone' reaches no more than 1.05 m above the present-day surface, which would be exceptionably low for a hunebed. Janssen (1856, 73-74) reported finding 'ash', modern glass, potsherds and ironware below the capstone in 1851, but also observed seven loose, larger boulders of granite 'at the other side of the road', which originally could have been part of this construction (Bakker 2004; Bakker 2005).

(Van Giffen 1925, 137-8; Van Giffen 1927, 67-75; Bakker 2004, 10-30; Bakker 2005b).

References

The year of publication for issues of periodicals that appear once in two or more years is referenced by the last year. For example, studies in *Palaeohistoria* 1971/1972 are referenced '(1972)'.

Publications that appeared in *Nieuwe Drentsche Volksalmanak* are referred to using the year for which this *almanac* was meant (and which was printed in heavy type on the front page). The actual date of publication at the end of the preceding year – which was also indicated on the front page of volumes 1-9 (for 1883-1891, printed in 1882-1890) – is ignored. This almanac has appeared every year except for volume no. 89 which covered 1971 and 1972.

A few other titles are found in footnotes. # indicates publications which I did not study myself, at least not recently.

DE ACOSTA, J. (1590) *Historia natural y moral de las Indias*. #

AHLERS, W. (2005) Jacob van Deventer, keizerlijk en koninklijk geograaf, *Jaarboek Twente* 44, 2005, 69-72.

ALESSANDRI, A. (1522) *Dies geniales*. Rome, 6 vols., repeatedly reprinted. #

ALI COHEN, L. (1844) De Hunebedden, uit een oudheidkundig en vooral uit een geologisch oogpunt beschouwd, *Mededeelingen uit het gebied van Natuur, Wetenschap en Kunst; vooral met toepassing op het bedrijvige leven. Verzameld en uitgegeven door Dr. L. Ali Coh*en 1, 1844, (23), 353-362, (24), 369-80, and one large plate with lithographs of D50-Noordsleen, D17 & D18-Rolde, D27-Borger, D6-Tynaarlo and D14-Eexterhalte by Cornelis Jan Bolt [1823-1879] after drawings by Jan van Ravenswaay [1789-1869] and his pupil Reinier van Harderwijk [1819-1849]. Reproductions: Arentzen 2006, 90; Van der Sanden 2007, 74.

VAN ALKEMADE, C. & P. VAN DER SCHELLING (1732-1735) *Nederlands Displegtigheden, vertoonende de plegtige gebruiken aan den dis, in het houden van maaltyden, en het drinken der gezondheden, onder de oude Batavieren, en vorste, graaven, edelen, en andere ingezetenen der Nederlanden, weleer gebruikelyk, nevens den oorsprongk dezer Gewoontens, en der zelver overeenkomst met die van andere Volken*. Rotterdam: Losel, 3 vols. #

ALSTORPHIUS, J. (1722) *Nobil. gravissimo viro, J. Nisinck, regionis Drentinae Deputato Amplissimo. S.P.D. Johannes Alstorphius*. Groningen: Officina Velseniana ('Scripsi Groningae Kalend Mart M. D. CC. XXII.'). [in Drenthe Archives, Assen: Gratama library, Joosting 306, bound behind J. ALSTORPHIUS, *Pallas Groning-Omlandica triumphans, seu Conjectanaea Philologica super nummo cuso in memorian Obsidionis & Liberationis Urbis Groningae. Anno M DCLXXII*. Groningen: Officina Velseniana, 1718].

ALTHAMER, A., *Commentaria Germaniae P. Cornelii Taciti Equitis Rom. libellus de situ, moribus & populis Germanorum*. Nürnberg: Johannes Petreius, 1536 # [2nd enlarged ed. of 1st ed. Nürnberg: Polypus, 1529 #].

[ANNIUS OF VITERBO] (1498) *Berosus Sacerdotis Chaldaici, Antiquitatum Italiae ac totius orbis libri V, Commentarijs Ioannis Annij Viterbensis*. Antwerp 1552 [(#, title cited after a later ed.].

TEN ANSCHER, T.J. (1988) *Een inventarisatie van de documentatie betreffende de Nederlandse hunebedden*. Amsterdam: RAAP-rapport 16.

TEN ANSCHER, T.J. (2010) *Leven met de rivier. De vindplaats P14 en de Noordoostpolder in Neolithicum en Bronstijd*. [to be published in 2010].

AREND, J.P. (1841) *Algemeene geschiedenis des Vaderlands*. Amsterdam: J. F. Schleijer, vol. 1 (1).

ARENTZEN, W. (2005) *Janssiana I: De verzameling L.J.F. Janssen*. Utrecht: W. Arentzen.[520]

ARENTZEN, W. (2006) *Janssiana II: L.J.F. Janssen en de Hunen*. Utrecht: W. Arentzen.

ARENTZEN, W. (2007) *Janssiana III: L.J.F. Janssen en het Gooi*. Utrecht: W. Arentzen.

ARENTZEN, W. (2009a) *Nicolaus Westendorp (1773-1836). Een uitmuntend oudheidkundige*. Utrecht: W. Arentzen. Ook: http://persistent-identifier.nl/?identifier=urn: nbn:nl:ui:13-3xz-y5r

ARENTZEN, W. (2009b) Nicolaus Westendorp, wegbereider voor de moderne archeologie, *Stad & Lande, het verhaal van Groningen, cultuurhistorisch tijdschrift* 18 (4), 2009, 10-15.

ARENTZEN, W. (2010) *W.J. de Wilde, 1860-1936, een fietstocht door Drenthe en de gevolgen daarvan*. [provisional title; my page references are to a pre-print].

ARNKIEL, T (1691) *Cimbrische Heyden-Begräbnisse* or *Cimbrische Heyden-Religion*, Hamburg. #

ATKINSON, R.J.C. (1956) *Stonehenge*. London: Hamish Hamilton [rev. ed. Harmondsworth: Penguin Books, 1979].

ATKINSON, R.J.C. (1976) Lukis, Dryden and the Carnac Megaliths, in MEGAW, J.V.S., ed., *To Illustrate the Monuments: Essays on Archaeology presented to Stuart Piggott*. London: Thames & Hudson, 111-124.

VON BAEDEKER, K. (1873) *Belgien und Holland. Handbuch für Reisende*. Coblenz & Leipzig: Verlag von Karl Baedeker.

---

520 The books Arentzen 2005-2009 are obtainable on CD from the author (Wout Arentzen, Afrikalaan 60, 3526 VN Utrecht) and accessible through www.dans.knaw.nl.

BAKKER, B., M. VAN BERGE-GERBAUD, E. SCHMITZ & J. PEETERS (1998) *Landscapes of Rembrandt. His favorite walks.* Bussum: Toth.

BAKKER, J.A. (1962-1963): in VAN REGTEREN ALTENA et al. 1962-1963.

BAKKER, J.A. (1964) VIII. De in 1853 op de Bosberg opgegraven "Haardsteden", in BAKKER, J.A. & J. YPEY Vroeg-Middeleeuwse vondsten uit het Gooi (6de tot 10de eeuw), *Mededelingen van het Museum voor het Gooi en Omstreken* VIII (1963/1964, 40-60), 56-58.

BAKKER, J.A. (1970) Diepsteekceramiek uit Hooghalen, gem. Beilen, *Nieuwe Drentse Volksalmanak* 88, 185-211.

BAKKER, J.A. (1978) Nordwestdeutsche Megalithgräber in niederländischen Berichten des 17. bis 19. Jahrhundert, *Die Kunde* N. F. 28-9, 1977-8 [1979], 21-31, pl. 1-2.

BAKKER, J.A. (1979a) *The TRB West Group. Studies in the chronology and geography of the makers of hunebeds and Tiefstich pottery*, Amsterdam: Universiteit van Amsterdam, Subfaculteit Pre- en Protohistorie. [reprinted with an 'In Retrospect' by J.A. Bakker: Leiden, Sidestone Press 2009].

BAKKER, J.A. (1979b) Protection, acquisition, restoration and maintenance of the Dutch hunebeds since 1734. An active and often exemplary policy in Drenthe (I), *Berichten van de Rijksdienst voor het Oudheidkundig Bodemonderzoek* 29, 143-88.

BAKKER, J.A. (1979c) July 1878 Lukis and Dryden in Drente, *The Antiquaries Journal* (London) 59-1, 9-18, pl. I-VI.

BAKKER, J.A. (1979d) Ein vergessenes Megalithgrab zu Leer (Ostfriesland), *Probleme der Küstenforschung im südlichen Norseegebiet* 13, 85-97, pls. 1-3.

BAKKER, J.A. (1980) Ein früher Krug der Westgruppe der Trichterbecherkultur, die Kammerverlängerung und der Beginn der Megalithgräber westlich der Weser, *Fundberichte aus Hessen* 19-20, 1979-1980, 119-29.

BAKKER, J.A. (1982) TRB settlement patterns on the Dutch sandy soils, *Analecta Praehistorica Leidensia* 15, 87-124.

BAKKER, J.A. (1983) Het hunebed G1 te Noordlaren, *Groningse Volksalmanak* 1982-1983, 113-200.

BAKKER, J.A. (1984) De opgraving in het Grote Hunebed te Borger door Titia Brongersma op 11 juni 1685, *Nieuwe Drentse Volksalmanak* 101, 103-16.

BAKKER, J.A. (1988) A list of the extant and formerly present *hunebedden* in The Netherlands, *Palaeohistoria* 30, 63-72.

BAKKER, J.A. (1989) Petrus en Adriaan Camper en de hunebedden, in SCHULLER TOT PEURSUM-MEIJER, J. & W.H.R. KOOPS, eds. (1989) *Petrus Camper (1722-1789), onderzoeker van nature.* Groningen: Universiteits Museum, 189-98.

BAKKER, J.A. (1990a) Prehistory visualised: hunebedden on Dutch school pictures as a reflection of contemporary research and society, *Berichten van de Rijksdienst voor het Oudheidkundig Bodemonderzoek* 40, 29-71.

BAKKER, J.A. (1990b) Views on the Stone Age, 1848-1931: the impact of the 1853 Hilversum finds on Dutch prehistoric archaeology, *Berichten van de Rijksdienst voor het Oudheidkundig Bodemonderzoek* 40, 73-99.

BAKKER, J.A. (1992) *The Dutch hunebedden, megalithic tombs of the Funnel Beaker Culture*. Ann Arbor: Michigan International Monographs in Prehistory, Archaeological Series 2.

BAKKER, J.A. (1993) De Romeinse muntschatten van Brandlecht (1620), Ringe (1654/55) en Emsbühren (voor 1713) in eigentijdse berichten, *Jaarboek voor Munt- en Penningkunde* 90, 5-21.

BAKKER, J.A. (1994) Eine Dolmenflasche und ein Dolmen aus Groningen, in J. HOIKA (ed.), *Beiträge zur frühneolithischen Trichterbecherkultur im westlichen Ostseegebiet: 1. Internationales Trichterbechersymposium, Schleswig, 4. bis 7. März 1985*. Schleswig, 1994 (Untersuchungen und Materialien der Steinzeit in Schleswig-Holstein 1), 71-78.

BAKKER, J.A. (1999) 'The Dutch megalithic tombs, with a glance at those of north-west Germany', in BEINHAUER et al. (1999), 145-62.

BAKKER, J.A. (2001a) 'Childe, Van Giffen, and Dutch archaeology until 1970', in METZ, W.H., B.L. VAN BEEK & H. STEEGSTRA , eds. (2001) *Patina. Essays presented to Jay Jordan Butler on the occasion of his 80th birthday*. Groningen and Amsterdam: Metz, Van Beek and Steegstra, 48-74.

BAKKER, J.A. (2001b) 'Opmerkingen over Drakestein vóór 1640', *Tussen Vecht en Eem* 19 (1), 2001, 4-10.

BAKKER, J.A. (2002) 'Hunebed de Duvelskut bij Rolde', *Nieuwe Drentse Volksalmanak* 119, 62-94.

BAKKER, J.A. (2004) *Kanttekeningen bij mijn publicaties en enige andere zaken*. Baarn: J.A. Bakker.

BAKKER, J.A. (2005a) 'De Steen en het rechthuis te Lage Vuursche', *Tussen Vecht en Eem* (Bussum), 23, 221-31.

BAKKER, J.A. (2005b) Funerary buildings from erratic boulders. The construction and function of the hunebedden, in LOUWE KOOIJMANS et al. (2005), 307-310.

BAKKER, J.A. (2009a) 'Hunebedden and Hünengräber: the construction of megalithic tombs west of the river Elbe', in SCARRE, C., ed., *Megalith quarrying. Sourcing, extracting and manipulating the stones, BAR Int. Ser. 1923 (Proceedings of XV world congress of UISPP, Lisbon, 4-9 September 2006)*, 209, 27-34.

BAKKER, J.A. (2009b) Chronicle of megalith research in The Netherlands, 1547-1900: from giants and a Devil's Cunt to accurate recording, in MIDGLEY, M.S., ed., *Antiquarians at the Megaliths, BAR Int. Ser.* 1956 (*Proceedings of the XV world congress of UISPP, Lisbon 4-9 September 2006*), 2009, 7-22.

BAKKER, J.A. (in preparition) *Hunebed D26 in het Drouwenerveld, verslag van de onderzoekingen.*

BAKKER, J.A. & A.L. VAN GIJN (2005) Megalith builders and sturgeon fishers. Middle Neolithic B: Funnel Beaker Culture and the Vlaardingen Group, 3400-2900 BC, in LOUWE KOOIJMANS et al. (2005), 281-306.

BAKKER, J.A. & W. GROENMAN-VAN WAATERINGE (1988) Megaliths, soils and vegetation on the Drenthe Plateau, in W. GROENMAN-VAN WAATERINGE & M. ROBINSON eds., *Man and Soils, Symposium of the Association for Environmental Archaeology 6, 20-23 September 1985 at Heemskerk.* Oxford (*BAR Int. Ser.* 410), 143-181.

BAKKER, J.A. & H. LUIJTEN (1990) "Service sets" and other "Similarity Groups" in western TRB pottery, in J. L'HELGOUAC'H, ed., *La Bretagne et l'Europe préhistoriques. Mémoire en hommage à Pierre-Roland Giot. Revue Archéologique de l'Ouest, Supplément* N° 2 – 1990, 171-187.

BAKKER, J.A. & W.A.B. VAN DER SANDEN (1995) Trechterbekeraardewerk uit natte context, de situatie in Drenthe', *Nieuwe Drentse Volksalmanak* 112, 132-148.

BAKKER, J.A. & J.D. VAN DER WAALS (1973) Denekamp-Angelslo: cremations, collared flasks and a Corded Ware sherd in Dutch final TRB contexts, in G.E. DANIEL & P. KJAERUM, eds., *Megalithic graves and ritual, papers presented at the III Atlantic Colloquium, Moesgård 1969.* Copenhagen 1973 (Jutland Archaeological Society Publications 11), 17-50.

BAKKER, J.A. & H.T. WATERBOLK (1980) *De Nederlandse Hunebedden. Rapport aan de Minister van Cultuur, Recreatie en Maatschappelijk Werk, en het provinciaal Bestuur van Drenthe.* Amsterdam, Groningen [typoscript].

BARRACLOUGH, G. (1994) The Times Concise Atlas of World History. London 1994.

BECANUS, J.G. (1569) *Origines Antwerpiae, sive Cimmeriorum becceselana novum libros complexa, Atlantica, Gigantomachia, Niloscopium, Cronia, Indoscythyca, Saxsonica, Gotodanica, Amazonica, Venetica et Hyperborea.* Antwerp: Christ. Plantijn, 1100 p. #

BECKER, C.J. (1947) *Mosefundne Lerkar fra Yngre Stenalder. Studier over Tragtbægerkulturen i Danmark.* Copenhagen (Aarbøger for Nordisk Oldkyndighed og Historie 1947).

BEEK, R. [ROY] VAN (2009) *Reliëf in tijd en ruimte. Interdisciplinair onderzoek naar bewoning en landschap in Oost-Nederland tussen vroege prehistorie en middeleeuwen.* Wageningen: Doctoral thesis Wageningen Universiteit, 641 p.

BEIMA, E.M. (1867) *De Aarde vóór den Zondvloed. Geschiedenis der voorwereld. Bewerkt naar het Frans en het Hoogduits.* Rotterdam & Leiden [based on L. FIGUIER (1862) *La Terre avant le déluge.* Paris: Imprimerie Générale de Chr. Lahure, and on O. FRAAS (1866) *Vor der Sindfluth. Eine Geschichte der Urwelt.* #

BEINHAUER, K.W., G. COONEY, C.E. GUKSCH & S. KUS, eds. (1999) *Studien zur Megalithik. Forschungsstand und ethnoarchäologische Perspektiven / The Megalithic phenomenon. Recent research and ethnoarchaeological approaches.* Mannheim-Weissbach: Beier & Beran.

BEKMANN, J.C. & B.L. BEKMANN (1751) *Historische Beschreibung der Chur und Mark Brandenburg*, vol. 2, *Von den Alterthümern der Mark.* Berlin, 345-452. #

VAN BERKEL, K. (2009) *Academisch leven. Over geschiedenis, karakter en veerkracht van de Nederlandse universiteit.* Amsterdam: Bert Bakker.

BERVOETS, J. (1992) Alexander Ver Huell (1822-1897), een levensbeschrijving. Zutphen: Walburg Pers.

BEUKER, J.R. (2008) Een vondst waar de vonken vanaf vlogen, *Nieuwe Drentse Volksalmanak* 125, 2008.

BEUKER, J.R. (2010) *Vuurstenen werktuigen, technologie op het scherp van de snede.* Leiden: Sidestone Press, 274 p.

BIBBY, T.G. (1956) *The Testimony of the Spade. Life in Northern Europe from 15,000 B.C. to the Time of the Vikings.* New York: Alfred A. Knopf / Random House: xviii + 414 + x p. Reprint 1957: London: Collins.

BIJVANCK, A.W. (1912) *Gids voor de bezoekers van het Museum Meermanno-Westreenianum.* The Hague: Gebroeders van Cleef.

BLAEU, J. (1662) *Grooten Atlas.* [Atlas van de Nederlanden, facsimile uitgave van de originele tekst en 65 kaarten uit den Grooten Atlas van Joan Blaeu, met een moderne inleiding van C. Broekema. Amsterdam 1973].

BLINK, H. (1892) Het ontstaan der diluviale gronden in Nederland, *Elsevier's Geïllustreerd Maandschrift* 1892, 185-96.

BOCK, H. (2008) *"Mobilmachung befohlen!". Arbeiten und Leben auf dem Lande in der nordwestlichen Altmark zwischen den Weltkriegen. Das Dorf Hanum.* Oschersleben: Dr. Ziethen Verlag.

BÖDIKER, H. (1828) Altertümer im Kreise Meppen, untersucht, endeckt und beschrieben ..., *[Wigand's] Archiv für Geschichte und Altertumskunde Westphalens* 2, 1828, 166-204.

BOELES, J. (1844) Het hunebed te Noordlaren, *Groningse Volksalmanak voor 1845*, 1844, 33-47.

BOELES, P.C.J.A (1951) *Friesland tot de elfde eeuw. Zijn vóór- en vroegste geschiedenis.* The Hague: Martinus Nijhoff, 2nd rev. ed.

BOESER, P.A.A. (1904) Levensbericht van Dr. W. Pleyte, *Handelingen en Mededeelingen van de Maatschappij der Nederlandsche Letterkunde te Leiden over het jaar 1903-1904*, 91-112.

BONSTETTEN, A. BARON DE [G.K. FREIHERR VON BONSTETTEN] (1865) *Essai sur les Dolmens et les Menhirs.* Geneva: J.G. Frick. #

[BOOM, H., A.L. LESTURGEON & D.H. VAN DER SCHEER] (1842-1847) *Drenthe in vlugtige en losse omtrekken geschetst door Drie Podagristen.* Reprints Assen 1947: Van Gorcum; Leeuwarden 1974: Van Seijen.

BOSCHMA, C. & J. PEROT (1991) *Antoine-Ignace Melling (1763-1831), reizend kunstenaar / artieste-voyageur.* Abcoude: Uniepers.

BOTS, H. & R. VISSER (2001) *Correspondance, 1785-1787, de Petrus Camper (1722-1789) et son fils Adriaan Gilles Camper (1759-1820).* Amsterdam / Utrecht: APA-Holland University Press (Lias, Sources and documents relating to the early modern history of ideas 28).

BOULESTIN, B., A. ZEEB-LANZ, C. JEUNESSE, F. HAACK, R.-M. ARBOGAST & A. DENAITRE (2009) Mass cannibalism in the Linear Pottery Culture at Herxheim (Palatinate, Germany), *Antiquity* 83, 2009, 968-82.

BOUMA, H. (1985) *Twee vernielde hunebedden te Hooghalen*, unpublished *doctoraalscriptie* BAI, Groningen.

BRANDT, K.-H. (1967) *Studien über steinerne Äxte und Beile der Jüngeren Steinzeit und der Stein-Kupferzeit Nordwestdeutschlands.* Hildesheim: August Lax Verlagsbuchhandlung (Münstersche Beiträge zur Vorgeschichtsforschung 2), IV + 210 text-p. + 43 pls. of objects + 34 pls. with distribution maps.

LE BRASSEUR, P.P. (1722) *Histoire civile et ecclesiastique du Comté d'Évreux.* Paris: Barois. #

BRINDLEY, A.L. (1983) The finds from hunebed G3 on the Glimmer Es, mun. of Haren, province of Groningen, The Netherlands, *Helinium* 23, 209-216.

BRINDLEY, A.L. (1986a) Hunebed G2: excavation and finds, *Palaeohistoria* 28, 27-92.

BRINDLEY, A.L. (1986b) The typochronology of TRB West Group pottery, *Palaeohistoria* 28, 93-132.

BRINDLEY, A.L. (2003) The use of pottery in Dutch *hunebedden*, in GIBSON, A., ed., *Prehistoric Pottery. People, pattern and purpose*, Oxford (*BAR International Series* 1156), 43-51.

BRINDLEY, A.L. & J.N. LANTING (1992) A re-assessment of the hunebedden O1, D30 en D40: structures and finds, *Palaeohistoria* 33/34, 1991-1992, 97-140.

BRINDLEY, A.L., J.N. LANTING & A.D. NEVES ESPINHA (2002) Hunebed D6ᵃ near Tinaarlo, *Palaeohistoria* 43/44, 2001/2002, 43-85.

BRONGERS, J.A. (1973) *1833 Reuvens in Drenthe. A contribution to the history of Dutch archaeology in the first half of the nineteenth century.* Bussum: Fibula-van Dishoeck.

BRONGERS, J.A. (1976) *Air photography and Celic Field research in The Netherlands.* Amersfoort: Rijksdienst voor het Oudheidkundig Bodemonderzoek (Nederlandse Oudheden 6), 147 p.

BRONGERS, J.A. (2002) *Een vroeg begin van de moderne archeologie. Leven en werken van Cas Reuvens (1793-1835). Documentatie van een geleerden-leven.* Amersfoort: Rijksdienst voor het Oudheidkundig Bodemonderzoek.

BRONGERS, J.A. (2006) Vroege belangstelling voor fossielen in Nederland, *Teylers Magazijn* December 2006, 9-11, ill. 1.

BRONGERS, J.A. & S.L. WYNIA (2005) *Wie is wie in archeologie. Proeve van een biografisch woordenboek van in Nederland en directe omgeving tot ca. 1960 op enigerlei wijze archeologisch actieven.* Amersfoort: Rijksdienst voor het Oudheidkundig Bodemonderzoek, 3rd ed.

BRONGERS, R. (1996) Komôf en fermidden fan Titia Brongersma, *It Beaken, Tydskrift fan de Fryske Akademy* 58, 1996, 14-25.

BRONGERSMA, T. (1686) *De Bron-Swaan, Of Mengeldigten ... Bestaande in Lof-Gedigten, Geestelijke stoffen, Gesangen, Af-beeldingen, Verjaar-gedichten, Lijk-klachten, Bruylofts-Sangen, Vertalingen, Byvallen, Omgeefsels, en Raatselen.* Groningen: Carel Pieneman.

BROOD, P. (2003) 'Maten', in GERDING et al. 2003, vol. 2, 585-6.

DE BRUIJN, J.G. (1977) *Inventaris van de prijsvragen uitgeschreven door de Hollandsche Maatschappij der Wetenschappen 1753-1917.* Haarlem: Hollandsche Maatschappij der Wetenschappen; Groningen: H.D. Tjeenk Willink.

BRUNSTING, H. (1947) Het grafheuvelonderzoek, in VAN GELDER, H.E, P. GLAZEMA, G.A BONTEKOE, H. HALBERTSMA & W. GLASBERGEN, eds., *Een kwart eeuw oudheidkundig bodemonderzoek in Nederland. Gedenkboek A. E. van Giffen.* Meppel: J.A. Boom & Zoon (IV + 608 p.), 1974, 223-253.

DE BUFFON, G.-L.L. (1749-1788) *Histoire Naturelle générale et particulière, avec le description du Cabinet du Roy.* Paris, L'Imprimerie du Roy, 36 vols. (8 additional vols. were published, until 1804, by Lacépède). #

BUIJTENDORP, T. (2007) Wetenswaardigheden uit de geveilde bibliotheek van Glasbergen en Van Giffen, *Westerheem* 56, 58-66.

BUTLER, J.J. & J.D. VAN DER WAALS (1967) Bell Beakers and early metal-working in The Netherlands, *Palaeohistoria* 12, 41-139.

Byvoegsels op de Nederlandsche Jaerboeken, inhoudende een Verhaal van de merkwaardigste geschiedenissen, die voorgevallen zyn binnen den omtrek der Vereenigde Provintien, sedert het begin des Jaers MDCCXVII. *Eenentwintigste Deel, Behelzende Byvoegsels op de Jaerboeken van 1756 tot 1759.* Amsterdam: Erven F. Houttuyn; Leiden: P. van Eyck & D. Vygh, vol. I [from 1770 or later].

VAN CALKAR, F.J.P. (1885) Diluviales aus der Gegend von Neu-Amsterdam, *Zeitschrift der Deutschen Geologischen Gesellschaft* 1885. #

VAN CAMPEN, J. (2000) *De Haagse jurist Jean Theodore Royer (1737-1807) en zijn verzameling Chinese voorwerpen.* Hilversum: Verloren.

[CANNEGIETER, H.] (1757) *Eerste Brief over byzondere Nederlandsche Oudheden. Bevattende ene Beschryving en verklaringe van enen ouden Grafkelder, onlangs by Anloo in den landschap Drente ontdekt als mede van de zogenaamde Donderbeitels en Vrouw* JACOBAES KANNETJES *enz. geschreven door enen Liefhebber der Nederlandsche Oudheden.* Arnhem: R. Brouwer. [anonymous publication].

CARTAILHAC, E. (1889) *La France préhistorique d'après les sépultures et les monuments.* Paris: F. Alcan.

CASPERS, C.M.A. (1994) 'Weg met de duivel? De rooms-catholieke Kerk en haar 'groot-exorcisme' van de zestiende eeuw tot heden', in ROOIJAKKERS, G., L. DRESEN-COENDERS & M. GEERDES, eds., *Duivelsbeelden. Een cultuurhistorische speurtocht door de Lage Landen.* Baarn: Ambo, 1994, 286-309.

CASSEN, S., ed. (2009) *Autour de la Table. Explorations archéologiques et discours savants sur des architectures néolithiques à Locmariaquer, Morbihan (Table des Marchands et Grand Menhir). Synthèse d'un programme de fouilles (*J. L'HELGOUAC'H *et* S. CASSEN *1986-1994) et d'une Action Collective de Recherche (ACR) 2003-2006.* Nantes 2009: Laboratoire de Recherches Archéologiques (LARA), CNRS, Université de Nantes, 918 p., 39 authors.

DE CAYLUS, A.C.-P. (1752-1767) *Recueil d'Antiquités Égyptiennes, Grecques, Étrusques et Romains.* Paris: J. Desaint, C. Saillant, N.M. Tillard, 7 vols. #

CHAIGNEAU, C. (in preparation) *Des pierres aux mots ... une histoire de la reconnaissance du fait mégalithique.* [a draft of part of this work was kindly sent to me by the author, Nov., 2007].

CHAIGNEAU, C., S. CASSEN & Y. LE GAUDION (2009) L'historiographie en Locmariaquer. Une première approche, in CASSEN, ed., 2009, 387-415.

CHILDE, V.G. (1950) *Prehistoric Migrations in Europe.* Oslo.

CLARKE, D.L. (1968) *Analytical Archaeology.* London: Methuen & Co Ltd.

CLUVERIUS, P. (1616) *Germaniae Antiquae libri tres.* Leiden. #

COERT, G.A. (1991) *Stromen en schutten, vaarten en voorden. Geschiedenis van de natte waterstaat in Drenthe (1400-1985).* Meppel: Boom.

COHAUSEN, J.H. (1714) *Ossilegium Historico-Physicum ...*, in NUNNINGH (1714).

COLONNA, F.M.P. (1739) *Histoire naturelle de l'univers dans laquelle on rapporte des Raisons Physiques, sur les Effets ... de la Nature. Enrichie de Figures en Taille-douce par Colonne.* Paris: Cailleau, 1739. #

CORDFUNKE, E.H.P., M. EICKHOFF, R.B. HALBERTSMA, P.H.D. LEUPEN & H. SARFATIJ, eds. (2007) *'Loffelijke verdiensten van de archeologie'. C.J.C. Reuvens als grondlegger van de moderne Nederlandse archeologie.* Hilversum: Verloren.

CUNLIFFE, B.(1999) *The ancient Celts.* London: Penguin Books.

CYPRAEUS, P. (1634) *Annales Episcoporum sleswicensium* (ed. by J.A. Cypraeus). Cologne 1634. #

DAMPIER, W. (1697) *New Voyage around the World.* #

DAMPIER, W. (1698*) Nieuwe reystogt rondom de wereld, waarin omstandiglyk beschreeven worden de land-engte van Amerika, verscheydene kusten en eylanden in Westindie, de eylanden van Kabo Verde ... in 't Engelsch beschreeven door William Dampier; en daaruyt vertaald door W. Sewel; met naauwkeurige landkaarten en kopere platen vercierd.* The Hague. #

DAMPIER, W. (1698) *Voyage Descriptions.* #

DANIEL, G.E. (1938) The megalithic tombs of northern Europe, *Antiquity* 1938, 297-310.

DANIEL, G.E. (1941) The dual nature of the megalithic colonisation of prehistoric Europe, *Proceedings of the Prehistoric Society* 7, 1-49.

DANIEL, G.E. (1958) *The Megalith Builders of western Europe.* London: Hutchinson.

DANIEL, G.E. (1960) *The prehistoric chamber tombs of France. A geographical, morphological and chronological survey.* London: Thames & Hudson.

DANIEL, G.E. (1962) *The Idea of Prehistory*, London: Watts.

DANIEL, G.E. (1967) *The Origins and Growth of Archaeology.* Middlesex: Penguin.

DANIEL, G.E. (1970) Megalithic answers, *Antiquity* 1970, 260-69.

DANIEL, G.E., ed. (1981) *Towards a History of Archaeology. Being the papers read at the first Conference on the History of Archaeology in Aarhus, 29 August – 2 September 1978.* London: Thames and Hudson.

DARVILL, T. (2006) *Stonehenge. The biography of a landscape.* Brinscombe Port, Stroud: Tempus Publishing Ltd.

DEHN, T., N. ENGBERG, V. ETTING, J. FRANDSEN, S.I. HANSEN, K. BORCH VEST, K. & J. WESTPHAL (2007) Bevaring og restaurering af fortidsminder, *Nationalmuseets Arbejdsmark* 2007, 273-90.

DEHN, T. & S.I. HANSEN. (2006) Birch bark in Danish passage graves, *Journal of Danish Archaeology* (Copenhagen), vol. 14, 23-44.

VAN DEURSEN, A.T. (1970) *Jacobus de Rhoer 1722-1813. Een historicus op de drempel van een nieuwe tijd.* Groningen: Wolters-Noordhoff.

DILICHIUS, W. (1604) *Urbis Bremae et praefecturum, quas habet, typon et chronicon.* Cassel. #

DIRKS, J. (1873) Reis naar Italie, September-November 1871, *Vaderlandsche Letteroefeningen* 1873, 20-56, 87-111, 188-208.

DRENTH, E. & A.E. LANTING (1990) Van een kruik die geen kruik bleek, *Nieuwe Drentse Volksalmanak* 107, 193-99.

DRENTH, E. & A.E. LANTING (1991) De chronologie van de Enkelgrafcultuur, enkele voorlopige opmerkingen, *Paleo-aktueel* 2, 42-6.

DRYDEN, H.E.L. & W.C. LUKIS (1878) [plans and descriptions of 40 Dutch hunebeds. Society of Antiquaries, London, partly also Drenthe Archives, Assen].

EBBESEN, K. (1992) Simple, tidligneolitiske grave, *Aarbøger for Nordisk Oldkyndighed og Historie* 1978, 47-102. #

EBELS-HOVING, B. (1987) Nederlandse geschiedschrijving 1350-1530. Een poging tot karakterisering, in EBELS-HOVING et al. (1987), 216-42.

EBELS-HOVING, B., C.G. SANTING & C.P.H.M. TILMANS, eds. (1987), *Genoechlicke ende lustighe historiën. Laatmiddeleeuwse geschiedschrijving in Nederland.* Hilversum: Verloren, 1987.

ECKHARD, M.P.J. (1734) *Duo perantiqua monumenta ... ex agro Jutrebocensi eruta.* Leipzig-Wittenberg. #

EICKHOFF, M. (2007) C. J. C. Reuvens als erflater. Twee eeuwen 'genealogieën' van de Nederlandse archeologie, in CORDFUNKE et al. 2007, 135-47.

EILSKOV JENSEN, L. & H. NIJBOER (1998) Titia Brongersma, een Friese dichteres in de 17ᵉ eeuw, *Fryslân, Nieuwsblad voor geschiedenis en cultuur* 4 (2), 3-5. [this comprehensive study is also on the internet].

EMMIUS, U. (1596) *Rerum Frisicarum historiae libri X.* Franeker: Gillis van den Rade.

ENDLICH, C., ed. (2005) *Kulturlandschaft Marsch: Natur, Geschichte, Gegenwart. Vorträge anlässlich des Symposiums in Oldenburg vom 3. bis 5. Juni 2005.* Oldenburg: Isensee-Verlag.

ENGEL, F. (1965) Tabellen alter Masse, Gewichte und Münzen, in JÄGER, H., ed., *Methodisches Handbuch für Heimatforschung in Niedersachsen.* Hildesheim: August Lax, 1965, 65-76.

ENGELBERTS, E.M. (1790) *De aloude staat en geschiedenissen der Vereenigde Nederlanden.* Vol. 3. Amsterdam: Johannes Allart, 161-84, spec. 181.

ENTZELT, C. (1579) *Chronicon oder kurtze einfeltige vorzeichnus / darinne begriffen / Wer die Alte Marck / und nechste Lender darbey sind der Sindtfluth bewonet hat / Auch anfang und ursach der Marck zu Brandenburg / und ire veranderung / Auch ankunfft / stamme und herkommen / aller Marggrauen zu Brandenburg / so jemals gelebt / bis zu dieser unser zeit. Durch den alten M. Christophorum Entzelt von Saluelt / Pfarherrn zu Osterburg.* Magdeburg: Mattaeus Giseken. [facsimile-edition: *Magister Christoph Entzelts Chronicon der Altmark 1579, with an introduction by P. Kupka.* Stendal 1925: Bibliophile-Reproduktions-Anstalt Leopold Schwarz, cf. WETZEL 2002].

VON ESTORFF, G.O.C. (1846) *Heidnische Alterthümer der Gegend von Uelzen im ehemaligen Bardengaue jetzt Königreich Hannover.* Hanover: Historischer Verein. #

EVANS, J. (1956) *A History of the Society of Antiquaries.* Oxford.

EXTEMPORÉ[521] (1844) 'Bij 't eerste gezigt der Hunebedden', *Drentsche Volksalmanak* 9, *voor het jaar 1845* [1844], 181.

FABRICIUS, K. & C.J. BECKER (1996) *Stendyngegrave og kulthuse. Studier over Tragtbægerkulturen i Nord- og Vestjylland.* Copenhagen: Akademisk Forlag A/S, Universitetsforlaget i København (Arkæologiske Studier XI), 399 p.

FERGUSSON, J. (1872) *Rude Stone Monuments in all Countries. Their age and uses.* London: John Murray [reprint Graz: Akad. Druck- u. Verlagsanstalt, 1976].[522]

FINKE, W. (1983) Ein Flachgräberfeld der Trichterbecherkultur by Heek-Averbeck, Kreis Borken. Vorbericht über die Ausgrabungen, *Ausgrabungen und Funde Westfalen-Lippe* 1, 1983, 27-32.

FOCKE, F. (1868) *Bilder aus der Oldenburgische Geschichte.* Jever. #

FOORTHUIS, W.[R.] & J. VAN DIJK (1987) De zaak Van Lier 1785, *Nieuwe Drentse Volksalmanak* 105, 35-44.

---

521 The real name of the author of this poem is unknown (pers. comm. H. Nijkeuter, 2007).

522 Fergusson's fig. 121 (1872, 321) is not hunebed D16-Ballo (as he indicated), but D18-Rolde, see section 'Ca. 1868 and following years'.

FRANKS, A.W. (1872) The megalithic monuments of The Netherlands and the means taken by the government of that country for their preservation, *Proceedings of the Society of Antiquaries of London*, 2nd ser. V (1870-1873), February 8, 1872, 258-67.

FRANKS, A.W. (1873) [Translation into English of the report of the King's Commissioner in Drenthe, L.J.G. Gregory, in *Provinciale Drentsche en Asser Courant*, which was first translated into French by L.O. Gratama], *Proceedings of the Society of Antiquaries of London*, 2nd ser. V (1870-1873), March 20, 1873, 475ff.

FREDERIK VII (1857) *Om Bygningsmaaden af Oldtidens Jaettestuer af Hans Majestaet Kong Frederik den Syvende til Danmark*, Copenhagen [2nd ed. Copenhagen: Berlingske Bogtrykkeri ved L.N. Kalckar 1862].

FREDERIK VII (1863) *De Hunnebedden. Op welke wijze in den ouden tijd gebouwd? Beantwoord door Z. M. Frederik VII, Koning van Denemarken. Eene voorlezing, gehouden in de jaarlijksche vergadering van het Koninklijk Genootschap van Oudheidkundigen, op het slot Christiaansborg, den 29 Mei 1857. – Tweede druk. Kopenhagen 1862. Uit het Deensch door Jhr. Mr. M. de Haan Hettema*. Leeuwarden: H. Kuipers.

FRIEDRICH, T. (2007) The strike-a-lights from the Ostorf graves, *Bericht der Römisch-Geramischen Kommission* 88, 2007, 415-23.

FRIJHOFF, W. (2010) *Meertaligheid in de Gouden Eeuw. Een verkenning*. Amsterdam: KNAW Press (Mededelingen van de Afdeling Letterkunde, Nieuwe Reeks, Deel 73 no. 2).

FRITSCH, B. & L. MITTAG (2006) Forschungs- und Zerstörungsgeschichte, in BOCK, H., B. FRITSCH & L. MITTAG *Großsteingräber der Altmark*. Halle (Saale): Landesamt für Denkmalpflege und Archäologie Sachsen-Anhalt & Landesmuseum für Vorgeschichte, 2006, 13-21.

FUCHS, J.M. & W.J. SIMONS (1977) *Het zal je maar gezegd wezen. Buitenlanders over Nederland*. The Hague: Kruseman.

GALLÉE, J.H. (1900-1901) Sporen van Indo-germaansch ritueel in germaansche lijkplechtigheden, *Volkskunde, Tijdschrift voor Nederlandsche Folklore* XIII, 89-99, 129-145.

GALLÉE, J.H. (1901) Henne, hunne en hunne samenstellingen, *Tijdschrift voor Nederlandsche Taal- en Letterkunde* 20, 46-58. [this important study was found by W. Arentzen].

[GALLITZIN, D.A.] (1789) *Lettres sur quelques objets de mineralogie à Mr le Professeur Petrus Camper*. The Hague. [anonymously published].

GEHASSE, E.F. (1995) *Ecologisch-archaeologisch onderzoek van het Neolithicum en de Vroege Bronstijd in de Noordoostpolder met de nadruk op vindplaats P14, gevolgd door een overzicht van de bewoningsgeschiedenis en de bestaanseconomie binnen de Holocene Delta.* Doctoral thesis Amsterdam Univerity (with a summary in English).

GERDING, M.A.W. (1997) *Johan Picardt (1600-1670), Drenthe's eerste geschiedschrijver.* Assen (Drentse Historische Reeks 6).

GERDING, M.A.W., P. BROOD, M. HILLENGA & H. NIJKEUTER, eds. (2003) *Encyclopedie van Drenthe.* Assen: Koninklijke Van Gorcum, 3 vols.

GEVERS, A.J. & A.J. MENSEMA (1985) *Over de hobbelde bobbelde heyde. Andries Schoemaker, Cornelis Pronk en Abraham de Haen op reis door Overijssel, Drente en Friesland.* Aphen aan den Rijn: Canaletto.

GIELIS, M. (1994) De duivel in het volksgeloof en in de rooms-katholieke verkondig-ing, in ROOIJAKKERS, G., L. DRESEN-COENDERS & M. GEERDES, eds., *Duivelsbeelden. Een cultuurhistorische speurtocht door de Lage Landen.* Baarn: Ambo, 1994, 329-55.

VAN GIFFEN, A.E. (1919) Mededeeling omtrent onderzoek en restauratie van het Groote Hunebed te Havelte, *Nieuwe Drentsche Volksalmanak* 37, 109-139.

VAN GIFFEN, A.E. (1924) Het hunebed te Rijs in Gaasterland, *De Vrije Fries* 27 (IV), 1924, 307-25, ill. 1-2.

VAN GIFFEN, A.E. (1925-1927) *De hunebedden in Nederland.* Utrecht: A. Oosthoek, 2 vols. and atlas.

VAN GIFFEN, A.E. (1927) *The hunebeds in The Netherlands.* Utrecht: A. Oosthoek [translation of VAN GIFFEN (1925), vol. I, and atlas]. #

VAN GIFFEN, A.E. (1930) *Die Bauart der Einzelgräber, Beitrag zur Kenntnis der äl-teren individuellen Grabhügelstrukturen in den Niederlanden.* Leipzig: Mannus-Bibliothek, vols. 44-45.

VAN GIFFEN, A.E. (1943a) De zgn. Eexter grafkelder, hunebed D XIII, te Eext, Gem. Anloo, *Nieuwe Drentsche Volksalmanak* 61, 103-15, figs. 16-20a.

VAN GIFFEN, A.E. (1943b) Het Ndl. Hunebed (DXXVIII) te Buinen, Gem. Borger, een bijdrage tot de absolute chronologie der Nederlandsche hunebedden, *Nieuwe Drentsche Volksalmanak* 61, 115-36.

VAN GIFFEN, A.E. (1944a) De twee vernielde hunebedden DVIe en DVIf bij Tinaarlo, gem. Vries, *Nieuwe Drentsche Volksalmanak* 62, 92-112.

VAN GIFFEN, A.E. (1944b) Een steenkeldertje, DXIIIa, te Eext, gem. Anloo, *Nieuwe Drentsche Volksalmanak* 62, 117-119.

VAN GIFFEN, A.E. (1944c) Twee vernielde hunebedden, DXIIIb en c, te Eext, gem. Anloo, *Nieuwe Drentsche Volksalmanak* 62, 119-125.

VAN GIFFEN, A.E. (1944d) Opgravingen in Drente, in J. POORTMAN, J., ed., *Drente, een handboek voor het kennen van het Drentsche leven in voorbije eeuwen*, vol. 1. Meppel: J.A. Boom & Zoon, 2nd enlarged ed., 1944, 393-568, figs. 1-65.

VAN GIFFEN, A.E. (1945) Het kringgreppelurnenveld en de grafheuvels O.Z.O. van Gasteren, Gem. Anloo, *Nieuwe Drentsche Volksalmanak* 63, 69-121.

VAN GIFFEN, A.E. (1951) Het grote hunebed D53, *Nieuwe Drentse Volksalmanak* 69, 102-4.

VAN GIFFEN, A.E. (1961) Een gereconstrueerd hunebed, *Nieuwe Drentse Volksalmanak* 79, 189-97.

VAN GIFFEN, A.E. (1962) Restauratie en na-onderzoek van het langgraf (D43) te Emmen, *Helinium* 2, 104-14.

VAN GIFFEN, A.E. (1969) *De Papeloze kerk. Het gereconstrueerde Rijkshunebed D49 bij Schoonoord, gem. Sleen*. Groningen: Wolters-Noordhoff (6th ed. 1972).

VAN GIFFEN, A.E. & W. GLASBERGEN (1964) De vroegste faze van de TRB-cultuur in Nederland, *Helinium* 4, 40-8.

VAN GIJN, A. (2010) *Flint in Focus. Lithic Biographies in the Neolithic and Bronze Age*. Leiden: Sidestone Press, 289 p.

VAN GINKEL, E., S. JAGER & W.A.B. VAN DER SANDEN (1999) *Hunebedden, monumenten van een steentijdcultuur*. Abcoude: Uniepers. [2nd ed. Abcoude: Uniepers, 2005].

VAN GINKEL, E. & L.[B.M.] VERHART (2009) *Onder onze voeten, de archeologie van Nederland*. Amsterdam: Uitgeverij Bert Bakker.

GIOT, P.-R. (1985) Historique des recherches, in *Megalithes en Bretagne, Exposition réalisée par la Direction des Antiquités historiques et préhistorques de Bretagne*. Rennes: Maison de la Culture, 7-17.

GOGUET, A.Y. [aided by A. C. FUGÈRE] (1758) *De l'Origine des Lois, des Arts et des Sciences, et de leur Progrès chez les Anciens Peuples*. Paris: Desaint & Saillant; The Hague: Pierre Josse. [translated into English (Edinburgh 1761), German (Lemgo 1760) and several times re-issued]. #

GONZÁLEZ-GARCÍA, A.L. & L. COSTA-FERRER (2007) Orientation of megaliths in Germany and The Netherlands, in E. PASZTOR, ed., *Archaeometry in Archaeology and Ethnography, British Archaeological Reports* S1647.

GOSLINGA, M. (2008) Schets van de geschiedenis van de fotografie in Drenthe tussen 1844 en 1910, *Nieuwe Drentse Volksalmanak* 125, 5-34. #

GOTJÉ, W. (1993) *De Holocene laagveenontwikkeling in de randzone van de Nederlandse kustvlakte (Noordoostpolder)*. Doctoral thesis Free University, Amsterdam, 1 april 1993.

GOULETQUER, P. (2009) Éteignez bien les braises, in CASSEN, ed., 2009, 463-9.

TER GOUW, J. (1874) Funeralia. Boerebegrafenis, *De Oude Tijd* 1874, 248-254.

[GRATAMA, L.O.] (1838) De Hunnebedden, *Drentsche Volksalmanak* 1838, 105-29, with a plate of hunebed D27-Borger. # [signed O.G., cf. VAN GIFFEN 1925, 219, no. 44].

GRATAMA, L.O. (1868) *Open brief aan het Collegie van Gedeputeerde Staten van Drenthe over de zorg voor en het onderhoud der hunnebedden, naar aanleiding der beraad-slagingen over dat onderwerp in de vergadering van Provinciale Staten van Drenthe van November 1867.* Assen: Van Gorcum en Comp.

GRATAMA, L.O. (1884a) De hunnebedden in Drenthe. Geschiedkundig overzicht over het gebeurde met dezelve – aard en inrichting – bestemming – ouderdom – stichting, *Nieuwe Drentsche Volksalmanak* 2, 23-50.

GRATAMA, L.O. (1884b) Heeft Tacitus met "Zuilen van Hercules in Germanië" de Drentsche hunnebedden bedoeld?, *Nieuwe Drentsche Volksalmanak* 2, 149-52.

GRATAMA, L.O. (1885) De hunnebedden in Drenthe II, *Nieuwe Drentsche Volksalmanak* 3, 22ff.

GRATAMA, L.O. (1886) *De hunnebedden in Drenthe en aanverwante onderwerpen.* Assen: Van Gorcum en Comp., VI, 236 p., ills. [updated reprint of Gratama 1884a-b, 1885 and other studies].

GRATAMA, L.O. (1887) Officiële verslagen omtrent oudheden in Drenthe van 1818 en 1819, *Nieuwe Drentsche Volksalmanak* 1885, 200-232. [VAN GIFFEN 1925, 217-8, no. 36 (a-m) listed them, but forgot the *Nadere Rapport*en of 1820].

GREGORY, L.J.G. (1879) De Hunebedden in Drenthe, *Provinciale Drentse en Asser Courant* 10 Maart 1879.

GRIMM, J. (1844) *Deutsche Mythologie*, 2nd ed. [1st ed. 1835; reprint: Basel, 1953]. #

[GRIMM, W.K.] (1824) [anonymous review of WESTENDORP 1822], *Göttingsche gelehr-te Anzeigen unter der Aufsicht der Königl. Gesellschaft der Wissenschaften* 70.-71. Stück, May 1, 1824, 689-711.

GROOT, D.J. DE (1988) Hunebed D9 at Annen (gemeente Anloo, province of Drenthe, The Netherlands), *Palaeohistoria* 30, 73-108.

GUMMEL, H. (1938) *Forschungsgeschichte in Deutschland.* Berlin: Walter de Gruyter & Co. (Die Urgeschichtsforschung und ihre historische Entwicklung in den Kulturstaaten der Erde I).

H[AASLOOP] W[ERNER], G. (1845) Hunnebedden en steenen gedenkteekenen, *Nederlandsch Magazijn ter verspreiding van algemeene nuttige kundigheden* 1845, 414-5 [signed G. H. W.].

HAASSE, H.S. (1978) *Mevrouw Bentinck of Onverenigbaarheid van karakter. Een ware geschiedenis.* Amsterdam: Em. Querido's Uitgeverij.

VON HAGEN, V. (1957) *Realm of the Incas.* The New American Library (Mentor books).

HAMCONIUS, M. (1609) *Frisia sev viris rebvsqve Frisiae illvstribvs. Libri dvo.* Münster: L. Raesfeldt.

HARKENROTH, J.Y. (1712) *Oostvriesche oorsprongkelykheden, van alle steden, vlekken, dorpen, rivieren enz ... .* Emden: E. Tremel. #

HARTOGH HEIJS VAN ZOUTEVEEN, H. (1883) Heeft Tacitus met de 'Zuilen van Hercules' in Germanië de Drentsche hunebedden bedoeld?, *Nieuwe Drentsche Volksalmanak* 1, 126-7.

HARTOGH HEIJS VAN ZOUTEVEEN, H. (1885) Wie waren de stichters der Drentsche hunebedden?, *Nieuwe Drentsche Volksalmanak* 4, 28-72.

HAYWOOD, J. (2001) *The historical atlas of the Celtic world.* London: Thames & Hudson [poorly translated as *Historische atlas van de Keltische beschaving.* Baarn: Tirion, 2001].

VAN HEERINGEN, R.M. (1989) The Iron Age in the western Netherlands. v, Synthesis, *Berichten van de Rijksdienst voor het Oudheidkundig Bodemonderzoek* 39, 159-62.

HEIZER, R.F. (1962a) *Man's Discovery of his Past. Literary Landmarks in Archaeology.* Englewood Cliffs N. J.: Prentice Hall.

HEIZER, R.F. (1962b) The background of Thomsen's Three-Age system, *Technology and culture* 1962, 259-66.

HELLINGA, G.G. (2007) *Geschiedenis van Nederland. De canon van ons vaderlands verleden.* Zutphen: Walburg Pers.

HERM, G. (1975) *Die Kelten, Das volk, das aus dem Dunkel kam.* Düsseldorf-Vienna: Econ. [Dutch translation: *De Kelten, het volk dat uit het duister kwam.* Baarn: Meulenhoff, 1992].

HERMANN, L.D. (1711) *Maslographia oder Beschreibung des Schlesischen Massel im Oels-Bernstädischen Fürstentum ... .* Brieg. #

HERODOTUS (1974) *Herodotos Historiën, vertaling Dr. Onno Damsté.* Bussum: Fibula-van Dishoeck, 3rd ed.

HEUPERS, E. (1979, 1981) *Volksverhalen uit Gooi- en Eemland en van de westelijke Veluwe, verzameld door E. Heupers, Van registers en commentaar voorzien door A.J. Dekker* [vol. 2 also by *J.J. Schell*]. Amsterdam: Instituut voor Dialectologie, Volkskunde en Naamkunde, I (1979, 307 p. with a preface by J.A. Voskuil, p. 7-19), II (1981, 307 p.).

HEUSSEN, H.F. VAN (1714) *Batavia Sacra, sive res Gestae Apostolicorum, qui fidem Bataviae primi intulerunt, in duas partes divisa.* Brussels: Foppens. #

HEUSSEN, H.F. VAN (1719) *Historia episcopatuum Foederati Belgii utpote metropolitani Ultrajectini, nec non suffraganeorum Harlemensis, Daventriensis, Leovardensis, Groningensis, et Middelburgensis ….* Leiden: Christiaan Vermey, 2 vols. #

HOFDIJK, W.J. (1856a) *Het Nederlandsche Volk geschetst in de eerste tijdperken zijner ontwikkeling.* Amsterdam: Gebroeders Kraaij. [lectures given in 1854/55].

HOFDIJK, W.J. (1856b) 'Inleiding' and 'Het Hunebed te Rolde', in W.J. HOFDIJK, *Historische Landschappen.* Haarlem: A.G. Kruseman, 1856, 1-26 and 29-56.

HOFDIJK, W.J. (1857) 'Eerste tijdvak, I', in W.J. HOFDIJK, *Schets van de Geschiedenis der Nederlanden opgehelderd met afbeeldingen.* Amsterdam: Gebroeders Binger, 1857, 1-3.

HOFDIJK, W.J. (1859) 'Voorbericht' and 'Voor-Historische Tijd', in W.J. HOFDIJK, *Ons Voorgeslacht in zijn dagelijksch leven geschilderd*, vol. 1. Haarlem: G. Kruseman, V-X and 3-20.

HOFDIJK, W.J. (1862) 'Voorwoord' and 'Een hunebed in de provincie Drenthe door H.D. Kruseman van Elten, te Brussel', in W.J. HOFDIJK, *Tafreelen uit de geschiedenis der ontwikkeling van het Nederlandsche volk. In de Kunstzaal der Maatschappij Arti et Amicitiae. Toegelicht door W.J. Hofdijk, Honorair Lid der Maatschappij.* Amsterdam: Gebroeders Binger, I-III, 9.

HOFSTEDE, P. (1766) *Bijzonderheden over de Heilige Schrift*, vol. 1. Rotterdam. #

HOFSTEDE, P. (1815) Beschrijving van de grafplaats, de gedaante hebbende van een hunebed, in het jaar 1809, bij Emmen in Drenthe, uit een heuvel opgedolven, *Letter- en Oudheidkundige Verhandelingen van de Hollandsche Maatschappij der Wetenschappen te Haarlem* I, 1815 [this is, actually, a report by J. Hofstede].

HOGESTIJN, J.W.H. & E. DRENTH (2001) In Slootdorp stond een Trechterbekerhuis? Over midden- en laat-neolithische huisplattegronden uit Nederland, *Archeologie* 10, 2000/2001, 42-79.

HOIJTINK, M. (2003) Een Rijksmuseum in wording. Het Archaeologisch Cabinet in Leiden onder het directoraat van Caspar Reuvens (1818-1835), *De negentiende eeuw* 27, 225-38.

HOIKA, J. (1993) [Review of BAKKER 1992], *Helinium* 33, 1993, 305-9.

[HOLWERDA, A.E.J.] (1906) *Ministerie van Binnenlandsche Zaken. Rijks Museum van Oudheden te Leiden. Verslag van den Directeur over het tijdvak van 15 Sept. 1904 tot 15 Sept. 1905.* The Hague: Ministerie van Binnenlandsche Zaken.[anonymous publication, written by A.E.J. HOLWERDA, Director of the National Museum of Antiquities and father of curator J.H. HOLWERDA].

HOLWERDA, J.H. (1906) Inleiding tot een archaeologie van Nederland, *Onze Eeuw* 6, 134-74.

HOLWERDA, J.H. (1907) *Nederland's vroegste beschaving, proeve van een archaeologisch systeem*. Leiden: E.J. Brill.

HOLWERDA, J.H. (1909) Hunneschans bij het Uddelermeer, *Oudheidkundige Mededeelingen uit 's Rijksmuseum van Oudheden te Leiden* 3, 1909, 1-52.

HOLWERDA, J.H. (1911) Praehistorische nederzettingen aan het Uddelermeer, *Oudheidkundige Mededeelingen uit 's Rijksmuseum van Oudheden te Leiden* 5, 1911, 5-17.

HOLWERDA, J.H. (1912) Opgraving aan het Uddelermeer, *Oudheidkundige Mededeelingen uit 's Rijksmuseum van Oudheden te Leiden* 6, 1912, 1-16.

HOLWERDA, J.H. (1913a) Opgraving van twee hunnebedden te Drouwen, *Oudheidkundige Mededeelingen uit 's Rijksmuseum van Oudheden te Leiden* 7, 29-50.

HOLWERDA, J.H. (1913b) Zwei Riesenstuben bei Drouwen (Prov. Drente) in Holland, *Prähistorische Zeitschrift* 5, 435-48.

HOLWERDA, J.H. (1913c) *Catalogus van het Rijksmuseum van Oudheden te Leiden. Afdeeling Praehistorie en Nederlandsche Oudheden. Supplement I: Opgravingen in Nederland*. The Hague: Ministerie van Binnenlandsche Zaken.

HOLWERDA, J.H. (1914) Das grosse Steingrab bei Emmen (Prov. Drente), *Prähistorische Zeitschrift* 6, 57-67.

HOLWERDA, J.H. (1925) *Nederland's vroegste geschiedenis*. Amsterdam: S.L. van Looy (2nd, enlarged edition).

HOLWERDA, J.H., M.A. EVELEIN & N.J. KROM (1908) *Catalogus van het Rijksmuseum van Oudheden te Leiden. Afdeeling Praehistorie en Nederlandsche Oudheden*. The Hague: Ministerie van Binnenlandsche Zaken.

HOOFT VAN IDDEKINGE, [J.E.H.] (1877) Nieuw licht over een duister tijdvak, *De Nederlandsche Spectator* no. 26, 202-204.

HOOFT VAN IDDEKINGE, [J.E.H.] (1879) Pleyte's Nederlandsche Oudheden, *De Nederlandsche Spectator* no. 28, 11-12.

[HOOFT VAN IDDEKINGE, J.E.H.] (1880) Nieuw licht over een duister tijdvak, *De Nederlandsche Spectator* 31, 246-247. [anonymously published, but the authorship was revealed by C. Vosmaer (1884)].

HOOFT VAN IDDEKINGE, [J.E.H.] (1881) *Friesland en de Friezen in de Middeleeuwen. Bijdragen tot de Geschiedenis, Rechtskunde, Muntkunde en Geografie der Friesche gewesten, inzonderheid gedurende de elfde eeuw*. Leiden: E.J. Brill, 228 p.

HÖTTGES, V. (1937) *Typenverzeichnis der deutschen Riesen- und riesischen Teufelssagen.* Helsinki. #

HUISKES, B. (1985) Van veldnaam tot vindplaats. Een onderzoek naar het verband tussen hunebedden en "steennamen" in Drenthe, *Driemaandelijkse Bladen voor Taal en Volksleven in het Oosten van Nederland. Orgaan van het Nedersaksisch Intituut der Rijksuniversiteit Groningen, nieuwe serie* 37 (3), 1985, 81-94.

HUISKES, B. (1990) *Steen-namen en hunebedden, raakvlak van naamkunde en pre-historie.* Amersfoort: Rijksdienst voor het Oudheidkundig Bodemonderzoek (Nederlandse Archeologische Rapporten, NAR 10).

HUISMAN, H. & W.A.B. VAN DER SANDEN (2003) 'Kolossale stenen' onder het veen. Het vermeende hunebed van Nieuw-Dordrecht, *Nieuwe Drentse Volksalmanak* 120, 129-137.

HUIZINGA, J. (1919) *Herfsttij der Middeleeuwen. Studie over levens en gedachtenvormen der veertiende en vijftiende eeuw in Frankrijk en de Nederlanden.* Haarlem: H.D. Tjeenk Willink. [translated by F. Hopman: *The Waning of the Middle Ages: A Study of the Forms of Life, Thought, and Art in France and The Netherlands in the XIVth and XVth Centurie*s. London: E. Arnold, 1924].

HÜSING, E. (1855) *Des Jod. Herman Nünning ... Westfälisch-Münsterländische Heidengräber aus dem Lateinischen übersetzt.* Coesfeld: Wittneven. [translation of NUNNINGH 1714 and COHAUSEN 1714].[523] http://diglib.hab.de/drucke/hl-129/start.htm?image=00149

ISINGS, J.H. (1975) Beschrijving van de plaat, in *Gulden Sporen met illustraties van J.H. Isings*, vol. 1. Groningen: Uitgeverij De Vuurbaak, 19-22 [this is a reprint of the *Toelichtingen* ('explanations') of Isings's school pictures by J.W. de Jongh, H. Wagenvoort and D. Wijbenga, in this case of plate '*Hunebedbouwers*' (Hunebed Builders) of 1959. Cf. Wijbenga 1960, 1975]

JACOB-FRIESEN, K.H. (1928) *Grundfragen der Urgeschichtsforschung.* Hanover (Veröffentlichungen der urgeschichtlichen Abteilung des Provinzialmuseums zu Hannover, vol. 1).

JACOB-FRIESEN, K.H. (1954) Johan Picardt, der erste Urgeschichtsforscher Niedersachsens, *Nachrichten aus Niedersachsens Urgeschichte* 23, 3-19.

JAGER, S.W. (1985) A prehistoric route and ancient cart-tracks in the gemeente Anloo (province of Drenthe), *Palaeohistoria* 27, 185-245.

JAGER, S.W. (1988) *Anloo-De Strubben, Kniphorstbos. Een archeologische kartering, inventarisatie en waardering.* Amersfoort: Rijksdienst voor het Oudheidkundig Bodemonderzoek (Nederlandse Archeologische Rapporten, NAR 7).

---

523 HÜSING's spelling of 'Nünning' is incorrect; it should be 'Nunningh'; see note 525.

JAGER, S.W. (1993) *Odoorn, het landinrichtingsgebied 'Odoorn' Een archeologische kartering, inventarisatie en waardering.* Amersfoort: Rijksdienst voor het Oudheidkundig Bodemonderzoek (Nederlandse Archeologische Rapporten, NAR 16).

JAGER, S.W. (1994) Anloo, *Nieuwe Drentse Volksalmanak* 111, 178-80.

JAGER, S.W. (1996) Emmen, *Nieuwe Drentse Volksalmanak* 113, 186.

JANSSEN, L.J.F. (1840) *Germaansche en Noordsche Monumenten van het Museum te Leyden.* Leiden: Lugtmans.

JANSSEN, L.J.F. (1848) *Drenthsche Oudheden*, Utrecht: Kemink & Zoon.

JANSSEN, L.J.F. (1850) Het Hunebed te Rijs, in Gaasterland, *De Vrije Fries* 5, 1850, 338-50.

JANSSEN, L.J.F. (1853a) Over de beschaving der allervroegste bewoners van ons Vaderland, afgeleid uit gevonden overblijfselen. (Eene archaeologische voorlezing.), *Oudheidkundige Verhandelingen en Mededeelingen van Dr. L.J.F. Janssen*, I. Arnhem: I.A. Nijhoff en zoon, 1-26.

JANSSEN, L.J.F. (1853b) Hilversumsche oudheden, *Oudheidkundige Verhandelingen en Mededeelingen van Dr. L.J.F. Janssen* I. Arnhem: I.A. Nijhoff en zoon, 137-60.

JANSSEN, L.J.F. (1853c) Nog iets over het Hunebed te Rijs, in Gaasterland, *De Vrije Fries* 6, 1863, 161-3.

JANSSEN, L.J.F. (1856) *Hilversumsche oudheden. Eene bijdrage tot de ontwikkelingsgeschiedenis der vroegste Europesche volken.* Arnhem: Is. Am. Nijhoff en zoon. [Reprint 2009, with a Preface by L. AMKREUTZ and an Introduction by W. ARENTZEN. Leiden: Sidestone Press].

JAŻDŻEWSKI, K. (1932) Zusammenfassender Überblick über die Trichterbecherkultur, *Prähistorische Zeitschrift* 23, 77-110.

JAŻDŻEWSKI, K. (1936) *Kultura Puharów Lejkowatych w Polsce Zachodniej i Środkowej* [mit deutscher Zusammenfassung: Die Trichterbecherkultur in West- und Mittelpolen, freie Übersetzung der wichtigeren und Zusammenfassung der weniger wichtigen Abschnitte, p. 323-409]. Poznań: Nakładem Polskiego Towarzystwa Prehistorycznego z zasiłkiem Senatu Uniwersitetu Poznańskiego skład główny w Księgarni Uniwersyteckiej Jana Jachowskiego w Poznaniu, 456 p. + 1081 drawings + 4 maps.

JAŻDŻEWSKI, K. (1965) *Poland.* London: Thames and Hudson (Ancient Peoples and Places 45).

JONGSTRA, A. (2010) *De Heldeninspecteur.* Amsterdam-Antwerp: Uitgeverij De Arbeiderspers.

JUNGMAN, B. (1904) *Holland.* London.

JUNIUS, H. (1588) *Batavia. In quae praeter gentis et insulae antiquitatem, decora, mores, aliaque ad eam pertinentia, declaratur quae fuerit vetus Batavia, quae Plinio, Tacito, & Ptolemaeo cognita.* Leiden: Officinia Plantinia. #

DE JUSSIEU, A. (1723) De l'Origine et des usages de la pierre de foudre, *Mémoires de l'Académie des Sciences* 1723, 6-9. #

KAHLKE, H.D. (1981) *Das Eiszeitalter.* Leipzig / Jena / Berlin: Urania Verlag.

KALB, PH. (1980) Neue Ergebnisse zur Megalithkultur auf der Iberischen Halbinsel, *Nachrichten aus Niedersachsens Urgeschichte* 49, 73-93.

KALTOFEN, A. (2008) Flachgrab der Trichterbecherkultur in Geeste, *Archäologie in Deutschland* 3, 2008, 45.

KAMLAG, B. (1988) *Hunebed D32d te Odoorn,* unpublished *doctoraalscriptie* BAI, Groningen.

KARROW, R.W., Jr. (1993) *Mapmakers of the Sixteenth Century and their Maps.* Chicago: Speculum Orbis Press. #

KARS, H. (1983) Het maalsteenproduktiecentrum bij Mayen in de Eifel, *Grondboor en hamer* 37, 110-20.

KARSTEN, P. (1994) *Att kasta yxan i sjön: en studie över rituell tradition och förändring utifrån skånska neolitiska offerfynd.* Stockholm (Acta Archaeologica Lundensia, Ser. in 8° no. 23).

KEMPIUS, C. (1588) *De origine, situ, qualitate et quantitate Frisiae, et rebus a Frisiis olim praeclare gestis, libri tres.* Cologne: Gosvinus Cholinus. #

KEYSLER, J.A. (1720) *Antiquites selectae Septentrionales et Celticae, qvibvs plvrima loca conciliorvm et capitvlarivm explanantvr, dogmata theologiae ethnicae celtarvm gentivmqve septentrionalivm cvm moribvs et institvtis maiorvm nostrorvm circa idola, aras, oracvla, templa, lvcos, sacerdotes, regvm electiones, comitia et monvmenta sepvlchralia, vna cvm reliqviis gentilismi in coetibvs christianorvm, ex monvmentis potissimvm hactenvs ineditis fvse perqvirvntvr. Cvm figvris aeri incisis. Avtore Ioh. Georgio Keysler Societatis Regiae Londinensis socio.* Hanover: N. Foerster.

KLEMM, G.F. (1836) *Handbuch der Germanischen Altertumskunde.* Dresden.

KLINDT-JENSEN, O. (1975) *A History of Scandinavian Archaeology.* London: Thames & Hudson.

KLINDT-JENSEN, O. (1976) The influence of ethnography on early Scandinavian archaeology, in J.V.S. MEGAW, ed., *To illustrate the Monuments. Essays on Achaeology presented to Stuart Piggott on the occasion of his sixty-fifth birthday.* London: Thames and Hudson, 1976, 43-48.

KLOK, R.H.J. (1979) *De hunebedden in Nederland. Zorgen voor morgen.* Bussum: Fibula-van Dishoeck.

KLOMPMAKER, H., H. NIJKEUTER & J. TISSING (1996) *Poëzie van hunebedden. Een cultuurtoeristische benadering.* Zuidwolde: Het Drentse Boek.

KNÖLL, H. (1952) Wanderungen, Handel, ideenausbreitung und Töpferwerkstatten bei der nordwestdeutschen Tiefstichkeramik, *Archaeologica Geographica* 3, Jahrgang 2, 1952, 35-40.

KNÖLL, H. (1959) *Die nordwestdeutsche Tiefstichkeramik und ihre Stellung im nord- und mitteleuropäischen Neolithikum.* Münster Westfalen: Aschendorfsche Verlagsbuchhandlung, 180 p., 1 + 24 maps, 45 pls.

KNÖLL, H. (1983) *Die Megalithgräber von Lengerich-Wechte (Kreis Steinfurt).* Münster (Bodenaltertümer Westfalens 12).

KOCH. E. (1998) *Neolithic Bog Pots from Zealand, Møn, Lolland and Falster.* Copenhagen: Det Kongelige Nordiske Oldskriftselskab (Nordiske Fortidsminder, Series B, vol. 16)., 575 p.

KOEMAN, C. (1983) *Geschiedenis van de kartografie in Nederland. Zes eeuwen land- en zeekaarten en stadsplattegronden.* Alphen aan den Rijn: Canaletto.

DE KONING, C. (1810) *De voorvaderlijke leefwijze en gewoonten hier te lande, van de vroegste tijden af, tot aan het einde van de zestiende eeuw.* Haarlem: F. Bohn,

KOOI, P.B. (1979) *Pre-Roman urnfields in the north of The Netherlands.* Groningen: Wolters-Noordhoff.

KOOPS, L. (2009) *Het geheim van het grootste hunebed – discussies over archeologie.* Borger: Hunebedcentrum.

KÖRNER, G. & F. LAUX (1980) *Ein Königreich an der Luhe.* Lüneburg: Museumsverein für das Fürstentum Lüneburg.

KOSSIAN, R. (2005) *Nichtmegalithische Grabanlagen der Trichterbecherkultur in Deutschland und in den Niederlanden.* Halle: Landesamt für Denkmalpflege Sachsen-Anhalt & Landesmuseum für Vorgeschichte, 2 vols.

KOSSIAN, R. (2007) *Hunte 1. Ein mittel- und spätneolithischer und frühbronzezeitlicher Siedlungsplatz am Dümmer, Lkr. Diepholz (Niedersachsen). Die Ergebnisse der Ausgrabungen des Reichsamtes für Vorgeschichte in den Jahren 1938 bis 1941. Mit Beiträgen von W.A. BARTHOLOMÄUS, P.M. GROOTES, B. SCHMIDT und W.-R. TEEGEN.* Hanover: Niedersächsisches Landesmuseum; Kerpen-Loogh: B. Gehlen, W. Schön.

KOSSINNA, G. (1909-1910) Der Ursprung der Urfinnen und Urindogermanen und ihre Ausbreitung nach Osten, *Mannus* 1, 17-52, *Mannus* 2, 59-91.

KOSSINNA, G. (1912) *Die Deutsche Vorgeschichte, eine hervorragend nationale Wissenschaft.* Mannus-Bibliothek 4, 1912.

KOSSINNA, G. (1921) Entwicklung und Verbreitung der steinzeitlichen Trichterbecher, Kragenfläschchen und Kugelflaschen, *Mannus* 13, 13-40, 143-65.

KOSSMANN, E.H. (2007) Nederland en Frankrijk, in E.H. KOSSMANN (2007) *Naoogst, samengesteld door H.L. Wesseling.* Amsterdam: Bert Bakker, 2007, 139-50 [a lecture in 1991].

KRAMER-CLOBUS, G.M.C. (1978) L.J.F. Janssen (1806-1869), an inventory of his notes on archaeological findspots in The Netherlands, *Berichten van de Rijksdienst voor het Oudheidkundig Bodemonderzoek* 28, 441-544.

KRAUSE, E. & O. SCHOETENSACK (1893) Die megalithischen Gräber (Steinkammergräber) Deutschlands. I. Altmark, *Zeitschrift für Ethnologie* 1893, Berlin, 105-71, pls. V-XIII.

VAN KUIK, J.M. (1897) Reis van Andries Schoemaker en Cornelis Pronk door een gedeelte van Drenthe, *Nieuwe Drentsche Volksalmanak* 1897, 21ff.

TER LAAN, K. (1949) *Folkloristisch Woordenboek van Nederland en Vlaams België.* The Hague & Batavia, G.B. van Goor Zonen's Uitgeversmij N.V.

LAMING-EMPERAIRE, A. (1964) *Origines de l'Archéologie Préhistorique en France. Des superstitions médiévales à la découverte de l'homme fossile.* Paris: A. et J. Picard [#, pers. comm. W. Arentzen].

LAMPO, H. (1967) *Toen Heracles spitte en Kirke spon, zijnde het verhaal van Charles-Joseph de Grave en zijn "République des Champs Élysées" waarin bewezen wordt dat Plato's Atlantis in de Nederlanden gelegen was.* Brussels-The Hague.

LANGEREIS, S. (2001) *Geschiedenis als ambacht. Oudheidkunde in de Gouden Eeuw: Arnoldus Buchelius en Petrus Scriverius.* Hilversum: Uitgeverij Verloren.

LANGEREIS, S. (2004) Van botte boeren tot beschaafde burgers. Oudheidkundige beelden van de Bataven, 1500-1800, in SWINKELS, ed., 2004, 70-105.

LANTING, A.E. (1983) Van heinde en ver? Een opmerkelijke pot uit hunebed D21 te Bronneger, gem. Borger, *Nieuwe Drentse Volksalmanak* 100, 139-46.

LANTING, J.N. (1973) Laat-Neolithicum en Vroege Bronstijd in Nederland en N.W.-Duitsland: continue ontwikkelingen, *Palaeohistoria* 15, 215-317.

LANTING, J.N. (1975) De hunebedden op de Glimmer Es (gem. Haren), *Groningse Volksalmanak* 1974-75, 167-180.

LANTING, J.N. (1994) Het na-onderzoek van het vernielde hunebed D31a bij Exlo (Dr.), *Paleo-Aktueel* 5, 39-42.

LANTING, J.N. (1997) Het zogenaamde hunebed van Rijs (Fr.), *Paleo-Aktueel* 8, 47-50.

LANTING, J.N. & A.L. BRINDLEY (2004) The destroyed *hunebed* O2 and the adjacent TRB flat cemetery at Mander (*Gem.* Tubbergen, Province Overijssel), *Palaeohistoria* 45/46, 2003/2004, 59-94.

LANTING, J.N. & J. VAN DER PLICHT (2000) De ^{14}C-chronologie van de Nederlandse pre- en protohistorie. III, Neolithicum, *Palaeohistoria* 41/42, 1999/2000, 1-110.

LAUX, F. (1989) König Surbolds Grab bei Börger im Hümmling, *Nachrichten aus Niedersachsens Urgeschichte* 58, 117-27.

LAUX, F. (1990) Die Trichterbechergruppen zwischen Elbe und Ems (Niedersachsen), in D. JANKOWSKA, ed. (1990), *Die Trichterbecherkultur, neue Forschungen und Hypothesen. Material des Insternationalen Symposiums Dymaczewo, 20-24 September 1988*. Poznań: Instytut Prahistorii im. Adama Mickiewicz w Poznaniu [&] Zakład Archeologii Wielkopolski IHKM PAN w Poznaniu, 1990, 181-195.

LAUX, F. (1991) Überlegungen zu den Großsteingräbern in Niedersachsen und Westfalen, *Neue Ausgrabungen und Forschungen in Niedersachsen* 19, 1991, 21-99.

LECH, J. (2008) Count Jan Potocki (1761-1815) and his place in the history of archaeology, in JASTRZEBOWSKA, E. & M. NIEWÓJT, eds., *Archeologia letteratura collezionismo, Atti del Convegno dedicato a Jan e Stanisław Kostka Potocki, 17-18 aprile 2007*, Rome 2008 (Accademia Polacca delle Scienze, Biblioteca e Centro di Studi a Roma), 125-48.

VAN LEEUWEN, S. (1685) *Batavia illustrata, ofte Verhandelinge vanden Oorspronk, Voortgank, Zeden, Eere, Staat en Godtsdienst van Oud Batavien, mitsgaders van den Adel en Regeringe van Hollandt, Ten deele uyt W. van Gouthoven, en andere Schryvers, maar wel voornamelijk uyt een menigte van oude Schriften en Authentijque Stukken en Bewijsen.* The Hague: Johan Veely, Johan Tongerloo & Jasper Doll, 29 + 1520 closely printed folio pages.

LEGRAND D'AUSSY, P.J.-B. (1799) Mémoire sur les sépultures nationales et les ornemens extérieurs qui en divers temps y furent employés, sur les embaumens, sur les tombeaux des rois francs dans la ci-devant église de Saint-Germain-des-Prés, et de sur un projet de fouilles à faire dans nos départemens, *Mémoires de l'Institut National des Sciences et Arts – Sciences Morales et Politiques* II, 411-699. Paris: Imprimerie de Baudoin [see Laming-Emperaire 1964; pers. comm. W. Arentzen]. #

DE LETH, H. (ca. 1765) *Nieuwe Geographische en Historische Atlas van de Zeven Vereenigde Nederlandsche Provinti*en. Amsterdam: H. de Leth, n. d. [photo-re-print Amsterdam: P.N. van Kampen en Zoon, 1970].

LIBERA, J. & K. TUNIA, eds. (2006) *Idea megalityczna w obrzadku pogrzebowym kultury pucharów lejkowatych* [viz. 'The megalithic idea in the burial ritual of the TRB culture']. Lublin-Cracow: Instytut Archeologii UMCS w Lublinie; Instytut Archeologii PAN, Oddział w Krakowie.

LIEBERS, C. (1986) *Neolithische Megalithgräber in Volksleben und Volksglauben. Untersuchung historischer Quellen zur Volksüberlieferung, zum Denkmalschutz und zur Fremdenverkehrswerbung.* Frankfurt am Main/Bern/New York: Peter Lang.

LIEBKNECHT, J.G. (1730) *Hessia subterranea.* Giessen. #

VAN LIER, J. (1760) OUDHEIDKUNDIGE BRIEVEN, BEVATTENDE *eene verhandeling over de manier van* BEGRAVEN, *en over de* LYKBUSSCHEN, WAPENEN, VELD- *en* EERTEKENS, *der* OUDE GERMANEN, *en in het byzonder de beschryving van eenen alouden Steenen Grafkelder, met de daarin gevondene Lykbusschen, Donderkeilen en Donderbylen, enz. By het* BOERSCHAP EEXT, *in het Landschap* DRENTHE, *ontdekt, in welke be-schryvinge zekere* BRIEF, *over byzondere* NEDERLANDSCHE OUDHEDEN, *zo opge-helderd als wederlegd word.* DOOR MR. JOANNES VAN LIER, *Oud Gedeputeerde Staate, thans Ontfanger Generaal en Medelid van den Loffelyken Etstoel des Landschaps Drenthe. Met noodige afbeeldingen opgehelderd. Uitgegeeven en met Voorreden en Aantekeningen vermeerderd door A.* VOSMAER. The Hague: Pieter van Thol.

VAN LIER, J. (1773) Ophelderende aanmerkingen over het xxxix artikul iv. boek van het Drentsche Landrecht, *Verhandelingen ter Nasporinge van de Wetten en Gesteldheid onzes Vaderlands* I. Groningen. #

VAN LIER, J. (1781*) Verhandeling over de Slangen en Adders die in het Landschap Drenthe gevonden worden. Met byvoeging van eenige aanmerkingen en byzonderheden, tot deze en andere slangsoorten betrekkelijk ... / Traité des Serpents et des Vipères qu'on trouve dans le Pays de Drenthe, au quel on a ajouté quelques remarques et quelques particularités relatives a ces especes de serpents et a d'autres ... .* Amsterdam: Erven Houttuin; Groningen: L. Huisingh.

[VAN LIER, J., J.H.P. VAN LIER & F.A. VAN LIER] (1792) *Tegenwoordige Staat van het Landschap Drenthe, Eerste en Tweede stuk.* Amsterdam etc.: J. de Groot etc.(reprint Groningen 1975: B.V. Foresta).[524]

---

524 This study by J. VAN LIER and two of his sons (1792) was followed by TONKENS's *Inleiding* (Introduction) (published in 1795, but written before 1790) in the same volume. The com-plicated editorial history of this book is discussed by Lunsingh Tonckens (1915) and Mulder (1950). Only the first title-page of the book used for the 1975 reprint has: *Hedendaagsche Historie of Tegenwoordige Staat van het Landschap Drenthe*; the title-page directly behind it has only: *Tegenwoordige Staat van het Landschap Drenthe*, as has the title-page of Tonkens's *Inleiding*. The three title-pages of another copy of the book (with the same dates, places and publishers, owned by W. Arentzen) have: *Tegenwoordige Staat van de Vereenigde Nederlanden; Behelzende het Begin der Beschryving van het Landschap Drenthe* and two times: *Tegenwoordige Staat van het Landschap Drenthe*.

LOCCENIUS, J. (1647) *Antiquitatem Sveo-Gothicarum, cum huius aevi moribus, institutis ac ritibus indigenis pro re nata comparatum libri tres.* Stockholm: H. Keiser [reprinted in 1654, 1670 and 1676; translated as *Swenske och Göthiske gamle Handlingar.* Stockholm 1726]. #

LONSAIN, B. (1915) Het reizen en het verkeer in den ouden tijd, *Nieuwe Drentsche Volksalmanak* 33, 163-87.

LORIÉ, J. (1887) Iets over Drenthe's bodem, *Nieuwe Drentsche Volksalmanak*, 183-197.

LOUWE KOOIJMANS, L.P., P.W. VAN DEN BROEKE, H. FOKKENS & A.L. VAN GIJN, eds. (2005) *The Prehistory of The Netherlands.* Amsterdam University Press, 2 vols.

LOUWE KOOIJMANS, L.P. (2007) Multiple choices – Mortuary practices in the Low Countries during the Mesolithic and Neolithic, 9000-3000 cal BC, *Bericht d. Römisch-Germanischen Kommission* 88, 551-80.

LUBACH, D. (1873-4) Over oude begraafplaatsen in Drenthe, bijzonder over de hunebedden, *Album der Natuur* 1873-4.

LUBACH, D. (1877) On the "Hunebedden", or Cromlechs in the Province of Drenthe in Holland, *The Journal of the Anthropological Institute of Great Britain and Ireland* 6, 158-66 [translation of LUBACH 1873-4].

LUGT, F. (1915) *Wandelingen met Rembrandt in en om Amsterdam.* Amsterdam: P.N. van Kampen & zoon.

LUKIS, W.C. (1879) Report on the hunebedden of Drenthe, Netherlands, *Proceedings of the Society of Antiquaries of London*, 2nd ser. VIII, 1879-1881, 47-55.

LUNSINGH TONCKENS, W. (1915) Een onbekend auteur, *Nieuwe Drentsche Volksalmanak* 33, 110-24.

LYELL, C. (1830-1833) *Principles of Geology, being an attempt to explain the former changes of the earth's surface, by reference to causes now in operation.* London: John Murray. #

MAASKAMP, E. [ca. 1812] *Voyage dans l'intérieur de la Hollande fait dans les années 1807-1812.* Amsterdam: E. Maaskamp [No date of publication given. A Dutch version of this book appeared about simultaneously].

MAJOR, J.D. (1692) *Bevölckertes Cimbrien: oder, die zwischen der Ost- und West-See gelegenen halb-Insel Deutschlands, nebst dero ersten Einwohnern ... .* Plön: T. Schmied. #

MANKELL, H. (2010) *De gekwelde man.* Breda: De Geus [Dutch ed. of *Den orolige mannen.* Stockholm: Leopard Förlag #].

MARIËN, M.E. (1952) *Oud-België van de eerste landbouwers tot de komst van Caesar.* Antwerp: De Sikkel. [also published in French as *Belgique Ancienne.* Antwerp: De Sikkel, 1952].

MARTIN, J. (1727) *La Réligion des Gaules tirée des plus pures sources de l'Antiquité.* Paris. #

MASSET, C. (1997) *Les Dolmens. Sociétés néolithiques et pratiques funéraires. Les sépultures collectives d'Europe centrale.* Paris: Editions Errance [2nd impression].

MATTHAEUS, A. (1698) *Veteris Aevi Analecta seu Vetera aliquot Monumenta quae hactenus nondum visa / collegit, edidit & observationes suas adjecit Antonius Matthaeus,* vol. I. Leiden: Fr. Haaring (10 vols, 1698-1710; 2nd ed. The Hague: G. Block, 1738).

M^cEVEDY, C. (1961) *The Penguin Atlas of Medieval History.* Harmondsworth: Penguin Books.

VAN MEERKERK, E. (2009) *Willem V en Wilhelmina van Pruisen. De laatste stadhouders.* Amsterdam-Antwerp: Atlas.

MEEÜSEN, W. (1983) *Het verdwenen hunebed D54a te Spier (gem. Beilen),* unpublished *doctoraalscriptie* BAI, Groningen.

MEINANDER, C.F. (1981) The concept of culture in European archaeological literature, in DANIEL 1981, 100-11.

VON MELLEN, J. (1679) *Historia Urnae sepulchralis Sarmaticae.* #

LE MENN, G. (1990) Menhir, dolmen, neologisms ou mots Bretons?, in J. L'HELGOUAC'H, ed., *La Bretagne et l'Europe préhistoriques. Mémoire en hommage à Pierre-Roland Giot. Revue Archéologique de l'Ouest, Supplément* N° 2 – 1990, 373-6.

MERCATUS, M. (1717) *Metallotheca Vaticana.* Rome. #

MICHELL, J. (1982) *Megalithomania. Artists, antiquarians and archaeologists at the old stone monuments.* London: Thames & Hudson.

MIDDLETON, C. (1745) *Germania quaedam antiquitis eruditae monumenta.* London. #

MIDGLEY, M.S. (1992) *TRB Culture. The First Farmers of the North European Plain.* Edinburgh University Press.

MIDGLEY, M.S. (2008) *The Megaliths of Northern Europe.* London-New York [Abingdon]: Routledge.

MINDERHOUDT, H.D. (1981) *Gedachten aan Picardt.* Coevorden 1981 (Picardtreeks 15b).

MITTAG, L. (2006) *Sagenhafte Steine. Großsteingräber, besondere Steine und Steinkreuze in der altmärkischen Sagenwelt.* Salzwedel: Akanthus & Johann-Friedrich-Danneil-Museum.

MOHEN, J.-P. (1997) *Standing Stones. Stonehenge, Carnac and the World of Megaliths.* London: Thames & Hudson [French ed. Paris: Gallimard, 1998].

MOLEMA, J. (1987) *Het verdwenen hunebed D43a op de Emmer Es te Emmen,* unpublished *doctoraalscriptie* BAI, Groningen.

DE MONTFAUCON, B. (1719) *L'Antiquité expliquée et représentée en figures.* Paris: Deleaune et al., 5 parts each in 2 folio vols. [reprinted in 1722; supplement vols. were added in 1724] # (pers. comm. W. Arentzen).

MOSER, S. (1998) *Ancestral Images. The Iconography of Human Origins.* New York. #

MULDER, R.D. (1942) Mr. Johannes van Lier (1726-1785), Drente's eerste wetenschappelijke natuuronderzoeker, *Nieuwe Drentsche Volksalmanak* 60, 33-64.

MULDER, R.D. (1950) De oudste medische dissertatie over Drenthe en haar verband met de "Tegenwoordige Staat", *Nieuwe Drentsche Volksalmanak* 68, 61-8.

MUSHARD, M. (1762) *Palaeo Gentilismus bremensis oder Ehemaliges Bremisches Heidenthum worinnen von den Götzendienst der alten bremischen Einwohner, von ihren Monumentis lapideis, oder Opferstädten, und was darunter befindlich behandelt wird* [manuscript, finished in essence in 1754, published by E. SPROCKHOFF in *Jahrbuch des Provinzialmuseums zu Hannover* N.F. 3, 1928 [Hildesheim-Hanover], 44-61.

NAARDEN, B. (2006) Witsens eilandgevoelens, in KLEIBRINK, M. & H. VAN OS, eds., *Cultuurgeschiedenis van het eilandgevoel, Symposion met oud-Lutje leden, 18-19 maart 2005, Schiermonnikoog.* Westerburen: M. Kleibrink, 2006.

NIEMEIJER, J.W. (1989) Het kunstenaarsalbum van Arnout Vosmaer, in NIEMEIJER, J.W., ed., *De verzameling van mr. Carel Vosmaer (1826-1888).* The Hague: SDU & Amsterdam: Rijksprentenkabinet, 148-69.

NIJKEUTER, H. (2001) *De 'pen gewijd aan Drenthe's dierbren grond'. Literaire bedrijvigheid in de Olde Lantschap, 1816-1956.* Doctoral thesis Groningen University. Groningen.

NIJKEUTER, H. (2005) Titia Brongersma, 'de tiende der muzen' geïnspireerd door de Olde Lantschap, in KLOMPMAKER, H. & H. NIJKEUTER (2005) *Dichter bij het hunebed.* Zuidwolde: Het Drentse Boek, 27-41.

NILSSON, S. (1838-48) *Skandinaviska Nordens Urinvånare, ett försok i komparativa ethnografien och ett bidrag till menniskoslägtets utvecklingshistoria.* Lund.

NILSSON, S. (1844) Bijdrage tot de ontwikkeling des Menschelijken Geslacht, *Tijdschrift voor Geschiedenis en Physiologie 1844,* 20-48 [translation of NILSSON 1838ff.].

NUNNINGH, J.H.[525] (1713) *Sepulcretum Westphalico-Mimigardico Gentile : Duabus Sectionibus PARTITUM, In Quarum Prima De urnis, in Altera De Lapidibus Ethnicorum Sepulcralibus Disseritur ... .* Coesfeld: B. Haustatt. [the 2nd ed., Frankfurt-Leipzig: M.A. Fuhrman, 1714, also contains COHAUSEN (1714). http://diglib.hab.de/drucke/hl-129/start.htm?image=00149. See also HÜSING's translation (1855)].

OKKEN, J.W.G. (1989) De verhinderde verkoop van de hunebedden te Rolde, 1847-1848, *Nieuwe Drentse Volksalmanak* 106, 74-86.

OKKEN, J.W.G. (1990) Mr. L. Oldenhuis Gratama en het behoud van de hunebedden, *Nieuwe Drentse Volksalmanak* 107, 66-95.

OKKEN, J.W.G. (2004) 150 jaar Drents Museum, *Nieuwe Drentse Volksalmanak* 120, 1-47.

OLAVS MAGNUS (1555) *Historia de gentibvs septentrionalibvs, earumque disversis statibus, conditionibus, moribus ... .* Rome: G.M. Viotti. #

OLEARIUS, J.C. (1701) *Mausoleum in museo, id est Heydnische Begräbniss-Töpfe, oder Urnae Sepulchrales welche – bey Jerichau, Köthen, Arnstadt und Rudisleben gefunden worden.* Jena: Bielcke. #

Ons eigen land. Uitgegeven door den Algemeenen Nederlandschen Wielrijdersbond, toeristenbond voor Nederland, ter gelegenheid van zijn vijf-en-twintig-jarig bestaan, 1 Juli 1908. n. pl., 4 vols.

OOSTKAMP, J.A. (1822) *Aardrijkskundig Schoolboek van de Provincie Drenthe.* Coevorden: D.H. van der Scheer [reprint Meppel: Krips Repro, 1977].

ORENSTEIN, N.M. (2001) *Pieter Bruegel the Elder, drawings and prints.* New Haven / London: Yale University Press.

OSTKAMP, S. (2007) De maagd en de wildeman. Een baardmankruik uit Deventer en zijn cultuurhistorische context, *Vormen uit Vuur, mededelingenblad Nederlandse vereniging van vrienden van ceramiek en glas* 198, 2007, 2-3, 42-57, 81.

OTTERSPEER, W. (1993) Een brief van Conrad Leemans uit 1846, *Nieuw Letterkundig Magazijn* 11, 1993, 29. #

PALLAS, P.S. (1771) *Reise durch verschiedenen Provinzen des Russischen Reichs.* St Petersburg: Kayserliche Akademie der Wissenschaften, vol. 2. #

PÄTZOLD, J. (1955) Eine Siedlung der Großsteingrableute unter Normalnull bei Oldenburg (Old.), *Oldenburger Jahrbuch* 55, 1955, 83-97. [= Gellenerdeich]

---

525 Nunningh's signature on the title-page of Hamconius's *Frisia* (1609) shows that he wrote his name without an umlaut: '*J. H. Nunningh / Dr. Schol. Vred[ensis]*' (UB Münster: http://miami. uni-muenster.de DSOViewerServlet?DocID=661&DvID=646 , 21.04.08). Cf. Gummel 1938, 67 n 3.

DE PAUW, C. (1768-9) *Recherches philosophiques sur les Amériquains, ou Mémoires intéressants pour servir à l'Histoire de l'Espèce Humaine.* Berlin. #

PELISIAK, A. (2007) The Funnel Beaker Culture settlements compared with other Neolithic cultures in the upper and middle part of the Dnister basin. Selected issues, State of research, *Analecta Archaeologica Ressoviensa* [Instytut Archeologii Uniwersitetu Rzeszowskiego] 2, 2007, 23-56.

PETERS, M. (2010) *De wijze koopman. Het wereldwijde onderzoek van Nicolaes Witsen (1641-1717), burgemeester en* VOC-*bewindhebber van Amsterdam.* Amsterdam: Uitgeverij Bert Bakker.

PICARDT, J. (1660) *KORTE BESCHRYVINGE van eenige Vergetene en Verborgene* ANTIQUITETEN *der Provintien en Landen Gelegen tusschen de Noord-Zee, de Yssel, Emse en Lippe. Waer by gevoeght zijn* ANNALES DRENTHIAE, *Dat zijn Eenige Aenteyckeninghen en Memorien, van sommige gedenckwaerdige Geschiedenissen, gepasseert in het Antiquiteet-rijcke Landschap* DRENTH, *van de Geboorte* CHRISTI *af, tot op desen tijdt. Mitsgaders een korte Beschrijvinge der Stadt, des Casteels, en der Heerlickheyt* COVORDEN. Amsterdam: Gerrit van Goedesbergh, 'Boeckverkoper op 't Water / aen de Nieuwe-brugh / in de Delfse Bybel', [printed] 't 'Amsterdam, Ter Drukkerye van Tymon Houthaak, in de Vogel Struis', in only 125 copies [see Figure 5]. 2nd ed. 1731, Groningen: Wed. Joannes Cost, in Latin instead of Gothic letters, spelling exactly as in 1660, no illustrations; identical 3rd ed. 1745, Groningen: W. Febens #. The 1st ed. was reprinted in 1971 (Meppel: Krips Repro N.V.) and in 2008 (Leiden: Sidestone Press, with a Preface by L.P. LOUWE KOOIJMANS and an Introduction by W.A.B. VAN DER SANDEN).

PIETERS, F.F.J.M. (1994) De menagerie van stadhouder Willem V op het Kleine Loo te Voorburg / La ménagerie du stathouder Guillaume V dans le domaine Het Kleine Loo à Voorburg, in SLIGGERS & WERTHEIM 1994, 39-59.

PIETERS, F.F.J.M. (2002) Het schatrijke naturaliënkabinet van Stadhouder Willem V onder directoraat van topverzamelaar Arnout Vosmaer, in SLIGGERS & BESSELINK 2002, 19-44.

PIETERS, F.F.J.M. & L.C. ROOKMAKER (1994) Arnout Vosmaer, topcollectioneur van naturalia en zijn *Regnum animale* / Arnout Vosmaer, grand collectionneur de curiosités naturelles, et son *Regnum animale*, in SLIGGERS & WERTHEIM 1994, 11-38.

PIGGOTT, S. (1950) *William Stukeley, an Eighteenth-Century Antiquary.* Oxford: Oxford University Press. [2nd rev. ed. 1983. London: Thames & Hudson].

PIGGOTT, S. (1976) *Ruins in a Landscape. Essays in Antiquarianism.* Edinburgh University Press.

PLEYTE, W. (1877-1902) *Nederlandsche Oudheden van de Vroegste Tijden tot op Karel den Groote. Afbeeldingen naar de oorspronkelijke voorwerpen of naar photographie-en met begeleidenden tekst en oudheidkundige kaart.* Chapter. I: *Friesland, Oostergo* 1877-79; ch. II: *Drente* 1880-82; ch. III: *Overijsel* 1885; ch. IV: *Gelderland* 1887-

?89; ch. V ('xvɪde Aflevering'): *Batavia, Gelderland II, Zuid-Holland I, Zeeland* 1901; ch. VI: *West-Friesland, Utrecht, Noord-Holland* 1899-1902. Leiden: E.J. Brill. [The book is a bibliographer's nightmare. The dates of issue are often not, or conflictingly, indicated on the title-pages or covers of subsequent fascicules (of which several are preserved in the library of the Leiden Museum, RMO); those given are based upon dates collected by A.E. van Giffen (in his copy in the former IPP-library), W. Glasbergen and W.J. de Boone. The publisher wrote 'Drenthe' and 'Overijssel' on the title-page, instead of 'Drente' and 'Overijsel', as Pleyte did himself in the text and on the plates. The numerals to the six chapters, which were left unnumbered on the general title-page, were added by me. Two fascicules appeared each year, initially, but the fact that the 16th fascicule was issued in 1901 (according to the title-page of the plates of chapter V), shows that this rate slowed down in later years. Van Giffen and Louwe Kooijmans et al. (2005) dated the last year of issue to 1903. Materials used for the publication, and meant for the unpublished chapters about Noord-Brabant and Limburg, are in the Pleyte archives in the RMO (loose pages numbered C1ff. in blue pencil, and in bindings Nederlandsche Oudheden 1-3). The loose pages of catalogue of J. Hofstede's collection are among the C-series (reproduced by Kooi 1979).]

PLEYTE, W. (1881) Hoog-halen, *De Nederlandsche Spectator* 10, 82-84.

PLEYTE, W., A. VAN DEN BOGERT & H. BOUWHEER (1889) *Uddel en Uddeler Heegde. Bijdrage tot de Geschiedenis van Barneveld.* Barneveld: G.W. Boonstra, cxciv + 113 p.

PLUIM, T. (1896) De Steen aan de Vuursche, *Eigen Haard* 18, May 2, 1896, 287-8.

LE PRÉVÔT, R. (1686) ["R. LE PRIVET" !], The Verbal Process upon the Discovery of an Antient Sepulchre, in the Village of Cocherel upon the River Eure in France, *Philosophical Transactions of the Royal Society* in London, No. 185, vol. 16 (1686-92), 221-6. #

RECH, M. (1979) *Studien zu Depotfunden der Trichterbecher- und Einzelgrabkultur des Nordens.* Neumünster (*Offa-Büch* 39).

VAN REGTEREN ALTENA, J.F, J.A. BAKKER, A.T. CLASON, W. GLASBERGEN, W. GROENMAN-VAN WAATERINGE & L.J. PONS (1962-1963) The Vlaardingen Culture, *Helinium* 2, 1962, 3-35, 97-103, 215-243, *Helinium* 3, 1963, 39-54, 97-120.

REINERTH, H. (1939) Ein Dorf der Großsteingräberleute. Die Ausgrabungen des Reichsamtes für Vorgeschichte am Dümmer, *Germanen-Erbe* 4, 225-42.

REUVENS, C.J.C. [manuscript maps and notes of his study tour in Drenthe, 1833], see BRONGERS 1973.

REUVENS, C.J.C., C. LEEMANS & L.J.F. JANSSEN (1845) *Alphabetische naamlijst behoorende bij de kaart van de in Nederland, België en een gedeelte der aangrenzende landen gevonden Romeinsche, Germaansche of Gallische oudheden; benevens de Romeinsche en andere oude wegen, enz. Begonnen door wijlen den Hoogleeraar C.J.C. Reuvens, voortgezet en uitgegeven door Dr. C. Leemans, Directeur van het Nederlandsch Museum van Oudheden, en Dr. L.J.F. Janssen, Conservator bij hetzelfde Museum.* Leiden: E.J. Brill, H. W. Hazenberg & Comp.

RHODE, C.D.& A.A. RHODE (1719) *Rhodisches Antiquitäten-Cabinet,* Hamburg 1719. #

RHODE, C.D. & A.A. RHODE (1720) *Cimbrisch-Hollsteinische Antiquitaeten-Remarques, Oder Accurate ... Beschreibung der in denen Grab-Hügeln derer alten Heydnischen Hollsteiner der Gegend Hamburg gefundenen Reliquien, ... welche durch häuffige Untersuchung und Ausgrabung derer Tumulorum aus selbigen hervorgehoben worden durch weyland Herrn Christian Detlev Rhoden ... und* [edited by] *dessen Sohn Andreas Albert Rhode ... .* Hamburg: C. Liebezeit, T.C. Felginger # (2nd impression Hamburg, 1728 #).

DE RHOER, J. (1770) *Oratio de fructu qui ex antiquitatis patriae studio in omne doctrinarum genus redit.* Groningen: Hajo Spandaw. #

DE RHOER, J. (n. d.) Eene plaatselyke beschryving van Westerwoldingerland, *Verhandelingen Pro Excolendo* (Groningen), vol. IV (2), 1ff. #

RICHTER, P.B. (2002) *Das neolithische Erdwerk von Walmstorf, Ldkr. Uelzen. Studien zur Besiedlungsgeschichte der Trichterbecherkultur im südlichen Ilmenautal. Mit Beiträgen von B. HEINEMANN und D. KUČAN.* Oldenburg (Veröffentlichungen der urgeschichtlichen Sammlungen des Landesmuseums zu Hannover 49).

V[AN] R[IJN], H. (1724) *OUDHEDEN EN GESTICHTEN VAN GRONINGEN EN GRONINGERLAND, Mitsgaders van het LAND VAN DRENT : Of Beschrijvingvan de Kerken, Kloosters, en Grafhuizen, die in de gemelde plaatsen van tijd tot tijd zijn gesticht : Benevens een verhaal van haare Begiftegingen, Vrijdommen, Voorrechten, Oversten. Daar ook bygevoegt is een lijst van roemwaardige en geleerde Mannen, die daar geboren zijn, of 'er gebloeit hebben. Uyt het Latijn vertaald, met AANTEKENINGEN opgehelderd, Door H.V.R.* Leiden: Christiaan Vermey. [This work is probably a translation of H.F. VAN HEUSSEN (1719) #, less probably of VAN HEUSSEN (1714) #].

RODDEN, J. (1981) The development of the Three Age System: Archaeology's first paradigm, in DANIEL1981, 51-68.

ROMEIN, J. (1932) *Geschiedenis van de Noord-Nederlandsche geschiedschrijving in de Middeleeuwen.* Haarlem: H.D. Tjeenk Willink & Zn. N.V.

ROOSEBOOM, H. (2008) *De schaduw van de fotograaf. Positie en status van een nieuw beroep: fotografie in Nederland, 1839-1889.* Leiden. #

ROSENOW, G. (1961) 50 Jahre Oldenburgisches Denkmalschutzgesetz, *Oldenburger Jahrbuch* 60 (2), 13-20.

RUMPHIUS, G. E. (1705) *D'Amboinsche rariteitenkamer.* #

DE SAINT SIMON, M.H. (1770) *Histoire de la guerre des Bataves et des Romains ... .* Amsterdam. #

VAN DER SANDEN, W.A.B. (2007) *Reuzenstenen op de es. De hunebedden van Rolde.* Zwolle: Waanders; Assen: Drents Plateau (Erfgoed in Drenthe 1).

SCHATEN, N. (1690) *Historia Westphaliae.* Neuhaus. #

SCHELE VAN WELEVELT, S. (1591-1637) *Hausbuch oder Chronik 1589-1637* [a manuscript of 1822 p., kept in the Osnabrück and Zwolle State archives. http://lehre. hki.uni-koeln.de / schele / provides the original manuscript and A. de Bakker's provisional translation].

SCHELTEMA, J. (1833) Berigt aangaande een oud altaar, (Dolmin) of een naar een Hunebed zweemend overblijfsel van de eerste bewoners dezer landen, in het dorp de Vuursche, in J. SCHELTEMA 1833, *Geschied- en Letterkundig Mengelwerk,* vol. 3(2), 33-45.

SCHILSTRA, J.J. (1974) *In de ban van de dijk. De Westfriese Omringdijk.* Hoorn: West-Friesland [4th ed. 1982].

SCHLICHT, E. (1962) Volkskunde en archeologie, in T.R.W. DE HAAN & J. NAARDING, eds., *De bijl in de baanderboom, volkskundige opstellen over de landschap Drente en de aan haar grenzende gewesten.* Wassenaar: Nederlands Volkskundig Genootschap / Neerlands Volksleven, 277-352 [= *Neerlands Volksleven* 12 (4), 1962, 321-430].

SCHLICHT, E. (1963) Suirboldus Ruhehaus, *Jahrbuch des Emsländischen Heimatvereins* 10, 1963, 9ff.

SCHLICHT, E. (1973) Kupferschmuck aus Megalithgräbern Nordwestdeutschlands [und den Niederlanden], *Nachrichten aus Niedersachsens Urgeschichte* 42, 1973, 13-52.

SCHNAPP, A. (1993) *The discovery of the past, the origins of archaeology.* London: British Museum Press [translation from the French, Paris 1993].

SCHONHOVIUS, A. (1547) *De origine et sedibus Francorum, de Chamavis, Bructeris, Tencteris aliisque....* [manuscript, published in MATTHAEUS 1698, reprinted 1738].

SCHULLER TOT PEURSUM-MEIJER, J. & W.H.R. KOOPS, eds. (1989) *Petrus Camper (1722-1789), onderzoeker van nature.* Groningen: Universiteits Museum, 189-98.

SCHULZ, W. (1959) Jacobus Tollius und die Großsteingräber bei Magdeburg. Ein Beitrag zur Geschichte der Vorgeschichtsforschung, *Jahresschrift für mitteldeutsche Vorgeschichte* 43, 121-26, pl. 4.

SEBIRE, H. [ca. 1990-2000] *Frederick Corbin Lukis & his family, one of the great men of the Victorian age.* Guernsey: Guernsey Museums & Galleries, n.d.

SEGER, H. (1930) Die Anfänge des Dreiperioden-Systems, in *Schumacher Festschrift zum 70. Geburtstag*. Mainz, 3-7.

SHERRATT, A. (1996) 'Settlement patterns' or 'landscape studies'? Reconciling Reason and Romance, *Archaeological Dialogues* 3, 140-59.

SINNINGHE. J.R.W. (1975) *Spokerijen in het Gooiland. Sagen, legenden en volkverhalen veelal uit de volksmond opgetekend*. Zaltbommel: Europese Bibliotheek,

SIPPEL, K. (1980) Die Kenntniss von vorgeschichtlichen Hügelgräber im Mittelalter, *Germania* 58, 137-46.

SJÖGREN, K.-G. (2003) *'Mangfalldige uhrminnes grafvar ...'. Megalitgravar och samhalle i Västsverige*. Göteborgs Universitet (Gatorc series B Gothenburg Archaeological theses 27).

VAN SLICHTENHORST, A. (1654) *XIV. boeken van de Gelderse geschiedenissen*, vol. 1. Arnhem: W.A. van Spaen.

SLIGGERS, B.C. (1982) *Het schetsboek van Cornelis van Noorde, 1731-1795. Het leven van een veelzijdig kunstenaar*. Haarlem: Schuyt & Co.

SLIGGERS, B.C. (2002) Het Naturaliënkabinet van de Hollandsche Maatschappij der Wetenschappen, in SLIGGERS & BESSELINK 2002, 45-142.

SLIGGERS, B.C. & M.H. BESSELINK, eds. (2002) *Het verdwenen museum. Natuurhistorische verzamelingen 1750-1850*. Blaricum: V+K Publishing; Haarlem: Teylers Museum.

SLIGGERS, B.C. & A.A. WERTHEIM, eds. (1994) *Een vorstelijke dierentuin. De menagerie van Willem V / Le Zoo du prince. La ménagerie du statholder Guillaume V*. Zutphen: Walburg Instituut.

SMIDS, L. (1694) *Poësye*. Amsterdam.

SMIDS, L. (1711) *Schatkamer der Nederlandsse Oudheden; of Woordenboek, behelsende Nederlands Steden en Dorpen, Kasteelen, Sloten en Heeren Huysen, Oude Volkeren, Rievieren, Vermaarde Luyden in Staat en Oorlog, Oudheden, Gewoontens en Lands wysen. Versierd met LX Verbeeldingen, van soo geheele als vervallene Heeren Huysen, Sloten en Kasteelen, meerendeels geteekend door ROELAND ROCHMAN. Nevens een Bladwyser, in de gedaante van een Land-Chronyk*. Amsterdam: Pieter de Coup.

SMIDS, L. (1737) *Schatkamer der Nederlandsche Oudheden... Tweede druk vermeerdert met aanteekeningen door Pieter Langendijk*. Haarlem: Joannes Marshoorn, XX, 417, 31 p. [2nd, enlarged ed. of Smids (1711)].

SMIDS, L. (1774) *Schatkamer der Nederlandsche Oudheden; of Woordenboek, behelsende Nederlands Steden en Dorpen, Kasteelen, Sloten en Heeren Huizen, Oude Volkeren, Rivieren, Vermaarde Luiden in Staat en Oorlog, Oudheden, Gewoontens en Lands wyzen. Versierd met LXIII Verbeeldingen, van zoo geheele als vervallene Heeren Huizen, Sloten en Kasteelen, meerendeels geteekend door* ROELAND ROCHMAN. *Nevens een* Bladwyser, *in de gedaante van een* Land-Chronyk. *De DERDE DRUK. Vermeerdert met Aanteekeningen door Pieter Langendyk. Van nieuws overzien; in Taal en Spelling naar den hedendaagschen smaak verbeterd, en met eene plaat en verscheide nieuwe Artikelen, en andere uitgebreider, vermeerderd* [door Theodorus van Brussel]. Amsterdam: Gerrit Bom, XXIV, 462, 22 p. [3rd, enlarged and revised ed. of Smids (1711)].

SMITH, R.A. (1926) *A Guide to the Antiquities of the Stone Age ...* . British Museum London (3rd ed.).

SPROCKHOFF, E. (1938) *Die nordische Megalithkultur.* Berlin-Leipzig: Walter De Gruyter & Co. (Handbuch der Urgeschichte Deutschlands 3)

SPROCKHOFF, E. (1966, 1967, 1975) *Atlas der Megalithgräber Deutschlands*, vol. 1: *Schleswig-Holstein* (1966); vol. 2: *Mecklenburg-Brandenburg-Pommern* (1967); vol. 3: *Niedersachsen-Westfalen, aus dem Nachlass herausgegeben von* G. KÖRNER *[und* F. LAUX] (1975). Bonn: R. Habelt [each consisting of a text-vol. and atlas].

STAAL-LUGTEN, C.M. (1976a) [*photographic inventory and typochronological analysis of the pottery from hunebed D19 at Drouwen*], unpublished *doctoraalscriptie* University of Leiden.

STAAL-LUGTEN, C.M. (1976b) Die verzierte TRB-Keramik des Hünenbettes D19 in Drouwen, Prov. Drenthe, *Analecta Praehistorica Leidensia* 9, 1976, 19-37.

STARING, W.C.H. (1856, 1860) *Natuurlijke historie van Nederland. De Bodem van Nederland.* Haarlem: A.C. Kruseman, vol. I (1856), 446 p.; vol. II (1860), 483 p.

STARING, W.C.H. (1858) De keijen der heidevelden of het Nederlandsch Diluvium, in *Voormaals en Thans. Opstellen over Neêrlands grondgesteldheid.* Haarlem: A.C. Kruseman, 79-106.

STEMMERMANN, P.H. (1934) *Die Anfänge der deutschen Vorgeschichtsforschung Deutschlands Bodenaltertümer in der Anschauung des 16. und 17. Jahrhunderts. Inaugural-Dissertation zur Erlangung der Doktorwürde d. Universität zu Heidelberg.* Quakenbrück: Handelsdruckerei C. Trute.

STRAAT, P. & P. VAN DER DEURE (1733) *Ontwerp tot een minst kostbaare, zeekerste en schielykste herstelling van de zorgelyke toestand der Westfriesche zeedyken; zonder dat het voortknagend Zeegewormte daar aan eenige hindernisse kan veroorsaken.* Amsterdam [2nd ed. 1735].

STRATINGH, G.A. (1847-1852) *Aloude staat en geschiedenis des vaderlands*, vol. I, *De bodem van de wateren* (1847), vol. 2(1), *De bewoners. Vóór en onder de Romeinen* (1849), vol. 2(2), *De bewoners. In en sedert het Frankische tij*dvak (1852). Groningen: R.J. Schierbeek.

VAN SWINDEN, J.H. (1812) *Vergelijkings-tafels tusschen de Hollandsche lengte-maten en den mètre; met het noodige onderrigt over dezelve maten.* Amsterdam: P. den Hengst et fils [reprinted in: RENTENAAR, R. (1971) *Van Swindens Vergelijkingstafels van Lengtematen en Landmaten. Uitgegeven en ingeleid door R. Rentenaar*, 2 vols. Wageningen: Pudoc].

SWINKELS, L., ed. (2004) *De Bataven, verhalen van een verdwenen volk.* Amsterdam: De Bataafsche Leeuw; Nijmegen: Museum Valkhof.

TAAYKE, E. (1985) Drie vernielde hunebeddden in de gemeente Odoorn, *Nieuwe Drentse Volksalmanak* 102, 125-144.

DEN TEX, E. (2004) Was basalt derived from water or from fire? Dutch tributaries to an 18th-century controversy, in J.L.R. TOURET & R.P.W. VISSER, eds. (2004) *Dutch pioneers of Earth Sciences*. Amsterdam: KNAW / Royal Dutch Academy of Letters and Sciences, 33-41.

THOMPSON. M.W. (1977) *General Pitt-Rivers. Evolution and Archaeology in the Nineteenth Century*. Bradford-on-Avon.

TILMANS, K. (1987) Cornelius Aurelius en het ontstaan van de Bataafse mythe in de Hollandse geschiedschrijving (tot 1517), in EBELS-HOVING et al. (1987), 191-213.

TISCHLER, O. (1890) [discussion after a lecture], *Korrespondenz-Blatt der deutschen Gesellschaft für Anthropologie, Ethnographie und Urgeschichte* 21, 111-12.

TOLLIUS, J. (1700) *Jacobi Tollii Epistolae itinerarii ex auctoris Schedis postumis recensitae, suppletae, digestae; annotationibus, observationibus et figuris adornatae cura et studio Henrici Christiani Hennini*. Amsterdam: Joh. van Oosterwyck [2nd ed. Amsterdam: Joh. Oosterwyck, 1714].

[TONKENS, J.] (1795) 'Inleiding' to [*Hedendaagsche Historie of] Tegenwoordige Staat van het Landschap Drenthe*. Amsterdam etc.: J. de Groot etc.[526]

---

526 TONKENS's *Inleiding* (Introduction) to [*Hedendaagsche Historie of] Tegenwoordige Staat van het Landschap Drenthe* was published in 1795 after his death in 1790, as a sequel to VAN LIER et al. (1792) and was bound with it. The Van Liers added a few notes to those of Tonkens. See note 524.

TREUER, M. G. (1688) *Kurze Beschreibung der Heidnischen Todten-Töpfe / in welchen die Heiden ihrer verbrannten Todten überbliebene Gebein und Aschen aufgehoben / unter der Erden beigesetzt / Und Bei den jetzigen Zeiten in der Chur- und Marck Brandenburg Hauffen-weise ausgegraben worden.* Nuremberg. #

TREVERUS, G.S.(1728) *Anastasis Veteris Germani Germanaeque feminae.* Helmstedt. #

TRIGGER, B. (2006) *A History of Archaeological Thought, Second Edition.* Cambridge, New York etc.: Cambridge University Press.

UFKES, A. (1992) *De inventarisatie van hunebed O2 van Mander.* Unpublished *doctoraalscriptie* GIA. Groningen.

VELTMAN, H. (1886) Das Grabmal des Königs Surbold, *Mitteilungen des Vereins für Geschichte und Landeskunde von Osnabrück* ('Historischer Verein') 13, 242-62.

VERDAM, J. (1911) *Middelnederlandsch handwoordenboek.* The Hague: M. Nijhoff.

VERHART, L.B.M. (2008) Jan Hendrik Holwerda and the adoption of the three-age system in The Netherlands, *Analecta Praehistorica Leidensia* 40, 2008 (Festschrift L.P. Louwe Kooijmans), 1-13.

VERLINDE, A.D. (1992) Denekamp, Archeologische Kroniek van Overijssel 1991, *Overijsselse Historische Berichten* 107, 177-9.

VERSFELT, H.J. (2003) *De Hottinger-Atlas van Noord- en Oost-Nederland.* Groningen: Heveskes Uitgevers.

VERSFELT, H.J. (2004) *Kaarten van Drenthe 1500-1900.* Groningen / Veendam: Heveskes Uitgevers.

VERSFELT, H.J. & M. SCHROOR (2001) *De Franse kaarten van Drenthe en de noordelijke kust 1811-1813.* Groningen: Heveskes Uitgevers.

VORTISCH, W. (1999) Geologisch-petrographische Untersuchungen an megalithischen Monumenten – Beispiele aus Portugal, in BEINHAUER et al., eds. (1999), 275-88.

VOSMAER, C. (1884) Levensbericht van J.E.H. Hooft van Iddekinge, *Jaarboek van de Maatschappij der Nederlandsche Letterkunde 1884,* 55-63.

DE WAAL, D. (2008) *Beschouwing over de Zuiderdijk bij De Weed en Oosterleek.* www. Oosterleek.biz/Beschouwing/Zuiderdijk.pdf (internet)

VAN DE WAAL, H. (1952) *Drie eeuwen vaderlandsche geschied-uitbeelding, 1500-1800. Een iconologische studie.* The Hague: Martinus Nijhoff, 2 vols.

VAN DER WAALS, J.D. (1972) Die durchlochten Rössener Keile und das Frühe Neolithikum in Belgien und in den Niederlanden, in H. SCHWABEDISSEN, ed., *Die Anfänge des Neolithikums vom Orient bis Nordeuropa,* vol. va: *Westliches Mitteleuropa,* ed. by J. LÜNING (*Fundamenta A3*). Cologne / Vienna: Boehlau Verlag, 153-84.

WÄCHTER, J.K (1841) Statistik der im Königreich Hannover vorhandenen heidnischen Denkmäler, *Hannoverscher Magazin*.

WAFER, L. (1700) *Tweede deel van William Dampiers Reystogt rondom de wereld, behelzende eene beschryving der togten na Tonquin, Achin, Malakka … .* The Hague 1700. #

WATERBOLK, H.T. (1960) Preliminary report on the excavations at Anlo in 1957 and 1958, *Palaeohistoria* 8, 59-90.

[WEDEL, G.W.U.] (1812) *Abhandlung über den Ursprung der alten Begräbniss-denkmäler im Departement Drenthe, zur Beantwortung der von der Kayserlichen Societaet der Wissenschaften zu Haarlem für den 1sten November 1812 aufgegebenen Preisfrage.* [anonymus manuscript, which was marked by a motto, archives Hollandsche Maatschappij der Wetenschappen in Noord-Holland Archives, Haarlem. The author's name was in a closed envelope marked by Wedel's motto. See the excerpt in Appendix 2A]

WESTENDORP, N. (1809) *Eerste Leerrede in de Nieuwe Kerk te Sebaldeburen, 1809, benevens een Oudheidkundige Verhandeling. Door den Predikant Nicolaus Westendorp.* Groningen: J. Oomkens, 187 p. [reprinted Assen: Van Gorcum, 1941, with 'Inleiding' (Introduction) by N.J.A.F. BOUMA & K. TER LAAN (p. 5-10)].

[WESTENDORP, N. (1812)] *Verhandeling over de Hunebedden. Ter beantwoording van de vrage, door de Maatschappy der Wetenschappen te Haarlem uitgeschreven, van inhoud vrage Welke Volkeren hebben de zoogenoemde hunebedden gesticht? In welke tyden kan men onderstellen, dat zy deze oorden hebben bewoond?* [anonymous manuscript, 152 p., marked by the motto 'À tous les coeurs bien nés, que la patrie est chère', archives Hollandsche Maatschappij der Wetenschappen in Noord-Holland Archives, Haarlem. The author's name and the date of Dec.25, 1812 were in a closed envelope marked by the motto. With 'Bijvoegsels' (Additions), 24 p., with a 2 p. letter, from early in 1813, ibid.].

WESTENDORP, N. (1815) Verhandeling ter beantwoording der vrage Welke volkeren hebben de zoogenoemde hunebedden gesticht. In welke tijden kan men onderstellen, dat zij deze oorden hebben bewoond?, *Letter- en Oudheidkundige Verhandelingen van de Hollandsche Maatschappij der Wetenschappen te Haarlem* I, 1815, 233-377.

WESTENDORP, N. (1819) Voorlezing over de oude grafheuvelen, voornamelijk met betrekking tot de Provincie Drenthe, *Antiquiteiten, Oudheidkundig Tijdschrift* 1.

WESTENDORP, N. (1822) *Verhandeling ter beantwoording der vrage Welke volkeren hebben de zoogenoemde hunebedden gesticht. In welke tijden kan men onderstellen, dat zij deze oorden hebben bewoond?* Groningen: J. Oomkens, xvi + 328 + 51 p. [revised and enlarged monograph edition of WESTENDORP (1815), same ills.].

WESTENDORP, N., ed., (1819-1826) *Antiquiteiten, een oudheidkundig tijdschrift, bezorgd door Nicolaus Westendorp*. Groningen: J. Oomkens. [part 2, 1823-6, was edited by N. WESTENDORP and C.J.C. REUVENS].

WETZEL, G. (2002) Zur Geschichte der archäologischen Forschung in der Altmark, in BOCK, H., ed., *Archäologie der Altmark 1, Hünengräber – Siedlungen – Gräberfelder*. Oschersleben (Beiträge zur Kulturgeschichte der Altmark und ihrer Randgebiete 7), 2002, 18-34.

WIBEL, F. (1869) Der Gangbau des Denghoogs bei Wenningstedt auf Sylt, *Berichte des Museums vaterländischer Altertümer* 29, Kiel. #

WIERINGA, J. (1968) Iets over de ligging van de hunebedden op het zuidelijk deel van de Hondsrug, *Nieuwe Drentse Volksalmanak* 85, 149-157.

WIJBENGA, D. (1960) Als stenen vertellen, in D. WIJBENGA, *Hunebedbouwers*. Groningen: Wolters-Noordhoff n.v. (De Jongh, J.W., H. Wagenvoort & J.J. Moerman, *Schoolplaten voor de vaderlandse geschiedenis*), 39-48 [often reprinted; cited here according to 1968 ed.].

WIJBENGA, D. (1975) Als stenen vertellen, in D. WIJBENGA, *Gulden Sporen. Met illustraties van J.H. Isings*, vol. 1. Groningen: Uitgeverij De Vuurbaak, 23-9. [reprint of WIJBENGA 1960].

DE WILDE, W.J. (1906) Een legendarische alomtegenwoordigheid, *Nieuwe Drentsche Volksalmanak* 24, 152-67.

DE WILDE, W.J. (1907) Een "Standaardwerk", *Nieuwe Drentsche Volksalmanak* 25, 68-102.

DE WILDE, W.J. (1908) Een populaire dwaling, *Nieuwe Drentsche Volksalmanak* 26, 86-139.

DE WILDE, W.J. (1909a) Een oude huisvriend, *Nieuwe Drentsche Volksalmanak* 27, 90-123.

DE WILDE, W.J. (1909b) De Steen van de Vuursche, *De Navorscher* 1909, 551-54.

DE WILDE, W.J. (1910a) De hunebedden in Nederland, *De Kampioen* 27, 242-4, 256-8, 277-80.

DE WILDE, W.J. (1910b) [Report of a lecture at Amsterdam by him], *Jaarverslag Koninklijk Oudheidkundig Genootschap 1910*, 9-13.

DE WIT, M.J.M. (1998) Elite in Drenthe? Een analyse van twaalf opmerkelijke Drentse grafinventarissen uit de vroege en het begin van de midden-ijzertijd, *Palaeohistoria* 39/40, 1997/1998. 323-73.

WOLFF, C. (1994) Die Beschreibung ur- und frühgeschichtlicher Funde in gedruckten Quellen des 15. und 16. Jahrhundert, *Bodendenkmalpflege in Mecklenburg-Vorpommern Jahrbuch* 1994, 191-217.

WORMIUS, O. (1643) *Danicorum Monumentorum Libri Sex*. Copenhagen: Joachim Moltkenius. #

WORMIUS, O. (1651) *Runir seu Danica Literatura Antiquissima ... Vulgo Gothicorum dicta luci reddita opera Olai Wormii*. Copenhagen [2nd ed.; the 1st ed. appeared in Copenhagen (and / or Amsterdam?), in 1636 #].

WORSAAE, J.J.A. (1843) *Danmarks Oldtid oplyst ved Oldsager og Gravhøje*. Copenhagen.

WORSAAE, J.J.A. (1879) On the preservation of National Antiquities and Monuments in Denmark, *Proceedings of the Society of Antiquaries of London*, 2nd ser., 1879-81, 56-68 [translated by A.W. Franks from *Mémoires de la Société des Antiquaires du Nord*, 1877].

WORSAAE, J.J.A. (1881) *Nordens Forhistorie efter samtidige Mindesmaerker*. Copenhagen.

VAN DER WOUD, A. (1990) *De Bataafse Hut. Verschuivingen in het beeld van de geschiedenis (1750-1850)*. Amsterdam: Meulenhoff.

VAN DER WOUD, A. (1998) *De Bataafse Hut. Denken over het oudste Nederland (1750-1850)*. Amsterdam / Antwerp: Contact [thoroughly revised ed. of VAN DER WOUD 1990: chapters1-3 revised, 4-5 partially rewritten, and 6 totally renewed].

VON WURZBACH, A. (1906-1911) *Niederländisches Künstler-Lexikon auf Grund archivalischer Forschungen Bearbeitet*. Vienna, 2 vols. [photographic reprint 1963, Amsterdam: B.M. Israël].

YPEY, J. (1961) 'Een aantal vroeg-middeleeuwse zwaarden uit Nederland', *Berichten van de Rijksdienst voor het Oudheidkundig Bodemonderzoek* 10-1, 368-94.

YPEY, J. (1982) Flügellanzen in niederländischen Sammlungen, in KRAUSE, G., ed., *Vor- und Frühgeschichte des unteren Niederrheins, Rudolf Stampfuss zum Gedächtnis*. Bonn, 1982 (Quellenschriften zur westdeutschen Vor- und Frühgeschichte, vol. 10), 241-67.

ZANDSTRA. E. (1959) *Onbekend Nederland, drieëntwintig speurtochten naar het leven der mensen*. Foto's: Bram Wisman. Kaarten: R.W. Michels. Amsterdam: Uniepers.

Zusammenfassung[527]

Untersuchungen von Megalithgräbern in den Niederlanden in den Jahren 1547-1911: Von 'Riesenbetten' und 'Säulen des Hercules' bis zu präzisen Untersuchungen

Die 53 noch vorhandenen und 24 verschwundenen niederländischen Großsteingräber, von denen der Grundriss oder die genaue Lokalisierung bekannt ist, sind Megalithgräber der Trichterbecherkultur. Meistens handelt es sich um Ganggräber. Sie befinden oder befanden sich im Nordosten des Landes, v. a. in der Provinz Drenthe, einige auch in den Provinzen Groningen und Overijssel, ein vermutliches in der Provinz Utrecht. Sie wurden zwischen 3350 und 3000 vor Chr. aus großen Findlingen der Eiszeit erbaut. Sie sind die westlichsten der norddeutschen und südskandinavischen Großsteingräber der Trichterbecherkultur (sog. West- und Nordgruppe, Abb. 1).

Dieser Aufsatz befasst sich mit der Forschungsgeschichte dieser niederländischen Großsteingräber vor dem Jahre 1912. Danach beginnt eine andere Ära mit den moderneren Grabungsmethoden von Jan Hendrik Holwerda und dann Albert Egges van Giffen. Eine allgemeine Einführung geht daran vorab (Teil A, Abb. 1-3).

Die Namen *hunebed* (NL, spr. hünebett) und *Hünengrab* (D) sind zusammengesetzt aus *Hun*, 'Riese' und *Bed*, Bett, bzw. *Grab*. Sie belegen, dass man seit uralten, vielleicht schon vorchristlichen Zeiten, Riesen für die Erbauer der Hünengräber hielt.

Ein Bericht von Anton Schonhovius aus dem Jahr 1547 sprach von Dämonen, Teufeln, und nennt ein Großsteingrab bei Rolde in Drenthe *Cunnus Daemonis*, 'Teufelsfotze'. Dieser Name zeigt deutlich, dass die heidnischen Riesen inzwischen von der Kirche diabolisiert worden waren. Ein Hünengrab bei Rolde – oder waren es die beiden Gräber nebeneinander, D17-D18? - wurde von Schonhovius als „Säulen des Herkules" gedeutet, die sich nach Tacitus (*Germania*, Cap. 34) ungefähr in Friesland befunden hätten. Auch wird von einem Brauch berichtet, Fremde durch den Eingang in ein Steingrab zu jagen und – bevor Bonifacius es verbot – auf den Steinen zu opfern. Jetzt wurden speziell Leute aus Brabant hin-

---

527 The following *Zusammenfassung* (Summary) and my comments in Appendix 2A-B were kindly translated into German by professor W. Haio Zimmermann (Wilhelmshaven-Bockhorn, Germany).

durch gejagt, geprügelt und mit Kot beworfen. Diese *Columnae Herculis / Duvels Cutz hodie* werden 1570 auf der ersten paläogeographischen Karte der nördlichen Niederlande abgebildet (Abb. 4). Zwischen 1568 und 1636 finden sie sich auf den Landkarten von Jacob van Deventer und anderen.

Auch nach der Reformation hielt man an der Deutung fest, Riesen hätten die Hünengräber errichtet. Diese findet sich 1660 in Text und Bild in den Schriften des calvinistischen Pastors Johan Picardt (1600-1670, Abb. 5). Er war hauptsächlich in den Niederlanden tätig, stammte aber aus Schüttorf, Grafschaft Bentheim (D), wo er auch die Kolonie Alte Picardie gründete (Abb. 6-8). Auch nach Hermann C. Conring (1665) waren die Lübbensteine bei Helmstedt (D) von Riesen errichtet worden. Picardt, der selber nicht in Hünengräbern gegraben hat, war der erste Geländearchäologe in den östlichen Niederlande und im angrenzenden Deutschland, der nicht nur die Hünengräber, sondern auch Grabhügel, Celtic fields, Burgen, Motten u.s.w. beschrieb. Ihm zufolge lag die Zeit der Hünengräber zeitlich 'ebenso lange vor den Römern, wie die Römer vor heute', also älter als etwa 1660 v. Chr. Dass er die Großsteingräber etwa den wichtigsten Besitz Drenthes genannt hat, wurde nie mehr von den Drenthischen Behörden vergessen.

Die erste archäologische Ausgrabung, die überliefert ist, verdanken wir der Dichterin Titia Brongersma (etwa 1648 geboren). Sie ließ 1685 in dem großen Hünengrab D27 bei Borger graben (Abb. 9). Sie schrieb zwei Gedichte über dieses Grab und verfasste einen knappen Fundbericht, in dem sie Keramikscherben, Knochenfragmente und 'Asche' erwähnt für ihren Freund Ludolph Smids, Dr. Medicus, Historiker und Bühnendichter. Er publizierte den Fundbericht und ein Gedicht über Titias Grabung. Darin werden Römer, Schwaben, Sachsen oder Dänen als mögliche Erbauer genannt. Später nannte er anstelle der Römer die Wikinger. Die 'fossilisierten' Knochen waren offenbar die Reste normal proportionierter Menschen und nicht von Riesen. Er schickte sie dem deutschen Arzt und Archäologen Chr. Schlegel. Dieser berichtete wiederum dem Archäologen Johann Christoph Olearius, dass die Erbauer der Hünengraber nicht Riesen, sondern normale Menschen seien. Daraufhin wurde von den deutschen Forschern Olearius (1701), Jodocus Hermann Nunningh (1713, 1714), Johann Heinrich Cohausen (1714) und Johann Georg Keysler (1720) die Riesentheorie endgültig verworfen. Nach Nunningh und Cohausen hatten die 'starken' germanischen Erbauer der Hünengräber nur Rollhölzer und als Hebel ihre Arme verwendet. Sonderbar ist, dass Smids in seiner Enzyklopädie (1711), in der er Titias Ausgrabung ausführlich bespricht (Abb. 9), doch wieder die Riesen als Erbauer der Hünengräber nennt. Einer der letzten Vertreter der Riesentheorie war Heinrich Christian von Hennin, Professor in Utrecht und Herausgeber von den von Jacob Tollius (1633-1696) nachgelassenen Reiseberichten aus Deutschland aus dem Jahr 1687. Hennin ließ 1700 Riesen als Erbauer von Hünengräbern bei Magdeburg (D) abbilden, obwohl Tollius selber nicht mehr an Riesen als Erbauer geglaubt hatte (Abb. 10).

Im Jahre 1706 wurde von Johannes Hofstede[528] und Abraham Rudolph Kymmell im Großsteingrab D17 bei Rolde gegraben. Ein genauer handschriftlicher Bericht mit Beschreibung der gefundenen Keramik liegt vor. Darin werden die in der Kammerfüllung zuoberst liegenden Gefäße als Behälter von später geopferten Speisen und Getränken gedeutet; die unteren Gefäße wären 'Urnen', d.h. Behälter von verbrannten Knochenresten. Letztere Deutung hielt sich bis Ende des 19. Jhs., erstere wird jetzt für alle Gefäße in Großsteingräbern angenommen. Dieser Bericht wurde erst 1847 publiziert, er scheint der Forschung vorher weitgehend unbekannt geblieben zu sein.

Nachdem der Pfahlwurm, auch Schiffsbohrmuschel genannt (*Teredo navalis*), 1730-34 alle hölzernen Ufer- und Seedeichbefestigungen entlang der Nord- und Zuider Zee, von Flandern bis Jever, zerstört hatte (Abb. 11) und infolge davon 1733 der moderne Deich mit Steinabdeckung erfunden wurde (Abb. 12), entstand ein reger Steinhandel. In Drenthe wurde 1734 nicht nur das Entfernen von Grenzsteinen strengstens untersagt, sondern auch Beschädigung von Hünengräbern, 'die ja überall erhalten werden sollten'. Dieses sehr frühe Denkmalschutzgesetz wurde 1790, 1809, 1818 und 1846 erneut bestätigt. Picardts temperamentvolle Worte, nach denen die Hünengräber ein einzigartiger Besitz Drenthes seien, haben dieses wohl mitbewirkt.

Nachdem im Jahre 1756 das Großsteingrab D13-Eext von Steinsuchern in einem Hügel entdeckt und beschädigt worden war, hat es der Steuereinnehmer von Drenthe, Joannes van Lier (1726-1799, Abb. 16) restauriert. Er schrieb dann 1760 ein Buch über das Grab und die daraus geborgenen Funde (Abb. 17-19). In einem langatmigen Text datiert er sie in eine Steinzeit, die einer Metallzeit voranging. Sein Herausgeber, Arnout Vosmaer, datierte das Grab in die Zeit vor ca. 450 v. Chr. Er meint, dass die Erbauer sicher keine Riesen waren, so seien z.B. die Treppenstufen, die in die Kammer führten, für Riesen viel zu klein. Wie die Altgermanen das Grab errichteten, wird nicht erklärt, stattdessen, dass Menschen solche Bauten errichten konnten. Zum Beweis führt er z.B. auf die zyklopischen Mauern der Inkas an. Van Lier bildete die Funde ab, soweit sie für ihn zugänglich waren (Abb. 19). Scherben wurden dabei leider nicht berücksichtigt. Ein Teil der Funde wurde dem jungen Prinzen, Wilhelm von Oranien, für sein inzwischen weltbekanntes Naturalienkabinett geschenkt.

Der berühmte Naturwissenschaftler, Petrus Camper (1722-1789), hat von 1768 bis 1781 einige Großsteingräber mit genauen Zeichnungen (Abb. 20-27) in einem Heft dokumentiert, in dem er auch Literaturzitate sammelte. Die Zeichnungen wurden von dem russischen Botschafter, Prinz Gallitzin, 1789 publiziert.

---

528 Der Grabungsbericht ist nur in Abschrifte erhalten. Er soll von dem Ausgräber 'S. Hofstede' verfasst worden sein. Ein S. Hofstede kommt aber in den Archiven von Drenthe nicht vor. Van der Sanden (2007, 60) vermutet, deshalb, dass es sich in Wirklichkeit um Johannes Hofstede [1685-1736] handelt.

Sie zeigen deutlich, dass die Eingänge sich in der Mitte der südlichen Langseite befanden, wie das schon 1760 Van Lier bei einigen Großsteingräbern festgestellt hatte. Nach Picardt (1660) lagen die Eingänge irrtümlicherweise im schmalen Westende.

1790 besprach und bildete Engelbert Matthaeus Engelberts (?1713-1807?) das Großsteingrab von Tynaarlo und Funde "aus den Hünengräbern" aus der Sammlung von Johannes Hofstede in sein allgemein zugänglichen Geschichtswerk ab (Abb. 28-29). Aber nur ein Teil der Funde stammte aus Großsteingräber.

Während P. Camper anscheinend nicht an einer ethnischen Deutung der Erbauer der Hünengräber interessiert war, war diese für seinen Sohn Adriaan Gilles Camper (1759-1820), der die nachgelassenen Schriften seines Vaters herausgab, von besonderem Interesse, ebenso wie die Frage nach der Datierung. Wir wissen das, weil er weitere Literaturzitate in das Heft seines Vaters nachtrug.

1808 formulierte er den Text zu einer Preisfrage der Haarlemschen Maatschappij der Wetenschappen mit dem Titel (übersetzt): 'Welche Völker haben die sogenannten Hünengräber erbaut und in welchen Zeiten haben sie in diesen Gegenden gewohnt? – Weil eine gute Beschreibung der Hünengräber in Drenthe und im Herzogtum Bremen noch fehlte, wird gefordert,

1.   sie mit ähnlichen Monumenten in Großbritannien, Dänemark, Norwegen, Deutschland, Frankreich und Russland zu vergleichen, und

2.   die Särge, Urnen, Waffen, Zierrate, Opfergeräte usw. aus den Hünengräber mit solchen zu vergleichen, die aus den Begräbnisplätzen der alten Germanen, Gallier, Slawen, Hunnen und der anderen nordischen Völker stammen, worüber Pallas verschiedene Besonderheiten berichtet hat.'

Inzwischen wurde im April 1809 das völlig intakte Großsteingrab D41-Emmen von einem Steinsucher entdeckt – die vier flachen Decksteine, die zehn Trägersteine und die Zwickelausfüllung dazwischen waren völlig von einem Erdhügel überdeckt und das Innere der Kammer war noch ein Hohlraum. Drei Tage später wurde es von einem Landmesser gezeichnet (Abb. 30), und der Steuereinnehmer Johannes Hofstede (1765-1848) schrieb einen detaillierten Fundbericht. Die Funde schenkte er dem König Ludwig Napoleon in Amsterdam.

Auf die Haarlemer Preisfrage hin erfolgten 1812 zwei Einsendungen: von dem holsteinischen Landedelmann Georg Wolfgang Ulrich Wedel und von dem Groninger Dorfpastor Nicolaus Westendorp (1773-1836). Auszüge aus der Einsendung von Wedel fügen wir unten in Beilage 2A bei. Westendorp gab ein umfangreiches Manuskript ab. Dieses war aber noch nicht fertiggestellt, noch immer trafen wichtige Bücher verzögert bei ihm ein, auch der Text selber bedurfte noch der Überarbeitung. Er versprach aber soviel, dass man den Abgabetermin bis Anfang 1815 verschob. Westendorp gewann den Preis. Seine Schrift wurde 1815 verkürzt in der Zeitschrift der Maatschappij publiziert (Abb. 33-35). In voller Länge wurde sie 1822 vom Autor selber als Buch mit etwa 370 S. herausgegeben. Westendorp kompilierte eine große Menge Fakten aus der Literatur und nahm die Hünengräber in Drenthe sowie mehrere westlich der Weser in Deutschland sowie die wichtigsten Fundsammlungen daraus in Augenschein. Ein guter Beobachter, wie Van Lier, P. Camper, und Hofstede (1809), war er aber nicht; Eingänge erkannte er nirgendwo, selbst dort nicht, wo Camper sie gezeichnet und Van Lier (1760) sie beschrieben hatte. Beeinflusst vom gedruckten Text von Picardt (1660), suchte er sie noch immer vergebens an der westlichen Schmalseite. Hünengräber waren seines Erachtens nie von einem Hügel überdeckt. Solche, die es doch waren, waren seiner Ansicht nach jünger, er hielt sie für Übergangsformen zu den Grabhügeln späterer Zeit. Von der Algarve bis nach Schweden (Abb. 36) wären sie von demselben Volk erbaut worden, wie es dieselben Mythen auch bezeugten. Mit Ausnahme der Kelten konnte er alle historisch bekannten Völker als Erbauer ausschließen. Die Kimbern hätten auch zu den Kelten gehört. Da Strabo zufolge (Buch III) Ephorus im 4. Jh. v. Chr. schon über Hünengräber bei Kap St. Vincent in SW-Portugal geschrieben hätte, waren sie sicher so alt, ja, selbst viel älter, weil damals der ursprüngliche Zweck offenbar schon längst vergessen war. Außerdem verjagten nach Herodot die Skythen an der Schwarzmeerküste die Kimmerier oder Kimbrier 'um 1500 vor unsere Zeitrechnung' [in Wirklichkeit erst im 8. Jh. v. Chr.]. Deshalb waren die Hünengräber sehr alt, 'ein Paar Tausend Jahre nach der Sintflut vielleicht'. Van Lier zufolge rechnete Westendorp mit einer Steinzeit, die einer Metallzeit voranging. Er spekulierte ausführlich über das ökonomisch-soziale Entwicklungsstadium der Großsteingraberbauer, wie auch Wilhelm Grimm das in seiner (anonymen) Rezension der Westendorp'schen Arbeit in den *Göttingschen gelehrten Anzeigen* (1824) tat. Da Ossian noch eine sehr bewunderte Autorität war und die Landwirtschaft und der Hausbau dieses Volkes noch unbekannt waren, mussten diese Versuche fehlschlagen.

In Kopenhagen arbeitete Christian Jürgensen Thomsen (1788-1865) damals an seinem Dreiperiodensystem (Seger 1930). Nachdem er 1825 Grimms Rezension gelesen hatte, schrieb er an Johann Gustav Gottlieb Büsching in Breslau, "damit Sie mich nicht für einen Plagiarius halten". Kurz zuvor hatte dieser ihm nämlich sein (noch embryonales) Dreiperiodensystem erklärt, das teilweise mit Westendorps Zweiperiodensystem vergleichbar war. Er meinte, dass Westendorp die Großsteingräber viel zu alt datiere und auch, dass er die Qualität der Keramik überschätze. Nachdem Gustav Friedrich Klemm Westendorps Theorien noch größtenteils in sein *Handbuch der germanischen Altertumskunde* (1836) übernommen hatte, wurde Klemms "Keltomanie" danach in Deutschland und anderswo bald allgemein verworfen.

Leonhardt Johannes Friedrich Janssen (1806-1869, Abb. 37), Konservator des Leidener Museums für Altertümer und der seinerzeit einzige in den Niederlanden tätige Berufsprähistoriker besuchte 1847 alle Großsteingräber, eine knappe Beschreibung publizierte er 1848. Er ging davon aus, dass die Gräber alle ursprünglich von einem Erdhügel überdeckt waren und dass der Eingang in der Mitte der Süd- oder der Ostseite lag. Janssen korrespondierte mit Kollegen in Deutschland und Skandinavien, erkannte auch schon, dass die Keramik aus den niederländischen Großsteingräbern der aus den mecklenburgischen sehr ähnlich war, für ihn blieb aber weiterhin das Zweiperiodensystem gültig. Eine Bestätigung dieses Systems war für ihn ein Fund von einem Stückchen Eisen und Tuffbröckchen zusammen mit tiefstichverzierten Scherben aus dem zerstörten Großstein-grab D44a-Zaalhof bei Emmen (Janssen 1848). Überzeugender für ihn war noch, dass in siebzehn 'Herdstellen', die 1853 bei Hilversum entdeckt wurden (Abb. 43; Janssen 1853b, 1856), sowohl steinerne Werkzeuge als auch ein Stück behauener Bentheimer Sandstein gefunden wurden. Janssen vermutete, dass der Sandstein von einem römischen Gebäude stammte. Demnach reichte die Steinzeit in den Niederlanden also offenbar bis in die Römerzeit. Er wurde aber vom Dirk West-broek mit Fälschungen bei der Nase geführt.

Westendorp (1822) hatte kurz beschrieben, wie man die Decksteine mit Sei-len, Rollhölzern und Hebebäumen über eine einfache hölzerne Schräge hoch be-wegen konnte. Der deutsche Forscher Hermann Bödiker (1828), sowie Janssen (1853a) beschrieben den Bau der Großsteingräber ausführlicher. Nach ihnen wur-den erst die Trägersteine aufgestellt, dann ein Erdhügel bis zu deren Schultern aufgeworfen und die Kammer mit Erde verfüllt. Danach wurden die Decksteine darüber geschoben. Diese Theorie ist der berühmten, jüngeren vom dänischen König Frederik VII (1857) sehr ähnlich. Verglichen mit der knappen Beschrei-bung Westendorps und der Weise wie man noch heute in Sumba Decksteine über eine hölzerne Schräge hochbewegt (Bakker 1999, 2009a), ist diese Theorie jedoch ein Schritt zurück.

Als die Allmenden in Drenthe verkoppelt wurden, war die Gefahr groß, dass die Großsteingräber von Privatleuten vernichtet wurden. Auf Initiative des Dren-ther Anwalts und Politikers Lucas Oldenhuis Gratama (1815-1887), der hier-über 1868 einen 'Offenen Brief' veröffentlichte, wurden fast alle niederländischen Großsteingräber in kurzer Zeit von der Landesregierung und der Provinz erwor-ben – ein Vorbild für angrenzende Länder, wo man damals noch nicht so weit war. Leider wurden die Gräber auch 'restauriert', dabei wurden nicht nur die Steine so gestellt, wie man meinte, dass es richtig sei, sondern auch Hügelreste wurden entfernt. Einen Extremfall zeigt Abb. 46. Westendorps Theorie (1815, 1822), dass Hünengräber keine Hügel gehabt hätten, wirkte sich hier fatal aus.

Der energische Londoner Archäologe, Augustus Wollaston Franks (1826-1897), Konservator des Britischen Museums und Mitglied und später Präsident der Society of Antiquaries in London, sah 1871 auf einer Reise Beispiele die-ser "Restaurierungen". Er veranlasste, dass Rev. William Collings Lukis (1817-1892) und Sir Henry Dryden (1818-1899) seitens der Society 1878 mehr als zwei Drittel der Großsteingräber vorbildlich vermaßen (Abb. 47-49, 52-53; vgl. Bakker 1979c). Zum ersten Mal in den Niederlanden zeichnete Lukis genau die gefundenen Scherben und die Feuersteinartefakte und siebte die Erde aus seinen Probelöchern. Es sollte bis 1970 dauern, bis das Sieben bei Untersuchungen von niederländischen Großsteingräbern Standard wurde.

Willem Pleyte (1836-1903) war von 1869 bis 1903 Konservator und Direktor des Leidener Museums für Altertümer, er führte selber keine Grabungen durch. In seinem Prachtwerk mit dem Titel (übersetzt): 'Niederländische Altertümer von den frühesten Zeiten bis zu Karl dem Grossen', (1877-1902), übernahm er die von König Frederik formulierte Theorie vom Aufbau eines Großsteingrabes und zwar auch Thomsens Dreiperiodensystem, das F. Wibel in seinem Bericht über den Denghoog auf Sylt (1869) beschrieben hatte, aber er verwendete diese Chronologie im Weiteren kaum. Mit Willem Hofdijk datierte er die Großsteingräber 'vielleicht' in die Zeit zwischen 3000 und 2000 v. Chr. Sein Argument waren die in ägyptischen Quellen erwähnten lybischen Tamehu, die nicht nur in Ägypten, sondern auch in Europa die Großsteingräber errichtet hätten

Buddeleien in Hünengräbern gab es bis etwa 1983, als die Kammerfüllungen der noch nicht untersuchten Großsteingräber 10 cm unter der Oberfläche mit durchlochten Betonblöcken abgedeckt wurden. In Berichten aus den Jahren 1848 und 1877 wird erwähnt, fast alle Hünengräber seien schon von Laien ausgegraben worden. Glücklicherweise stimmte das nur zum Teil, und so konnten Holwerda in den Jahren 1912-13 und vor allem Van Giffen ab 1918 und ab 1968 deren Nachfolger systematische Ausgrabungen durchführen. Mit seinem Atlas der niederländischen Großsteingräber (1925-1927) orientierte sich van Giffen weitgehend an Dryden's Plänen (Bakker 1979c). Es war wohl kein Zufall, dass Ernst Sprockhoff für seine drei Atlanten der deutschen Megalithgräber (1966, 1967, 1975) dieselbe Größe wie Van Giffen sie für seinen Atlas wählte.

Reports from 1812 and 1809 on megalithic graves on Fehmarn and elsewhere in Holstein, Germany[529]

Berichte von 1812 und 1809 über Megalith-gräber af Fehmarn und anderswo in Holstein

(2A) Georg Wolfgang Ulrich Wedel, Erbherr auf Freudenholm bey Preetz in Holstein (1812)

Abhandlung über den Ursprung der alten Begräbnissdenkmäler im Departement Drenthe, zur Beantwortung der von der Kayserlichen Societaet der Wissenschaften zu Haarlem für den 1sten November 1812 aufgegebenen Preisfrage

Kommentar von J.A. Bakker

Für die Preisfrage der Hollandsche Maatschappij der Wetenschappen zu Haarlem sandte außer Nicolaus Westendorp ('Abhandlung A') auch Georg Wolfgang Ulrich Wedel eine Abhandlung ein ('Abhandlung B'). Beide taten es gemäß Vorschrift anonym, mit Kennwort.[530] Die Angaben zu ihrer Person lagen in einem verschlossenen Umschlag. Nur der des Gewinners wurde geöffnet; die der Verlierer hätten, so besagte es eine Vorschrift, vernichtet werden sollen. Das geschah glücklicherweise nicht, auch der Umschlag von Wedel blieb in Haarlem erhalten. Dort wurde er vor wenigen Jahrzehnten geöffnet (De Bruijn 1977). Für den Text der Preisfrage und Westendorps Abhandlung A verweise ich auf meinen früheren Aufsatz. Abhandlung B wurde laut dem im Kuvert beigefügten Zettel durch G.W.U. Wedel aus 'Freudenholm den 1sten Julii 1812' nach Haarlem geschickt.

---

529 Because Wedel's study is written in German, my comments are given in that language (Appendix 2A). The same is true for Appendix 2B.

530 Wedels Motto war '*Et regum cineres, extructo monte quiescunt, Lucani Pharsalia L. 8, v. 686*'.

Wedels Abhandlung wurde von der Haarlemer Kommission zur Beurteilung der Preisfrage als weniger gut als Westendorps Abhandlung beurteilt. Als der Abgabetermin schließlich auf den 1.1.1815 verschoben wurde, um Westendorp zu ermöglichen, seine umfangreiche Abhandlung abzurunden, sandte Wedel keinen überarbeiteten Text mehr ein.

Da Abhandlung B völlig unbekannt ist und schwer zugänglich im 'Noord-Hollands Archief' in Haarlem lagert (Stücke der Hollandsche Maatschappij der Wetenschappen, Abt. 'Prijsvragen') und mir einiges daraus für die Geschichte der archäologischen Forschung und der Kenntnis heute nicht mehr erhaltener Denkmäler in Holstein wichtig erscheint, lege ich hier längere Auszüge vor (in Kursivschrift, im Gegensatz zu meinem Kommentar)[531]. Abhandlung B hat eine Länge von 9 + 81 Seiten. Gemäß der Vorschrift wurde nicht in z.B. gothischer Schrift, sondern in lateinischer Schreibschrift abgeliefert. Wedel fügte aber seinem im Kuvert verschlossenen Zettel mit seinem Name folgende Bemerkung hinzu *'Der Verfasser bittet …, ihm, im Falle seine Abhandlung gekrönt würde, es zu erlauben, sie aus seinem Original Manuskripte drucken lassen zu dürffen, indem er auf das eingesandte Mspt. in jedem Falle gänzlich Verzicht Leistet'*. Schreibweisen wie '*Goettern*' statt '*Göttern*' und '*aeussern*' statt '*äussern*', vielleicht auch einige Lesefehler, könnten Wedel zu dieser Bitte veranlasst haben.

Nach Wedel waren die 'Normannen' um 854 die Erbauer der 'Hühnenbetten'. Westendorps Abhandlung A ist auch aus heutiger Sicht viel einleuchtender als B.

Wie Wedels Beweisführung läuft, zeigt die 'Inhaltsanzeige' seiner Arbeit:

Inhaltsanzeige

---

531 Abhandlung B, die Beurteilungsbriefe der Abhandlungen B und A der Kommissionsmitglieder der Preisfrage von 1813 sowie von Abhandlung A von 1815, und Westendorps Abhandlung von 1812, wurden 1993 von mir fotokopiert – auf Wunsch stelle ich sie gern zur Verfügung. Selbstverständlich zitiere ich Wedels Zeilen wortwörtlich (in Kursivschrift). Zur Verdeutlichung sind die Buchstaben (a)-(h) und die Ziffern [1]-[9] eingefügt.

III Zweiter Abschnitt, die eigentliche Preisfrage betreffend

Die Abhandlung Wedels ist ein typisches Werk aus einem Studierzimmer, mit vielen Zitaten, z. B. aus Saxo Grammaticus, Chroniken und aus der weiteren historischen und archäologischen Literatur (108 Titeln, S. 1-7). Die Arbeit ist überwiegend kompilatorisch, ziemlich altmodisch und wenig originell. Von heute aus betrachtet ist sie chronologisch schwach, da sie anscheinend alle 'Urnen' und anderen Funden aus den verschiedenen Stufen der Urgeschichte und wohl auch des frühen Mittelalters als aus den 'Hühnenbetten' stammend, oder dazu gehörig beschreibt. Z. T. handelt es sich dabei auch um Nachbestattungen in Megalithgräbern, um Funde im freien Gelände und vermutlich auch aus post-megalithischen Grabhügeln.

Aus Abschnitt II.8 (S. 32-44), '*Von Sachen die sich in den Hühnenbetten gefunden*', zitiere ich hier ziemlich viel um Wedels systematische Sammlerbuchhalterei, noch ohne viel typochronologisches Wissen, zu zeigen. Hier und dort befinden sich darunter Schätze, wie die verkohlten Gerstenkörner in einer „Urne". Dass alle Töpfe 'Urnen' genannt werden, ist ganz normal; in den Niederlanden war dies vor 1900 nicht anders.

(a) '*... sind die Urnen, theils mit Asche allein, theils mit Asche, Knochen und Erde gefüllt, worin man zuweilen Menschenhaare am Boden in die Runde gelegt, auch allerlei kleines Geraethe findet.*

Beim Verbrennen der Todten wurde hoechst wahrscheinlich auch den Goettern geopfert, wie mir der Umstand glaublich macht, weil ich drei etwas angebrannte und dadurch wohl erhaltene Gerstekoerner besitze, die ich zwischen Knochen und Asche in einer Urne gefunden. Um die Urnen herum, seltener unter denselben, liegen die mit ihnen vergrabenen Alterthümer, welche auf das Geschlecht und Gewerbe der Todten Beziehung haben. Gemeiniglich sind die Urnen so fest mit Steinen verwahrt, dass viele Sorgfalt dazu erforderlich ist, sie unzerbrochen zu Tage zu foerdern.

Die Form der Urnen und ihre Groesse ist ausserordentlich verschieden, und sind sie im Norden von 4 bis 12 Zoll hoch, und mit Ausnahme der wendischen ohne Fuesse. Einige haben einen bis zu vier Oere, oder kleine Handhaben, andere keine. Gewoehnlich sind die Urnen rund mit langen oder creysfoermigen Strichen, auch mit Puncten und Strichen auswaerts verziert. Theils sind sie von sehr feiner, theils von grober sandiger Erde verfertigt, und schwaerzlich, roetlich, gelblich, grau oder bleistiftmaessig von Farbe, einige auch auswaerts und inwendig gleichsam glasirt. Von dieser letztern Art besitze ich zwei Fragmente einer schwarzen Urne, etwa 12 Zoll hoch an der aeussern Seite mit Puncten à la Grecque geschmückt, von einer bewunderenswürdig schoenen Form. Eine in der Lausitz ausgegrabene, mithin wendische Urne von einer ganz eigenen Gestalt, war ehemals zu Gottorf, laut Olearii Gottorfischen Kunstkammer pag. 77 und deren Tab. 36 n°. 3 gelieferten Abbildung.

Nach der Zahl der Urnen pflegen dabei, eben so viele Keile von Feuerstein, auch wiwohl seltener, dergleichen Opfermesser zu liegen, welches wie ich muthmasse, einen religioesen Grund hat, um Incantationen und Daemonen vom Grab ab-zuhalten. …

Was nun seltnere Massen der Urnen anlangt, so hat man 6 Stücke von dün-nem Goldbleche 1685 beim Pflügen auf Munkoe bei Fühnen mit Asche gefüllt gefunden, die saemtlich nach der Koeniglichen Kunstkammer in Kopenhagen ge-kommen, und wovon die groesste nur 5 Loth, die übrigen aber 4 Loth und ein Drachma gewogen.[532] So hoechst selten goldne Urnen sind, so merkwürdig ist es auch, dass diese in zwei Reihen auf einander gesetzt, und die drei unten bedeckt gestanden mit den drei oebern, durch Goldfaeden verbunden gewesen, laut Olgeri Jacobaei, Museo Regio pag. 57 und dessen Auctorio pag. 12fg. nebst Tab. 14. Fig. 8, wo eine dieser Urnen abgebildet, sich findet.

Eine schoene crystallene Urne unterwaerts eifoermig gestaltet, oben mit einer doppelten creisfoermigen, 16 Loth an Gewicht haltenden Einfassung vom fein-sten Golde, wurde 1673 bei der Kirche zu Braemsnäs in Norwegen, unter einem Verdecke von Erz, das meist verwittert war, zwischen vier Feldsteinen vermacht gefunden, welche hoechste Seltenheit sich ebenfalls in vorgedachten Koeniglichen Kunstkammer befindet und Tab. 14. Fig. 6, beim Jacobaeo abgebildet, und in dessen Auctorio pag. 12. beschrieben worden.' (S. 33-35).

Nach Beschreibung einer *'glaesernen, inwendig vergoldeten, bei Giördslev auf Seeland 1637 ausgegrabenen Urne'* (Wormius, Monumenta Danicorum, S. 21), einer ähnlichen in Dresden (Keysler, Fortsetzung der Reisen, S. 1078, 1137), folgt: *'Eine marmorne Urne, und in selbiger einen goldenen Ring fand der Pastor Rist in der Gegend der Elbe teste novis litterariis maris Balthici 1699 pag. 94, welches vermuthlich die naemliche Urne ist, deren Rhode in den cimbrischen Antiquitaeten Remarques pag. 43, als schwarz mit rothen Adern durchdrungen gedenkt, wo er zugleich von einer steinernen Urne Nachricht gibt, die der Doctor Rustorf bei Kiel gefunden. Ich selbst sah 1803 bei dem Herrn Pastor Holst in Kiel, wie er mir seine hoechst schaetzbare Mineraliensammlung zu zeigen die Gute hatte, eine Urne von Felsstein in Gestalt eines Kohlkopfes, auswaerts in die Laenge canellirt, und für die grobe Masse, sauber gearbeitet, inwendig ausgeschliffen, fast spiegelglatt und gleichsam glasirt.*

---

532 1 Lot = 14,6 gr., 1 Apotheker-Drachme = 3,65 gr (Engel 1965, 68).

Einer grossen ehernen Urne sesqui congii mensuram capientis, die in Fühnen ausgegraben worden, gedenken die nova litteraria maris Balthici 1700 pag. 341. So fand ein Bauer zu Malente 1782 bei Grabung eines Lochs zu einer Thorstütze 2 Fuss tief,[533] eine sehr schoene bunte grosse metallene Urne mit zwei kleinen krausgearbeiteten Henkeln versehen, die er leider barbarischerweise, in Hoffnung darin enthaltener Schaetze zerschlagen.' (S. 36-37).

Ein metallenes Gefäss mit einem durch kupferne Nägel angenieten Henkel (1719 aus einem großen Hünenbett bei Höwisch in der Altmark, nach Keysler Antiquitates selectae septentrionalis 1720, S. 319ff.) und mehrere andere in der Literatur erwähnte Urnen aus Norddeutschland und Südskandinavien werden noch erwähnt (S. 37-39).

'Was insonderheit die nordischen Hühnenbetten anlangt, so hat man darin ausser den gewohnlich thoenernen Urnen, einigen Stücken Bernstein, etwas Raeucherwerk einer Corallenschnur, kleinen steinernen Goetzen, einem Halsbande von ehernen Corallen und kleinen Ringen, und einem grossen sauber gearbeiteten ehernen Ringe zum Kopfschmucke, dessen Camerer pag. 200 seiner Merkwürdigkeiten der holsteinischen Gegenden gedenkt, und letztere beide Fig. 13 & 14 abgebildet geliefert, naemlich:'

Es folgt eine lange systematische Auflistung der Funde (S. 39-44):

'1. von Gold' (u. a. die schon genannten Goldfunde);

'2. von Silber: Selten findet man etwas von Silber; indessen waren doch im Gothenberge bei Malente, ein Schloss, einige kleine Messer und Schnallen, nebst einem unverarbeitetem Stücke dieses Metalls vorhanden ... Wie ich denn selbst, vor Jahren, beim Goldschmidt Geerz in Eutin einen Armring mit einen daran befestigt haengenden Dolche, beides von Silber gesehen, den er sich gekauft hätte, wenn ich damals die hoechste Seltenheit dieses Stückes auch nur geahndet.

'3. von Kupfer und Erz, das ist einem gemischten gelben Metalle: Urnen, grosse Spitzhaemmer, Streithaemmer, Wurfpfeile, Schwerter, Spiesse, Dolche, Opfermesser, Opferbeile, Sporen mit einem blossen Stachel, Steigbügel, Pferdestangen, Ketten und zum Pferdegeschirr gehoerige Zierrathen, Schaabmesser für Gerber, Scheermesser, andere Messer, wovon eins oben mit einem Pferdekopfe verziert gewesen, Pfriemen, lange Haarnadeln, Naehnadeln, Stecknadeln, Haarkneipen, Kopfringe, Armringe, kleine Ringe, runde einfache Hemdsknoepfe, Schnallen, Halsbaender, kleine Hütchen, ein kleines Anker, eine runde vergoldete Dose mit grauem Pulver, eine schmale lange Platte mit 12 rundlichen Knoepfen dicht nebeneinander, Tönnchen, Stoepfel, runde Lampen, Goetzenbilder, und endlich ein Messerheft, dunkelblau und weiss emaillirt mit einem oberhalb sehr sauber gegossenen, auf einem Dudelsack blasender Krieger, das ich selbst besitze.' (S. 39-42).

---

533 One schleswig-holsteiner Fuß = 0,287 cm (Engel 1965, 65-6), but I do not know whether it was also current on the Danish island of Fyn (Fünen). It was probably used by Wedel on the Isle of Fehmarn and elsewhere in Schleswig-Holstein (see below).

Ebenso ausführlich sind die Listen der zu den folgenden Kategorien gehörenden Funde, die ich aber weglasse (S. 42-43):

'4. von Eisen';

'5. von Zinn: Von diesem Metalle besitze ich ein doppeltes, durch Schraubengaenge verbundenes, meist verwittertes Büchschen, vermutlich eine Balsamdose';

'6. von Feuerstein';

'7. Von Felsgestein, Basalt, Sand[stein] und feinen Kiesel und anderen Steinen'.

Es folgen (S. 43-44) einige schwierig klassifizierbare Funde. Eine in einem Riesenbette gefundene brennenden Phosphorlampe (Rhode, Nov. litterar. maris Baltici, 1792, S. 181; Antiquitaeten Remarques S. 101, 159ff.) scheint Wedel *'noch nicht über allen Zweifel erhoben zu sein'*, da Rhode dies nur auf Aussage der Arbeiter meldet.

Hiermit sind Wedels buchhalterische Talente – und wie es jetzt scheint, seine Naivität – genügend dargestellt, und ich beschränke mich weiter auf Passagen, die mir interessant erscheinen, weil sie hauptsächlich auf originalen Berichten Wedels beruhen:

(a) *'Uebrigens gibt die Beschaffenheit der in den Hühnenbetten gefundenen Sachen, ihr höheres, oder geringeres Alter zu erkennen, indem diejenigen, worin blos steinerne und eherne Geräthe und Waffen vorhanden, weit aelter als solche sind, in welchen sich nebst jenen, auch eiserne finden, was dem verdienstvollen Alterthumsforscher Christian Detlev Rhode in novis litterariis maris Baltici 1699 pag. 91 sehr richtig zu bemerken Anlass gab; ...'* (S. 11-12).

(b) *'Dass auch in Holstein Hühnenbetten von einem sehr hohen Alter vorhanden gewesen, auch einzeln vielleicht noch sind, erhellte daher unzweifelhaft, weil man nicht nur eherne Waffen so verwittert gefunden, dass sie von der Feuchtigkeit in einem hohen Grade angegriffen sind, sondern ich auch in meiner Sammlung von Alterthümern eine Spiessspitze, einen Wurfpfeil und ein Opfermesser besitze, worauf ein dem feinsten grünen Lack aehnlicher aerugo nobilis, gleich auf den aeltesten griechischen und römischen Münzen sichtbar.'* (S. 12).

Dass Wedel selbst aktiv gegraben hat und ein guter Beobachter war, zeigen folgende Zitate:

(c) *'Gewoehnlich bestehen die Graeber in den Riesenbetten aus grossen einwaerts gerade gespalteten und winkelrecht 6 Fuss lang und 3 Fuss breit [1,72 x 0,86 m] erichteten rohen Feldsteinen, die mit kleineren Steinen und Fliesstücken gleicher Art sorgfaeltig verkeilt, und mit Erde befüttert sind. In einer Tiefe von etwa 3 Fuss [0,86 m] pflegt der Grund mit kleingeschlagenen Feuersteine gleichsam gepflastert und fest gestampft zu sein, welcher Platz, nach der gemeinen Meinung, für die ustrina gehalten wird, und worauf nach Südosten hin, die Urne sorgfaeltig zwischen Steinen vermacht zu sein pflegt. So fand ich es wenigstens in verschiedenen unter meiner Anleitung aufgegrabenen Hühnenbetten in Holstein. Graeber von Bedeutung sind nach aussen mit grossen Steinen umsetzt, und mit einem oder zwei grossen, oben runden und unbearbeiteten Deckelsteinen belegt. Die mehresten Graeber aber deckt nur ein Erdhügel von 4 biss 5 Fuss Hoehe [1,14-1,43 m].' (S. 29-30).*

(d) 'Hiernaechst nehme man zum Aufgraben der Hühnenbetten Leute an, die mit Behendigkeit zu arbeiten im Stande sind, und behalte man ja diejenigen zu dieser Arbeit bei, die sich bereits einige Fertigkeit darin erworben haben. Ihnen sind, ausser gemeinen Spaten und Hebewerkzeugen, auch leichte kleine Stangen, Grabscheite und breite Meissel von gut verstahltem Eisen zu geben, um damit in der Naehe der Urnen behutsam arbeiten zu koennen.' (S. 46-47).

Folgende 'Hühnenbetten' in und beim Gothenberge, bei Malente im Amt Eutin, werden von Sprockhoff (1966, S. 64-65) nicht erwähnt - oder handelt es sich vielleicht um den mutmaßlichen erweiterten Dolmen 246 nördlich vom Gronenberg oder Stubbenberg (S. 64, Beilage 26, Atlasblatt 99)? Es folgt die Beschreibung aus dem Jahr 1812:

(e) 'Ein gleiches beweist auch die taegliche Erfahrung in Holstein, indem zum Beispiel zu Malente, Amts Eutin, in und beim Gothenberge, wo hoechst wahrscheinlich die merkwürdige Schlacht zwischen Koenig Gottfried von Daenemark und Carls des Grossen gleichnamigten Sohne zum Nachtheile der Franken vorgefallen, es hohe runde, auch nicht sehr hohe rundlicht, theils oben flache, theils spitzige und auch laenglicht und am Ende abgerundete, theils an einer Seite runde, und an der entgegengesetzten breit und schraeg ablaufenden Hühnenbetten mit und ohne Steinumgebungen, gibt, hiernaechst auch in geraden Linien gehende Reihen von Grabhügeln auf dem Zarnekauer Felde und der Krummenser Weide unfern, Eutin gefunden werden.' (S. 25).

Hierzu lese man auch folgende Stelle:

(f) 'Was nun die Hühnenbetten an und für sich selbst anlangt, so gibt es Hügel und steinerne Graeber, worin nur eine Urne, zuweilen auch keine, und einige Alterthümer sich finden, aber auch Hügel mit mehreren grossen und kleinen Urnen, die Familiengraeber gewesen zu sein scheinen, dagegen aber auch Hügel, worin eine sehr grosse Menge von Urnen dicht bei und über einander vorhanden sind, wie z. B. im nungedachten Gothenberge, ...' (S. 26-27). Siehe auch die schon genannten Silberfunde im Gothenberge.

Auch das Steingrab auf dem Bracker Felde im Amt Eutin scheint nicht von Sprockhoff (1966) erwähnt zu werden:

(g) '... wie auch mir selbst von einem eifrigen Alterthumsgraeber Namens Facius berichtet worden, dass auf dem Bracker Felde Amts Eutin, ein Grab unten am Fusse eines hohen Berges sich befinde, vor dessen Oeffnung ein grosser Stein gelegen. Dieses Grab sei viereckig mit Feldsteinen ausgesetzt, dessen Mundloch aber so enge gewesen, dass er nur mit Mühe hinein gekrochen. Er habe im Finstern nur zwei Streithaemmer und Keile heraus zu fühlen vermogt. Zu Ende desselben

zu kriechen habe er aber nicht gewagt, theils aus Besorgniss, in diesen langen Behaeltniss zu ersticken, theils aus Furcht, dass der ganze Berg hohl sein koennte, und er in einen Abgrund stürzen moegte.' (S. 28)

Viel wichtiger als alles andere scheint mir aber der folgende, von mir un-verkürzt zitierte Bericht aus dem Jahr 1809. Darin zähle ich neun, von Wedel beschriebene, heute nicht mehr erhaltene Grabmonumente bei der Bergmühle auf Fehmarn [1]-[9] auf:

(h) '... wenn ich mir noch die Bitte erlaube, ein hoechst merkwürdiges Denkmal der Vorzeit ausfuehrlich beschreiben zu dürfen, welches ich selbst 1809 auf der Insel Femarn in Augeschein genommen, und der dort cantonnirenden Herrn Lieutenant von Pagendorm sorgfaeltig aufzunehmen, und abgezeichnet an die Societaet der Alterthümer nach Copenhagen einzusenden ersucht, da, soviel mir bekannt, kein Monument dieser Art je, von einem Alterthumsschriftsteller be-schrieben, vielweniger bildlich dargestellt worden, dessen Veranlassung und ei-gentliche Bestimmung gleichvoll unlaeugbar, einen hoechst untersuchungswür-digen Gegenstand für Alterthumsforscher und die Geschichte des Mittelalters ausmacht.

[1] Auf dem Avendorfer Felde, am westlichsten von der Wulfener Mühle fand ich naemlich eine von Osten nach Westen aufgeworfene, mit grossen Felssteinen umsetzte Erhöhung, circa. 240 Fuss lang, 20 Fuss breit [ca. 68,65 x 6,70 m]. Viele Steine waren bereits weggeschaft worden, indessen, von Graebern hier Keine Spur zu bemerken.

[2] Unfern davon nordoestlich befindet sich ein runder Hügel mit einem Altare [Dolmen] von Osten nach Westen, ebenfalls mit sichtbaren Beweisen der Verwüstung bezeichnet.

[3] Oestlicher nach der Wulfener Mühle hin ist ein von Süden nach Norden auf-geworfener Begraebnisshügel, circa. 380 Fuss lang, 20 Fuss breit [ca. 108,70 x 6,70 m], worin eine grosse Menge Graeber dicht neben einander von Osten nach Westen bemerklich war. Runenschrift fand ich ungeachtet der ungeheuren Menge von Feldsteinen nirgendswo. Die Deckelsteine ohne Ausnahme, waren vernichtet, und viele Bohrloecher an selbigen, und ihre Beschaffenheit bewiesen, dass sie in neuern Zeiten, was nirgend geduldet werden sollte, mit Pulver gesprengt worden.

[4] Zu diesem Hügel führt noerdlich, von Osten nach Westen, eine, gleich einer Brücke aufgeworfene, circa.100 Fuss lange, 20 Fuss breite [ca. 28,60 x 6,70 m], zur Seite mit Steinen eingefasste Erhoehung, die aber laenger gewesen zu sein schien. Auch hier war kein sichtbares Merkmal vormaliger Graeber. Vieles war verwüstet, und der Begraebnisshügel selbst, an mehreren Stellen mit Kartoffeln be-baut. An dessen Ende nach Norden befanden sich die groesten Steine, und hoechst wahrscheinlich das Grab eines Anführers.

[5] Oestlicher, mithin naeher nach der Mühle, fand ich einen runden Hügel mit zwei Graebern von Süden nach Norden, wo auf dem einen, ein ungeheu-er Deckelstein, aber in der Laenge gespalten, vorhanden war, ohne irgend eine

Spur, dass dieses durch Menschenhaende bewirkt worden, da einwaerts die bei-den Stücke, wie gehobelt glatt und kein Merkmal angewandter Keile aeusserlich sichtbar war.

[6] Oestlicher nach der Mühle, befindet sich wieder ein mit Steinen von Osten nach Westen eingefasste Erhoehung etwa 20 Fuss breit [ca. 6,70 m], *auf welcher dicke und alte Hagedornstaemme standen. Diese Erhoehung war indessen gaenz-lich verwüstet.*

[7] Noch östlicher, hart an der Wulfener Mühle, ist ein Platz circa.100 Fuss lang, 20 Fuss breit [ca. 8,6 x 6,70 m] *von Süden nach Norden mit grossen Steinen eingefasstt, der sonst nichts zu bemerken Anlass gab.*

[8] Ostwaerts von der Mühle steht ein Altar [Dolmen], *dessen platter Deckelstein in der Richtung von Osten nach Westen etwa 14 Fuss lang* [ca. 4,00 m], *auf sieben in der Runde gesetzten Steinen ruhte.*

[9] Am oestlichsten endlich waren zwei über 400 Fuss lange, circa. 20 Fuss breite [ca. 114,40 x ca. 6,70 m], *mit grossen Steinen eingefasste, etwa 30 Fuss von ein-ander parallel laufende Erhoehungen von Süden nach Norden, wovon die west-liche mehr südlich nach der Ostsee, die oestliche aber mehr noerdlich landwaerts ging, wo auf beiden ebenfalls nichts von Graebern oder sonst etwas zu bemerken war.'* (S. 21-23).

Demnach befindet oder befand sich ein Bericht des Leutnants von Pagendorm von 1809 im Topografischen Archiv des Nationalmuseums in Kopenhagen. Sprockhoff (1966, S. 66-67, Bergmühle) hat diese neun Monumente nicht mehr angetroffen, weist aber auf eine ausführliche, reich illustrierte Beschreibung des Pastors Harries von 1837 hin. Dieses Manuskript befindet sich im Archiv des Landesmuseums in Schleswig. Sprockhoffs knappe Auszüge erlauben zwar keinen gründlichen Vergleich der Texte von Wedel und Harries, aber es scheint mir, dass Harries nach den angegebenen Maßen und dem Wortlaut zu urteilen Wedel fast wörtlich folgt, also eine Kopie von dessen Bericht benutzt haben muss. Harries schreibt aber ausführlicher aus eigener Anschauung, und er ergänzt den Bericht mit fünf deutlichen Zeichnungen (Sprockhoff 1966, Taf. 60 Mitte, 62 oben und unten, 63 oben und unten). Davon lassen sich vorerst die Nummern [3] mit Taf. 62 unten, und [9] mit Taf. 63 oben identifizieren. Es wäre interessant, festzustel-len, ob sich in den 28 Jahren nach 1809 viel verändert hat.

Als ich diesen Arbeitsstand erreicht hatte, war mir klar, dass sich ein genauer Vergleich der Handschriften von Harries, Wedel und Pagendorm (Kopenhagen) durch einen Mitarbeiter des Museums Schloss Gottorf lohnen würde. Ich schlug meinem Freund und gutem, sehr tüchtigem TBK-Kollegen, Dr. Jürgen Hoika [1941-2006], vor, dass wir beide zusammen diese Arbeit machen sollten. Dazu ist es leider nicht gekommen. Es stimmt traurig, dass wir beide dieses Projekt in der Zeit unseres Ruhestandes nicht zusammen durchführen können. Leider kann ich deshalb nur diesen Beitrag vorlegen. Mit den Handschriften in Schleswig und Kopenhagen, und einer Geländebegehung auf Fehmarn und im ehemaligen Amt Eutin kann in Zukunft sicher mehr erreicht werden.

(2B) H. Wilder und J.D. Gundelach (1809)

Steingräber bei Burg, Vitzdorf, Gahlendorf und Petersdorf auf Fehmarn [534]

Herr Christian Adamsen, Redakteur der berühmten dänischen Zeitschrift *Skalk*, hat das in Beilage 2A erwähnte Bericht von Leutnant vom Pagendorm in Jahre 2010 vergeblich im Archiv des Nationalmuseums in Kopenhagen gesucht. Dabei entdeckte er aber andere Berichte über Megalithgräber auf Fehmarn, die 1809 als Antworten auf eine Enquete der 'Königlichen Commision zur Aufbewahrung der Alterthümer' in 1809 geschrieben wurden.

Ich danke C. Adamsen dafür, dass ich hier Ausschnitte aus diesen Berichten vorlegen darf; sie ergänzen den obigen Bericht Wedels. Ich übernehme nur die Passagen, die von Steingräbern handeln, die ausführliche Berichte über Altertümer in der Kirche von Burg, die Erwähnung der Ruine des Schlosses Glambeck usw. lasse ich aus. Die Unterstreichungen und die Umrechnungen in [ ]-Klammern sind von mir.[535]

J.A. Bakker

Burg und Oster-Kirchspiel [VIII.144]

> *'I. Die in der Kirche der Stadt Burg vorhandenen Alterthümer und Notizen von ehemaligen merkwürdigen Begebenheiten. ...*
>
> Unter 'Notizen' wird bemerkt: *'Auf einem an einem Gewölbpfeiler mitten in der Kirche* [von Burg] *aufgehängten Brette wird unter anderen angeführt, "daß König Erich von Pommern im J. 1420. Femern zerstört habe." (Eine Begebenheit, die aus der Geschichte hinlänglich bekannt ist und wovon die Landleute auf Femern noch immer mit fabelhaften Zusätzen reden.)' ...*
>
> *II. Die außer der Kirche auf dem Felde des Osterkirchspiels unter freyer Himmel sich befindenden Alterthümer. ...*
>
> *2) Ist zu bemerken die sogenannte <u>Vitzdorfer Steinkiste</u>. Diese ist eine Höhle, die an den Seiten mit ziemlich großen Steinen umgeben und oben mit einem sehr dicken runden Feldsteine, dessen Diameter wenigstens 4 Fuß* [1,15 m] *hält, bedecket ist. Der Raum der Höhle ist inwendig über 4 Fuß hoch* [1,15 m]*, nach hinten 3 Fuß breit* [0,86 m]*, und durch die fast oben so breite Oefnung beym Eingange kommt man auf 3 Stuffen hinein. Im Hintertheile der Höhle ist ein kleiner steinerner Sitz. Bey der zerstörung Femerns durch obgedachten nordischen König Erich soll (wie die Sage lautet) einer von den wenigen Einwohnern dieser Insel, die damals das Leben retteten, sich in dieser Steinkiste verborgen haben. Sie liegt an der östlichen Seite der Insel, beinahe 400 Schritte von der Seeküste, in*

---

534 These reports are complementary to Wedel's report about megalithic tombs on Fehmarn and also written in German.

535 1 schleswig-holsteiner Fuß = 1 hamburger Fuß = 12 Zoll; 1 Zoll = 2,4 cm. 1 (gemeine) deutsche Meile = 7532 m, eine alte hannoversche Landmeile = 9323 m (Engel 1965).

einem Fleck Landes, der vormals zu dem Vitzdorfer Felde, jetzt aber zu dem Gute Catharinenhof gehört. Wahrscheinlich ist sie ein Ueberbleibsel des Heidenthums aus der grauen Vorwelt. Wenn die Femerschen bauern das hohe Alter eines Dinges nachdrücklich bezeichnen wollen, so pflegen sie gewöhnlich zu sagen: "Dat is so ohld, as de Vitsdöpper Stehnkis."

Diese Beschreibung ergänzt Sprockhoff (1966, 97; Karte 27, Tafel 61 oben, 'verschollen') sehr wesentlich. Er schrieb 'Steingrab, nach einer alten Zeichnung zu urteilen ein Dolmen, wohl nu rein Deckstein. Rundhügel?' Die Abbildung (bei Sprockhoff) und obige Beschreibung passen gut zusammen.

3) Ist <u>östlich von Gahlendorf</u>, nicht weit vom Dorfe auf der dazu gehörenden Weide ein dicker langer Stein; der auf etlichen Steinen von verschiedener Größe ruht und sich von hinten nach voran allmählig herabsinkt. Der Raum unter demselben ist da, wo der Stein am höchsten ist, so groß, daß ein Kind von 8 Jahren bequem darunter stehen kann.

Diese Beschreibung ergänzt Sprockhoff (1966, 97; Karte 27, Tafel 61-unten, 'verschollen', 'das Opfergrab') wesentlich. Die Zeichnung Tafel 61-unten stimmt mit dieser Beschreibung gut überein.

Anmerk: Dieses ist alles, was ich in dem Osterkirchenspiele von Femern von Altherthümern itzt kenne. Der ehemalige <u>Steinofen</u>, der westlich von der Stadt auf dem Stadtfelde [von Burg] auf einer kleinen Anhöhe errichtet war, bestand aus einem großen 4-eckigten Steine, der auf kleineren Steinen sich stützte, und hatte eine ziemlich geräumige Oefnung. Aber er ist nun seit 30 Jahren fort, weil man die Steine, welche dazu gehörten, gesprengt und zu Steinzäunen der Koppeln gebraucht hat. Eine nahe dabey befindliche Viehtränke, Steinofensoll (i.e. Steinofentränke) genannt, erhält noch sein Andenken.

Geschrieben zu Burg auf Femern d 4te Octob. 1809, H. Wilder[536]

Petersdorf Ksp. [VIII.146]

d 12te Oct 1809, Iohann Daniel Gundelach [537] ...

Grabhügel (Riesen- oder Hünen-Hügel) auch heidnische Altäre sind nach der Vorschrift nicht mit Gewißheit zu finden. Es sind aber in diesem Wester Kirschpiele an verschiedenen Orten zusammen geordneten Steinmassen gewesen, von einigen weiß man nur aus der Erinnerung, von anderen, sind noch Theile und Spuhren vorhanden.

---

536 Hans Wilder war Compastor zu Burg Ksp. in 1801-1834.

537 Johann Daniel Gundelach war Prediger zu Petersdorf Ksp. in 1783-1818. Da mir eine topografische Kentniss des ehem. Ksp. Petersdorf fehlt, kann ich nicht sagen, welche von den von Gundelach (1809) genannten Steingräber mit denen in den Beschreibungen bei Wedel (1812, s. Beilage 2), Harries (1837, in Sprockhoff 1966) und Sprockhoff (1966) übereinstimmen. Die Steingräber von Albertsdorf, Wulfen, Bergmühle und Bisdorf, die es jetzt größtenteils nicht mehr gibt, lagen alle auf dem Meßtischblatt Petersdorf.

Eine kleine Viertel Meile von Peterstorff *nach Westen findet sich auf einem allmählich sich erhebendem Felde, das zu* Kopendorff *gehöret, ein Hügel, wo auf großen Steinen ein anderer großen geruhet hat, wodurch ein Raum eingeschlossen wurde, der drey Fuß Höhe* [0,86 m], *ein fast eben so große Breite, und nach einer Seite eine Oefnung gehabt hat. Das ganze mag 10 Fuß ins Gewiete messen* [2,85 m]. *Die untern Steine liegen noch, nur etwas aus der Lage verrückt. Der obere ist zum theil herunter. Man hat sie durch Pulver gesprengt.*

Dicht dabey siehet man an der östlichen Seite viele meist geschlossenen Steine, und am südlichen Ende derselben noch einen 3 Fuß hohen, 1¼ Fuß breiten und 8 Fuß langen Gang [0,86; 0,36; 2,29 m], *der sich nach Süden öfnet, welcher durch einen hintern Stein und durch Seiten Steinen jeder Art wird, fehlt etwas der Stein zur oberen Decke. Diese Steine haben nicht die Größe, wie sie bey zwei ersten Verbindung sich findet.*

Fünf hundert Schritte etwa weiter in derselben Richtung nach Küste und ebenfalls auf einem zu Kopendorff *gehörigen etwas hochgehendem Felde ist wieder ein auf ähnlicher Ort ersichtiger Hügel. Ein großer Stein macht eine Wand, daran liegen auf jeder Seite zwey nicht so große Steinen, der obere ist gesprenget und herunter. Der innere Kammer enthält 3 Fuß 3 Zoll in der Breite, zwey Fuß in der Höhe, und ist 8 Fuß lang* [Br. 0,93 m, H. 0,57 m, L. 2,30 m] *mit eine Oefnung nach Westen.*

<u>Auf dem Schlagesdorfer Felde</u> ist eine viertelmeile von Peterstorff *nach Nordwest ein Hügel, wo bis vor wenigen Jahren auf derselbige Art verbundene Steine gewesen sind, die aber nachher zu Koppel-Befriedigungen weggefahren sind.*

Das ist auch mit etwa so aufgeführt gewesenen Steinen an einer anderen Stelle von <u>Schlagesdorfer Felde</u>, so wie auf einer kleinen Erhöhung beim so genanten Fester [?] See in den Boiendorfer Feldern geschehen. ...'

Bei der Stadt Burg [s.o, VIII.144] wurde demnach der <u>Steinofen</u> im Stadtfelde um 1780 gesprengt und vom Bansdorfer Kirchspiel [VIII.60] auf Fehmarn wurden keine Megalithgräber erwähnt.

Appendix 3

Additional notes to some of the illustrations

Ad the Frontispiece. Shown are 93 pots, 12 axes and 10 beads from hunebed D19-Drouwen. The original number of pots from the chamber was much larger, however (Staal-Lugten 1976a, b).

Ad Figure 2. Van Giffen's 'Drouwen style' and 'Havelte style' (1927) are indicated to the right. 'Havelte' was subdivided into 'Early' (*Vroeg*) and 'Late' (*Laat*) by Van Giffen. Later 'Middle Havelte' (*Midden*) was added (Bakker 1962-1963; 1979a, viz. Brindley's horizon 6). The cal BC dates on the left differ slightly from those estimated by Lanting & Van der Plicht (2000).

Ad Figure 3. Johan Herman Isings [1884-1977] consulted the Dutch experts about every detail of this school picture 'HUNEBEDBOUWERS', from 1959 (Bakker 1990a). The illustration measures 96 x 67 cm and is signed Isings '59. The clothes are simplified versions of Bronze Age clothes found preserved in Danish barrows. The house to the left is the 'cult house' of Tustrup, Denmark. The oversized quasi-Lower Saxon house is a copy of the reconstruction of TRB houses in Huntedorf 1 (Reinerth 1939). The smaller house to the right, which is of realistic size, is a copy of those found in the lake-side village of Buchau in southern Germany. Pottery would have been made within a house to avoid draughts and the normally cut trees lying in the yard would have been removed because at night one could trip over them. The ceramic 'frying-pan' in the lower left-hand corner is a copy of one from the Stade region near Hamburg. Given what is now known about the economy, an oxen-drawn cart with two or four massive wooden wheels would also have been present in addition to the cow behind the fence and the *ard*-plough carried by the man. After fifty years, this magnificent 'diagonal' composition remains inspiring.

Ad Figure 4. The Latin title means 'The situation of ancient Frisia under Emperor Augustus, according to the sources'. This map is an inset of a map of Friesland-Groningen drawn by Sibrandus Leo and printed in *Theatrum Orbis Terrarum*, edited in 1579 and following years by Abraham Ortelius and issued at Antwerp by Gilles Coppens.[538] The reproduction is from the 1595 edition, which mentions for the first time '*D. Joachimus Hopperus describebat*' ('designed by Mr. Joachim Hopper'). See Van der Sanden (2007, 51) for a coloured illustration (with trimmed right and lower margins).

Ad Figure 5. This print of Picardt's portrait (Picardt 1660, fol. 33) is signed '*GVGoedesberg Excudit*', '*P. Holsteÿn Sculp.*' and '*H. Nÿhoff Pin*'. Gerrit van Goedesbergh was the publisher (as indicated at length on the title page). P. Holsteijn was the Haarlem engraver Pieter Holsteijn [ca. 1614-1687], who is named Pieter Holsteijn II by Von Wurzbach (1910). H. Nijhoff, the painter of the portrait was only known by this (lost) painting to J. Immerzeel, in 1843 (Von Wurzbach 1910). Except for the (outsized) print of a portrait of Hans Adolph count of Bentheim, which is signed HDM, all other portraits in Picardt (1660) are signed *P. Holsteÿn Sculp.* and by the publisher, without naming the painter. Although Picardt's illustrations of prehistoric events, including those reproduced here in Figures 6-8, are unsigned, they were probably made by P. Holsteijn II. He must have travelled to Coevorden in Drenthe and Bentheim or Steinfurt in present Germany to reproduce the eight painted portraits for these prints. While there, Holsteijn could perhaps have drawn hunebeds for the first time from nature, but his prints of prehistoric events, including hunebeds and Celtic Fields, may just as well have been based on sketches provided by Picardt. The map *fol. 1* with speculatively reconstructed ancient place names is signed '*Int Ruijge geteÿckent van* Doctor I. Picard' ('rough drawing by Doctor I. Picard'). The illustrations of hunebeds (Figures 6 and 8) are no accurate renditions.

Ad Figure 7. Picardt (1660) was one of the first to connect cremation with the hunebeds:

> '*Some giants were buried in flat soil, others under barrows, others again were cremated and their bones were collected in pots and jugs of fired clay which were buried under* [hunebeds]. *Cremation of the dead was common in ancient times among most Heathens.*' (Picardt 1660, 32-33, abbreviated).

As in Figure 8, normally sized men are peacefully mingling with the giants, in contrast to Figure 6 and Picardt's description.

Ad Figure 9. The print of Titia Brongersma's excavation in hunebed D27-Borger, in 1685, by the Amsterdam engraver Jacobus Schijnvoet [1673-1744] is pure fantasy. The illustrated tomb is similar to Picardt's drawing (Figure 6), and the excavation took place in the chamber, not outside it. For lack of better images of hunebeds this illustration, which measured 17 x 12 cm, was reproduced by Keysler (1720, Fig. 2) and, without people, by Stukeley (*Itinerarium curiosum*, 1724; cf. Mohen 1999, ill. p. 131).

---

538 Hopper's map was partly based on Jacob van Deventer's map of ancient Friesland from before 1558 (Versfelt 2004, maps 3-4; Karrow 1993), which does not show the COLUMNAE HERCULIS.

Ad Figure 11. Although he claims to have drawn the print 'from life', Elias Baeck [1679-1747], from Augsburg in Bavaria, probably never saw this event himself. Behind the sailing vessel, the distant silhouette of Amsterdam is barely visible The personification of Fame is shown to the right, but without her usual wind-blown sail and with her hands raised in despair because Dutch prosperity appears to have gone. The German text reads:

'Abildung deren höchst schädlichen unbekandten See-Würmer, welche aus West-Indien,[539] zu erst nach Ost-Friesland, in den Texel, und Amsterdam gekommen, und alldorten unbeschreiblichen Schaden verusache.[540]

'Was dieses bald zu End lauffende 1732. Jahr durch das mächtige Element des Wassers an verschiedenen Orthen vor unbeschreiblichen Schaden geschehen, kan mit keiner Feder nicht genügsam beschrieben werden, So entsezlich nun dieses traurige begeben zu sehen ware, so wird es Holländischen Berichten nach von Tag zu Tag schlimmer wegen der Abendtheuerlichen menge deren See-Würmen, solche seijnd verschiedener Länge u: Grösse, haben sehr harte Köpff, geben sich unten an die Pfähle, u: zernagen die gröste balcken von grund aus bisz an dass oberste vom Wasser, das solche wie ein Sieb durchlöchert, alsdan fallen, oder durch die Fluthe des Meers um gestossen werden, und zu ettlich 1000. an Land treibend kommen; die Unter-Intendanten deren Deichen von Drenterland,[541] nahe beij Nord-Holland, haben den General-Staaten bericht ertheilet dasz in selben Quartieren 1122. balcken, in die länge von 4000. Ruthen durch diese Würme abgenaget, und dero Schaden, auf eine Million und 600000 florins Holländischen sich beläufet, die Geestmer-Amt, Schaegen und Niedorp haben ein gleiches berichtet mit dem Anschlusz, dasz ihre Einkünfften nicht mehr suffisant wären obgedachten Schaden herzustellen, wan die General-Statten[542] ihnen nicht aus der allgemeinen Cassa eine mächtige hülf von Geld u: Materilien fourirten,[543] man hat an vielen Orthen Gegen-Deichen gemacht, und in einigen anderen Plätzen, wo die Gefahr am augenscheinlichsten nehmen die beij den Deichen wohnende Bauren die Flucht sich anderwärths hin mit ihrem Viehe u: Haus-Rath zu retiriren aus Forcht einmahl unversehens durch die Fluth verschlungen zu werden; die General-Staaten haben disertalben schon den 18. Octob. einen Fast- und Bett-Tag durch alle ihre Provintzen angeordnet mit Befehl an die Prediger, von was Religion sie seijen, das Volk zur Andacht und Busz zu ermahnen um den Zorn Gottes zu besänfftigen, der ihnen eine Plag zu geschickt, worauf der gäntzliche Ruin des Staats erfolgen könte; besonders lebet die Provinz Ost-Friesland in höchster Bekümernüs, wie auch die Städte Alcmaer, Horn, Enckhuysen, Medemblic, etc. so das meist von diesem Ungeziffer ausstehen, welches das Unglück noch grösser macht, so greiffen

---

539 To be corrected into OST-INDIEN.
540 To be corrected into *verursachen.*
541 To be corrected into *Drechterland,* which is part of Dutch region of West-Friesland, north of Amsterdam. The towns of Alkmaar, Hoorn, Enkhuizen and Medemblik, mentioned below, are located in West-Friesland. Dutch West-Friesland is part of the province of Noord-Holland and is not to be confused with the Dutch province of Friesland – between West-Friesland, Drenthe and Groningen – which is called 'Westfriesland' in Germany and Denmark
542 To be corrected into *General-Staaten.*
543 To be corrected into *fournirten.*

diese Würmer auch die im Haffen vor Ancker ligende Schiffe an, diese entsetzliche Würme sein gleich den grossen Seiden Würme, oder den Blut-eglen, haben so harte Köpffe, die mit einem hammer kaum können zerschlagen werden, wan man solche aus dem Wasser an die Luft bringet so crepieren sie gleich. E. Baeck à H. fecit et exc. a. v. ['Drawing and print from live by E. Baeck à H.']'.

What 'à H.' meant is unknown to me.

Ad Figure 13. In the right upper corner of this anonymous drawing of hunebed D53-Havelte is written: *De Huinebedden by Hesselte / In Drenth 16 Septemb^r : 1732'*. Hesselte, predecessor of Havelte (founded in AD 1310), is a deserted village (*Wüstung*), near the present-day village Darp. The name 'Hesselte' was still current in the 18th century, but has now been replaced by 'Darp' and does not occur on modern topographical maps (Gerding et al. 2003, 180, 384-5, 402 and pers. comm. H.T. Waterbolk). Because hunebeds D53 and D54 are 2.7 km away from the centre of Havelte, and only 1.3 km from Darp / Hesselte, they were sometimes named after Darp (De Wilde 1910) or Hesselte. Figure 13 is assigned to Cornelis Pronk by the Drents Museum, but Pronk's 1732 drawings of D53-Havelte and D54-Havelte have a different style.

Ad Figure 14. A pencil inscription in the upper right corner reads *Hunnebed te Midlaaren, Dingsdag 30 July, 1754* ('Hunnebed at Midlaren, Tuesday July 30, 1754') and in another hand is written *C. Pronk*. In the opinion of G. Overdiep, with whom Van der Sanden (2007, 62) concurred, the gentleman standing between the stones and smoking a long clay pipe was the antiquarian Andries Schoemaker (1660-1735). Because Schoemaker died in 1735 (and Abraham de Haen in 1748), this is not possible. Evidently, Pronk kept drawing hunebeds, 22 years after Schoemaker had pointed them out to him. Or did Pronk produce copies of earlier sketches on later dates? Cf. Figure 25.

Ad Figure 18. The numbers indicate: (1) windmill of Eext; (2) church of Borger; (3) church of Eext; (4) hunebed D14-Eexterhalte; (5) D13; (6) stone steps of D13; (7) surface of the barrow. The situation before 1756 is shown in the inset 'LETT. A' at the top; D13 is the barrow (5) to the right; an earthen tumulus is on the left.

Ad Figure 19. Composed from Van Lier 1760, plates II-IV. The figures clockwise are pl. II: 1; II: 3; II: 4; II: 5; II: 2; IV: 1; II: 6; III: 6; III: 8; IV: 3; IV: 2; III: 7; III: 5). The collared flask (below, right; III: 5) is from hunebed D12-Eext Es – it is the first illustration of a decorated TRB-pot in The Netherlands. According to Van Lier (1760), the two 'urns' (upper left; II: 1-2) were partly filled with burned bones, 'as probably were the other urns which passed into other hands'. The axes (II: 3-4; IV: 1-2) and long chisel (II: 5) were made 'of flint-like stone'. The marble (II: 6) is probably a natural concretion of pyrite or markasite. The 'oil lamp' with hollow stem (III: 6) is now explained as a sucking cup, or *biberon*, for small children. Most of the artefacts were found between the first and the second floor in the chamber, the biberon perhaps above the upper floor. The hammer-axe (IV: 3) and the arrowhead (III: 8) were found in loose earth, which derived from the barrow. How Van Lier thought that the small axes were mounted in a wooden mace is shown below in the middle (III: 7). According to W.C. Lukis, pls. E3 and F4 (of 1878 manuscript), the ornamented 'bottle' was said to have been found together with the ornamented amphora (Figure 29: 2) in D12-Eext Es. J.N. Lanting (1973, appendix 2), assigned the stone hammer-axe (IV: 3) to the 'Emmen' battle-axe type. The barrow of D13 was made in two phases. The first reached up to the tops of the orthostats and dates from the TRB period; the second phase, which covered the capstones until the 18th century, dates from the Bell Beaker period, as well as the Emmen battle-axe (IV: 3) and the arrowhead (III: 8).

Ad Figure 20. The title of P. Camper's upper drawing reads 'Hunnen Bed near Annen on the carriage road, west side'. The '3-10' in the right lower corner means 3 v[oet] and 10 d[uym]. The measures are in *voeten* (31.4 cm) and *duymen* (2.6 cm).The title of the drawing of hunebed D13-Eext, reads 'A. 5 voet 10 duim [1.73 m] wide, 4 v. 6 d. [1.41 m] high. B. 5 v. 4 d. [1.67 m] wide, 4 v. 6 d. [1.41 m] high 12 v. [3,77 m] total length. 7 v. [2.42 m] width. Burial-chamber (*Grafkelder*) near the Windmill of Eext in Drenthe. See [Van Lier 1760]'.

Ad Figure 21. Petrus Camper wrote on and under his drawing of D14-Eexterhalte: 'HUNNEN BED outside EEXT [viewed] from the south side. 59 v. [18.5 m] long' and 'This large heap of stones seems to have made more than one hunebed; most [stones] are displaced, and many small stones have fallen to the ground and are covered by sand; these beds are more complete than those of N. Laren, however. Van Lier describes these [hunebeds] on p. 8. One can reach it closely enough by a coach, the distance south of the chamber is hardly more than ¼ hour's walk' Actually, the hunebed is *one* large tomb, not 'more than one', as Camper suspected. The two hunebeds 'of N[oord] Laren' are D3- and D4-Midlaren, cf. Figures 25-26. Van Giffen (1925, 172-4) discussed Figure 21 in detail. It was seen from the WSW. Prince Gallitzin (1789) reproduced this drawing (Table V). N.B. Van Giffen (1925, 169, 173-4, 185, 214 (24) 229, 239) systematically, but erroneously referred to the author as 'Prince de Radzivil' instead of Prince de Gallitzin.

Ad Figure 22. Camper added further to his drawing of hunebed D14-Eexterhalte: 'A and B mark the two largest stones. The circumference of A is 26 v. [8.14 m], the stone is 10 v. 2 d. [3.19 m] long, 6 v. [1.88 m] wide. B is 29 v. [9.01 m] in circumference'. Van Giffen (1925, 172-4) discussed Figure 22 in detail. It was seen from the north, showing only the middle part east of sidestone Z1. Prince Gallitzin (1789) reproduced this drawing as Table VI. N.B. Van Giffen (1925, 169, 173-4, 185, 214 (24) 229, 239) systematically, but erroneously referred to this author as 'Prince de Radzivil' instead of Prince de Gallitzin.

Ad Figure 24. Petrus Camper wrote under the drawing of hunebed G1-Noordlaren: 'Hunnen Bed to the west of Noordlaren, standing in the cornfield not far from the road, from the distance it looks like a coach. Drawn from the east side.' His granddaughter wrote below 'The 1st of August, 1832 these stones still had exactly the same position, F. B., born C.'. Frederica Theodora Ernestine Camper [1799-1834] was married to Professor Jacob Gijsbert Samuel van Breda [1788-1867].

Ad Figure 25. The measures given of hunebed D3-Midlaren are Camper's, the lines below were written by his granddaughter. The tree sketched in pencil to the right should help to join Figures 25 and 26 together.

Ad Figure 26. Outside the left margin is written 'here follow № 1 on the preceding page'. Pencilled lines indicate the contours of hunebed D4-Midlaren. Camper's granddaughter added to his drawing of hunebed D4-Midlaren: 'The 1st of August, 1832 these stones still had exactly the same position, F. B., b[orn] C.'

Ad Figure 27. In 1781, Petrus Camper lived in Klein Lankum near Franeker in Friesland. He wrote under his drawing of hunebed O1-De Eese: 'The hunebed lying in the Steenwyk Heath, not far from Friesland, is rather large and consists of very large stones, all loose and moved apart from each other. The largest seems to be A, with a circumference of 25 v. 2 d. [7.9 m]. One side of B was in the ground and it could have been larger. The largest [stones] lay in the middle, the western stones seemed smaller than the eastern ones. The axis was not east and west, but closer to SW-NE. It seems as if the earth surrounding it covered it like a tumulus; there were also 2 Tumuli close by visible, as indicated by C [upper right, difficultly visible]. One drives from Wolvega to De Blesse, from there via Peperga [and] Steggerda to the Heath in one long hour and a half. See the large map of Schotanus. Stell. W. western end.'

Ad Figure 28. The upper view is drawn from the SSW, similar to Van Giffen's 1918 photograph (Atlas 1925-27, pl. 14). The lower view seems to have been drawn from a lower vantage point, with the view from the SW. Because the style of drawing is different, the original sketches may have been made on different occasions (but it is not clear why both rather similar views were published by Engelberts).

Ad Figure 29. No. 2 is a barely recognisable picture of the complete, *tvaerstik* decorated TRB amphora 'from Eext' (Pleyte 1880-2, pl. XLIX: 4), which may have come from hunebed D12-Eext Es.[544] Nos. 1, 3 and 4 may be the completely distorted pictures of undecorated TRB pots. According to Engelberts, no. 4 with a 3.7 cm wide mouth, a 6.7 cm wide body and a height of 6.1 cm, could be a tearflask, but the illustration shows no collar and has little similarity to an undecorated a collared flask (is it a medieval *Kugeltopf*?). No. 5 is a medieval pot. The polished stone perforated axes, nos. 6-8, and the polished axes nos. 9-11, were made

---

544 Van Giffen (1927, note 5 on p. 20-1) discussed the locality of this amphora at length. He noted that Van Lier (1760) did not record it among the artefacts from hunebed D13-Eext and suggested that it derived from hunebed D12-Eext Es. He did not mention Engelberts's illustration. This assignment is confirmed by Lukis, who illustrated it (ms. 1878, pl. E: 3) as 'said to have been found together with' the collared flask ('bottle') from D12 (his pl. F4, then in Museum Utrecht).

of flint or 'German agate'; no. 11 is of a rare type in Drenthe (cf. Bakker & Van der Sanden 1995). That most axes are shown with vertical sides may be an erroneous simplification, but on the other hand, nos. 6-8 may be perforated *Breitkeile* of the Rössen or even early TRB period.[545] No. 7 broke when the perforation was made, after which another perforation was made (cf. Van der Waals 1972, p. 43: L.16). The ceramic 'discs', nos. 12, 12*, and 13, are Carolingian loom-weights, the same type that L.J.F. Janssen later found in great number in Dorestad, the famous commercial town of that period (Janssen 1848, 16n, 152-4); he thought that they were weights for fishing nets. Van Lier (1760) had thought that they were discs for throwing.[546] In December, 1809, J. Hofstede presented King Louis Napoleon of Holland with three disci of his collection, after the King's visit to Drenthe – probably they were the three in Figure 29.[547] They had been 'excavated in the neighbourhood of a tumulus near Eelde' (Pleyte archives C82: C45-47; cf. Bakker 1979b. 59; 1990b, 75). The ox-horn hammer, no. 15, was perhaps a modern jeweller's tool. No. 14 seems to be a *lusus naturae* and the unnumbered object between 13 and 12* is difficult to interpret. No. 16 is a ceramic model boat, which is 13 cm long, 4.3 cm wide (Pleyte 1880-2, pl. LXV: 6) and is reported to have been found in hunebed D15-Loon.[548] Another one (Pleyte 1880-2, pl. LXV: 7) turned up later and is labelled as 'found in Drenthe'. Van Giffen (1927, 91) dated these ceramic model boats to the Carolingian period and noted that J. Hofstede did not mention the model in his short report of his excavation in hunebed D15-Loon in 1809. Apparently J. Hofstede fell victim to inventive stories of traders who knew that objects with known localities would yield more. Westendorp (1815; 1822, 10), who was not aware that nos. 5 and 12-16 probably had not been found in hunebeds, paid some attention to them in his text. Hofstede presented his model boat to King Louis Napoleon, in 1809, who placed it in the Royal Museum in Amsterdam, from where it travelled later to the Leiden Museum.

---

545 See Brandt 1967, 11-9 and chronological table opp. p. 156: '7. *Donauländische Äxte*' and Van der Waals 1972.

546 The *discus* illustrated by Van Lier (1760, pl. V, 1) is not identical to those in Engelberts's illustration (Figure 29).

547 Louis Napoleon [1778-1846], brother of Emperor Napoleon Bonaparte, was King of Holland ('*Koning Lodewijk*') from 1806 to 1810. His 'Kingdom of Holland' consisted of the present-day provinces of The Netherlands, without Limburg and the Flandrian part of Zeeland ('Zeeuws Vlaanderen'), plus Ostfriesland, Jever, Kniphausen and Varel in present-day Germany, from 1807-1810 [Varel till 1808]. In 1810-1813 all these provinces were part of the French Empire. When this king visited Drenthe in 1809, its *Land-Drost* (Bailiff), Petrus Hofstede [1755-1839], wanted to please him and urged his ten years younger brother Johannes Hofstede [1765-1848] to present his whole collection to the King.

548 J. Hofstede wrote in the Catalogue of his collection, which was donated in 1809 to King Louis Napoleon's museum in Amsterdam, that the ceramic model boat was '*found under the stone hunebed between Loon and Taarloo* [i.e. D15-Loon],… [and] *the only one known of its kind*' (Van Giffen 1927, 61-2). Some of J. Hofstede's finds in the Amsterdam museum were later moved to the Leiden museum; the remaining pieces came via The Hague into the Leiden museum in 1826 (Van Giffen 1927, 51). Curiously Engelberts described the model boat as 'made of wood' (1790, 171). Van Giffen (1927, 61-2) considered the facture of both model boats as being medieval. No. 5 and No. 16 (Figure 29) were probably made in the medieval pottery workshops near Eelde, in the province of Groningen.

Ad Figure 31. The pots were very well drawn by P.A.C. Buwama Aardenburg on ¾ actual size in pencil, pen and watercolour. The flask was 'red' and the other two pots were 'ash-grey'. The three pots were also illustrated by Pleyte (Drente, 1880-82, pl. V: 1-3) and Van Giffen (1927, p. 30, text-fig. 4, copied from Pleyte), but the profile of the collared flask in Buwama Aardenburg's drawing is completely different from the one in Pleyte's illustration. Both drawings show groups of three vertical [stab-and-drag] lines on the shoulder, but Pleyte had an additional horizontal stab-and-drag line on the neck-shoulder transition, made with a pointed stamp.

Ad Figure 34. This print of sections of hunebed D41-Emmen, at its discovery in 1809, was probably made by C.C. Fuchs (Westendorp (1815, 1822, pl. II). The original drawing by P.A.C. Buwama Aardenburg is in Archief Hollandsche Maatschappij der Wetenschappen, Noord-Holland Archives (cf. Figure 30).

Ad Figure 44. Not one of the visitors pays any attention to the hunebed itself. The rather insipid text runs: 'NEW HUNS AT AN OLD HUNNEBED / "And did that Hun sleep under this, papa?" / "Yes, my child – and he has not risen yet"'[549] Alexander Ver Huell[550] [1822-1897] was a famous designer of innumerable humoristic and moralistic cartoons (Bervoets 1992). He visited Drenthe between July 15 and 23, 1858, and drew the hunebeds D6-Tynaarlo, D13-Eext and D14-Eexterhalte, a view in the village of Gieten, and a few persons (Gemeente-archief Arnhem VH 44:8: 'Drente').

In 1880, Ver Huell published a short series of plates that was named *Pijlspits-slijpersnakroost* ('Offspring of the arrowhead polishers'). The first lithograph shows a family of arrowhead polishers (*Denkende Beeldjes, schetsen uit de portefeuille van A. Ver Huell*. Arnhem, P. Gouda Quint 1880, pl. 1, lithographed by Maarten Bos and heavily corrected by Ver Huell. See Bervoets 1992, 200 for the original drawing). Ver Huell devoted no other illustrations to prehistoric subjects but he made a few other sketches on archaeological subjects (pers. information Dr. J.A. Bervoets, 2009).

Ad Figure 46. The lichen-free parts show that the stones had been covered by a barrow reaching up to the base of the capstones. The soil was removed to below the foundation stones under some of the orthostats as shown by the kerbstone in the front. Hardly any of the artefacts reached the Assen museum. See Figure 40 for the situation in 1847, when the barrow was still intact.

Pleyte's view of hunebed D15-Loon (1880-82, pl. LXIV: 1) copied this photo precisely, but the skyline was placed ¾ cm higher for unknown reasons. He added a vertically mirrored (!) plan of D15 (pl. LXIV:2), a drawing of an 18 cm long point-butted stone *walzenbeil* (pl. LXIV: 3) and six further pieces of TRB pottery

---

549 *NIEUWE HUNNEN BIJ EEN OUD HUNNEBED* / *"En sliep die Hun daar nu onder, papa?"* / *"ja, kind – en hij is nog niet opgestaan"*. In Bakker 1979b, I dated this print incorrectly to 1857, the error was copied by Van Ginkel et al. 1999, 144 and Van der Sanden 2007, 192.

550 Alias Jhr. Mr. Alexander Willem Carel Maurits Ver Huell (Jhr. means Jonkheer, Mr. means Master of Laws, LL.M).

from the tomb (pl. LXV: 1-6).[551] Two Veluwe type Bell Beakers were illegally dug up from the entrance area of D15 in 1979 (Van Ginkel et al. 1999, photograph of one beaker on p. 120).

Ad Figure 47. 'Sheet of measurements' of 'Drouwen N° III. Gemeente of Borger' [D26-Drouwenerveld] on 'July 12 1878' by Henry Dryden Bar.[t] The measurements of the position of the orthostats from long tangent lines are projected on virtual lines in the hunebed. '3/6' means 3 feet, 6 inches. Wavy lines show where rims of stones disappeared into the ground. The places where the capstones rested on the top of an orthostat are indicated by a small oval. One foot is 30.48 cm, one inch is 2.54 cm,

Ad Figure 48. Ink and water-colour by Henry Dryden Bar.[t] and Rev.[d] William Collings Lukis, 'Drouwen N° III, G[emeente] of Borger' [D26-Drouwenerveld], July 12, 1878, Plan XVI'. Dryden noted that 'measuring took 3¼ hours'. Lukis, who dug a pit in the entrance passage to establish the depth of the floor, and sieved its contents, wrote

> *The floor of the entrance passage is 3 feet 2 inches below the present surface level.[552] In searching for the floor I found a few fragments of urns'* (collection Society of Antiquaries, London. These sherds were not drawn by Lukis).

Ad Figure 49. The chamber has had 9 PS, but capstones D1, D2 and D4 are missing at the western end.[553] The three stones to the left and the four stones to the right are remnants of a kerb. 'Hunebed near Gieten. Drenthe. / Gem : of Anlo. / View looking South. / W.C. Lukis. F.S.A. 8 July 1878' and at the top 'Plate V / Church of Rolde'. Lukis drew no clouds and his pencil drawings are nicer. The steeple of the church of Rolde is shown on the horizon to the right. Lukis also drew a view of the southern side of the hunebed, on the following day (Plate VI). He wrote in his description:

> *'Vestiges of the mound, 33 yards long by 20 yards wide, are still traceable.*
>
> *Innumerable fragments of plain and ornamented Urns are in the earth close under the surface near a boundary post opposite the entrance passage. Burnt human bones may also be found. I gave many fragments, part of the cutting edge of a stone axe, and a square-ended flint arrow point to the Assen Museum. Dr. Pleyte, of the*

---

551 Pleyte 1880-82, Pl. XLV: 7-8 are medieval ceramic model boats from other locations, one of which was assigned to hunebed D15-Loon (see notes 248, 345, 548).

552 As rendered in 'Section B E G looking E' in Figure 48.

553 Van Giffen (1925, 40-3; atlas-pl. 31) recorded that capstones D1 and D4 were absent and that a fragment of capstone D2 lay in the chamber in 1918, which was the middle part of the capstone, which had been split into three pieces. The longitudinal cleaving traces are indicated on the plan (atlas-pl. 31). With reference to the report by the Schulte of Anloo (1818), Van Giffen concluded that, after 1818, capstone D1 or D4 had been taken away. According to him, capstone D2 was 'shifted to the east and resting on Z3, Z3'and Z4' – this was not D3, as the plan would suggest.

Leiden Museum possesses many fragments which he has found here, and among them polished portions of four clay pot covers.

Janssen has marked seven capstones as existing in his time, and notes the absence of an eighth stone only. He has reversed the position of the monument in his Table of Diagrams by which the entrance passage appears to be placed on the north side. He says that a claystone axe was found here and refers to [Janssen 1840], N.°. 17. Van Lier Pl. III.5 / p. 191.'

Lukis illustrated the artefacts found on pl. F: 1 & 3; pl. G: 5-6, 7; Pl. H.[554]

Ad Figure 51. The illustrations are taken from J. & B. Wilgus, 'The magic mirror of life: an appreciation of the camera obscura', http://brightbytes.com/cosite/notaco.html). The camera lucida was invented by William Hyde Wollaston in 1807. 'It was a reflecting prism which enabled artists to draw outlines in correct perspective. The paper was laid flat on the drawing board, and the artist would look through a lens containing a prism, so that he could see both the paper and a faint image of the subject to be drawn. He would then fill the image.' (anon. 'Adventures in Cybersound. Magic Machines: A History of the Moving Image from Antiquity to 1900', http://www.acmi.net.au/AIC/MAGIC_MACHINES_1.html). For working outside, the drawing board is mounted on a tripod. 'It requires tremendous skill in use and no highly competent artist … would waste the time required to setup and use the instrument in the field when it is more efficient and instantaneous to sketch with eye and hand. The only place for the instrument was in the kit of a professional artist from the nineteenth or twentieth century, but limited to accurate copying of complex contours in controlled situations… The basic practical problem with the instrument derives from the fact that you have to position your eye so that it focuses at the same time to the reflected image in the prism and your pencil point on the paper. If you move your eye during the drawing or lift the pencil you have to begin the job of repositioning or realigning eye, image and pencil all over again.' (R. Woodrow, http://www.newcastle.edu.au/discipline/fine-art/theory/analysis/lucida-x.htm). But W.C. Lukis used the camera lucida to draw the hunebed stones as exactly as possible (photographic equipment with its wet glass plates was still too cumbersome). Although, as late as 1976, R.J.C. Atkinson (1976) used a camera lucida to draw megaliths, such images are now captured photographically. A camera lucida is still mounted, however, on microscopes for drawing thin sections.

Ad Figure 52. 'Great Hunebed, Borger. Drenthe. W.C. Lukis 13 July 1878 / view looking WSW / Plate XIIb'. What instrument Dryden is using is unclear. Plate XIIa is a 'view looking NNW' to hunebed D27, drawn by Lukis on the same day (Society of Antiquaries, London).

---

554 The trapezoidal arrow-head pl. G: 7 was also assigned to hunebed D14 in Lukis's text, but his description of this drawing tells that it was 'found by W.C.L. Hunebed of Bronger n° III. near Borger', viz. hunebed D23-Bronneger.

Ad Figure 53. According to H. Dryden, 'The lines represent the <u>central</u> lines of the chambers. / The red strokes I I show position of entrances. "Ent?" means Entrance doubtful / Magnetic meridian taken to be 15° 50′ West of true North / H. Dryden 1878.' The hunebeds indicated are, from top to bottom: D40, D43, D21, D38, D13, D22+D26, D41+D45, D7, D16, D24, D9, D14, D25, D5+D46 or D47, D20, D10+D28, D27, D17 or D18, D19, D6, D30. The pencilled notes are Van Giffen's, written about 1920.

Ad Figure 54. These hunebed builders seem ill-suited in their animal skins, like the people in Picardt's 1660 illustrations (Figures 6-8). Although much action is shown, the four men in the foreground appear astonishingly awkward, hardly able to manage the large boulder using cords, a lever and another tree stem. The standing man with a spear, looking like a chieftain, supervises their attempts. He carries an ill-fitted battle-axe in his girdle. Next to him are a sitting woman (with a clumsily rendered left leg) and a funnel beaker. That some of the men are tattooed is hardly visible. The hunebed is completely free-standing, without dry masonry between the orthostats or an enclosing barrow. A lady who balances a funnel beaker on her head and a child are passing in the background. Actually, apart from tattoos and the carrying of burdens on the head, nothing is added to the existing hunebed iconography.

Ad Figure 55. Bueninck's view is from the east, from the former train station Vries-Zuidlaren on the Assen-Groningen railway line. The flat heaths on the Pleistocene Drenthe Plateau are clearly illustrated. The line behind the shepherd's head indicates the primeval valley of the stream Wester Diep or Schipborgse Diep. Behind it is the Hondsrug ridge with a farm, a windmill, trees and yellow rye. Basalt poles with white heads mark the State-owned hunebed reserve.[555] Presently this view is completely blocked by trees. See Bakker (1990a, 32-4) for a detailed discussion.[556] (Van Ginkel et al. 1999, ill. p. 146). Bueninck's school picture was used in reverse for the cover of this book.

Ad Figure 66. The original dry masonry between the kerbstones, which was made of slabs, is replaced by smaller rounded stones in concrete. The two hunebed chambers D43S and D43N are seen in the background. Note kerbstone R17 to the left of the kerb and Stone X in the foreground within the restored barrow. Cf.

---

555 According to Van Giffen (1925, 244), State-owned hunebeds were so marked between 1918 and 1925, but here it happened before 1901 (in 1880, when D6 was bought by the State?). The visual angle of this school picture is shown in a 'commentary' booklet by G.J.A. Mulder (Bakker 1990a, fig. 2).

556 J.H. Textor, became station-master of the Vries-Zuidlaren station in 1870; he excavated pottery fragments from the chamber of nearby D6-Tynaarlo, part of which W.C. Lukis acquired in 1878. Lukis found two TRB sherds 'on the floor' (his pl. B: 3-4) and excavated several 'in the entrance passage' of D6. He deposited these artefacts in the Assen Museum and drew them together with earlier collected pottery from D6-Tynaarlo in the museum (see his manuscript text to Plan II and his plates B: 1-4; D: 1; Ia: 1-10, 12; Ib: 1-11, and Ic: 1 in the archives of the Society of Antiquaries of London), altogether 28 pieces. However, one large decorated tureen fragment was assigned by Pleyte (1880-82, pl. XI: 1, an almost identical drawing) to 'Angelslo'. Otherwise, Pleyte illustrated no pottery from D6-Tynaarlo (1880-82, cf. pl. LXI).

Pleyte's lithographs (1880-82, pls. XIII-XIV, based on photographs taken by J. Goedeljee in 1874: the oak trees have just been planted and the barrow soil was not yet completed with soil from elsewhere by Van Giffen in 1960.

Ad Figure 67. The use of one large capstone enabled the builders to widen the chamber. Restored positions of chamber orthostats and kerbstones are shown hatched. Faint traces of extraction holes seemed to indicate, however, that the kerbstones stood nearer to the chamber originally.

Index of the Dutch hunebeds

There are **53 extant hunebeds** in the Netherlands (G1, D1-32, D34-D47, D49-D54).

Excavated were **24 sites of demolished hunebeds** (*F1, *G2, *G3, *G5, *D6a, *D13a, *D13b, *D13c, *D31a, *D32a, *D32c, *D32d, *D33, *D35a, *D37a, *D39a, *D43a, *D44a, *D52a, *D54a, *D54b, *D54c, *O1, *O2).

There are **3 suspected sites of demolished hunebeds** (**G4, **D8a, **D8b).

Finally the Stone of Lage Vuursche (***U1) may or may not be a hunebed remnant.

As far as known, these **77-81 hunebeds were passage graves, except 1 dolmen** (*G5), **1 passage grave or cist** (*D13c), **2 cists** (*F1, *D13b), and **1 suspected cist** (**D39a).

The hunebeds are indicated by a capital letters for their *Provincie* (province) and a serial number. In Drenthe, the demolished tombs have the number of the most near extant hunebed and a small serial letter (e.g. *D6a). This registration system is an adapted form of Van Giffen's (1925). In the provinces of Friesland, Groningen, Overijssel, and Utrecht, the hunebeds are simply indicated by the letter F, G, O or U and a serial number.

See Appendix 1 (p. 202-227) for a short description of each tomb and Figure 57 (p. 201) for its location. *N, NO, O, ZO, Z, ZW, W, NW* in the hunebed names are cardinal and intercardinal directions, *bos* means wood and *veld* means [former] common heath land; it is linked to the name of the village of the former owners (e.g. *Valtherveld*, 'common heath of Valthe').

*F1-Riis / Rijs (Rijsterbos) [**cist**] – 5, 10, 27, 130, 200, **202**

G1-Noordlaren – 10, 20, 97, 100, 130, 132, 147, 163, 165, 200, **203**, 231, 295-296, Figures 24 & 58

*G2-Glimmen-N (Glimmeres) – 20, **203**, 235

*G3-Glimmen-Z (Glimmeres) – 20, 36, **204**, 235

G4-Onnen (Onneres) – **204

*G5-Heveskesklooster [**dolmen**] – 5, 9, 19, 36, 200, **204**, 216, Figure 59

D1-Steenbergen – 31, 35, 130, 165, **203**, 205

D2-Westervelde – 130, 165, **205**

D3-Midlaren-W (Steenakkers) – 35, 64-65, 91, 98, 100, 162, 165, 167, 169, 174, **205**, 295-296, Figures 14 & 25

D4-Midlaren-O (Steenakkers) – 35, 91, 99-100, 165, 167, 169, 174, **205**, 295-296, Figure 26

D5-Zeijen (Noordse Veld) – 108, 134, 153, 180, 196, **205-206**, 301, Figure 53

D6-Tynaarlo (Hunebedstraat) – iv, 20, 100-101, 114, 122-123, 125, 142, 147, 167, 169-170, 175, 180, 190, **206**, 229, 298, 301, Figures 28, 35, 39, 44, 53 & 55

*D6a-Tynaarlo-O [until 1998: 'D6e-f-Tinaarlo'] – 20, **206-207**, 235, Figure 60

D7-Schipborg – **207**, 301, Figure 53

D8-Anloo-N (Kniphorstbos) – 78, 91, 96, 110, 153, **207**, Figure 23

D8a-Anloo-Z1 (Kniphorstbos) – **208

D8b-Anloo-Z2 (Kniphorstbos) – **208

Index of Persons

Co-authors ('et al.'), translators, editors, publishers and booksellers are generally not included. Titles and predicates are usually omitted. The articles *de, 't, van, van den, van der, von* in surnames are placed after the main names. Only the initials of first names are given. Monarchs and the like are found under their first names.